ALWAYS
almost
modern

David Carter is Professor of Australian Literature and Cultural History at the University of Queensland. From 2001 to 2006 he was Director of the university's Australian Studies Centre. He has written widely on Australian literature, publishing, and popular culture. His books include *Dispossession, Dreams and Diversity: Issues in Australian Studies* (Pearson 2006), *A Career in Writing: Judah Waten and the Cultural Politics of a Literary Career* (ASAL, 1997), and the edited volumes *Making Books: Contemporary Australian Publishing* (UQP, 2007) and *The Ideas Market: An Alternative Take on Australia's Intellectual Life* (MUP, 2004). He is currently writing a history of Australian books in the American marketplace.

ALWAYS
almost
modern

AUSTRALIAN PRINT
CULTURES AND
MODERNITY

David Carter

AUSTRALIAN SCHOLARLY

First published 2013, Australian Scholarly Publishing Pty Ltd

7 Lt Lothian St Nth, North Melbourne, Vic 3051 TEL: 03 9329 6963 FAX: 03 9329 5452
EMAIL: aspic@ozemail.com.au WEB: scholarly.info

ISBN 978-1-925003-10-9

Cover design Art Rowlands   *Typesetting* Sarah Anderson

This book is typeset in Minion Pro 10.5/15

CONTENTS

INTRODUCTION

The essays brought together in this volume were written—I was rather shocked myself to discover—over a period of twenty years from the late 1980s. The earliest is an essay on the different modes of realist writing developed in mid-twentieth-century Australia in response to distinctively modern forms of social crisis (Chapter 9 below); it was first published in *The Penguin New Literary History of Australia*, a project supported by The Australian Bicentennial Authority. Understandings of literary history, *Australian* literary history and cultural modernity have all been challenged and transformed over the last two and half decades since that publication, and it has been both disconcerting and reassuring to realise that this early essay pursues questions that in different ways I am still pursing today: the modernity of writing which is not always overtly modernist; the relations between artistic modernism and broader apprehensions of modernity; the intersection of intellectual and political 'isms' with artistic modernism; and the nature of cultural nationalism, not least its *inter*nationalism. Topics or approaches that on one level I feel I've turned to only recently have on another level and in other forms been working away in my thinking about Australian culture over more than twenty years.

I did not always have the vocabulary then to name some of the major developments in literary studies and cultural history with which I might now align my writing—the emergence of the history of the book or print culture studies; new studies in modernity; and the 'transnational' turn in literary, cultural and historical work—but there are certainly continuities as well as shifts in method and matter. Work in cultural and media studies has also intervened in my engagements with Australian culture since 1988, meaning that to see literary or critical writing for me now is to see it, not simply in its 'social context', but more specifically within a print or cultural economy, in relation to other media and forms of entertainment, and, as that implies, in relation to a public space and a marketplace (even where that relationship is conceived purely negatively).[1] These are some of the main themes connecting the essays in the present volume. At their centre is the question of modernity, addressed or attacked from different perspectives and with very different 'raw materials', across literary and popular fiction, upmarket and downmarket magazines, art works or talk about them (Chapter 3), and film and television (Chapter 13).

Always Almost Modern: writers, artists, critics and intellectuals have worried away at the nature of Australia's relationship to the modern since the late-nineteenth century at least. Whether in the 1880s or the 1980s, commentators have repeatedly discovered that the nation's culture was on the verge of modernity; that the signs of modernity were gathering but had not yet, not quite, been consolidated; that the latest great novelist or poet or playwright or painter was a sign that the nation had finally caught up, or *grown up*, for modernity was often linked to cultural maturity (that step beyond colonial status). It is still difficult for us not fall into this reaction, taking the latest international success in any cultural field as a sign of success for the whole culture and for us personally—they've made it, *we've* made it. This response, of course, is an effect of nationalism, manifesting the force of 'imagined community', but it is also a symptom of Australia's colonial/ postcolonial situation, that sense of living in a cultural province or 'suburb' in relation to the modernising cultural metropolises, so dramatically and schematically described by Pascale Casanova—or closer to home by A.A. Phillips's resonant notion of the 'cultural cringe'.[2] Provincialism seems to be the very opposite of metropolitan modernity, and the fact that we are a long way away (itself of course a very partial cultural geography) is routinely converted into the sense that we are or were a long way behind. Geographical distance is translated into cultural belatedness.

One way of leaping over this belatedness is to reverse its terms, to claim that Australia was *always already* or *almost always modern* (and I'm happy for my title to be misread momentarily). Australia, so the argument goes, is modern not through gradual cultural evolution or sudden modernist revolution but through being 'born modern'. This way of projecting Australian culture is discussed in the first essay below, 'Weird Scribblings on the Beach'. But while this vision neatly transforms dull provinciality into a radical form of originality, it scarcely escapes the colonial bind.

INTRODUCTION

Australia has typically been seen as too modern and not modern enough: 'too modern' in the sense that it lacked any deep cultural roots or tradition of its own, folk or high, that it was too young, too raw, too superficial, too philistine; 'not modern enough' in the sense that it lagged behind the Greenwich meantime of modernity, that it was not (yet) sophisticated, fashionable, cool, conflicted or urban enough to be truly modern. Against these assumptions, often deeply embedded within Australian cultures and subjectivities themselves, more recent work has explored the forms of 'provincial modernity' or 'colonial modernity' (terms which would once have been thought oxymoronic); or, in another formulation, 'vernacular modernities'.[3] If Australia was provincial there is little reason for assuming that it was more so than most of Britain or America or Europe outside a few great modernist 'conurbations'; and to discover Sydney's or Melbourne's modernity is to discover in turn the 'provincialism'—the localness rather than the universality—of Paris, London and New York.

Of course we cannot 'write off' Australia's position of relative weakness or subordination within international or global cultural systems. Both cultural production and reception are affected inevitably by Australia's position as a 'medium-sized English-language culture', and the effects are registered at local, national and international levels.[4] This is to say nothing about the originality or creativity of Australian literature or painting, cinema or TV—this scarcely needs now to be asserted or defended—but it is to begin to say something about the conditions under which that creativity operates and its chances of finding publication or distribution at home and abroad. Modernism/modernity has been one critical frontier for these concerns. Earlier work on Australian literature and art—up until the 1980s—was focused primarily on high culture and high modernism, charting Australia's ignorance, rejection or belated uptake of modernist styles and understandings. Such views depended either on a nationalist model of cultural evolution in which Australia's early assertion of cultural nationalism in the 1880s–1890s had to wait until the mid-twentieth century to be tempered by or integrated into the modern tradition (at which point it would be mature, deeply 'individual', distinctively Australian and truly universal all at once); or, alternatively, the perspective was that of the established modernist canon which again produced a sense of Australia's distance and belatedness. Instead of Picasso and Ezra Pound we had the

Jindyworobaks and Ern Malley, and even then not until two or three decades after the avant-garde moment.[5]

In *The Black Swan of Trespass*, his landmark though controversial study from 1979, Humphrey McQueen ranged widely across literature, art and philosophy looking not for the *arrival* of modernism in Australia (a metaphor suggesting importation) but its *emergence*; that is, where modernist preoccupations gained traction in Australia because of their intersection with immediate, local concerns, whether of technique, professionalism or politics.[6] Subsequent studies, especially those focused on the role of women artists in the first half of the twentieth century, have broadened our vision to include a much wider range of art forms, career choices, and institutional circumstances, and to follow artists beyond national boundaries into much wider circuits of influence and inspiration. Such studies dissolve modernism (as a strict set of stylistic *or* intellectual features) into a more flexible, open-ended modernity, concerned as much with social change as with developments within the 'story of art' itself.[7]

In this perspective what becomes significant is less the position of individuals or artefacts *on* modernism than their position *within* modernity; this enables us to read the 'modernity' of texts that are partly or even wholly resistant to modernism but engaged, nonetheless, with their own contemporaneity. This was the case for the periodicals examined in Chapters 3–5 and Chapter 8: *Art in Australia, Aussie, Vision* and *All About Books*; for the proletarian realism discussed in Chapters 6 and 9; and for the 'middlebrow' book culture discussed in Chapters 7 and 8.

Over the last decade or so a whole new phase of studies in Australian modernity has emerged, focused less on artistic or intellectual modernism than on popular modernity—on the new forms of commercial culture and entertainment and the new modes of fashion and consumption, the new audiences and publics, to which they gave rise.[8] From the late-nineteenth century to the 1920s, the availability of cheaper print materials, new fiction, and new magazines with better quality illustrations, and the new phenomena of cinema and cinema-going, of jazz dancing, radio, recorded music and the gramophone, together produced a new modern culture in Australian cities and beyond, reinforced by such developments as the department store, modern advertising and the application of 'scientific business methods'.[9] This was also a newly international or transnational culture, although Australian entertainment was already thoroughly integrated into international networks.[10] Cinema and radio not only broadened culture's reach it changed its time-space coordinates. Australians could watch the same movies at the same time—but not necessarily in the same way—as their contemporaries in Great Britain or North America. If they had an enormous thirst for 'imported' cultural forms, especially those of modernising America, they fashioned their consumption to their local circumstances: 'in the process they forged an identity as modern Australians and modern citizens of the world.'[11] As Jill Matthews writes in her study of 1920s Sydney: 'International modernity was gradually adapted and Australianised in Sydney then proudly performed to the rest of the country and returned to the world... Rather than the last station on the line, a backwater ten years behind Europe and America as some both at the time and since have asserted, Sydney was a busy port of call in the ceaseless international ebb and flow of commerce and ideas that underpinned cosmopolitan modernity.'[12] While Sydney was Australia's largest and perhaps most cosmopolitan city, the point can be generalised.

The effects of the new work on modernity are thus much more significant than a simple shift of focus from high to popular culture, for they fundamentally alter our models of modernity and modernism. As Philip Mead puts it: 'Both modernity and modernism look very different today from what they used to, even a decade ago... The idea of modernity, as much as its history, is no longer the preserve of an exclusively Euro-American intellectual seminar.'[13] From a local perspective, the relationship between Australian culture and modernity is pushed beyond import/export metaphors to much more interactive models of cultural networks, communication circuits, and cultural flows in both or multiple directions. In Robert Dixon's account, the new approach to modernity

> takes issue with the assumption that modernity is first invented in the
> metropolitan centre and then exported to the colonial peripheries, which are
> always, by definition, belated. Instead it seeks to re-envisage the cultural landscape
> of empire or the world system as a set of interdependent sites, as a network of
> relations rather than a one-way transfer of culture and authority ... an interactive,
> transnational network in which specific local conditions of metropolitan and other
> centres are mutually formative of the responses of the whole economy.[14]

Australia is revealed not simply as the passive recipient of cultural imports but as an active participant in the global diffusion of vernacular modernities, not as belated but as engaged, productive, and itself 'modernising'. And the insights derived from the new popular cultures can be driven back into our understanding of contemporary literature, of 'modern reading and writing', of books as part of modern entertainment as well as intellectual life.

If the domination of Australian publishing, writing and reading by the British book trade remains an incontrovertible fact, 'domination' was never the whole story, for the imperial network itself could function as a vector of modernity not merely as a force for cultural conservatism. British domination *connected* Australian readers and writers to London's book culture producing a sense of contemporaneity with that metropolitan book world (something lost in the post-war years and replaced, from the 1970s, with the sense of an autonomous Australian book culture). Books, authors, ideas and aspirations could travel in both directions. We can redeploy to other cultural domains Veronica Kelly's description of the transnational theatre world as 'a de-centred competitive trade in theatrical commodities—whether performers, scripts or productions— wherein the perceived entertainment preferences and geographies of non-metropolitan centres were formative of international enterprise'.[15]

These concerns are paramount in my current research, first into Australian middlebrow culture and second into relations between Australian books and American publishers.[16] As suggested earlier, both the reconfiguration of modernity/modernism and the transnational turn in literary, cultural and historical studies emerged after many of the essays collected in *Always Almost Modern* were first published. Yet looking back over them I find many of these concerns anticipated or struggling to find expression. 'Weird Scribblings on the Beach', as indicated, examines one response to the anxiety of belatedness, a recurrent mode of argument that discovers Australia to have been always and already modern, in its nature if not its culture. 'Critics, Writers, Intellectuals' traces the emergence and transformation of the modern critic and modern criticism in Australia as applied to Australian literature. Chapters 3–6 examine a sequence of Australian magazines, from *Art in Australia*, which first appeared in 1916, to the short-lived 'little magazines' of the early 1930s, analysing in turn their complex reactions to the modernism and the modernity which surrounded them. In a context in which book publication was seriously underdeveloped, periodical publication becomes a major focus for understanding how books and reading and literary value circulated in Australian society.[17]

'The Mystery of the Missing Middlebrow' makes a first foray into describing the emergence of a middlebrow book culture in Australia, its rise and fall from the 1920s to the 1960s, and its possible ongoing manifestations into the present. It argues that the emergence of the idea of a 'middlebrow' and of the institutions which supported it were quintessentially modern phenomena, shaped by the apparent split of culture into antagonistic 'highbrow' and 'lowbrow' domains in the early twentieth century. The next essay examines one key local site of the middlebrow, the magazine *All About Books* (1928–38), which was all about Australians 'keeping up' with contemporary developments in the book world.

Chapters 9 and 10 return to the middle decades of the twentieth century but from a different perspective, focussing on the intersection of political, intellectual and literary commitments that emerged in the face of that series of cataclysmic events—from the Great War and the Soviet Revolution to the Depression, the Spanish Civil War, the rise of fascism and the threat of a second world war—which appeared to signal a crisis in every aspect of civilisation. The apprehension of social crisis was political but it was also framed by the context of social modernity and artistic and intellectual modernism, as represented in the great mid-century novels of Eleanor Dark and M. Barnard Eldershaw (Chapter 10). One response to social crisis was a commitment to communism and socialist realism, examined briefly in 'Realism, Documentary and Socialist Realism' (Chapter 9) and in 'Communism and Carnival' (Chapter 11) which highlights the surprising example of Ralph de Boissiere's post-war Caribbean-Australian novel *Crown Jewel* (1952).

By the 1950s, modernity had taken on a quite different complexion from between the wars—suburban rather than urban, domestic rather than public, and focused on the consumption of household goods rather than fashion or glamour. Chapter 12 looks at the phenomenon of Nino Culotta's (John O'Grady's) bestselling novel *They're a Weird Mob* (1957) which itself performs something of a suburban 'modernisation' of the Australian (male) identity. Chapter 13, 'The Wide Brown Land on the Silver Screen', shifts media and period to analyse representations of land and nature in Australian cinema and television. My interest there is in the significant changes from the 1980s in the kinds of landscape and nature which most fully signify the nation and in their complex, politically volatile engagements with Aboriginality. Finally, 'Good Readers and Good Citizens' examines the limits but also the potential productivity of national frames for understanding Australian literature or culture. It draws on work from media studies to suggest different ways of modelling transnational cultural 'transfers' and of understanding literature as 'a form of public-commercial-aesthetic institution comparable to cinema, television or popular music'. First published in 1999, half-way through the two decades covered by the essays in this volume, it might be seen as a 'theorisation' of the processes of understanding Australian literature and culture pursued by the other essays but also as a hinge between earlier and later ways of conceiving Australian literature as a national and transnational (or 'translocal') literature.[18]

I have resisted the impulse to update essays and have made only minor changes for sense or syntax, occasionally shifting tense or deleting obsolete references to better address the contemporary reader. I have also left in place some points or examples which are repeated (with variations) across more than one essay. Each essay stands on its own; and in addition these repeated points indicate certain touchstones in my own understanding of Australian literature and modernity to which I continue to return. Most of these essays have been published previously and publishing details are including in the notes for each chapter where this is the case. 'Weird Scribblings on the Beach' first appeared in *Southerly*; '"Esprit de Nation" and Popular Modernity' in *History Australia*; 'Communism and Carnival' in *Australian Cultural History*; 'The Wide Brown Land' as two separate essays in the *Journal of Australian Studies*. An earlier version of 'Critics, Writers, Intellectuals' was published in *The Cambridge Companion to Australian Literature*, edited by Elizabeth Webby and 'The Mystery of the Missing Middlebrow' appeared in *Imagining Australia* published by the Australian Studies Committee at Harvard University. 'Realism, Documentary, Socialist Realism' first appeared as a chapter in *The Penguin New Literary History of Australia*, edited by Laurie Hergenhan, which was also a special issue of *Australian Literary Studies*. My biggest debt is to this journal and its editors Laurie Hergenhan and Leigh Dale: Chapters 6, 8, 10, 12, and 14 all first appeared in *Australian Literary Studies*. Acknowledgements are due to the editors of these journals and volumes for their comments and suggestions on earlier drafts of the essays and for their permission to reprint them here. Chapters 3 and 5 are previously unpublished. Acknowledgements are also due to colleagues and correspondents including Patrick Buckridge, Robert Dixon, Laurie Duggan, Allan Gardiner, Peter Kirkpatrick, Russell McDougall, Richard Nile, Tom O'Regan, Roger Osborne, Susan Sheridan and Gillian Whitlock.

WEIRD SCRIBBLINGS ON THE BEACH
Modernity and Belatedness

This essay began life as an interest in Nevil Shute's bestselling novel, *On the Beach*. Published in 1957, the year of Sputnik, Shute's novel describes the last months of all human life following a nuclear war. As the radiation cloud heads south, Melbourne becomes the last place on earth—appropriately, according to the comment widely attributed to Ava Gardner, the female lead of Stanley Kramer's 1959 film of the book. My interest was in the novel's after-life, especially the way it had entered into a series of mushrooming discourses around modernity via its bestselling reception, its imbrication with popular Cold War discourses on the Bomb, the making of Kramer's film, its local reception and so on.

At a conference in London on Australian popular culture, there was fall-out of another kind which pointed me instead towards the present essay. Andrew Milner delivered a paper entitled '*On the Beach*: Apocalyptic Hedonism and the Origins of Post-Modernism'. He used Shute's novel as an exemplary text to evidence what he called 'Australia's own distinctively postmodern condition'.[1] The experience of listening to the paper was uncomfortable, even uncanny, as Milner articulated some of my own half-formulated thoughts about the significance of the novel's cultural recurrence.

I'll return to Milner's argument in detail later. But as I watched my original enthusiasm for a study of *On the Beach* go up in smoke another project began to rise from its ashes. For it occurred to me that the argument

1

Milner was making was generic. That is, it belonged to a *type* of argument that commentators, especially literary commentators, had been making in Australia since at least the mid-nineteenth century. What he was doing for postmodernism had earlier been done for a whole range of modernisms and their precursors.

Let me attempt to describe the recurrent form of this argument as concisely as possible. It is to claim that Australia has always already been what European or American culture has only recently discovered as its own modernity. What emerges in the metropolis as a new philosophical or art movement (which might then be generalised as the modern condition, the postmodern condition, or the human condition) is defined in Australia as the *Australian* condition. The aesthetic or the epochal is rewritten as the very essence of Australia.

Explicitly or implicitly, the argument involves the claim that in a special sense Australia got there first: that Australia was modern before modernity, and now postmodern before postmodernity. But this modernity is achieved on a different plane from in the metropolitan cultures. Australia is not modern by the sophistication of its high culture, by its intellectual or aesthetic avant-gardes. If anything, the absence of these cultural structures is the first principle of the argument. Emphasis falls instead on what we might call the *pre*-cultural, even the pre-historical: nature, environment, landscape. Australia was 'born' modern (or postmodern) in the peculiarities of its landscapes and the peculiarly pre-cultural social life determined by this environment; or in its sheer otherness and distance from 'the chatter of cultured apes/Which is called civilisation over there'.[2]

We can find a statement more or less in these terms for many, if not quite every, post-romantic art movement: late-romantic gothic, symbolism, realism, aestheticism, modernism, and now postmodernism. It is a paradoxical argument which proclaims Australia's modernity and lack of modernity in the one breath. It finds a radical originality which, however, is likely to be expressed in terms of absence rather than presence, of the primitive rather than the modern. High modernism too, of course, could apprehend itself in terms of the primitive. In the Australian case, however, we will need to define a specifically postcolonial problematic.

I hesitate to begin my series of examples with Marcus Clarke's all-too familiar account of 'weird melancholy' as the 'dominant note of Australian scenery'. For this text is still potent enough to seduce unwary users into falling for its gothic version of Australian nature, or at least for its gothic version of the Australian mind:

> What is the dominant note of Australian scenery? That which is the dominant note of Edgar Allan Poe's poetry—Weird Melancholy ... The Australian mountain forests are funereal, secret, stern. Their solitude is desolation. They seem to stifle, in their black gorges, a story of sullen despair ... All is fear-inspiring and gloomy ...
>
> Australia has rightly been named the Land of the Dawning. Wrapped in the [mists] of early morning, her history looms vague and gigantic ...
>
> In Australia alone is to be found the Grotesque, the Weird, the strange scribblings of nature learning how to write ... the dweller in the wilderness acknowledges the subtle charm of this fantastic land of monstrosities.[3]

Clarke in fact was writing something like a publicity blurb; and recognising good copy he used it more than once. But the force of his description, if that's the right word, cannot be denied (neither can it be explained by references to Clarke's gloomy temperament). Re-reading the text now, as the first in my generic series, what is most striking is Clarke's unprecedented alignment of Australian nature with what might be considered a metropolitan *avant-garde*. In the first version of the text, Clarke refers to the stories of Hoffman and Hawthorne as well as Poe, linking them by the wonderful phrase 'weird delight'.[4] Of course the romantic gothic was no longer new when Clarke was writing in the 1870s. What was still new was the symbolist appropriation of Poe. The gothic, in short, could still carry the shock of the new.

Clarke's text, I would argue, needs to be read as something more than just another case of the aestheticisation, through a familiar European discourse, of an unfamiliar antipodean landscape. For he is drawn to the margins rather than the mainstream of contemporary western high culture: to the new, the perverse, the 'weird'. In locating these qualities within Australian *nature* he effects those startling reversals that still carry force: the primeval discovered as the modern, the prehistoric as the unprecedented, 'the strange scribblings of nature learning how to write'.

One of the tropes available to colonial settler cultures as a way of understanding themselves is that of belatedness. This is a colonialist metaphor: a colonial culture is by definition a belated culture. Whether judged against the traditional universal standards inscribed at the metropolitan centre or against the modernity no less inscribed there, it is as if the new society is always catching up, always arriving but never quite there. For most of the nineteenth century what we lacked according to this figure was *history*, and without history there was no literature, no civilisation. As Clarke puts it, 'this our native or adopted land has no past, no story'.

But the scale of comparison begins to shift at just about the time that Clarke was writing. Increasingly, from the late nineteenth century, what we lacked was not so much history as *modernity*. Here was another version of colonial belatedness in which modernity comes to be associated with an always-lacking cultural maturity: we were not yet quite modern, we had not yet quite grown up.

Yet the discourse of modernity also allowed another cultural trajectory: the possibility of a radical originality in the peripheral culture in which the very absence of history makes modernity peculiarly our own. Perhaps Clarke's genius was to have been the first to glimpse this possibility of an Australian culture discovered in the very weirdness of modernity, in that uncanny moment when the pre-historical meets the post-historicist. By being the last we become the first.

This was not necessarily an argument for modern*ism*. My point is rather to define a particular structure of apprehension which is only possible within the discourse of modernity. What is apprehended is the familiar postcolonial dilemma of belatedness, which is also the dilemma of originality and origins. Of course, my reading of Clarke is 'weird' in its own right. With its redolent spirit-of-place rhetoric, his text might more readily be located in a lineage which extends forward to P.R. Stephensen, the Jindyworobaks and the radical nationalists. This is the dominant genre in which distinctiveness, usually a sort of environmental distinctiveness, is asserted against cultural belatedness: 'a gum tree is not a branch of an oak'.[5]

But what interests me is the *excess* of the arguments comprising my genre, the excess that turns to metropolitan modernism in order to define Australian distinctiveness. Twenty-odd years after Marcus Clarke, and in explicit opposition to him, A.G. Stephens strangely repeats the structure of his argument but with a different reference to modernity:

Verlaine's cult of Faded Things, extolling the hinted hue before the gross colour, finds a natural home in Australia—in many aspects a Land of Faded Things—of delicate purples, delicious greys, and dull, dreamy olives and ochres. Yet we have been content to let strangers foist upon us the English ideals of glaring green and staring red and orange; we have permitted them to denounce our grave harmonies of rock and vegetation, with shadow laid on tender shadow, light on dusky light ...

Englishman Marcus Clarke has even called our gum-tree 'melancholy', our forests 'funereal'.[6]

Stephens, by contrast, describes the gum-tree as 'many-bosomed': to observe it is 'to receive an aesthetic education'. Here indeed the aesthetic dimension of symbolism is to the fore: the gumtree is 'unconventional'. The landscape is no longer prehistoric but once again its unconventionality, its difference, can only be apprehended through the otherness of modernity. Once again it is nature not culture, not history but the lack of history, which is figured in terms of the modern. The colonial figure of belatedness is reversed—but at what cost? In a sense, as I will suggest, at the cost of history, which might be why we are condemned to repeat the argument.

Clarke and Stephens together suggest another feature of the genre: their reference points are not English but the weird or unconventional American and Continental. Precisely because of the colonial relation no English modernity can be visible: modernity was anti-English. In a related case, D.R. Jarvis has shown how the development of the *Bulletin*'s 'egalitarian poetics' occurred between a negative account of Oscar Wilde and aestheticism and a positive account of Emile Zola and realism.[7]

This is something we will meet at each stop on the way from weird melancholy to apocalyptic hedonism. But following Stephens's text from 1901, there is a significant gap in my series. My account does suggest new ways of reading important twentieth century pieces such as Stephensen's *Foundations of Culture in Australia* (1935–36)—reading its modernity as well as its romantic nationalism in terms of Stephensen's own involvement with modernism. *His* references are to Americans and English émigrés (Theodore Dreiser, Sinclair Lewis, Eugene O'Neill, Norman Douglas, D.H. Lawrence, Aldous Huxley). But there are no very clear examples to fit my case until after the Second World War.

Why might this be so? Largely, I think, because of the way that positions within cultural politics divided up between modernism, anti-modernism and nationalism. There were internationalist positions proclaiming the utter contemporaneity of modernity wherever it occurred, in Paris, Moscow or Melbourne.[8] There were anti-modernists calling for a return to tradition. And, increasingly, there were nationalists. For them the modernity of the national culture depended not upon the imported faddishness or decadence of modernism but upon its own progressive historicity. In none of these cases was the otherness of the modern possible as a figure for the oneness of the national culture. The sheer proliferation of modernist discourses made this unlikely.

Nevertheless there are two revealing limit cases, two arguments which do approach the structure I have indicated. They come, significantly, not from within modernism at all but from the extremes of anti-modernism and cultural nationalism. The first case is *Vision*, the Lindsayite magazine which first appeared in Sydney in 1923. *Vision* rejected the primitivism and 'complex superficiality' of modernism in favour of Beauty and creative passion, defined in romantic, vitalist terms.[9] What is interesting for my purposes, though, is what we might call the contemporaneity of the magazine's anti-modernism. Rather in the spirit of what they attacked, *Vision*'s editors (Jack Lindsay for the most part) wrote anti-modernist manifestos. They named and capitalised 'Modernism'; in many ways they knew their modernism better than anyone else in the country. As Humphrey McQueen has written, *Vision* 'was up-to-date in a way that almost no other local publication had managed. Its contributors scoured the cultural presses of the world in search of decadence to attack.'[10]

It is not surprising, therefore, to find in *Vision* another instance of the argument that leaps over belatedness, in this case the belatedness that it self-consciously and perversely identifies with modernism. Again, we can be first by being last. The magazine's opening Foreword is constructed throughout in terms of such reversals and oxymorons: modernism is old, 'provinciality' is new. The modernist is a 'cultured savage' for whom the great works of the past are an 'unimaginable future'. The task of renaissance falls uniquely to Australia: 'If Australia alone in the world is doing this— and we see no evidence for any other conclusion—then the Renaissance must begin from here, and both the onslaught of expression and the analytic attack must begin from here also.' The essential 'youthfulness of Australia' is also the essence of art itself. In short, the terms of the genre are repeated, if inverted. We will be more modern, that is more vital, than modernism.

My second limit case arises within the anti-modernism of nationalism. Nationalism finds its image reflected in realist art, and it is virtually inevitable that the realism it prefers will be celebrated as a local development. From this point it is only a short step to the argument that we got there first, that at least a certain kind of realism was first made in Australia. As such, this indigenous realism is not merely an historical art movement but an essential quality of the national life (drawn at once from landscape and society). Realism in such an argument is understood as progressively modernising, a series of new starts.

There are hints of this position throughout the forties; but let me cite a late and striking version of it, from A.A. Phillips. The opening essay of his collection, *The Australian Tradition*, begins in the following dramatic manner:

> When the Australian writers of the nineties achieved a revolution in nineteenth
> century Anglo-Saxon letters, setting fiction free from the cage of a middle-class
> attitude and a middle-class audience ... [11]

This essay, on the craftsmanship of Henry Lawson, first appeared in 1948. Its wonderful opening was aimed very precisely at the English departments which would not read Australian literature. But in our terms, Phillips is also claiming the radical originality of Australian culture in terms of its modernity. The writers of the 1890s were the first to discover a *proletarian* realism, a form of realism which, like Stephens's symbolism, is both marginal and quintessentially modern, and so epochal in the progressive history of art forms. And once again it is by discovering the essential qualities of Australian life in literature that we have anticipated the cultural modernity of the rest of the world.[12]

For Phillips, post-war, the relationship to modernity had altered. He is writing 'after' modernism, and the argument is historical for the first time. The 'way of life' thus takes precedence over landscape although they are still virtually synonymous; and the modernist *movement* is absent. Modernism, in this sense, was no longer contemporary. Because of its historicising, the argument is less involved in the dramatic reversals of our earlier cases than with a sort of precocious evolution. What Phillips seeks to define is a progressively modernising realism which in the terms of my argument defines the original and originary modernity of Australian culture and its *continuing* modernity, its 'anti-belatedness'. This is generalised as the 'democratic theme', defined in the essay of that name.

The Australian Tradition can be read as a single extended argument around the theme of belatedness, most famously in the essay 'The Cultural Cringe'. Belatedness, however, is a recurrent concern for Phillips because of the organicist nature of his own model of historical development which poses maturity as the culture's goal. The metaphor assures its own irresolution, for the sense of a deep and progressive national tradition must always be qualified by a sense of its incompleteness: maturity is always about to be achieved, but there is still a lack; we are still not quite adequate to the present.

A little later on, and in an explicit response to Phillips, there is an argument which takes the obvious next step. Phillips argues that the Australian tradition is a modern tradition, but makes only a passing claim to any more general condition of modernity. By contrast, this is precisely the claim H.P. Heseltine makes: that the essentially modern elements in the modern condition are the essentially Australian elements of the Australian condition.

Heseltine's essay, 'The Literary Heritage', was first published in *Meanjin* in 1962. It is still arguably a nationalist piece yet it represents a fundamental shift in the rhetoric of national culture. Heseltine belongs to the new post-war generation of university trained critics who turned their attention to Australian literature in the 1950s and 1960s. Somewhat unusually he had studied in the USA. 'The Literary Heritage' is a major rewriting of *The Australian Tradition* which draws on all the resources of this modernising experience.

Heseltine first takes three common versions of the Australian literary tradition: Phillips's 'democratic theme'; the theme of evolution from colony to mature nationhood; and the theme of confrontation with the landscape. He finds that each has much to support it but none is adequate to define 'the very centre of the Australian imagination'. Given such a romantic formulation it is not surprising that he next considers romanticism itself by way of a contemporary argument, this time from Herbert Piper, to the effect that Australian literature is romantic in a residual way that marks it off 'from the modern European literature which rejected Romanticism at least a generation ago'.[13] There's a nice figure of colonial belatedness.

Heseltine explicitly rejects and reverses the charge of backwardness. Australian literature is indeed, historically, a romantic or post-romantic phenomenon. However:

> Due to certain circumstances of history and geography, it came much *earlier*
> than European literature to deal with a number of key themes of late Romantic
> awareness ... Australian literature, in fact, early took as its central subject what is
> still one of the inescapable concerns of all modern literature.[14]

Australia, once again, was modern before modernism. Heseltine's reference-point is Lionel Trilling's 1961 essay, 'On the Modern Element in Modern Literature'.[15] Here we have a Nietzschean version of the modern: society as the rationalisation of cruelty, the artist as alienated outsider, and modern literature as the exploration of the 'primal non-ethical energies'. Heseltine's references again are all non-English: Trilling himself, Dostoevsky, Nietzsche and, one imagines, contemporary existentialism.

The distinctive or, rather, generic aspect of Heseltine's argument is the further claim that the qualities which define the very modernity of the modern also define the very 'Australianness of Australian writing': 'that peculiarly modern element in modern literature which ... Australian literature so early laid hold on'. From the beginning, Australian literature has known nihilism, nothingness, the 'horror of primal experience', 'the terror at the basis of being'; and these are its recurrent concern, from Marcus Clarke to Henry Lawson to A.D. Hope and Patrick White.

Indeed Heseltine's argument can be understood as a rewriting of the whole history of Australian literature in the image of White's novel *Voss* (1957). The history is rewritten so that *Voss* can appear as its culmination. Modernity and Australianness are completely aligned, as *Voss* 'fuses almost all those aspects of Australia's literary heritage which define both its modernity and its Australianness'. Heseltine thus clinches the argument towards which Phillips only gestured by aligning the original and originary modernity of Australian culture with its essential and 'continuing' modernity:

> The fundamental concern of the Australian literary imagination ... marked out by
> our national origins and given direction by geographic necessity, is to acknowledge
> the terror at the basis of being, to explore its uses, and to build defences against its

> dangers. It is that concern which gives Australia's literary heritage its special force and distinction, which guarantees its continuing modernity. (166)

Ironically, of course, this is an argument that could occur only after the institutionalisation of the modern in the academy, as a modern tradition. Heseltine's modernism is no longer that of the schools or movements, no longer avant-garde.

There is a further irony in the essay's postcolonial politics, for it is still governed by the figure of belatedness. It finds new ways to talk about landscape and hints at the role of social formations, but Heseltine repeats the absenting of history, of an historical culture and cultured society, which Marcus Clarke had initiated. To underline this point and its postcolonial ambiguity we might compare his argument with those surrounding the near-contemporary London exhibition of Australian painting: the famous Whitechapel exhibition of 1961.

Here the work of Sidney Nolan, Albert Tucker, and Arthur Boyd, among more than fifty Australian artists, was packaged by and for a London audience in terms of what Bernard Smith has called the 'myth of isolation': the myth that Australian art had been virtually isolated from 'the Renaissance tradition' and subsequently 'from any European tradition older than impressionism'.[16] In other words, from the perspective of London, Australian art was celebrated as exotic, primitive, pre-social and, once again, outside history. The very modernity of the paintings was a result of their innocence in relation to modernism. (We can recognise similar gestures today in the reception of Australian film and Aboriginal painting.) These are familiar appropriative manoeuvres from the colonising metropolis especially when in decline: vitality is imported back to the metropolis from the outposts of empire. The irony is that Heseltine has no defence against this colonisation, for he is already inside its rhetoric.

Having traced this argument about Australia's original modernity for almost a century, we may now find Andrew Milner's startling claims about Australia, *On the Beach* and postmodernity quite predictable. In exemplary postmodern fashion it finds its texts in popular culture, not in nature, human nature, high culture or local traditions. In *On the Beach*, Milner finds an 'apocalyptic hedonism' which 'importantly prefigures much of what has become characteristic of contemporary postmodern sensibility'.[17]

More than that, however, Milner's concern is 'the extent to which Australia in particular can come to exemplify the postmodern in general' (200). However, we define postmodernity, 'it is surely not difficult to recognise in Australian society and culture its peculiarly adequate instance' (200).

Australia, in short, was postmodern before postmodernism. And the condition of this postmodernity is again Australia's belatedness, defined by a series of absences. We are postmodern without ever having been fully European. Indeed we are post-historical without ever having been fully historical: postmodernism announces 'the end of history to a culture which has never known that it has begun' (200). Clarke's primitivism finds a strange, reverberant echo in the postmodern present.

Milner's argument is dense and in many way persuasive. He details the post-Hiroshima, consumerist dimensions of the postmodern which might well have a specific local resonance. There *is* an important sense in which Australia's 'post-imperialism' is its postmodernism. Milner notes the significance of his wholly North American frame of reference (which recalls our earlier cases): the postmodern 'remains peculiarly visible from a New World, extra-European vantage point' (195). He is playfully conscious of the excess of his own argument: 'in the coincidence of a nuclear arms race and a general economy of affluence, the whole of the West finally had Australianness thrust upon it' (202).

But the generic aspects of the argument remain. Once again Australian culture is located outside history and culture. Its modernity is defined by the sheer absence of those structures which produce modernity elsewhere. The intellectual, artistic condition *there* becomes the very way of life or national consciousness *here*. Again Australian belatedness is rewritten as originality.

What the generic repetitions tell us is not to read this as historical description at all, but as a kind of conceit, an extended rhetorical figure (*chiasmus* perhaps). It also tells us about the position of the speaker. For despite its postmodernism, the authority of Milner's piece is still that of the traditional culture critic: the culture doctor able to diagnose the general condition of the society via its cultural symptoms. And despite its ability to name postcolonialism, indeed to rename it post-imperialism, Milner cannot but repeat the ambiguous politics of Heseltine and his predecessors which suggest that real history takes place elsewhere and that the Australian postmodern is a kind of primitive, originary postmodern, scarcely conscious of its own origins or its own modernity—indeed requiring European/North American postmodernism to name and know itself.[18]

This is not the place to commence an alternative Australian cultural history—one which might, for instance, highlight the successive, piecemeal and incommensurate discourses of modernity which have found their place in Australia (in a complex series of relationships to its postcoloniality). It would be tempting to discover in the recurrence of this genre of literary commentary a key to Australian culture. We might even pose it in the same terms: as virtually the *last* white-settler colony, Australia was the *first* to discover its own postcolonialism. But I would argue in quite the opposite direction. The more examples we find the less we should expect to discover anything material about the distinctiveness of Australian culture in such accounts.[19] What we might discover, instead, is something more interesting about the postcolonialism Australia *shares* with other white-settler colonies. So my general conclusion is a warning against general conclusions: against any attempt to treat Australian culture as a discrete organism, a general condition or state of mind. From whatever perspective this is done it will be caught inevitably under the sign of belatedness. There is a weird sort of melancholy about apocalyptic hedonism after all.

CRITICS, WRITERS, INTELLECTUALS
Australian Literature and its Criticism

Australian literary criticism in the 1990s found itself in the unfamiliar circumstance of being front-page news. Controversies about the ethical and historical responsibility of literature and criticism, and a series of high-profile scandals about the identities of some celebrated authors, brought into the public domain debates about literary theory that might otherwise have remained within the university. There have been more than faint echoes of the American 'culture wars' over political correctness and the destruction of the canon. We have become familiar with talk about a crisis in literary studies. In the pages of the higher journalism, the universities have been accused—in one sense correctly—of having abandoned literary values and tradition for theory, ideology or pop.

Literary criticism in the universities has undergone dramatic changes over the last three decades, although changes in the classroom have almost certainly been less dramatic. There has been a new confidence in the relevance of literary studies to broader issues of cultural and political importance, such as questions of race and ethnicity in the nation's history. But the changes in literary studies have also been driven by anxieties about the point of literary criticism in a postmodern or 'post-media' world. Literary studies has typically become a kind of *cultural* studies.[1] This has increased its scope and worldliness, but perhaps, too, its sense that there are significant cultural dynamics that exist well beyond traditional notions of the literary.

Outside the universities there are prominent independent critics and 'public intellectuals' who publish regularly in newspapers and magazines and appear at writers festivals, and who almost certainly have a more direct influence than academic critics on publishers, readers and editors. Academic literary criticism nonetheless probably still dominates the reception of Australian literature *as* Australian literature, especially its shaping into histories, even as it is frequently attacked for being at once too specialised, and so unable to communicate with ordinary readers, and not specialised enough, overstepping its proper disciplinary boundaries.

These debates remind us that the meanings and institutional sites of literary criticism and so the ways of being a critic in Australia have undergone significant shifts, especially since the mid-twentieth century. At different times the authority of criticism has been concentrated in literary associations of educated gentlemen, in newspapers and periodicals, in informal networks of writers and critics, and in professional practice within the academy. While the history of ideas would suggest strong lines of continuity and influence, for example in the recurrence of romantic, evolutionary metaphors describing the national literature, a focus on institutional changes indicates rather the discontinuities in the meaning and function of literary criticism in Australia. It would be difficult to write the history of Australian criticism around a series of seminal books or an evolving tradition of major critics, not because of the quality of the criticism itself but because of the inconsecutive nature of its institutional and social contexts. It is tempting nevertheless to tell the story as one of evolutionary progress from simplicity to diversity or from colonial ignorance to postcolonial enlightenment. But one of the effects of recent work in literary history and cultural studies has been a renewed sense of the complexity—and originality—of earlier cultural formations in Australia. The situation of culture in Australia must be understood not merely in terms of insularity or belatedness. Australia has always been a point where a complex pattern of cultural flows converged—and then diverged throughout the structure of local cultural institutions. A model of cultural transference and transformation is more useful in describing this pattern than cultural evolution or 'becoming'.

Literature and talk about literature have played a central role since at least the 1830s in debates about the status of the national culture. Literary criticism has rarely been about literature alone; at stake has been the nature of civilisation, culture and 'character' in Australia and the authority to speak in their name. In the nineteenth century, debates about the national culture turned on its relation to tradition. In the twentieth century they have more often expressed a postcolonial anxiety about the status of the national culture's modernity. This in turn has expressed itself as anxiety about the status of the literary critic and, more particularly, the literary intellectual. What kind of critics or intellectuals should the national culture sustain? What was the appropriate relationship between critics and writers or writers and readers? What was the relationship between local culture and intellectual movements from elsewhere?

This essay traces the significant role of literary criticism in defining attitudes to modernity in Australia and in struggles over cultural authority; the relation of criticism to other public discourses; the shaping of criticism by notions of 'high' versus 'popular' cultures; institutional changes governing where and how criticism was practised; shifts in how the critic or intellectual has been conceived; perhaps even the rise and fall of the critic in Australia.

CRITICISM AND THE INCIPIENT NATION

Early twentieth-century critics inherited from the nineteenth century a set of beliefs about national literatures that would remain influential in Australian criticism until the 1970s. Perhaps most revealing is the recurrence over a century or more of the critical judgement that the beginnings of a national literature could be discerned but that it had not yet fully arrived. Frederick Sinnett, in 1856, found 'some small patches' of the potentially vast fiction fields that had 'been cleared, and fenced, and cultivated'. Two decades later, Marcus Clarke found in Adam Lindsay Gordon's verse 'something very like the beginning of a national school of poetry'. Two decades more, and H.G. Turner could claim only that 'Australian literature begins to assume some definiteness of form'. A.G. Stephens, no friend to the critical views of Clarke or Turner, saw in Henry Lawson and 'Banjo' Paterson 'something like the beginnings of a national school of poetry'. Vance Palmer in 1905: 'even now the national movement is beginning'. P.R. Stephensen in 1935: 'we are on the threshold of Australian self-consciousness, at the point of developing Australian nationality, and with it Australian culture'. And Vincent Buckley in 1957: 'we are still not quite modern

… yet we are on our way to being mature'. The national literature or culture was always emerging but never fully emerged. As Miles Franklin remarked, 'Native literature remained chronically incipient'.[2]

The recurrence of this judgment suggests the lack of continuity in local literary institutions. It also reveals how widely shared was a particular notion of literature and its relationship to nation, race and civilisation. As Brian Kiernan has argued, the concept of a national literature emerged well before the political nationalism of the late-nineteenth century.[3] From the 1830s, the idea of an Australian literature was connected to the social and moral development of the nation. An earlier neo-classical view of literature as the index of a society's level of civilisation was absorbed in romantic theories of literature as the expression not merely of individual genius but of the genius of the nation or race, its essential spirit or character. In setting the model for Australian literature, Nettie Palmer wrote, in 1929, 'it is Shakespeare that proves England a nation'.[4] In what kind of literature, then, would Australian nationality be proved?

Literature had this exalted role, above any of the other arts, because of its seemingly more organic relationship to place and race: in Palmer's words, it was 'the basis, the soil of the arts'.[5] Behind such arguments lie evolutionary ideas regarding the influence of environment on national character. Kiernan refers to the specific influence of Taine's *History of English Literature* (1863) with its 'scientific' approach to literature as determined by race, environment and epoch.[6] In a country 'without history' such as Australia, the environment would be most influential. Literature would adapt to the environment; the environment would express itself through a literature 'racy of the soil'.[7] Despite Clarke's famous speculation that the 'dominant note of Australian scenery' was 'Weird Melancholy', evolutionary thinking generally suggested a more optimistic view of the national character which became fundamental to both nationalist and imperialist attitudes: 'the great body of our nascent literature is cheerful and vigorous, as becomes the pioneer writers of a young and hopeful country'.[8] The idea that Australia was pioneering a literature often led to the romantic notion that it should be a literature of pioneering. Such evolutionary assumptions generated the constant search for the emergence of the national literature; but the recurrent sense that it had not yet fully emerged was inevitable given that it was expected, impossibly, to express the whole 'national life and character'.

It is easy, nonetheless, to underestimate the level and complexity of colonial literary activity both in the spread of its institutions—by mid-century there was a thriving if volatile newspaper and magazine market—and in its intellectual range as the English tradition was defined through classical, continental and American romantic and religious knowledges, and then again through knowledge of the local. While there were few books published on local literature, criticism flourished in newspapers and magazines.[9] Essays on literature were part of a more general field that included writings on moral, philosophical and religious subjects. Discussions of the national literature were part of a wider discourse about the progress of civilisation in the colony. Criticism was not a matter for literary experts—there were in this sense no literary critics—but rather a field for all cultivated men and very occasionally women. If the ideal was that of the man of letters, few other than journalists saw themselves as professional writers, let alone full-time literary critics.

It is also easy to underestimate the contemporaneity of colonial culture. Imperialism carried its own kind of internationalism. The imperial connection did not mean only that local culture was provincial. It could also mean cosmopolitanism, a sense of near simultaneity with literary and intellectual issues in London, Europe and America. Towards the end of the century, however, these cosmopolitan links became less rather than more important in elite literary circles. A narrower form of British affiliation came to dominate official culture as the new imperialism flourished and as romanticism settled into Victorian moral hygiene. Even for an enthusiast such as H.G. Turner, the proper 'service' of Australian literature was 'to supplement and perchance in minor departments replace the magnificent body of writing to which our lucky stars destined us to be heirs'.[10] Turner was bemused by the popular success of Paterson and Lawson, for he could not see their modernity. Cosmopolitanism re-emerged in a more populist, nationalist and anti-imperialist cultural formation, particularly around the Sydney *Bulletin*.

THE RISE OF THE CRITIC

The *Bulletin* was a distinctively modern phenomenon in the 1880s and 1890s. It addressed a new kind of citizen and consumer; it identified the public or national interest against established interests; its city was a place of energy and spectacle; it was ironic; it spoke for the here and now.[11] Its nationalism was a statement of its modernity, a way of placing Australia in the contemporary world. Its work in literature had similar effects, democratising and modernising the relation between writers and readers, and helping to bring a new kind of writer and writing into being. The *Bulletin* was central in the widespread feeling that 'something like the beginnings of a national school of literature' had emerged by the century's turn. Australian literature could be seen to have its own time and place, no longer merely as a 'supplement' to English literature. This development was understood in evolutionary terms but we can understand it now in terms of institutional changes: a new class of readers, the rise of popular journalism, the professionalisation of writing careers, and the emergence of an inner-city literary 'bohemia'.[12]

What was new about A.G. Stephens's work on literature, as critic and editor of the *Bulletin*'s literary section, the Red Page, was not a new literary theory but the way he modernised the business of criticism. This was the effect of literary realism overlaying the late-romantic heritage but also of Stephens's journalistic context. The *Bulletin* was a popular commercial weekly, not a literary magazine. This format demanded a local, contemporary focus and delivered a new kind of audience to Stephens which he made his own, even if it lacked traditional forms of cultural capital. His criticism was almost wholly focussed on contemporary writing or the contemporary 'force' of earlier writers.[13] He wrote not through populist identification with his readers or fellow-writers but as one engaged in the same cultural enterprise, criticising in order to educate, entertain, improve, and exemplify 'the possibilities of work in literature' in Australia.[14] The *Bulletin* provided him with evidence of thousands of readers and writers 'quickening' across the continent, and Stephens defined his role in relation to this burgeoning national movement.

If Stephens was Australia's first professional literary critic, institutionally he was a professional journalist whose authority to talk about literature— and a wide range of other subjects—was general and amateur rather than specialist.[15] The profession of critic was still in its earliest stages. Stephens was the most original figure in a vigorous public culture of literary journalism, perhaps best represented in its witty and biting theatre criticism. In this commercial sphere the literary and the journalistic, the popular and the high, inhabited the same public space. Stephens had a journalist's sense of the craft of writing alongside an elevated, ideal notion of the literary. This combination enabled him to give the idea of a national literature a more popular meaning, while at the same time elevating popular reading and writing to questions of national and literary significance. His modernising literary nationalism was expressed in the radical break he saw between the colonial past and the emerging national present. Stephens shared the common view that literature should be both local and universal, but Australia, he argued, was no longer a matter of externals, incidental to the permanent truths. For the Australian writer, it was the necessary site of the universal, to be embraced not transcended: thus Stephens's insistence on the 'wealth of novel inspiration for the writers who will live Australia's life and utter her message'.[16] It was this mix of high and popular values that enabled the *Bulletin* and its Red Page to establish, not a new literary elite, but something like a 'national literary club' for a new generation of writers.[17]

Stephens's credentials as much more than a 'literary nationalist' are by now well established. His focus on the contemporary meant, no less, a focus on the international (this was not the opposite of 'national'; 'colonial' was). On the Red Page 'discussions and printings of Australian literature ran side by side with reviews of Stephen Crane, Kipling, Mark Twain, Gorki, Oscar Wilde, Olive Schreiner, Bernard Shaw, D'Annunzio, Henry James and many others'.[18] 'Cosmopolitan' was one of Stephens's preferred terms of praise, even if his list of writers who were 'essentially Australian, yet cosmopolitan' comprised only three rows of asterisks.[19] Critics have also defended Stephens from mere nationalism by showing how he judged Australian literature always on a 'universal' scale. Most famously, he celebrated Franklin's *My Brilliant Career* as 'the very first Australian novel' yet judged that it was 'not a notable literary performance'.[20] But the appeal to universal values is something of a mannerism in Stephens's criticism and it is likely to be the aspect of his writing least interesting to readers today. It reveals most clearly the limits of the journalistic sphere and the orthodox dimensions of Stephens's taste for 'artistic emotion' and 'ideals of beauty'.[21] It was difficult on this scale for realism ever to make it to the very highest artistic level. Modernism had even less chance, and Stephens's sense of the new would remain in the 1920s what it had been in the 1890s. The same might be said of Christopher Brennan despite his precocious appreciation of French Symbolism.[22]

MODERNISM AND THE NATIONAL CULTURE

The *Bulletin* continued into the twentieth century as Australia's principal magazine of review, producing new offshoots such as the *Bookfellow* and the *Lone Hand*. But by the 1920s its modernity had disappeared into a conservative, patriotic nationalism that was anti-cosmopolitan. Its literary pages were still varied and sometimes contentious—its weekly appearance encouraged conversation and debate on literary matters—but there was little of the creative pressure that Stephens had brought to bear. The Red Page itself was not noticeably nationalist. Essays and reviews covered much the same ground as any middlebrow English magazine. A few essays on art and nationality by Louis Esson and Vance Palmer were just one minor part of the mix and were answered in the predictable way with arguments about universality or individual greatness.[23]

The language of criticism was largely that of the romantic nineteenth century and the middlebrow twentieth century, as critics praised writing that was natural, simple, noble and sincere. But that language was increasingly under pressure. The Red Page of the early 1920s worried away at the manifestations of modernity all around it—Cubism, Futurism, Freud, Joyce, Pound, jazz, free verse and free women. America is ubiquitous, for it presented a special kind of problem. While American literature represented all the worst aspects of modernity—sex-obsessed, feminised and mass-produced—it also showed a distinctly American energy that could suggest just what Australian literature lacked. The *Bulletin* and other magazines, such as the *Triad*, that defined the Australian literary scene in the early twenties were on the cusp of a new 'modern' understanding of culture. As commercial magazines, most of them, they had a strong sense of their own contemporaneity. They could identify themselves with the world of Shaw, Wells, James, Conrad or Synge. But the 'ultra-moderns'—the 'neurotic-erotic moderns'—were another case altogether.[24] Modernism was characterised through a sense of *unbalance*, whether as ideas divorced from emotion, style distorting nature, or an overload of abstraction, introspection or sex. If one thing defined this moment of extreme modernism for its critics it was the way form seemed to be unhinged from feeling in violation of the 'natural' laws of artistic expression which called for their organic unity. Represented thus, as lacking form or as nothing but form, modernism was unnatural, primitive, and pathological, or merely fashionable, artificial, a confidence trick. It was typically the product of literary schools, cults or 'isms' not individual vision. By contrast, an optimistic pastoral tradition set the frame for Australian literature.

There was nothing unique about this Australian response to modernism nor were Australian critics 'behind the times', for modernism was still marginal in contemporary culture. But the sense of Australia as distant and different confirmed critics in their overwhelmingly dismissive response. Even for critics unenthusiastic about nationalism, Australia could be seen as a refuge from the twin aspects of modernity: the decadence of Europe, manifested in the fractured forms of modernist art, and the degraded modern culture of America, from jazz to cinema. Both were seen as alien to an Australia defined as young, vigorous, cheerful and manly, with a culture as wholesome as its climate.[25] Against a modern world divided into 'isms' or massed into an anonymous market, Australia was projected as still a 'living culture', a classless organic community, a unified nation.

In such terms criticism politely excused itself from having to think its way through the intellectual challenges of modernism. Australia's national characteristics belonged to a pre-industrial pastoral world cleansed even of Lawson's darker notes. These responses were not just ideological but also institutionally determined in that, unlike in America and England, there was no fully-fledged, distinct class of 'literary intellectuals'. The bohemian circles of writers that formed in the 1880s and 1890s had not developed into a permanent intelligentsia. Literature was reviewed in numerous papers but the mode was genial amateurism rather than intellectual authority. The magazines were broad in their contents and readership; even a dedicated journal of arts and letters such as the *Lone Hand* was proudly middlebrow. The universities had little to do with contemporary Australian literature. There was virtually no place within mainstream Australian literary culture where modernism—as a set of ideas, a movement—could be given an intellectual response. A fragmentary intelligentsia existed in more political domains, in socialist or rationalist movements for example, but these were marginal. Ideas of the nation as an ideal, democratic community did not encourage the concept of a separate class of intellectuals.

THE NATIONALIST PROJECT

It was against this background that literary nationalism—and the career of the nationalist intellectual—achieved its modern form, most prominently in the work of Vance and Nettie Palmer and P.R. Stephensen.[26] Although they inherited romantic, evolutionary notions of culture and shared with conservatives a belief in Australia's essential vitality, their nationalism was defined by a distinctly modern sense of social and cultural crisis. Its meaning lay not in celebration of a pastoral tradition but in the problem of modern democracy. Its formative moment was the emerging split between high and 'mass' cultures. Nationalism, in this view, was a contemporary movement; indeed, alongside the Irish revival, it was an *international* movement in which emerging or revived vernacular cultures would underwrite the creation of new, democratic societies worldwide.

The Palmers applied a general post-war analysis of cultural malaise to the specific situation of Australian culture. Their nationalism was a complex phenomenon: cosmopolitan in its sense of other national literatures, isolationist in its dislike of cosmopolitan modernism; populist but never certain that the public existed; more confident than Stephens about the deep origins of a national culture but more pessimistic about its continuity into the present; intellectual in calling for a serious, committed Australian literature, but anti-intellectual in the privileging of literature above abstract thought or modern 'isms'. Nonetheless, even if its solutions were inevitably more symptom than cure, nationalism between the wars did name an unresolved problem, the problem of colonial identity. Shorn of their organicism and populism, certain aspects of literary nationalism can—once again—strike us as surprisingly modern in their sense of a radical originality in Australian culture: for example, despite its romantic racism, Rex Ingamells's notion that Aboriginality was part of the contemporary meaning of Australian culture.[27]

From the other side of modernism, the Palmers worked the image of Australia's 1890s into a powerful myth of origins in which 'conscious literature' and folk ways were fused in the ideal image of an organic national culture. Such a myth 'solved' the problems of modernity and colonialism together. The writer should be at one with the reader, with the culture, the people and the soil, in a living relationship, an idea linked to the bush where individuality and community could still be imagined democratically as united. For Nettie Palmer the key notion was *intimacy*, the evolution of an intimate relation between writer and environment, writer and audience.[28] This was the message of Australia's 1890s, all but lost it seemed in the modernising twenties. On one side, provincial or colonial attitudes still prevailed; on the other, the new trends of cosmopolitanism and commercialisation threatened what fragile traditions had earlier been laid down. Without its own strong cultural life, Vance Palmer argued, Australia was peculiarly vulnerable to the cheapening (even feminisation) of culture, above all in the rootless cities and standardised suburbs.[29]

The heroic task of the contemporary writer and critic was to resist these forces and bring forth a common culture. Palmer found its modern expression in the *novel*, with Conrad as one model.[30] Against the general elevation of poetry, Palmer's commitment to the novel was symptomatic of the modern form of nationalism and was shared with a generation of literary nationalists who emerged in the 1930s. The novel was the art form, above all others, in which individual and social expression could be fused. In this sense, the ideal form of the novel was an ideal image of the national culture itself.

The modernity of the Palmers' nationalism can also be seen in their 'life project' as nationalist literary intellectuals, articulating a new image of the writer and *critic* as a public intellectual defined by his or her responsibility to serious literature and to the national culture. They worked to separate the vocation of intellectual from the uncommitted professional literary journalism that surrounded them. But there remained an anxiety, at once structural and ideological, towards the notion of the 'intellectual' as distinct from the 'writer'. Australia lacked *serious* critics and an 'impersonal critical atmosphere', but the notion of a professional intellectual or writing class was foreign to the idea of a national culture in touch with its popular roots. Yet there was no responsive or unified public for Australian writing. Where the people should have been, there instead was the mass audience, 'in its promiscuousness, vagueness and lack of any kind of unity'. Where, then, did the genuine culture and its 'peculiarly Australian kind of democracy' exist?[31] Among the people, or only among a small band of intellectuals after all; in social institutions or only in literature? The nationalist project was driven by these anxieties, alternating between pessimism at what had been lost or ignored and optimism that despite everything a distinctive culture persisted at the core of our national character, almost by definition, because it *was* the national character.

While mid-century nationalism extended Stephens's understanding of the national culture, it also represented a *narrowing* of what literature in Australia could mean. This was not simply a matter of the limits of the nationalist critical vocabulary, but an effect of the professionalisation of literary work in Australia in which the Palmers were centrally engaged. Throughout their criticism, they made clear distinctions between serious literature and everything else. In doing so they were defining the cultural authority of the critic. The narrowing of the field was in this sense a necessary effect of their efforts to give Australian literature depth and tradition, to make it worthy of intellectual work. But although the Palmers came as close as anyone to the public 'life of letters', their careers indicate the uncertain institutional status of the literary critic at least until the 1960s. Their work fell structurally between the professional and the amateur, with a significant degree of cultural authority legitimised through their public roles in literary journalism, but with no secure institutional location. The career of the freelance intellectual was partly choice, partly a virtue made out of necessity.

LITERARY INTELLECTUALS AND CULTURAL CRISIS

Despite the recurrence of nationalist language through to the 1950s it is misleading to see an unbroken nationalist mainstream dominating Australian criticism. Nationalism was crossed by a mix of traditional, vitalist, bohemian and communist tendencies that made up the web of literary conversation. The more 'intellectual' forms of nationalism took their bearings from European and American models as well as local traditions.

Literary nationalism had an ambivalent status, at once commonplace and marginal in the field of culture. That Australian culture had its source in the bush; that it was popular rather than intellectual and cheerful rather than gloomy; that it first took shape in Lawson and Paterson; that environment and national character together made it distinctive: such ideas were widespread. But only rarely were they shaped into a coherent intellectual program or cultural critique. Thus while most discussions of Australian literature assumed a 'nationalist' framework underscored by pastoral or post-Anzac myths, the militant nationalism of the Palmers, Stephensen and others was a minority position. As they attempted to distinguish the vocation of the intellectual from occasional literary journalism, nationalist intellectuals occupied one small corner of the literary field while arguing its centrality.

Literary nationalism had yet to find any authoritative statement or institutional identity. The strongest sense among the nationalist intelligentsia throughout the 1930s and 1940s was still of 'the inconsecutive nature of our literary life' and the feeling that the nationalist argument needed 'stating over and over'.[32] The forms of criticism remained ephemeral, their brief lives passing in the weekly or monthly papers. The *Bulletin* offered some continuity, some space for intellectual contestation, otherwise the critical density of periodical and book publication was mostly lacking. Expressions of anxiety about the national culture, its absence, betrayal or unfulfilled promise, were far more common than confident statements of the Australian tradition.

Further, political events in the 1930s—the Depression, the rise of international fascism and communism, the Spanish civil war and approaching world war—changed the meaning of democratic and nationalist arguments. These events were not seen as external to Australia (or to literature) but symptomatic of a deep crisis in its national culture, embedded within a crisis in civilisation itself.[33] Fascism abroad was linked to censorship and conservatism at home. Nationalism had to be distinguished from the complacent patriotism of the mainstream press and politics. For many writers, literary culture was at once politicised and 'intellectualised' by these events. The early thirties saw a number of little magazines influenced by radical political and artistic theories.[34] New writers' organisations were established, or, in the case of the Fellowship of Australian Writers, re-organised around a more explicit understanding of the writer's social responsibility. Novelists and critics turned to writing pamphlets on culture, democracy and freedom. The 'crisis of civilisation' demanded an engagement with new political and artistic ideas *together*, and in this crossover of aesthetic and political discourses the literary intellectual was called into being.

This was the moment of Stephensen's *The Foundations of Culture in Australia*. 'We are,' he wrote, 'being *forced* into national consciousness.' His essay is famous as an aggressive reprise of environmental language, but it is less well known as a call for intellectuals. 'An act of intellectual self-consciousness, an *act of thought* performed now, by those equipped to do the thinking for this nation, is necessary.' Stephensen found no sustaining tradition, no literature of contemporary Australia. He wanted 'a finer, less sensational, less *journalistic*, Australian literature'; in short, a more intellectually sophisticated and modern literature.[35]

THE AUSTRALIAN TRADITION

In 1942, a special 'Crisis Issue' of the new magazine, *Meanjin*, appeared (its name suggests the role Aboriginal culture played in the search for a national sense of belonging which also motivated the Jindyworobak movement).[36] It was symptomatic that in the space of a year or so, *Meanjin* had moved from a poetry magazine to cultural politics. By 1943 it had become a quarterly, the form of the most serious reviews and expressive of its distance from 'mere' journalism. *Meanjin* was a new kind of magazine in Australia, a magazine for literary intellectuals. Much of its talk was 'self-reflexive', discussions of the role of the writer or critic and of magazines. Cultural commentary, philosophy, literary criticism, history and anthropology appeared alongside verse and fiction in what seemed like a shared public sphere of liberal values. Editor C.B. Christesen was committed to opening up lines to European literature and philosophy, aligning Australian intellectual life with a 'modern tradition' which he understood in terms of an enlarged humanist realism.

Despite the broad range of its articles, literature remained at the centre of *Meanjin*'s interests as the medium through which cultural values were created and sustained. Christesen saw his magazine as 'a literary forum ... a document of our aesthetic development'.[37] He wanted it to produce 'a core of sound literary criticism'. It is important, while recognising the magazine's commitment to nationalist cultural politics, not to underestimate the role it played in sustaining the formal study of Australian literature. Alongside *Southerly*, *Meanjin* enabled the regular publication of extended critical studies. The two quarterlies 'virtually introduced the formal critical essay into twentieth century Australian literary criticism'.[38]

Perhaps the most important shift to which *Meanjin* contributed was a new confidence in talk about an Australian tradition. The *presence* of an Australian tradition comes to replace that sense of its loss or absence which had produced earlier nationalist arguments. The previous decade had seen a substantial output of new fiction and poetry that seemed both modern and distinctively Australian. M. Barnard Eldershaw's *Essays in Australian Fiction*, had, in 1938, taken the unprecedented step of devoting a whole book to individual studies of contemporary novelists (four male and four female writers).[39] Women played a much larger part in Australian literature and its criticism in this period before its institutionalisation in the universities. The newly-available density in the literary tradition was underscored by developments in the writing of Australian history, which, earlier than literature, had become the subject of a serious body of work, from W.K. Hancock to Brian Fitzpatrick. The late forties sees a concentration of articles in *Meanjin* on literature and the democratic tradition including Manning Clark's first two contributions, on mateship and tradition.[40]

The notion of an Australian cultural tradition received its authoritative statements in a series of major books in the 1950s: Vance Palmer's *The Legend of the Nineties*, A.A. Phillips's *The Australian Tradition* and Russel Ward's *The Australian Legend*.[41] These books were historical studies of a social tradition: 'the evolving personality and the evolving traditions of the Australian community, as reflected in the works of our writers'.[42] Although the socio-political rather than environmental aspects of nationalism now received greater emphasis, the image of the bush contained both meanings at once. Realism and democracy, it was assumed, went together. Australia's unique historical experiences had given rise to distinctively Australian attitudes, democratic, nationalist and popular, which were manifested at first unconsciously in ballads and folk song and then consciously in the literature of the 1890s. These same ideals *still* defined what was most valuable, and most Australian, in Australian society and culture. That was the point of the argument, sharpened for nationalist intellectuals by their sense of a new struggle between true and false popular cultures and true and false democracies during the Cold War. When *Overland* magazine began in 1954, connected to the Communist Party and the Realist Writers movement, it could name itself heir to a continuous democratic and realist Australian tradition.[43] Communist intellectuals shared this democratic nationalist reading of Australia's literary history but articulated a more politically-conscious working-class tradition within nationalism.[44]

What is easily forgotten is the newness of this understanding of the Australian tradition after the war, particularly its radical democratic edge. The sense of a tradition with historical density extending back into the nineteenth century and forward into contemporary literature was scarcely available earlier, to even the most optimistic nationalists, although it had always been foreshadowed.

For Phillips, by contrast, there was a 'democratic theme' in Australian literature reflecting the 'spirit of the nineties'. Its effects could be found in a wide range of contemporary writers as a belief in 'the Common Man', a determination to do without the 'fripperies' of aesthetic practice—though Phillips could also refer to Joseph Furphy's 'literary modernism'—and a 'preference for revealing the simple verities rather than the sophistications of human nature'.[45] Phillips was university-educated but, like Marjorie Barnard and Flora Eldershaw, wrote as an informed amateur (in the fullest meaning of the word). The amateur critic in this sense was closer to the figure of the public intellectual than was the academic specialist, in a period when the bulk of the criticism of Australian literature was still written outside the university.

The notion of an Australian tradition gave new complexity and depth to nationalist cultural history. But it also simplified and narrowed the *literary* history. The body of a strong democratic and realist tradition immediately produced its shadow; an alternative stream of 'Australian literature' which could only be seen as alien, belonging neither to its time or place or to its public, but *there* nevertheless—colonial verse, Christopher Brennan and, more recently, Patrick White. Underlying the 'tradition' was still an organic, evolutionary model of the national culture, emerging from colonialism into national self-consciousness and then, soon if not quite yet, to 'unself-conscious' maturity. Ironically, nationalist criticism revealed its limitations most clearly where it also found its strengths, in its understanding of literature as a social phenomenon.

AUSTRALIAN LITERATURE AND THE UNIVERSITIES

Meanjin and *Southerly* went further than any previous journals in bringing together academic and amateur work. One part of the nationalist argument had long been that Australia *had* a literature and it should be studied. Some Australian literature had been researched and taught in universities since the 1920s.[46] This work was uncontroversial because it remained clearly supplementary to the English department's core business. By the 1950s, however, the place of Australian literature in the universities became contentious, first because of the pressure of the newly-articulated Australian tradition, second because of changes in the English departments themselves. Lectures sponsored by the Commonwealth Literary Fund were also important, bringing non-academic critics such as Miles Franklin into the universities while giving younger university critics the chance to exercise their professional skills on Australian literature.

In 1954 *Meanjin* initiated a forum on the question of 'Australian Literature and the Universities'. The academic contributors were not hostile to Australian literature but they were sceptical as to whether it possessed the necessary cultural capital for the real work of English, as a training in critical standards and 'sensibility'. Only Vance Palmer argued differently, proposing 'Australian studies' rather than literature in isolation.[47] Nonetheless the density which now cohered around the Australian tradition was felt more widely than by nationalist intellectuals alone. In the two decades following the war, a new generation of professional critics entered Australian English departments, trained in the modern tradition and armed with the vocation of 'English' and its methods of ethico-formalist criticism.[48] Such views intensified the centrality of criticism itself in the literary domain; they also revealed Australian literature as a 'new' field scarcely touched by modern criticism and demanding its close scrutiny. *Was* there a tradition? Was it a *literary* tradition? Did it coincide with the *best* Australian literature?

The decade from the mid-1950s saw the institutionalisation of Australian literature in that its locus shifted from the ephemeral forms of general magazines, newspapers and occasional books of 'amateur' criticism to the university, critical quarterlies, and eventually books of criticism. Vincent Buckley's return to the question of Australian literature and the universities in 1959 summed up a process that had already begun in critical articles: the necessity of applying the same 'standards' to Australian literature as were applied to English literature. What was needed, Buckley argued, was critical discrimination in forming a properly articulated canon of Australian authors based on 'some agreement about their relative value'; and then, more reluctantly, 'some link between Australian literature and Australian history or sociology: if only to stop the swamping of our literature by sociological interests and criteria'.[49] The latter reference was to nationalist criticism. A work should be analysed, not as an 'adjunct' to sociology, but as a 'document in the history of Australian attitudes and sensibility': 'It would [then] be a *literary* analysis all the way'. This slight shift of focus from sociology to sensibility had major consequences in redefining the autonomy of both the literary text and literary criticism. The national historical framework remained but it was removed from the centre of properly literary concerns.

The institutionalisation of literary criticism within the universities meant arguing Australian literature back into the mainstream of English or European literature, back into a modern tradition. (Strangely, then, the new criticism was generally very narrow in its own intellectual reference points. It seldom stretched far beyond the reach of Arnold, Eliot and Leavis.) The literary works that were most highly valued were those seen as aligning Australian reality with European culture in a synthesis, either of the Australian and the traditional or the Australian and the modern, which was taken to define the *maturity* of Australian literature. Maturity was also figured in terms of emerging 'individuality' in literary works (as opposed to social or 'sociological' concerns). This approach favoured relatively neglected, complex, 'European' writers such as Brennan and Henry Handel Richardson. An extraordinary number of studies of these two writers was produced from the 1950s to the 1970s.[50] The argument towards maturity was also a reflection of the critics' own 'mature' institutionalisation.

In the process of revaluation, literary values were discerned less in formal characteristics than in moral, 'metaphysical' or 'spiritual' questions.[51] These were grasped as universal in contrast to ephemeral sociological interests. Discovering literary greatness was not as important as discovering the right kind of 'literariness'. Brennan's poetry was valued upwards: although a failed *oeuvre* it was the right kind of failure, compared to Paterson who represented the wrong kind of success. In a series of publications from the early 1950s Australian writers past and present were subject to critical scrutiny.[52] Colonial writing was revalued, especially poetry, because again it showed the right kind of literariness; poetry in general was revalued against the nationalist preference for realist prose. Canonical authors like Lawson were reinterpreted for the metaphysical beneath their social themes.

Re-interpreting the high nationalist moment of the 1890s against 'strictly literary standards', G.A. Wilkes concluded:

> Lawson is memorable not for the part of his work ... that reflects the temper of his age, but for the part that transcends it, while Furphy's work is important not for its democratic temper or offensively Australian bias, but for its exploration of issues that are not local, but universal in their reference. ... The best poetry written at the time [Brennan] is unrelated to social and political movements, as is the work of the most notable novelist to emerge [Richardson].[53]

Buckley provided a similar revaluation in 'The Image of Man in Australian Poetry', the lead piece in his *Essays in Poetry, Mainly Australian* (the casual authority of the titles suggests the weight of the institution).[54] Brennan, not Lawson, was the pivotal figure, producing 'the first genuinely unselfconscious Australian poetry ... representative of the human condition in a way, and with a depth, which makes Lawson's attempt at representative statement appear no more than striking of an average'. The notion of poetry shaping Buckley's essays carries within it all the weight of the modern tradition, from Arnold to Eliot.

'Brennan stands like a Colossus between the world of our first nationhood and the world of our modern endeavours'. This remarkable figure grounds Buckley's subsequent account, leading to a model of synthesis at once familiar from earlier critics and radically new in the literary history it describes. *Southerly* and the *Bulletin*, especially under Douglas Stewart's editorship of the Red Page (1940–61), had maintained a strand of Australian literature, especially poetry, based on a more vitalist, individualist ideology than the nationalist tradition.[55] Many of the twentieth-century poets featured in the influential 1958 *Penguin Book of Australian Verse* were not easily accommodated in the nationalist canon, but they now became the very definition of Australian literature's modern maturity. Buckley traces a line from Brennan to Kenneth Slessor and R.D. Fitzgerald then to Francis Webb, James McAuley, A.D. Hope, Judith Wright and Stewart himself. This was the evolution that mattered, not the democratic tradition. Australian poetry was reaching 'spiritual maturity', a 'deepening of sensibility to the point where the land is conceived ... in terms which are at once spiritual, moral, sensory, and directed to the drama of human existence'. The poets were *individual*; and while not 'in any obvious or insistent way, Australian' each had 'begun to bring together into a satisfying synthesis the objective and the subjective ... European culture and Australian fact'. Buckley insisted that his arguments for 'a literature strongly rooted in a local place and atmosphere are not at all the same as the arguments for a nationalist bias and stereotype'.[56]

MODERNITY AND MATURITY: PATRICK WHITE AND THE CANON

The nationalist social tradition was rendered superficial in relation to true literary meaning, and *obsolete*, as if belonging to an earlier, 'immature' moment in the culture's development. The argument with nationalism was partly about redefining the image of Australian modernity. Buckley rewrote the history of Australian poetry to show the contemporary poets as its deepest evolutionary outcome. In another influential essay, H.P. Heseltine rewrote the history of Australian literature so that Patrick White emerged as its modernity and its maturity.[57]

Heseltine defined the 'literary heritage' (not 'tradition') as 'that element of our most accomplished literary works which makes known their Australianness'; he thus makes literary standards coincide with distinctive national qualities. Heseltine takes three common versions of the Australian tradition: Phillips's 'democratic theme'; confrontation with the land; and evolution from colony to nationhood. Each has a point, he argues, but none is adequate to define 'the very *centre* of the Australian imagination'. Calling on Lionel Trilling's notion of 'the modern element in modern literature', Heseltine, who had studied in America, modernises the Australian canon by claiming that it is this modern element that defines the 'Australianness of Australian writing'. From the beginning, Australian literature expressed 'the terror at the basis of being', an apprehension that continued from Clarke to Lawson to Hope and White. White's *Voss* provides the ultimate synthesis, for it 'fuses almost all those aspects of Australia's literary heritage which define both its modernity and its Australianness'. This was a powerful form of argument that did not reject the nationalist tradition but absorbed it, giving it a new depth and modernity.

The sudden emergence of White's novels *The Tree of Man* and *Voss* was a major event in the history of Australian criticism. The two novels took themes deeply embedded in nationalist history but treated them in a symbolic or 'metaphysical' manner that appeared to contradict the democratic, realist tradition. For some, White was an un-Australian writer, anti-realist and anti-democratic.[58] For a critic like Buckley, by contrast, he was just the kind of writer who might be canonised—another case of 'spiritual maturity'— whether or not his works were totally successful literary achievements.[59] White's fiction seemed to be at once highly individual, firmly within a modern tradition, *and* distinctively Australian. Critics linked him to contemporaries such as Hope and McAuley (and Sidney Nolan) and to Brennan as precursor, even though they often remained uncomfortable with his 'anti-organic' symbolism and disdain of the genteel.[60]

For many nationalist critics, White caused a troubled revaluation of the Australian tradition, already under stress from the weight of critical re-interpretation. Such was the power of White's canonisation that to reject him was virtually to announce one's own marginality. White could be accommodated by broadening the notion of realism to include, say, 'psychological realism' or by changing the grounds of the tradition itself. *Overland* shifted its talk from the Australian 'tradition' to the Australian 'myth'.[61] John McLaren argued that White was 'the latest contributor to a distinctly Australian tradition, which rises from the hostility of the landscape to man's efforts to tame it'. Phillips added a footnote to the 1966 edition of *The Australian Tradition* to the effect that, in *The Tree of Man*, White had 'succeeded in reconciling a sensitive interpretation of Australian life with a keen feeling for the spiritual mysteries'. By the mid-sixties, in short, the new language of metaphysical depth had won the day even within nationalism itself.

The re-defined Australian literary tradition was confirmed in a series of books. Buckley's *Essays in Poetry* contained individual studies of Slessor, Fitzgerald, Hope, Wright and McAuley. Grahame Johnston's collection, *Australian Literary Criticism*, reprinted Wilkes on the 1890s, Hope's seminal 'Standards in Australian Literature', and individual essays on Brennan, John Shaw Neilson, Fitzgerald, Slessor, Wright, Hope, McAuley, Lawson, Furphy, Richardson, Martin Boyd, Xavier Herbert and White. Geoffrey Dutton's more generous *The Literature of Australia* included broader essays, some in the nationalist vein, but was again dominated by essays on individual writers in the canon.[62] Wilkes's *Australian Literature: A Conspectus* drew the orthodox themes into a book-length study. White in fiction, Hope and McAuley in poetry, provided the culmination of its story: their work represented 'the extension of European civilisation, and the assertion of an indigenous culture' coming together 'to produce a literature that is both distinctive and mature'.[63] Despite its different intellectual provenance, Wright's 'romantic-idealist' study of traditional and environmental influences in her *Preoccupations in Australian Poetry* could be recruited to the cause. It would take another generation before the postcolonial potential of Wright's—or Brian Elliott's—criticism could be perceived.[64]

POLITICS AND PROFESSIONALISATION

As John Docker has argued, the anti-nationalist tenor of the new academic criticism was not only an effect of its institutionalisation but also of its political context within what Buckley called the 'peculiarly Australian intellectual cold war'.[65] Literature was a key battlefield in this ideological struggle because of its traditional significance as the bearer of both national and universal meanings. Although for most critics, the move beyond nationalism was a matter of applying appropriate professional rather than political standards in criticism, the influence of the cold war notion of the 'end of ideology' was pervasive. For others, like Buckley and McAuley, there was a more conscious project of wresting the cultural meanings of the national literature away from left-leaning nationalist or communist intellectuals. McAuley's opening editorial in *Quadrant* met point by point the foundational principles of cultural nationalism by redefining the core concepts of Australianness, modernity, democracy, tradition, liberalism and literature.[66] As Susan Lever has argued, the poetry published in *Quadrant*, although apolitical, worked to underwrite the magazine's ideological project.[67] The 'ordered, rational, decorous' poetic language spoke eloquently for civilised tradition against the twin evils of nationalism and modernism (communism, for McAuley, was a form of both).

To see the cultural field polarised into antagonistic ideological camps dramatises the fact of a fundamental struggle over cultural authority in the 1950s and 1960s among literary intellectuals. It captures the *institutional* distance between nationalist and 'new' critics. But it is misleading if it suggests utterly opposed notions of literature or literary criticism. Underlying debates over the meaning of the Australian tradition was a common 'expressive realist' aesthetic based on organic form and fidelity to individual experience. Christesen, Phillips and the Palmers shared with the academic critics a belief in literary autonomy, in 'disinterested criticism', and in the universal values of great literature.[68] So did most communist writers. On the other hand, modernism remained as difficult for Hope and McAuley as for nationalist critics, while for others it could be accommodated from an academic distance as a modern tradition. Buckley and Wilkes were as committed to defining the distinctive qualities of Australian literature as were nationalist critics. Some, like Heseltine or Vivian Smith, although within the circle of the new academic criticism, were not anti-nationalist in their wider intellectual sympathies. There was a broadly shared assumption (not shared by McAuley) about the natural links between literature and the values of liberal humanism.

Interestingly, like earlier commentators, authoritative university critics such as Buckley, Hope and McAuley still derived much of their cultural status from *outside* the university, as poets, and therefore as committed 'amateur' readers rather than academic specialists. Christopher Lee has described a complex set of sceptical, sometimes hostile responses among writers, literary journalists—and academics themselves—to the professionalisation of the criticism of Australian literature.[69] Institutionalisation brought with it the suspicion that the role of academic was less than adequate to the role of writer or (less commonly) the intellectual. Buckley argued that literature was not really a university subject at all in the sense that other subjects were.[70]

As Patrick Buckridge suggests, the commitment by university critics to Australian literature must be understood in positive not merely negative, anti-nationalist terms.[71] Buckley's commitment to literature was part of a broader commitment to the intellectual life, which saw literature as profoundly expressive of the human condition. Wilkes's criticism was as often scholarly as evaluative or anti-nationalist, as in his studies of Brennan. The new criticism *could* render Australian literary works as complex, morally-serious texts in ways that nationalist criticism had rarely managed.

There was also an ongoing stream of 'middle-ground' criticism that remained largely unaffected by the intellectual cold war, for example the monumental work of H.M. Green, memorable for its discussions of print culture, or Cecil Hadgraft's regular books. A less narrowly evaluative concern with literary history and scholarship continued alongside ethico-formalist analysis in *Australian Literary Studies* (launched in 1963). Novelists, poets and journalists continued to review in the newspapers, although academic critics became increasingly prominent. Nonetheless, despite being a minority position in some respects, it was the mode of evaluative criticism that captured the intellectual high ground, such that its frameworks came to dominate criticism of Australian literature into the 1980s, to become the 'common sense' of critical practice, and to make *careers* in Australian literature possible long after the cultural politics of its founding moment had dissolved. Later critics such as Brian Matthews and Brian Kiernan, with no cold war campaign against nationalism, show its influence: Matthews in his analysis of Lawson as a kind of proto-existentialist, Kiernan in reading the fiction canon through the theme of the 'individual and society'.[72] The dominant mode of criticism was the formal academic essay on an individual text or writer; concerns with cultural history were pushed to the margins although they would never quite disappear.

LITERARY CRITICISM AND LITERARY THEORY

Australian literary criticism in the 1970s remained marked by its founding moment as a university study. Australian literature was widely taught although its typical status was as an 'option' added to the core English curriculum. More criticism than ever before was being published in a range of established magazines including *Meanjin, Southerly, Overland, Westerly* and *Australian Literary Studies*. The formation of the Association for the Study of Australian Literature (ASAL) in 1977 represented both the culmination of the critical enterprise of the previous two decades and the stirring of new developments beyond its orthodoxy. Australian literature was now academically respectable but many of its younger advocates also wanted it to be more than 'merely' academic. Although ethico-formalist criticism remained dominant, Australian literature also became the vehicle for a revised cultural politics.

The 1970s saw a period of complex neo-nationalism in Australian culture and historiography. In intellectual terms this neo-nationalism was founded in a critique of 'old' nationalism, denounced for its racism, sexism and lack of theoretical rigour, most famously in Humphrey McQueen's *A New Britannia*.[73] But the critique was also anti-imperialist, hence predisposed towards new articulations of nationalism. The influence of New Left neo-Marxism, especially in history and politics departments, was decisive.[74] If there were certain Australian traditions to be rejected, there were others to be reclaimed. A revitalised interest in national histories coincided with new movements in Australian fiction, poetry, drama, journalism and cinema.

Against these movements the university could look like the last refuge of imperialist attitudes, especially English departments. The institutionalisation of Australian literature could appear *too* successful given the dominance of formalist studies. Most of the important books which helped redefine attitudes to Australian literary studies came from outside the English department: McQueen's books, Anne Summers's *Damned Whores and*

God's Police (1975), Miriam Dixson's *The Real Matilda* (1976), David Walker's *Dream and Disillusion* (1976), Tim Rowse's *Australian Liberalism and National Character* (1978), Drusilla Modjeska's *Exiles at Home* (1981), Richard White's *Inventing Australia* (1981) and Sylvia Lawson's *The Archibald Paradox* (1983). From within English, John Docker's *Australian Cultural Elites* (1974) expanded the boundaries of literary criticism into a politically-informed history of ideas which, amongst much else, argued the sexist basis of the 'Sydney' tradition of vitalist idealism, from Brennan to Hope and White.

Feminism and neo-Marxism were linked via the central concept of *ideology* through which accepted versions of Australian history and culture were criticised and politicised. Both radical nationalist and conservative liberal traditions were critiqued. The claims to universal truth or ideological disinterest which had sustained the academic institutionalisation of Australian literature were directly challenged. Still, new theories of *textuality*, structuralist or poststructuralist, had a less immediate effect in literature departments. A radical historiography was not necessarily linked to radical notions of the text or the 'linguistic turn'. If literary criticism was slow on the up-take perhaps this was because the one thing structuralist, poststructuralist and neo-Marxist theories shared was scepticism about the autonomy of the literary text—and with that went the late-romantic notions of authorship, individuality and organic form which had sustained the critical enterprise.

There was a perception in the 1970s and early 1980s that criticism of *Australian* literature was particularly resistant to 'theory', that is, to the examples of feminist, Marxist, structuralist and poststructuralist theories which were rapidly emerging in the academy, as if theory were foreign both to the nationalist sympathies of Australian studies and to the concerns of a literary criticism still involved in justifying Australian literature's place in the university. A survey of the mainstream critical periodicals in this period nevertheless reveals shifts in the critical agenda. While formal studies of individual texts and authors still dominate, feminist terms and notions of ideology begin to appear in literary essays. Across all journals, interestingly, race becomes a recurrent issue (*The Chant of Jimmie Blacksmith* was an important catalyst).[75] Numerous articles indicate that contemporary Australian drama in this period posed unfamiliar questions about genre and ideology, and new Australian fiction and poetry soon demanded similar rethinking beyond the boundaries of expressive realism. Contemporary American literature became a more important reference than the English tradition for contemporary Australian work. Still, explicit theorisation remained the exception—spectacularly so in two articles by Don Anderson which managed to refer to Northrop Frye, Marx, Freud, Barthes, Macherey and Lévi-Strauss.[76] Anderson's subjects—Christina Stead and Patrick White—suggest that there remained an inverse relation between an interest in nationalism and an interest in theory.

Outside mainstream literary criticism, however, a flourishing sub-culture of informal reading groups emerged in the 1970s among students and younger academics, perhaps with some parallels to the writers' associations of the 1930s except that the *literary* no longer dominated. The novelist or literary intellectual was replaced by the 'cultural theorist', and before too long careers in 'theory' could be pursued. It was precisely the collapse of literary autonomy and the anti-empirical 'excess' of theory that seemed liberating. New theoretical work was consumed with enormous energy, not surprising when even Frye could come as a revelation. Raymond Williams, Terry Eagleton and Frederic Jameson led back to Marx, Lukács, Benjamin, Adorno and Russian Formalism, or to Althusser, Macherey and Foucault; Barthes led back to Lévi-Strauss and Saussure or forward to Derrida and de Man; Lacan and Kristeva led back to Freud. The trajectories closely followed those being pursued in British and North American universities, including the high-tension debates about 'foreign theory', but Australian work soon developed its own dynamics governed in part by its postcolonial situation.

One indicative occasion was the *Foreign Bodies* conference on 'Semiotics in/and Australia' held in February 1981, with papers subsequently published by the Local Consumption Collective (the titles are richly suggestive).[77] *The Foreign Bodies Papers* included three essays specifically on literature although perhaps only one which would have been recognised as 'literary criticism'. The interest, instead, was in the construction of authorship, the authority of critic and teacher, the literary institution, and the nature of literary textuality and textual politics; the references are to Foucault, Barthes, Baudrillard, Lacan, Eagleton, Deleuze and Derrida. This was indeed a foreign world to the earlier post-war generation of critics. The location of the conference and publication outside the mainstream periodicals and other disciplinary forms suggests well enough where poststructuralism stood in 1981.

By the early eighties some critique of the poverty of theory in Australian literary studies was being voiced 'within' the field itself. The notions of individuality and value which had established the modern canon appeared oppressively moralistic in the face of the new literary movements and naïve, indeed anti-intellectual, in their understanding of textuality. This was made strikingly clear in the hostile response accorded the 1981 *Oxford History of Australian Literature*. For some of the book's reviewers at least, the ideological bias of its criticism, its unquestioning assumption of authority, and its inability to deal with history or the national culture were almost scandalously evident.[78]

The 'arrival' of literary theory was announced controversially, and in one sense prematurely, at the 1982 ASAL conference. Papers included Sneja Gunew on 'discourses of otherness', drawing on Foucault and Kristeva; Ian Reid on the status of the literary text and canon, drawing on Marxist, semiotic and reader-response theory; Graeme Turner and Delys Bird on the theorisation of Australian studies alongside cultural studies; and Carole Ferrier on 'proletarian fiction', using Marxist and feminist theory.[79] All except Ferrier were then teaching in newer interdisciplinary contexts rather than in traditional English departments. Other papers, although more orthodox critically, introduced feminism and Aboriginal literature.

Although it would be the best part of a decade before the full impact of poststructuralist or deconstructive theories was absorbed into the mainstream of Australian literary criticism, the new tendencies represented by these papers dramatically redefined the field of Australian literature and its criticism over the course of the 1980s. Modjeska's *Exiles at Home* and Reid's *Fiction and the Great Depression* contributed to a positive re-reading of the fiction of the 1930s and 1940s through feminist and Marxist categories. Feminist criticism had the single greatest influence in reshaping the nature of Australian literary studies through to the mid-1990s, not only in its critique of the masculinism of the nationalist tradition and the established canon, but positively in the rediscovery of mid-century women writers and the recovery of colonial romance and autobiographical genres. These genres had been invisible or negative examples to both nationalist and 'universalist' critics. *Gender, Politics and Fiction*, edited by Ferrier, continued the process of re-reading authors marginalised in the canon on the basis of gender, genre, politics or ethnicity. Communist, social realist and working-class writings were all the subject of new research.[80]

As early as 1984, Docker could attack the new formalism of High Theory, although the main force of his book, *In a Critical Condition*, was to savage the ideological freight of the 'metaphysical orthodoxy' still dominant in Australian criticism. Other works explicitly signalled their debts to structuralist and poststructuralist theory. Graeme Turner's *National Fictions* examined national traditions and myths across both cinema and literary texts, bringing literary criticism and cultural theory together. The book's impact was muted, perhaps because its literary references were mostly canonical although its method pointed elsewhere. Turner began with the proposition that ideologies or cultures rather than individuals produce meanings: 'As the culture produces its texts *it* prefers certain meanings, thematic structures and formal strategies. Within these ... we find the ideology of the culture'.[81] Such a proposition could still be scandalous in literary studies although already commonplace elsewhere. Kay Schaffer's *Women and the Bush* began from a similar point, this time bringing feminist and psychoanalytical theory to bear on the gendered mythologies of land and identity. Although orthodox in critical vocabulary, Adam Shoemaker's *Black Words, White Page* helped establish Aboriginal writing as a subject internal to Australian literature. Mudrooroo's *Writing from the Fringe* theorised the issue from a black perspective.

These changes in criticism are summed up in Ken Gelder and Paul Salzman's 1989 study of contemporary fiction, *The New Diversity*.[82] The book included no chapters on individual authors but was organised around particular genres, including popular genres, and around issues of cultural difference and exclusion—gender and sexuality, politics and history, Asia, regionalism, the migrant experience, and Aboriginality. The book is a study of the relationship between textuality and ideology. Similarly, although its organising principles were looser, the 1988 *Penguin New Literary History of Australia* had no essays on individual authors but instead, among other topics, essays on Aboriginal writing, women's writing, political fiction, children's literature, autobiography, and literary production. The fact that it was only mildly theoretical and aimed at the middle ground makes it all the more significant of how far changes in the critical institution had by this time been accepted.

For many in Australian literary studies, structuralist and poststructuralist theories arrived almost simultaneously. One effect of this delayed and compressed arrival was their agglutination into the single category of 'theory' which could then be opposed to 'normal' practice. A more interesting effect has been the relative importance accorded to the social and political rather than philosophical or linguistic dimensions of theoretical work. The general force of (post)structuralist theory in Australia was registered in a framework already defined by feminist and Marxist categories and by the critique of nationalism they provided. While postcolonial criticism has a complex theoretical relation to both feminism and Marxism (which it has largely displaced), in practice its critical modes have been largely complementary to them. Thus by the late 1980s some notion of 'textual politics' had become constitutive of contemporary criticism. Criticism became critique, 'deconstruction' became a shorthand for work on ideology, and semiotic play was taken as a sign of subversion. But while deconstruction and semiology have been influential, the revision of textual analysis and literary history has been more generally weighted towards questions of gender, race and nation.[83] We can observe the shift in Robert Dixon's work, from a neutral history of ideas in *The Course of Empire* to a politically-conscious, deconstructive critical history in *Writing the Colonial Adventure*.[84] In the latter, which treats popular genres and journalism alongside high art forms, the influence of Marxist 'ideology critique' is overwritten by poststructuralist and postcolonial concerns with representation and subjectivity. Although the focus is on texts—on the narrative shaping of ideologies—the framework is cultural history.

POSTMODERNISM—POST-CRITICISM?

By the late-1980s most literary studies departments included Australian literature courses in an array of options that diluted the traditional core function of English literature. Notions of literary autonomy persisted, of course; poststructuralism could be routinised as little more than a new style of 'close reading'; and teaching and criticism continued, inevitably, to produce canons. But criticism—at least within the academy—developed a new relation to the process of canon formation, less concerned with maintenance or defence than with challenging the process of canonisation, revealing its exclusions, and dissolving it back into (political) histories of production and reception. Simon During's *Patrick White* is an indicative text. Although in the guise of a single-author study, it pursues its subject not through the individual 'vision' but through cultural institutions and 'as part of a transitional moment in the emergence of postcolonial Australia'. The effect is profoundly non-canonical and the book was controversial among literary journalists and some established critics.[85]

Australian literary history has been thoroughly re-written since the early 1980s. It is almost impossible now to think 'Australian literature' without thinking women's writing, Aboriginal writing, or ethnic minority writing.[86] In the 1990s, in what we might call the second wave of theoretical innovation, postcolonialism became increasingly important in articulating notions of identity and difference, in work on colonial and indigenous writings, and in shifting analysis away from Australia's national distinctiveness to what it might share with other settler colonies.[87] Queer theory has emerged too, but as yet without the same inevitability. 'Australian literature'— the construction of Australian literature through the process of canon formation—has sometimes been seen not as the oppressed space of national identity and freedom, but as the oppressive dominant asserting its power by excluding a range of different voices which it is the task of criticism to argue back into the field. Certainly the field of Australian literature has been given new breadth, depth and diversity.

In some ways the canon has merely been modernised once more, its past realigned with its present to accommodate new literary developments such as Aboriginal literature. More profoundly, the sense of an Australian literature or tradition has been dispersed across a wide range of written, oral and visual forms such as autobiography, biography, travel and history writing, journalism, essays, crime, romance, science fiction, cinema and television. The literary is no longer a pure category. Thus, the question of what constitutes 'literary criticism' is no longer self-evident either: is it something distinct or merely a branch of cultural studies or history? Recent critical work, for example, has included studies of explorer narratives; representations of 'the Centre'; indigenous narratives across different media; the Eliza Fraser stories; travel writing; even gardening. Those trained in literature might write about media, republicanism or the Aboriginal sacred, while writers from 'outside' literary studies such as Stephen Muecke or Meaghan Morris have as much to say to it as those within the field.

Such developments have been international, but they have a particular edge in Australian criticism because of the potential proximity of cultural politics to national politics, for example around issues of race. The cultural dynamics of Australia's place in the world have also shifted. In both positive and negative ways, Australia can now be seen as *exemplary* rather than merely supplementary; exemplary, for example, of such postmodern and postcolonial conditions as McKenzie Wark describes when claiming that 'the great virtue of Australian culture is its unoriginality—that it borrows shamelessly from all manner of foreign sources, that it adapts and collages'.[88] The anxieties about maturity and universal values that drove 'modern' criticism in Australia have suddenly disappeared, not because they were solved but because they ceased to pose interesting questions. Australia has become an exporter of work in postcolonialism, cultural studies, feminism, Foucault and more, or rather one point in a circulation network in which import/export metaphors no longer make the best sense.

Inevitably the approaches that rose to prominence in the 1980s and 1990s can be represented as a new orthodoxy. Despite their oppositional rhetoric they have become more or less constitutive of the critical institution. The textual revelation of 'transgressive' elements in literary works—the dominant mode of criticism by the mid-1990s—can be as routinised, romanticised and ahistorical as any earlier method. There have, subsequently, been signs of a shift towards a more 'positive' cultural history of literary institutions and practices which goes beyond negative critique alone. At least this is one strand in a field that shifts from semiotics to sociology, and from sexual politics to textual scholarship. Certainly the anti-canonical moment has (in the new century) lost some of its energy and purpose as the discipline itself has sometimes seemed under siege from adjacent fields within the academy, such as cultural studies, and from outside the academy, from opinion columnists, politicians or disenchanted English teachers. While the force of anti-canonical critiques must still be recognised, a new consolidation around the positive practices of criticism is beginning to emerge, for example in new interests in questions of 'literature and ethics' or in the history of print cultures and publishing in Australia.[89]

If literary studies reasserted its centrality when linguistic and semiotic-based theories altered the nature of work across the humanities, it did so at the cost of any secure sense of literature as a privileged or distinct domain of meaning. Hence the disquiet among some sections of the literary world both inside and outside the academy. Literary criticism in the university has responded in a number of ways, sometimes reaffirming the tradition of modernity or the avant-garde notion of literature as a permanent opposition; sometimes reinventing work on texts as discourse analysis; sometimes turning literary criticism into cultural studies or cultural history; and sometimes reaffirming the deep significance of textual play. Perhaps Vincent Buckley's notion that literature was not really a university subject sufficient to itself has been proven correct, although not at all in the sense he intended.

DRAWING THE LINE
Art in Australia and the Contemporary Modern

Art in Australia was the first commercial magazine devoted to the fine arts and craft in Australia. Indeed across its lifespan from 1916 to 1942 it was the only such magazine in the mainstream print market.[1] It was initially edited by its main progenitor, Sydney Ure Smith, together with Bertram Stevens, also editor of the *Lone Hand*, and Charles Lloyd Jones, later manager of the David Jones department store. When Art in Australia Ltd was established in 1921, the three became the company's directors, and from the November 1921 issue Ure Smith and Stevens alone were listed as editors. Following Stevens's death in February 1922, poet and journalist Leon Gellert became Ure Smith's co-editor. In her detailed study of Ure Smith's career, Nancy Underhill insists on the active role played by his collaborators, but as she also makes clear, Ure Smith was the only one among the editors with a primary interest in the visual arts and extensive connections in the art world.[2] He was a practising artist, art patron and entrepreneur, President of the Sydney-based Society of Artists from 1921 and a trustee of the National Art Gallery of New South Wales from 1927. He was also a partner in Smith and Julius, Sydney's classiest advertising agency. The agency opened important professional and business contacts to Ure Smith, and also provided work for many emerging local artists. According to Lloyd Rees, its studio functioned as 'something of an unofficial art centre of Australia-wide significance'.[3]

Ure Smith thus worked across the commercial and artistic realms on a daily basis, and although the commercial imperative was often seen in the magazine's pages as the enemy of true Art, *Art in Australia* was always and unapologetically located within the marketplace. It was expensive, at the outset more expensive than the imported British fine arts magazine *Studio*, and each issue 'was more like a deluxe special publication than a serial magazine on contemporary art'.[4] It did become more 'magazine-like', moving to quarterly publication in early 1921, bimonthly from July 1930 to December 1933, then quarterly again in March 1934, with a reduced cover price.[5] Nonetheless, in design and format each issue maintained high production values, part of the magazine's commitment to fine art publication but also an aspect of its modernity. Each issue was sixty pages or longer, comprising around twenty reproductions, many in colour, together with short essays of appreciation usually on individual artists, usually Australian, printed on quality paper with generous typeface and spacing. In ways that manifest Ure Smith's own interests, the magazine brought together equal commitments to fine art, craft values, and modern developments in printing technology and design, especially the new technologies for colour reproduction which were important to the art market and to advertising alike. The reproductions which appeared in the magazine allowed for the first time the wide circulation of art images in colour—and, not least, images of Australian art. And as Underhill remarks, 'Once technology offered colour reproductions of art and ideas about them to the public, the question as to who constituted the art community became more urgent'.[6]

In this respect, *Art in Australia* was less highbrow or exclusive than in its high cover price and specialist appearance might suggest. It was never simply a magazine for and about connoisseurship—nor primarily a magazine for *criticism*. One of the editors' principal aims as stated in its opening editorial was 'to bring artists into closer association with the picture buying public'; that is, to create both a public *and* a market for art in Australia and for Australian art in particular. In other words, the magazine was addressed from the outset to the marketplace, both the emerging art market and the burgeoning magazine market of the period. As an editorial from 1919 put it, 'The commercial basis of art may be scorned, but cannot safely be ignored'.[7] Thus *Art in Australia* was not set up in opposition to the general commercial magazines that surrounded it but was launched into the same print economy rather than into a more specialised field of professional art criticism—although its presence over more than two decades would help to bring that art criticism into being.

II

Art in Australia opens up two areas of enquiry, for periodical studies and studies in modernity respectively. The first concerns the problematics of how we read and the degree to which we should read a magazine as a single entity, a text in its own right, especially for those magazines with an extended life span where we might have the equivalent of a hundred book-length texts and even more individual authors, illustrators, editors, and so on, challenging any attempt to bring all the pieces together into a coherent story. What interests me here is not the process whereby as readers we produce a kind of discursive coherence for a magazine's heterogeneous contents, something that is most often intellectually productive and, in any case, probably inevitable, but in a way the opposite, how a magazine's complex relations to a print economy or marketplace produce an irreducible sort of heterogeneity, always something more than the sum of its discursive parts and more than its editorial platform. In what ways is this ordinary fact about magazines culturally significant?

The second and related question is how to read a cultural artefact, a magazine in our case, in the context of its *own* modernity—its 'contemporary modernity'. This is a question of particular importance for artefacts from this critical hinge period for modern print and other cultural forms, the late-nineteenth to the mid-twentieth century. How, in other words, might we bracket out our own 'post-modernism', our location *after* the formation of diverse modernisms into a modern tradition. What did the present look like before we knew who the winners were in the competition of artistic movements and before the victors' histories had been written?

The first issue probably besets all magazine and newspaper historians. On one level it's the problem of sheer volume, the sheer mass of print and visual materials that any periodical of more than a few years' existence presents to the historian or critic. But on a more interesting level, it's a question about the nature of magazines and their 'magazine-ness', and equally about the periodicity of periodicals. I'm sure I'm not the only magazine historian to be struck—again and again—by the sheer abundance and heterogeneity of a magazine's contents within individual issues and across multiple issues, an effect multiplied when we take in other contemporary magazines and papers until the whole print economy seems to be booming. Of course, there's an enormous amount of redundancy in this economy, and certainly in a situation such as Australia's circulation numbers and the pool of prospective writers could be limited (in fact a small number of Australian magazines were able to achieve high circulations, although *Art in Australia*, not surprisingly, was never one of them).[8] But the sense of discovery, of seeing something anew in this diversity, remains. So much so that I find I want to do more than just note the abundance, I want to celebrate it, almost I might say to *liberate* it, to let it loose into the neat, canonising world of capitalised Literature or Art. Even as we trace the sentimental, conservative, misogynist, racist, parochial, populist or merely commercial enthusiasms of the magazines of the period—for they nearly all have at least one of these qualities—the sheer abundance can have a radical effect, bringing back into view the writing and reading that time forgot, all that which gets left behind in the processes of tradition or canon formation.

This kind of heterogeneity and contemporaneity is just as likely to be a product of the marketplace as of competing intellectual or political positions, although the two need not be opposites. As such, it will be truer of certain kinds of magazines than others: less true of the magazines that until recently were most often studied—modernist or avant-garde 'little magazines' which are more likely to be driven by a single principle or platform—and much more the case for the relatively devalued form of the general commercial magazine, with its typical mix of entertaining features, 'literary matter', paragraphs, essays and sketches, pages of advertising, society or women's pages, photographs of scenery, socialites or celebrities, book news and theatre reviews, public commentary, answers to correspondents, and bad jokes—the mainstream magazine form of the late nineteenth and early twentieth centuries.[9] This emphasis has a specific Australian application too, especially for those periods seen as relatively barren in terms of significant, canonisable literary or artistic achievements. Frequently, these are periods, like the Australian 1920s, understood either as before modernism arrived or before an authentically Australian modernism found expression. To put it in shorthand, instead of the absence of modernism we discover the abundant presence of diverse kinds of modernity, manifested in a busy public print culture.

But this point also reminds us that such heterogeneity or abundance is in large part a mundane and unremarkable fact about such magazines (this is one of the remarkable things about them); that is to say, it is an institutional or even industrial effect rather than a set of explicit editorial intentions, an effect of a magazine's variable relations to the marketplace, to other magazines and other media, and to advertisers, contributors and consumers. Whatever discursive coherence we are able to read back into the diverse contents and forms within a magazine—and that's much of what we do when we read as critics or historians—these institutional or structural effects will mean that the magazine, in its cultural workings *as* a magazine, cannot be reduced to any single discursive logic. The dialectic between heterogeneity (or more simply variety) and coherence (maintaining the magazine's distinctive identity in a competitive marketplace) is an inevitable one for these commercial *periodical* forms, dependent as they were on largely freelance contributors, both amateur and professional, on advertisers, and on a broad and 'promiscuous' readership. While the readership for *Art in Australia* was defined more narrowly it was still conceived as a public.

III

Because of its role as the only Australian art magazine in the period, a period defined by the shifting pressures of cultural nationalism, post-war imperialism, artistic modernism and 'mass culture', *Art in Australia* is a key document in understanding Australia's place within the histories of both modernism and modernity, especially the story of modernism's 'belated' emergence in Australia. Its standing in this history is at best mixed. *Art in Australia* promoted a pastoral landscape tradition as the strong line of Australian art, although criticism has tended to overlook the fact that the bulk of the art works and objects displayed in its pages had no obvious connection to the nation, and landscapes did not crowd out other genres or art forms. Its heroes in the pastoral line were Arthur Streeton, the great founding figure, Hans Heysen, and the younger Elioth Gruner (although again the range of Australian artists it found noteworthy was very much wider). The magazine gave virtually no space to and did little to encourage intellectual interest in the contemporary movements around cubist or post-cubist art. We might agree that its 'failure to reproduce the work of leading European Modernists was not overcome by its fine colour illustration of Australian work'.[10] More than that, it played host to some of the most militant anti-modernist polemicists—L. Bernard Hall, J.S. Macdonald, Howard Ashton, and Lionel and Norman Lindsay. Indeed, in this company, Lionel Lindsay, later the author of Australia's most famous anti-modernist manifesto *Addled Art* (1942), looks positively avuncular. Adding all this together, *Art in Australia* becomes culpable in the history of Australian modernism, a major force in its retardation.

But as commentators on the magazine have also noted, this was only part of the story. *Art in Australia* regularly aligned itself with modern tendencies in the arts, if not those tending towards abstraction. It kept a watching brief on the self-styled Contemporary Group of painters in Australia and, perhaps belatedly, devoted a special issue to the group in September 1929. It published an issue dedicated to the 'New Australian Landscape' in September 1926, featuring works by Gruner, George Lambert, John D. Moore, Margaret Preston, Kenneth Macqueen, Vida Lahey and Roy de Mestre, featuring works more or less 'post-impressionist' in approach. In December 1927 it published a special Margaret Preston number (followed, it's true, by a Lionel Lindsay number in March 1928; but Lindsay was one of Preston's supporters). In the mid-twenties, the magazine also included some modernist writing, notably from Katharine Susannah Prichard.[11] If it was concerned to promote the solid achievements of Australian art, the magazine was also constantly on the search for its contemporary developments, those which would, in effect, give Australia a modern—or at least a contemporary—art of its own. Although it showed no sustained engagement with European or American modernism, it did report on emerging trends in English painting, and in design, sculpture and architecture. This was a 'conservative' position in the sense that these developments were at best only mildly post-impressionist, but they *were* contemporary not drawn from the past. Much of the magazine shared Roland Wakelin's perception that, following Cezanne, 'the most noticeable characteristic … in modern English painting is a feeling for formal design and insistence on drawing, emanating mainly from the Slade School'.[12] Most famously, *Art in Australia* became something of a house journal for Preston, then, as now, recognised as Australia's most significant modernist artist, even celebrating her 'frank and primitive originality'.[13]

It requires only a little exaggeration, then, to claim that *Art in Australia* was the most aggressively anti-modernist and (among) the most comfortably 'modern' of Australian magazines. The second half of the equation demands greater qualification, for it fails to take account of a number of other periodicals that welcomed modern art or modern style in varying degrees—upmarket commercial papers like Ure Smith's other magazine the *Home* (1920–42) or *BP Magazine* (1928–42), a travel, fashion and society magazine published by the Burns Philp Company, and little magazines such as *Stream* (1931) or *Manuscripts* (1931–35). Still it has a point, for it would be seriously misleading to characterise *Art in Australia* simply in terms of its anti-modernism or its preference for pastoral landscapes. Faced with the magazine's apparent contradictions—contradictions doubled by the *Home*'s constant promotion of modern design and decoration—the search for a deeper point of stability or a framework of coherence becomes almost irresistible. The most common and persuasive version of this is to argue that for Ure Smith and some at least of his contributors, the principles of modern design, their stress on simplified form, colour and bold patterning, were perfectly suited to the decorative or 'lesser' arts, to craft, interior decorating, industrial design, photography and advertising. But when it came to high art forms, to painting, drawing and sculpture, bearing all the weight of tradition and the ideals of Truth and Beauty, the traditional pre-modern hierarchy of genres and materials and the established representational principles of volume, tone and light remained unchallenged. As Underhill writes, 'Ure Smith fundamentally concurred with the academic view that fine and commercial art occupied separate aesthetic orders. Both had to strive for excellence but under distinct headings'.[14] Or Humphrey McQueen:

> The reason for the ready acceptance of Modernism in commercial items was directly related to the resistance to Modernism in works of art ... The fact that Modernist designs were used in commodity production was precisely why they could not be accepted in art ... Surrealist photographs could be featured in the *Home* since photographs were not considered 'art', because they were mechanically and mass produced.[15]

So Ure Smith and his magazine could be pro-modern in one dimension, anti-modernist in the other.

The logic of this split is reinforced—if also to some degree confused—by the contrast between Ure Smith's two magazines: *Art in Australia* lending its weight to conservative tastes in the fine arts, the *Home* promoting modernity in decoration, design, photography and fashion. The modernity of the *Home* was possible because 'Ure Smith's great interests, graphic design, photography and interior decoration, were sites of modernity and were freed of the aesthetic constraints placed on the fine arts.'[16] The *Home* could be advertised in *Art in Australia*—in a way *Art in Australia* could never advertise itself—under a heading announcing that 'Modernism has reached Australia': 'The wave of modernism which has flooded the intellectual centres of civilised countries has penetrated Australia. It is already perceptible in its art, its music, its architecture, its household furniture and decoration, its literature, its photography and its landscape gardening.'[17] It claimed for itself 'a lighthearted aestheticism which is the keynote of Modern Life, but it takes many things very seriously.'[18] While acknowledging the force of the contrast—which again has as much to do with the position the magazines claimed within the periodical marketplace as with Ure Smith's personal values—it can lead to a very selective view of both publications. *Art in Australia*, as suggested, had an interest in including a wide range of art forms and styles, if never those of the avant-garde, while the *Home* was as interested in antiques and stately homes, say, as in modern architecture and fabric design. *Both* publications were governed by regimes of 'good taste', although this carried a different burden in each. Note, too, in the sentence quoted from the advertisement for the *Home*, how art, music and literature are included under the modernist rubric; *their* modernism could be embraced at least when seen as an attribute of lifestyle or taste.

Finally, the division between the highest and weightiest forms of fine art and the rest is reinforced by its gendering. An interest in colour and pattern, in craft or fashionable design, was at once acceptably modern and essentially feminine. Preston's and Thea Proctor's art could be appreciated as working within traditionally female and minor genres such as still life, flower painting or the decorative arts, because they left the serious business of landscape or portrait painting largely untouched. For Caroline Jordan, '*Art in Australia* chose to represent Modernism as a marginal, decorative, feminine practice'. Preston and Proctor could be promoted because 'their work was consistent with notions of "woman's place" within the artistic hierarchy. Despite their prominence, they fulfilled a minor, complementary feminine role within the whole.'[19] Again, while this account makes sense of a good deal in the magazine, the neat dichotomies are misleading. If certain commentators dismissed the 'design-oriented modernism' of key women artists of the 1920s as 'decorative and frivolous',[20] such a view seriously underestimates the significance Ure Smith himself accorded to design and decoration, to the professional status of female as well as male artists, and, indeed, to the 'female' sphere more broadly; 'fashion' for Ure Smith was not (or not automatically) a dismissive term. And beyond Ure Smith himself, the magazines, across their whole contents, do not allow such minimisation. When Proctor and Preston were valued for their design, colour or drawing, they were not being trivialised but rather aligned with the forward momentum of Australian art.[21] Helen Topliss has shown how artists like Preston, Grace Cossington-Smith, Grace Crowley and others turned the notion of a separate female artistic sphere to their own advantage, for they were better positioned to respond to the technical challenges of modernism. Working from within the limits imposed by the art institutions, they were able to create a new modernist art practice whose principles would increasingly infiltrate and transform the dominant naturalism and establish a new professional status for women artists.[22] These transformations were possible both despite and because of *Art in Australia*.

IV

For present purposes I want to approach from a different direction, starting not from the end of a modern tradition and working backwards, as it were, in the attempt to bring neglected artists into the modernist camp, but from somewhere closer to its beginning, to the moment when Streeton, Heysen, Gruner, the Lindsays, Lambert, Wakelin, Proctor and Preston could *all* appear contemporary, if not all modern in the same way; to a moment when Augustus John and William Orpen could be seen as in some sense *more* contemporary than cubism or futurism, which could appear to have already come and gone. In other words, my interest is in the magazine's position *within* modernity rather than its position *on* modernism.

What sense of the present emerges from across the magazine, and how did it articulate its own contemporary modernity? How did the contemporary look in this moment—after impressionism, even in a sense after *post*-impressionism, but before post-impressionist modernism was consolidated as the inevitable outcome of art's progressive history? How was the emergence of Australian art to be understood in this context? This set of questions also requires thinking about the kind of magazine *Art in Australia* was; or, to put it another way, it means *not* reading it as a failed modernist little magazine. It also means trying to avoid the critical habit of 'barracking' for modernism, as if we always were or would have been on the side of the progressive avant-gardes, as if we always already knew the historical outcomes. We can make little sense of *Art in Australia* if we simply divide the magazine into pro- and anti-modernist positions, those on the side of history and those resisting its tide, those behind the times and those at the cutting edge. It is virtually impossible for *our* sense of modernism not to be anachronistic in this sense. After all, we know that William Orpen did not become the great British artist of the twentieth century.[23] How that might have looked in 1920, even if one were well informed about European modernism, is quite another matter.

One hint is simply the range of positions contained within the magazine: the fact that for its editors and, one assumes, for most of its readers Preston could sit more or less comfortably alongside Lambert, Streeton, Gruner, Heysen and Norman Lindsay in the magazine's pages. Despite the radical differences between these artists, we need to accept that at least provisionally, between the magazine's covers, they constituted a field of interrelated positions—the magazine constituted them as a field—that could be grasped coherently under the sign of the contemporary (and in particular the Australian contemporary). At the same time, it was in the nature of the magazine and in its interests, as I will suggest later, that this coherence was of a relatively weak and unsystematic kind. Although a dominant figure at a number of points in the magazine's history, Norman Lindsay's polemics, for example, are quite atypical—almost a form of bad manners—and never carry the force of a manifesto for the magazine itself.[24]

Nonetheless it is possible to discern a particular narrative of art's modern history that emerges across the pages of *Art in Australia* and which defines as closely as anything its sense of its own present moment. Although it is easy to see its perspective—from our position—as *already* belated, it is precisely this narrative and its consequences for understanding the present that we need to take seriously. For a start it is made to do a lot of work in the magazine in making sense of the modern, while it also emerges casually across a wide range of reviews and essays of very different persuasions.

The magazine's sense of its own contemporaneity is defined, first, against the academic practices of nineteenth century British and European painting. Academic painting had become increasingly decadent in the Victorian period, especially in its sentimental, anecdotal 'picture making' and mere illustration, and this continued today among 'painter-platitudinarians'.[25] Impressionism (sometimes 'realism') was seen to have provided the necessary corrective, returning art to its fundamental traditions of truth to nature *and* individual artistic vision, the truth of light, form and atmosphere rather than anecdote, whether in the realism of Manet or the heightened subjectivity of Monet. This anti-academic revolution also defined the moment of Australian art. The painters of the late-nineteenth and early twentieth centuries were part of *this* modern history of painting. And although the impressionism of these painters was no longer new, we should not underestimate the novelty in the 1920s of the idea of a contemporary tradition of Australian painting. Indeed this could still be seen as an *emerging* phenomenon, still in the process of formation. As Laurie Duggan points out, 'until the 1920s the work of the Heidelberg painters was not well known'.[26] The first generation of Australian painters were still active, still contemporary, the continuity of the tradition still undecided (hence the investment in Gruner and Lambert). To be exercised by the question of how the landscape tradition would be developed by the emerging generation of painters was by no means simply reactionary in 1920.

In European art, to return to the main narrative, but perhaps in Australian art too, impressionism itself had eventually reached a dead end or two, losing itself in the impression for its own sake, in either extreme subjectivity or extreme abstraction, or, in the classic symptom of modernist excess, in the domination of theory over truth and beauty. (Whistler, for example, could only be saved from his own theories by his practice.) The contemporary moment, in this limited sense, was 'post'-impressionist:

> The design of the impressionists was soft, fluid, vaporous, preferring atmosphere to outline. The modern movement seeks to give a rendering of nature that is firm, solid, definite. Unity, simplicity and strength are the qualities that the modern spirit seeks.[27]

Post-impressionism at its worst took the impressionist tendency towards abstraction, subjectivity and fragmentation to its extremes, but at its best it corrected the balance in painting's evolution, rediscovering the principles of construction, form, draughtsmanship and good drawing that academic art had increasingly trivialised.

This was exactly the moment at which or in which *Art in Australia* positioned itself: a moment of transition in which the key note of the present was associated not with modernism or the avant-garde but with this *new* emphasis upon design, craftsmanship, technical application and formal structure. This was precisely the set of terms through which 'modern art' could be apprehended and appreciated—in painting as well as in craft and the decorative arts—but also precisely the set of terms with which a line could be drawn and modernism or *ultra*-modernism rejected. On one side it reaffirmed what were seen as the traditional or fundamental values of good painting and drawing; on the other it could accommodate post-impressionist experiments with colour, form and pattern in so far as these were seen as moving beyond the limits of impressionism, finding a way *back* to structure and draughtsmanship, but also, for some, taking them forward—clarifying, revivifying, freshening up the true values of art. So Lionel Lindsay could admit 'Modernism … has been useful to art'.[28] It was a position, or field of positions, that could be at once post-impressionist and *pre*-impressionist in its tastes. At best, the new practices, even if sometimes startling, were rediscovering the common sense of the masterpieces of the past. But exactly how this would work itself out, and the range of ways in which it might do so, remained an open question.

My interest is to attempt to capture this sense of transition and contemporaneity not to dismiss the magazine as simply behind the times—cautious at best, defensive, complacent or downright reactionary at worst. It was all those things, but something else as well. Its characteristic position 'in between' (between the end of impressionism and the future of post-impressionism) can be read in its persistent anxiety over the *dullness* of Australian art. It was as if its writers sensed they were at the end of a tradition or movement but were unable to see beyond it in any sustained way. Dullness could be turned into sincerity, but reviewers could seldom resist expressing disappointment at, say, the Society of Artists' annual exhibitions. The best one could say was that the shows did 'creative art no harm'.[29] More disturbing were the reviews of the London Exhibition of Australian Art in 1923–24 which found 'a sameness, a kind of monotony [and] lack of experiment'.[30] While the magazine defended Australian art against these charges, the need for something new was widely expressed in the magazine's submissions.

Thus while there was no sustained engagement even with Cezanne, let alone cubism, Art in Australia aligned itself with certain modern trends in the British art world, from the Slade School and New English Art Club to contemporary painters, if not to Roger Fry's essays on cubism and post-impressionism (which in any case were published in book form only in the late 1920s). As argued earlier, despite its sometimes spectacular anti-modernist essays on 'artistic Bolshevism', in Christopher Brennan's wonderfully overdetermined phrase,[31] it would be a mistake to see the magazine as scandalously belated or reactionary in its take on contemporary art. It aligned itself with a still-evolving 'modern' tradition in which British painting, and so, potentially, Australian painting, were now in the mainstream (and it sought the mainstream not the avant-garde margins). P.G. Konody, critic for the London Observer and for some years the magazine's English correspondent, expresses the magazine's own kind of post-impressionism when he describes the modern age positively as an 'age of experiment' but then, in a recuperative gesture, embraces the diversity of contemporary styles and influences as so many 'experiments in beauty'.[32] He charts a necessary movement away from impressionism and towards what he calls 'a rebellion into insistence on shape'. The problem was that this was now being pursued 'through almost every exaggeration possible'.

This history of the present helps explain what might otherwise seem inexplicable, the magazine's championing of George Lambert as embodying the future directions of Australian art (and Lambert was rarely a landscape painter). Along with de Mestre and Wakelin, Lambert was seen to have corrected an imbalance in Australian art, even in the pastoral tradition the magazine elsewhere celebrated, that matched the imbalance produced by European impressionism. In Basil Burdett's words, this was a bias towards 'sensibility' at the cost of 'an art of the intelligence'.[33] This characteristic note of modernity in Art in Australia was repeatedly dated to Lambert's return to Australia from England in 1921. In rather startlingly gendered imagery, he was described as 'like a tonic to a rapidly drooping body'.[34]

The message Lambert had brought back from Europe was, in the simplest terms, the need for good draughtsmanship and good technique: 'Get your machinery first... Learn your trade... Stick to drawing and painting'.[35] The *force* of this otherwise unremarkable message came from that understanding of an unresolved contemporary moment outlined above, and the uncompromising manner—sometimes startlingly modern—in which Lambert expressed it. 'Forget about the mystery, and the greatness and the sacredness of art while you plug hard at learning your job, making a machine; that is, a human machine that can see and draw accurately'.[36]

In the catalogue to a 2007 retrospective exhibition devoted to Lambert, Anne Gray has made a qualified case for his modernism in terms close to the historical narrative I've suggested. Lambert 'assimilated the continuing tradition, basing his work on long-established artistic conventions and sources', but at the same time he often depicted his subjects from 'a close-up modernist perspective', he created 'a kind of abstract patterning of paint on the surface of the canvas', he 'simplified and flattened his forms', he 'looked at his subjects as decorative arrangements of lines, forms and colours'.[37] What looks like academic realism can be seen, from another perspective, as a 'formalist approach to art ... an aesthetic viewpoint which directed attention to design and to the formal aspects of art and away from the sentimental, intuitive method of painting'.[38] In 1922, Gray records, Lambert told a reporter that 'he agreed with the "bolshevics (sic) of art"', that a picture could be resolved into its components just as a piece of music could be analysed into its parts'. He had become more sympathetic to the ideas of the cubists and futurists on returning to Australia, for 'the man who invented cubism at least had an idea'.[39] He praised C.R.W. Nevinson's *Looking Down on Down Town New York*, shown in the European Art Exhibition in Sydney Town Hall in 1923, in terms that recur in *Art in Australia*'s engagement with the contemporary, admiring its 'hard and definite forms ... severe and geometrical arrangement' and 'reduction to essentials'. That last phrase was critical in the magazine's sense of what was necessary in the modern.[40] Lambert's importance, Gray argues, was in his insistence on 'decisive drawing' and the importance of design, precisely the qualities that enabled his work to be considered alongside that of Gruner, Preston and de Mestre, despite what might appear now to be its mannerist anachronism.

Lambert's return to Australian art thus signalled the arrival of that new understanding of drawing, design, and 'patient mechanism', the return from impressionism and the excesses of post-impressionism, that seemed *most contemporary*. The symbolic function of these attributes is that they were simultaneously modern and, in Burdett's terms, 'entirely traditional' (Burdett was the best informed about modern art of all the magazine's regular contributors).[41] Gruner's new work in the 1920s was evaluated in similar terms, as having acquired a 'greater attention to form, more careful organisation of design; greater reticence of sentiment [and] a classic restraint'.[42] Again and again these were the terms of praise, advancing towards and retreating from a modernist renewal. De Mestre's painting represented 'a modification of the extreme abstract attitude preserving great simplicity of form'; those expecting 'rabid ultra-modernism' would find, if they looked correctly, 'a very good sense of values and a charming and refined sense of colour'.[43] The special number of September 1926 devoted to 'A New Vision of Australian Landscape' celebrated a range of very different artists, from Lambert to Preston to Daryl Lindsay; while none of the works, the editors note perhaps regretfully, had 'a particularly wild character' they were linked by the idea of 'simplification and reduction to essentials'.[44] The *old* landscape was still welcome, if rather too familiar: 'It advances like a huge tide—washing its way into a thousand households, filling up our open spaces on living-room walls, ascending the stairway and overflowing into bedroom and attic'. By contrast, and in a memorable phrase, here was the Australian landscape translated 'into the curt speech of the present day'.[45] For a moment, a whole other sense of modernity seems about to open up— urban, future-directed, utterly novel. But the logic is ultimately realist, for the Australian landscape 'lends itself to a simpler, harder treatment. It is severe in form and outline'.

Writing of the Contemporary Group in 1929, Burdett drew a parallel between 'the essential phase of Australian art at present and the reaction after French impressionism in Europe':

> The ephemeral character of so much of the work being done … its banality and
> lack of invention, has led [the Contemporary Group] to seek more permanent
> forms. In the search they have come to realise that observation is one thing
> and pictorial organisation another, a truth which was being lost sight of in the

casual rendering of effects of light. So continuity is assured. Various aspects are exploited. Light, form, even movement, are analysed in the hands of divisionists, cubists, simultaneists. Disinterested art, for art's sake, is pursued until, like the divisionist's form, the semblance of things disappears entirely. But from them grow other things. Their discoveries are embodied in more traditional forms and made intelligible to a wider audience, and, through it all, we find that our apprehensions have been quickened and the world about us made more rich and vital.[46]

This is a fascinating play across the boundaries of modernity and tradition, discovering the logic of modernism *within* Australian art while drawing it back into the logic of continuity, the renewal rather than rupture of traditional forms, and hence towards an art for a 'wider audience', not for highbrows or artistic bolshevists.

These were also the terms in which the radically different visual forms of Preston's art could be celebrated, with a slight shift of language from the more masculine 'draughtsmanship' to the more feminine 'design'. In the special Preston number of December 1927, the lead essay, by A. Radcliffe-Brown, argues that 'the difference between the art of 1890 and the art of 1910–1930 [shows] itself in a different treatment of design':

the modern movement seeks to give a rendering of nature that is firm, solid, definite. Unity, simplicity and strength are the qualities that the modern spirit seeks. In the excesses and exaggerations of the movement, little as we admire them, we may see what is aimed at.[47]

Preston's art appeals as much to the intelligence as to the eye, and in one of the best phrases of the decade, 'it seeks a design which is and appears to be constructed'. Thus the movement of her work towards the 'utmost simplicity of form', the key note of the contemporary modern.

V

There's a great deal more that could be said—with over two decades of the magazine as raw material—about the discursive field of modernity as represented in *Art in Australia*, emphasising either the points of convergence around key terms such as design and craft or the faultlines that appear around the very same terms. The notion of draughtsmanship, for example, could elevate one or all of Norman Lindsay, Lambert and Preston to the premier position in Australian art. For some, modern commercial design was the very antithesis of art, for others it was the very synthesis of modern design principles. But I want to shift the analysis away from the rhetorical to the institutional, for if *Art in Australia* was on the cusp of a new understanding of modernity, as I have suggested, it was so not merely in the words or concepts it had at its disposable for making sense of contemporary art, but also in its form as a magazine and in its relationship to professionalisation and what we might call the rise of the modern critic.

Clearly the magazine had a select group of favourites both among artists and critics. As A.G. Stephens remarked, 'too much praise has been given to too few people'.[48] But while one of its prime tasks was to define the strong lines of succession in Australian art, its canonising function was relatively weak and dispersed. There were very few artists major or minor who were not noticed, and a broad range of art forms, major and minor, was included— not only painting and sculpture but etching, wood cuts, black and white illustration, fabrics, figurines, even Norman Lindsay's model ships, were valued as art. (In a cruel if unconscious joke at Lindsay's expense, given his horror of the primitive, one of his model ships shared a double-page spread with artefacts from British New Guinea.)[49] The magazine identified itself, not with any particular movement or style, but with 'the whole field of artistic effort in Australia that is worth attention'.[50] This inclusiveness was not so much an intellectual principle as a function of the magazine's positive relationship to the art marketplace—and, again, to the print marketplace as well. So too its orientation towards the contemporary; its interest in art history seldom extended beyond the late nineteenth century and the vast bulk of its articles and reproductions concerned recent and contemporary art. Its diverse, even contradictory viewpoints sat comfortably together (or rather appeared in succession) as an unremarkable feature of the magazine in its commercial and public forms, with little intellectual pressure to force them into confrontation with each other.

At the same time, especially over its first decade or so, we can follow the magazine itself being pulled in different directions, towards the different kinds of magazine it might be, as an up-to-date, commercial art review. We can read different versions of its relationship to modernity as it moves backwards and forwards, even in one issue, between the models of coterie fine art publishing, general literary journalism, professional art criticism, or the little magazine. The point is that the magazine's engagement with modernity goes beyond the individual dispositions of its various editors and contributors, and must also be considered as a kind of institutional effect of the way it was positioned in the print culture of its time and place. Although the magazine would only ever have a small and 'self-elected' audience, this audience was never imagined as comprising exclusively other art professionals or other producers, a characteristic modernist formation. Whatever the actual size and composition of its readership, the magazine's address is to an imagined public, Burdett's 'wider audience', which in its emerging forms also meant consumers who wanted contemporary art in their homes—and modern advertising in their magazines. It was as a commercial magazine that *Art in Australia* engaged with the modernising dynamics of the marketplace, even while other aspects of its publication suggest a kind of 'pre-modernist' cultural formation. I do not mean to suggest that every commercial magazine will therefore be modern or modernising simply by being commercial; and yet some kind of pressure in that direction is exercised by the relationship of the magazine to consumers. In *Art in Australia*'s case, its very *raison d'être* was the emerging phenomena of a professional art market, which existed in a complex dialectic with the growth of the market for modernising consumer fashions.

The magazine's orientation towards an emerging art market was matched by a discourse of professionalisation—both the professionalisation of the artist and the emergence of the professional critic. Again we find the magazine on the cusp between older and newer forms, between forms of amateurism, including connoisseurship but also more generous notions of appreciation, and new kinds of professionalism, including that of the modern intellectual. Few if any of its writers can be thought of as professional critics, although some made part of a living through newspaper reviewing. Gallery directors and established teachers such as Macdonald or Hall were certainly art professionals but they were not primarily art critics. Most critics and reviewers were practising artists writing about other artists for non-specialist readers, not critics writing for critics, and the magazine's reliance on the freelance and amateur market for its contributors was one factor producing its low-pressure diversity of views. Indeed it produces some tension in the magazine between the professional artist's and art patron's concern with defining proper aesthetic understanding and good taste, on the one hand, and a determined amateurism, on the other, which insisted that art, like good taste, could be understood in the language of common sense (or perhaps the language of literary journalism).

Those pivotal notions defining the present—the essentials of draughtsmanship, technique or craft—were equally critical in defining the professionalism of the modern artist. Lambert's position as 'the arbiter of "progressive" taste'[51] depended not only upon his insistence on good drawing and mechanics but equally his insistence on artistic professionalism. Indeed the two amounted to much the same thing. Lambert's argument is striking, not just for its advice about technique but for his sense of what he calls 'the business of painting and drawing':

> Learn your trade before you begin to think about art or criticise it ...
>
> [G]et rid of all that nonsense about art and artistic. Stick to drawing and painting...
>
> [M]ake yourself as efficient in your own work as any young student in any other branch of industry or profession.[52]

Art is 'hard, very hard work'. Once again, though, the terms were double-edged, pointing backwards towards tradition and realism, and forwards towards technical and formal innovation. On the one hand, they defined exactly what separated the serious artist from the rest, implying a form of training and professional commitment, much more than a simple disposition towards art; this could be brutally unsentimental, a kind of scientific or mechanical dissection of form, as in Lambert's machine image quoted earlier or in Preston's defining essay 'From Eggs to Electrolux'.[53] In this sense, craft had a distinctly modern resonance. On the other hand, it could serve a common sense representational understanding of technique; as J.F. Bruce put it: 'look after the craft and the art will look after itself'.[54] Whereas many of the magazine's critics would have agreed with Lionel Lindsay, that 'any but the simplest ideas are dangerous to painting', Preston described a radically different conception of the artist, not just as a technician, but as a kind of intellectual. She could sound rather like Lambert in the process—Art is 'mind before matter', 'work hard with constructive brains'—but for Preston questions of form become intellectual questions. The artist becomes a member of the intellectual vanguard, not pleasing the Man in the Street but *making* 'The Man to Think'.[55]

With Basil Burdett's increasing presence in the magazine from the late 1920s, we can begin to see something like the emergence of the modern professional critic. Burdett was a journalist and founder of Macquarie Galleries, among the earliest of the new dealer galleries in Sydney. In both modes he represented a move beyond the amateur to the modern professional and he constantly defined his speaking position in his criticism by its relationship to the modern. De Mestre argued that critics should be trained for their profession just as art students were.[56] When introducing the Contemporary Group in September 1929, the editorial invokes 'that band of intellectual enthusiasts to whom Art is the most vital factor in the world—that small body whose knowledge and judgement the public respects and trusts—a vanguard marching ahead of public taste'.[57] The phrasing here suggests a cautious but potentially radical shift in the magazine's own positioning towards modern criticism, or rather it balances older and newer notions of the relationship between criticism and public taste. Again the magazine looks both ways—encouraging this new professionalism while remaining deeply sceptical of any kind of theorisation or separate intellectual sphere, any idea that criticism might have a kind of equivalence to art itself.

Professionalisation was also at stake in the magazine's interest in commercial and industrial design. The word itself (alongside 'craft') was a way of invoking professional art and a professional art market. Here again the argument that modernism was acceptable in Ure Smith's magazines as long as it was confined to the feminised domestic or decorative arts needs qualification. Praising Preston's work because it 'insisted fiercely … on the importance of design' was to make it central to the modern potential of Australian art.[58] In other words, neither the decorative nor the domestic carried negative connotations; neither did the industrial or commercial (at least not in *these* modes and these moments in the magazine). For Thea Proctor there was no contradiction between Preston's artistic 'genius' and valuing her woodcuts as 'an ideal wall decoration for the simply furnished house'.[59] For Ure Smith:

> The prejudice against the more modern art in Australia is difficult to understand.
> Modern design in fabrics used for women's clothing, curtains, furniture, rugs,
> glass, china and lighting fixtures are imported every month … and they are all

readily appreciated. Many of them are designed by modern artists, yet we are confronted with the inconsistency of a woman in a gown designed by a modern French artist and completely surrounded by the products of a modern decorative artist's brain, condemning 'modern' work, by an Australian artist, which would fit in so well with her modern home. To quite a number of people, anything 'modern' can be appreciated in anything except pictures.[60]

It is difficult not to read the feminisation of the modern here as a slighting form of domestication, but the passage also expresses a kind of insight that Ure Smith grasped and which enabled the magazine's interest in modernity; that is, the exchange of visual forms between modern art and commercial design, the interplay between fashion and modernity, and the infiltration of the domestic into high art. It was precisely in these terms that *Art in Australia* could celebrate as a sign of the new application of art to industry, and as a sign of its own modernity, the invitation by the Ford Motor Company to Lambert, Proctor and Ure Smith to assist in designing colours for their new range of cars (in December 1929).[61] For Preston, design becomes an intellectual principle informing and transforming all art; for Ure Smith, all art is in danger of becoming 'good taste'. The point for the present argument might be the need to take *both* positions, both imperatives towards the modern, seriously in any history of modernity in Australia.

Art in Australia was situated—or found itself—on the cusp of a new understanding of modernity, not least, of course, a new understanding of modern art. It was after impressionism but before modernist post-impressionism in the sense I have been suggesting; that is, before the articulation of a modernist tradition. In this sense it was also *after* post-impressionism: if, on one level, the magazine delivered a reassuring discourse about good taste and tradition in art and design, on another its editors and authors constantly worried away at the problem of the present, sorting out the productive possibilities of contemporary art from the merely ephemeral, the dead-end or the downright dangerous. It found its definition of the contemporary through a series of key principles, if we can call them that—draughtsmanship, professionalisation, craft, design, simplicity and the reduction to essentials—which were flexible enough to draw together a whole series of otherwise incommensurate art interests and styles. It found its modernity, not in the avant-garde, but where tradition and modern developments intersected, folding back into each other or unfolding into something new. This set of terms or principles cannot be resolved into a single discourse, much less boiled down to the magazine's 'position', for it was also on the cusp generically and institutionally between older and newer forms—of the artist, the critic, the consumer, the marketplace and the magazine form itself—at a time before the institutions of high modern culture had been established in Australia.

'ESPRIT DE NATION' AND POPULAR MODERNITY
Aussie Magazine 1920–31

THE CHEERFUL MONTHLY

Social and political histories have established Australia's 1920s as a period of 'intense domestic turmoil', even as the national settlement around White Australia, protectionism, arbitration and Empire was reaffirmed.[1] Cultural histories have given a different emphasis, positioning the twenties as a crucial decade in the story of Australian modernity, as the full effects of changes in work and leisure patterns, gender relations, consumption and entertainment begin to make their impression on Australian society.[2] The force of these histories has been to identify women as key agents of modernity, as well as the locus of anxieties about its transformations; to trace the overlapping trajectories of popular culture, professionalisation, consumption, subjectivity and 'heterosexual modernity'; and more generally to locate Australia within a transnational history of modernity, not a belated recipient of the modern but a site of and for modernisation in its own right.

One manifestation of these overlapping social changes was *Aussie* magazine, launched in Sydney in April 1920. Alongside its more famous contemporaries, the *Bulletin* and *Smith's Weekly*, *Aussie* was at the centre of the processes by which the community of the nation was re-imagined after the First World War through a certain form of populist nationalism; but while the rhetoric of this nationalism is familiar, its function as a mode of apprehending modernity has largely been ignored. *Aussie* was not a political or intellectual journal but a general commercial magazine of humour, opinion, literary entertainment and review. If it styled itself editorially 'The Organ of Australianism', it also claimed to be 'The Cheerful Monthly'. As *such* it was able to address a national (and modern) rather than sectional readership.

There is a broader point here beyond my reading of *Aussie* as a single case study: a question about how such magazines are to be read, and how they work as evidence in cultural histories. In the interwar years, magazines and newspapers filled the broad cultural field, complementing more than competing with the commercial theatre and cinema. As ephemeral *periodical* forms, they were often relentlessly modernising in their engagement with the rhythms of contemporary urban life, its new products and its cultural styles; and therefore they could be critical in mediating modernity for their readers. This is especially the case for the typically, often wildly, heterogeneous commercial magazines of the early twentieth century, magazines that depended upon addressing a diverse reading public—or, better, addressing the diverse capacities of a 'general public'—even as they sought to establish a distinctive identity among their competitors. Neither the magazines nor their meanings for readers can be reduced to their explicit 'positions'; nor were they simply the sum of their contents.

It is surprising that *Aussie* has not played a larger role in the writing of Australian cultural history. It appeared monthly for more than a decade to 1931—from the immediate post-war period to the Depression—with sales of 80,000 by 1924, plus a further 20,000 in New Zealand, then still part of a trans-Tasman cultural marketplace.[3] The magazine claimed to be carrying the Aussie diggers '*esprit de corps* into a peace-time *esprit de nation*' (April 1920), and it had good grounds for doing so. Its first series had appeared in France in January 1918, the most successful and professional of the many trench magazines.[4]

To date, only the war-time *Aussie* has been brought into the historical archive, even though the peace-time magazine was launched, in effect, as a brand new monthly paper.[5] As such it is an important artefact in its own right, not just as an expression of post-war nationalism, but for its mode of participation in the print culture of its time and place—for how it existed as a magazine for both its readers and writers—and for its contradictory participation in the modernity of 1920s Sydney. Although it continued to proclaim its identity with the digger experience, the new *Aussie* was never only a returned serviceman's magazine. Instead, it explicitly broadened its address, re-inventing itself in terms of a civilian, indeed a civic, discourse, fit for the public sphere and the marketplace.

As a commercial magazine, but one lacking its own staff of permanent writers, *Aussie* relied on the local circles of freelancers, from professional journalists and an occasional university man to amateur poets and paragraphers. Founding editor, Phillip L. Harris, was a journalist from a publishing family (publishers of the *Hebrew Standard*, the main Jewish newspaper in Sydney). He was succeeded in 1923 by freelance writer Walter Jago, editor of the *Lone Hand* from 1919 to 1921, second President of the Fellowship of Australian Writers, and husband to Henry Lawson's daughter Bertha. Vance Palmer wrote articles, short fiction and many of *Aussie*'s editorials until mid-1923.[6] Indeed, most of the well-known Australian writers of the 1920s were published in its pages, including E.J. Brady, Fred Broomfield, Zora Cross, Dulcie Deamer, Louis Esson, Mary Gilmore, Will Lawson, Lennie Lower, Les Robinson, Dale Collins, Hilary Lofting, Mabel Forrest, Hugh McCrae, Ernest O'Ferrall, Roderic Quinn, A.G. Stephens and John Le Gay Brereton. Unk White, Emile Mercier and Percy Lindsay were among the regular cartoonists. The magazine was published by New Century Press, one of Sydney's major presses, which had a stable of magazines extending from *Humour* through to the *Lone Hand* and, from 1929, *Australian Quarterly*. As late as September 1931, a competition in which readers sent in their favourite quotations from Australian poems showed readers from all the mainland states. About two-thirds were from the bush or country towns, one-third from city areas. *Aussie*, in short, was a significant part of the vibrant, crowded print culture that characterised 1920s Australia.

A reader of *Aussie* bought a magazine full of humorous cartoons and 'literary matter' in the broadest sense—verse, very short stories, comic paragraphs, jokes, anecdotes, brief essays and opinion pieces. The cartoons, verse and stories appeared on about twenty of its fifty pages, and found their humour in stock urban types and situations: hen-pecked or drunken husbands, large families, long-suffering clerks, baffled policemen, foolish lovers, frustrated gardeners, dentists, clergymen, landladies, mothers-in-law, feminists and flappers. 'Aussiosities', the department for digger anecdotes, covered two or three columns. For the more serious reader, there was 'Bookish', a page or two of book news about anything from H.G. Wells or the rise of travelling libraries, to the American Civil War and the latest Zane Grey ('Something like 50 pages deal with the psychological storms induced by a rather improbable kiss').[7] 'Stagery' offered two pages of theatre news and reviews, while 'The Aussie Woman' department spread across three to six pages, featuring an essay on Mary Gilmore for example, in May 1922, the first in a series on Australian women poets. Although the mode was popular and entertaining, *Aussie* also addressed its readers in their public being, as *interested* readers keeping up with both political and cultural affairs.

In the midst of the cartoons and tall stories, the magazine's politics were limited to one or two editorial pages and a small number of cartoons. Here, a relatively narrow range of themes concerned with the national good were reiterated: the incompetence or self-serving of politicians and bureaucrats; the instability of imperial relations and the post-war settlement in the Pacific; the promotion of Australian manufacturing, tariff protection, and industrial co-operation; resistance to imported American 'tripe'; and, above all, eternal vigilance in defending White Australia. A typical cartoon, a racetrack scene drawn by G.K. Townshend, shows the favourite, 'Australian Sentiment', being blocked by 'Foreign Influences', 'Sectarianism', 'Professional Patriotism' and 'Anti-Australianism' (May 1922). The punter 'Aussie Public' looks on in anguish as the bookie, labelled 'Selfish Interests', gloats at the spectacle. This just about sums up the paper's populist nationalism, although there is also an ongoing scrutiny of national and imperial affairs.

Aussie remained cheerful about its own fate until its final issue in December 1931, although it had become increasingly monovocal. Almost certainly it suffered a fatal decline in advertising revenue due to the Depression, but we might also see its disappearance as a sign that the heyday of the independent commercial magazine was over.[8] The particular combination of humour, literature, reviews and public affairs that *Aussie* presented was being challenged on a number of sides: by the more sophisticated and immediate forms of entertainment offered by cinema and radio; by the modernisation of daily and weekly newspaper formats; by the professionalisation of journalism and the decline of the freelance market;

and by increasing market segmentation, for example, the emergence of new women's magazines directed at a specific caste of consumers.

DO YOU DANCE THE NEW DANCES?

Aussie's identification with the returned digger reveals a powerful affective dimension of early-century nationalism: the sense of the nation as a *generational* experience. For the generation born in the years leading up to Federation and still young during the war, there was, perhaps, a natural temptation to identify their own experience and aspirations with those of the nation. This identification gave new meaning to the familiar image of Australia as a young nation and its associations with virility, health, sunshine and freedom; it was a nation newly united through war and with its future in the hands of a rising generation. In announcing the new paper, Harris thus drew the magazine, the digger-reader and the nation together as if they shared the one 'generational' history:

> *Aussie* is now in civvies ... The Digger is now a civilian ... In his new role he
> [*Aussie*] wishes to convey to the civvie Aussie that spirit of cheerfulness and
> patriotism which characterised the Digger Aussie ...
>
> *Aussie* ... has grown into full and virile manhood ...
>
> *Aussie* will be a patriotic, ambitious member of the community, with a strong
> Australian personality, appealing to the patriotism and national humour and
> interest of ALL Australians. He will collect and distribute the best anecdotes,
> sketches and cartoons ... and have as strong an appeal to the interest of all classes
> as the battlefield *Aussie* had for the Digger.
>
> *Aussie* will contain the best work of the best Aussie writers and artists. (April 1920)

'Aussie' was personified as a young adult male, with the outline of the nation forming the profile of his head (Cape York makes a prominent nose, Arnhem Land a manly chin).

Like *Smith's Weekly*, *Aussie* continued throughout the 1920s to record and celebrate larrikin and laconic tales from the Front in its Aussiosities department; but that was about the extent of its diggerism outside of Anzac Day. The more significant subject of the magazine's address was the young single man and woman, the new family man or young mother, the emerging clerks and shop assistants. Again the appeal was strongly generational. Its focus was contemporary city or town life not digger nostalgia. The front cover of the first issue showed the figure of 'Aussie' changing out of his uniform into civvies—stiff collar, tie and waistcoat, not overalls—in a setting that evokes a suburban bedroom or lodgings.[9] A later cover, 'Following in his Father's Strides' (October 1921), shows mother at her sewing machine cutting down a pair of father's trousers for junior, a perfect combination of family self-reliance, maternal transmission, and masculine lineage.

This is the audience implied across the magazine's contents: the young working-class or middle-class man and woman, perhaps especially the 'sub-professional' middle class. These provide the scenes for its stories, sketches and cartoons, and for the bulk of its advertisements. A typical issue featured advertisements for art and business courses, insurance, ready-to-wear suits, lawnmowers, Lactogen, vinegar, nerve tonics, toiletries, alcoholic spirits, watches, sports clothes, gramophones and pianos. It could even extend to advertisements for London shipping lines, though more representative of its address to readers was the magazine's regular spot for Fluxite, do-it-yourself home soldering for repairing saucepans and other household goods. If some advertisements were directed merely to good housekeeping, others were more aspirational, inviting readers not merely to improve but to modernise themselves. An advertisement from April 1928 for the State Savings Bank of Victoria contrasted the 'old thrift', saving for a rainy day, for old age and hardship, with the 'new thrift', saving for 'A Home; The Delights of Travel; The Pleasures of Music, Art and Literature; The Benefits of Scientific Invention; [and] Better Holidays'. In the same issue, Gordon and Gotch advertised *Harmsworth's Home Doctor*, with a special appeal to Young Married People ('a complete manual of Sexual Hygiene'). This emerging class—or generation—of consumers and citizens symbolised the new, young nation itself, committed to self-improvement and modernisation at a national level.

Aussie's version of the new Australian citizen was thus a modern one, 'young Australia' surrounded by motor cars, radios, jazz, flappers and flat-dwellers and involved in modern forms of work and consumption. This modernity was not always celebrated, but it was where the magazine found the comedy and energy of contemporary life. Like the advertisement for the very modern Gillette Safety Razor, it might have asked: 'Do You Dance the New Dances?' (April 1923). A different aspect of its modernity was its emphasis on the development of Australian manufacturing industries rather than pastoralism. There is little bush mythology, at least in the early years; just enough perhaps to gather these older strands into the present moment. After all, if Dad and Dave became stock characters in the 1920s, they did so as part of contemporary urban popular culture, on stage, cinema and radio. Similarly, the dynamism of *Aussie*'s arguments and amusements came predominantly from the contemporary urban world of work and leisure, even if its politics sometimes evoked the bush.

DISCIPLINING THE DIGGER

Seen as contemporary rather than residual, the magazine's editorial positions can be understood as an expression in another sphere, and in a popular, commercial journalistic form, of the liberalism that marked a new generation of Australian intellectuals in the early decades of the century. As both Tim Rowse and Gregory Melleuish have shown from their very different perspectives, central to this liberalism was the notion that society was evolving beyond the class war towards co-operative forms of production and government.[10] Co-operation was advanced in the name of efficiency and development, hence the bias towards manufacturing rather than rural industries. *Aussie* ran a series on 'Australia's Optimistic History': lengthy didactic stories by Ernest Osborne, each disclosing to a sceptical local interlocutor the virtues of a particular Australian industry.

The early 1920s represent a critical period for these liberal understandings. Despite the lessons of the war years, co-operation seemed further away than ever. Sectionalism infected politics and industry, and government was incapable of advancing national development. Modernity, which had once promised 'scientific government', now seemed to offer only degeneration towards forms of mass government and mass culture. The state's interventions, far from advancing co-operation, had only made the people less self-reliant and less conscious of national purpose. It was precisely in the face of this crisis in optimistic liberalism that *Aussie* asserted its own cheerful nationalism. The opposite of 'cheerfulness' was not simply pessimism but social discord and division.[11]

The very sense of unity the magazine carried back into civilian society generated its own sense of threats multiplying from within the nation. The ordinary cheerful 'Aussie' was surrounded by the noisy, disputatious figures of self-interest and 'bad Australianism'. At the centre was the class war of Capital versus Labour, but the divisions were also manifested as religious sectarianism, party politics, a self-interested press, and jingo imperialists (indeed, an editorial suggested that the 'loud-voiced, anti-Australian crowd of flag-waving Imperialists' was 'probably more injurious to true Australianism than the red-raggers', June 1921). The magazine's own populism was prone to anxieties that the people themselves had become the mass, 'trusting blindly in a power that is powerless' (July 1923). The nation's future was threatened on all sides by profiteers, strikers, imperialists, bookmakers, publicans, wowsers, snobs, parsons, propagandists, bureaucrats and politicians.

Aussie's cheerfulness, in this context, contained a disciplinary dimension. There was cultural work to be done in guiding the digger and thereby the wider national audience into exemplary citizenship. Its writers found the Australian soldier's distinctive character, perhaps surprisingly, in self-discipline. For Palmer, this characteristic described an ideal democratic body represented by the Australian army in the recent war: 'It could be depended upon to recognise the need for discipline at the proper time, and, more important, to exercise self-discipline ... it was keen on asserting a peculiarly Australian kind of democracy' (August 1920). The contrast in war-time was with the enforced discipline of the traditional (British) army. In peace-time, it was either the undemocratic urban mass, the 'panting, sweating crowd occupied in cheering some politician, or welcoming some prince or general from overseas', or the 'excrescence' of modern bureaucracy. For Ex-Digger, 'the twin brother of that frilled discipline which the war exposed as a sham necessity, an expensive, exasperating and dangerous excrescence, and a cloak for the worst kind of inefficiency, lives corpulently in our civil life; and its home is the Public Service' (May 1922).

Aussie's populist nationalism could express radical opinions: anti-capitalist, anti-imperialist, anti-clerical, and anti-ruling class. But if this involved political critique, indeed a call for good government, it was also always anti-governmental, bound to be dissatisfied by any mediating forms of state, class or institutional organisation. Predictably the magazine was drawn to forms of self-government and co-operative community:

> The life of a country ought to be based on the activities of small groups—scientific, agricultural, artistic, and so on—and the more power such groups have the less likelihood there is of the Government becoming centralised and inefficient. 'Do it

yourself' is a good motto for Australians, though that need not mean a scrambling individualism. Voluntary co-operative movements, both in agriculture and industry, are the right lines of development for Australia. (October 1921)

In the future, *Aussie* predicted, men 'will form societies outside Parliament to promote irrigation, co-operative farming, town-planning' (May 1922). It found signs of hope in the New States Movement and equally in plans for abolishing all governments except the national. Both ideas expressed the utopian notion (open both to socialist and fascist inflections) of self-governing local communities combining organically into a single national community. The vision was ultimately for a politics without politics, government without governments. White Australia, indeed, was just such a piece of 'anti-political politics', based not upon class or clout but upon self-government and self-reliance: the nation imagined in terms of the individual and communal body. The magazine could even prefer royals to politicians as representatives of the people.[12] Increasingly, under Walter Jago's guidance, White Australia comes to absorb all other aspects of *Aussie*'s politics. Thus the magazine's anti-governmental rhetoric was ultimately consonant with the governing consensus:

> Australians, with all their political differences of opinion, formed their Commonwealth to guard the only white man's continent in the world for the development of the higher races and higher civilisations (as they, the Australians, see these things). High above economic exploitation they have placed social considerations, and these are not to be stultified by racial adulteration. Nor is that which has been done to establish social efficiency to be ruined by the competition within their land of other peoples with lower economic and social standards. (April 1930)[13]

It would be difficult to find a more complete statement of White Australia ideals and anxieties; all it lacks is the account, offered elsewhere, of 'young white Australian girls being gathered in from Chinese hovels ... all over Australia' (May 1929).

BRAINS AND EFFICIENCY

Jago's editorials lack the radical edginess of those from the magazine's early years, an indication not just of Jago's professional limitations but also that the particular volatilities of the early twenties had dispersed. After 1925 the magazine had more recourse to mawkish celebrations of pioneer virtue, agrarianism and mateship, and to reminiscences of the literary world of the 1890s. In the Dad's Number of August 1929 (the reference *is* to Dad and Dave), Jago writes:

> When we speak of Dad, we do not visualise the family man who scoots with
> insane haste about the city streets, dressed to the ears with neck-tie and collar. Dad
> conjures up for us the collarless man with a chest like a bag of wheat; the outsize
> in chest being necessary to accommodate his courageous and hospitable heart.
> Some passably good men have been known to wear collars and ties during working
> hours, but none has panned out gold value per ton equal to Dad's ...
>
> Figures do not matter; we know instinctively that without Dad, without Mum,
> without Dave and Sarah, we might well be without Australia at all. (August 1929)

'Dave' was also recruited, for 'Dave never goes on strike, while in the cities and industrial centres hardly a day of the year passes when the artisans of some trade or other are not on strike' (January 1930). Even so, agrarianism was not the dominant note in *Aussie* but a kind of elevated rhetoric available to it for special occasions such as this one-off number. The passage above was written for the harassed urban 'family man' it describes, perhaps to reassure him that 'we are all pioneers, each with his job to do in the building of a new nation' (January 1930).

Otherwise, the magazine's politics were more attuned to modernity than rural nostalgia. *Aussie* summed up its approach in the slogan 'Brains and Efficiency' (March 1928). It demanded 'sane, well ordered Government' (June 1923) and 'sane, disciplined management of child welfare, fresh air, good food, healthy homes' (July 1923). It called for modern training and education, and the scientific administration of industrial, public and domestic life:

> Australians have cast aside the prejudices and musty theories of old-world
> conservatism. Our immense undeveloped resources, our almost illimitable wealth-
> potentialities; the vastness of our continent, and the sparseness of our population,
> have combined to convince us of the imperative call for the most efficient, most
> economic and most scientific handling of our problem.

> A nation lives by and through its industries; and we are reminded that that
> nation is the wealthiest and most advanced which has the greatest number of
> its citizens properly employed in the widest variety of industries, trained and
> equipped by education and technical training to grapple with every new situation
> and new problem which goes to make up the battle of life—whether individual or
> national. (March 1928)

This scenario has little space for Dad or Dave. Indeed, 'the old haphazard rule-of-thumb methods, hallowed by tradition, are not only out of place … they are a distinct menace under present-day conditions' (April 1928). Specialised Teachers and University Chairs of Commerce were the magazine's heroes for the future. Osborne saw the modernising moral even in Anzac Day, for the war had 'made it necessary for Australia to become a manufacturing nation … Australia's birth as an industrial nation was begotten by its Anzacs' (April 1927).

BOOKS AND READERS

If *Aussie* had nothing more to offer than its populist discourse of nation and race, its interest for the historian or cultural critic would be limited. But while the magazine's patriotic politics played both a framing and binding role, it would be a mistake to attribute too much of its appeal directly to its platform; a mistake, in particular, about how the magazine worked *as* a magazine for its diverse readers. Similarly, 'ideology critique' provides only a very partial account of the magazine as text. It is in the nature of general, commercial papers not to be consumed whole or with equal engagement across the full range of their contents. *Aussie*'s opinion pages probably had no more effect than the editorials of daily newspapers today. It was in the magazine's own commercial interests to be diverse, within the limits it could tolerate. Different departments, in the hands of different writers, were more or less autonomous, and a variety of perspectives was guaranteed by the paper's reliance on freelance contributors. It would be misleading, then, to imagine 80,000 militantly patriotic readers in the spirit of Jago's editorials; indeed there's evidence to suggest that Jago's own nationalism was viewed as a mild eccentricity.[14] More important than the platform was its broader address to a new readership imagined as young, modern, literate and largely middle class.

Doubtless, for most readers, it was the undemanding entertainment of the magazine's fifty or so 'literary' pages, its reviews or the 'Aussie Woman' section that proved most attractive. At best this writing had only modest literary or intellectual aspirations; unlike its contemporary the *Triad*, it is difficult to imagine anyone buying *Aussie* to establish (or lift) their cultural credentials. But cumulatively, across its whole range, the magazine did assume for its readers a certain level of 'cultural literacy' and 'public interest', and, no less relevant, a degree of leisure time and a desire to be up to date. If the cultural literacy worked in terms of breadth rather than depth, perhaps even a sort of innocence rather than sophistication, it did address a reading *public* (in a more than casual sense of the term). *Aussie's* literary pages inhabited the world of popular journalism and commercial entertainment rather than projecting any notion of a separate literary culture; to put it more positively, the literary culture it projected was still part of the public domain, whether as 'literature' or 'entertainment'. As such, *Aussie* and other general magazines of the 1920s occupied much the same cultural space as the commercial theatre, and both would suffer a similar dispersal as cinema, radio and new print forms proliferated towards the end of the decade.

This particular register of book talk is a familiar one from the print cultures of the late-nineteenth and early-twentieth centuries, but it has been a difficult phenomenon for cultural history to describe with any certainty.[15] *Aussie* was clearly 'popular' in its forms of address, but the term is both too broad and too narrow to describe the magazine's literary range with any accuracy. It fails to make the distinctions *Aussie* itself made between good books and 'tripe', while it also misses the 'serious' notions of books and reading that *Aussie* and similar magazines activated, even as they welcomed the latest popular novels. *Aussie* could compare American and French bestsellers, noting that the latter were achieved 'by books with literary quality' (March 1923); in the same issue it paused 'to reflect upon the modernity of the novel' and praised Sinclair Lewis's *Main Street* as 'a book that is not only a literary work of art, but is a bitter satire on his own countrymen'. It could welcome the appearance of *Vision* magazine as 'the cleverest exposition of the modern youth's attitude towards modern life that has ever been published in Australia' (June 1923). In the institutional context of a robust journalistic culture, an Arnoldian or vitalist faith in literature's public role met an enthusiastic interest in the contemporary book world—in what might best be called the public world of books. In the absence of well-established, autonomous institutional sites, this book world could extend to include university figures such as Le Gay Brereton, 'men of letters' such as Palmer, professional journalists, freelance essayists, and amateur contributors of the occasional sketch or paragraph. In part, *Aussie* manifests an older form of journalistic modernity, most familiar in the earlier *Bulletin*, but its contemporary interests were also attuned to the means and aspirations of the rising generation, experiencing modern urban life 'for the first time' after the war.

Nor did *Aussie*'s populist nationalism translate simply into literary chauvinism. Its review pages were filled with brief discussions of the most newsworthy contemporary figures from the British book world—Wells, Shaw, Galsworthy, Conan Doyle and a host of lesser known figures. It printed a series of 'knowing' satirical descriptions of Ruskin, Carlyle, Ibsen, Strindberg, Emerson, Zola, Shaw, Wells, Galsworthy and Wilde, suggesting its readers were familiar with their works or at least their reputations (August 1921). 'Highbrow', though, was a dirty word, understood to mean narrowly intellectual, effetely aesthetic, or simply un-Australian. A short story published in December 1921 pits a smiling, patronising Highbrow against a 'coarse' Lowbrow. The Highbrow reads Flaubert but not Henry Lawson and is aggressively challenged by the Lowbrow for his ignorance. Nonetheless, the bulk of the fiction the magazine reviewed consisted of the latest bestsellers and popular genre fiction from London or New York—westerns, mysteries, crime and historical romances—although it also had a running gag over many issues at the expense of romance bestseller Charles Garvice. Reviews happily recommended a 'good tale', a romance that 'shouldn't be missed' or a 'first-class thriller' at the same time as deriding American slickness, 'ridiculous' Sax Rohmer, and Marie Corelli, 'a crude artisan in mystical trash' (February 1922). Later in the decade, Australian books were criticised for being too influenced by 'Yankee "slick stuff," manufactured like a cocktail according to formula' (April 1928). Nonetheless, romances, adventures and crime continued to fill its columns.[16]

The world of *Aussie*'s book review pages, in short, was that of the contemporary British (and American) book world, embracing both popular and middlebrow tastes—Wells and Shaw at one end, Zane Grey at the other—with very little to suggest that this was in any way foreign to the magazine's readers and writers, or that their aspirations were simply colonial. Rather it was their source of the contemporary, of modern stories and styles, of new pleasures and provocations. When new Australian books were available they were welcomed, especially popular novels from the New South Wales Bookstall Company, while Katharine Susannah Prichard's *Black Opal* was celebrated as 'truly Australian' because based on 'the love for the Square Deal and Mateship, which is the Australian character' (November 1922). It was only towards the end of the magazine's life that Australian books could be reviewed with any regularity. Fred Broomfield, Walter Murdoch, Nathan Spielvogel, Nina Murdoch, Frank Dalby Davison, M. Barnard Eldershaw, Brian Fitzpatrick, James Devaney—and D.B. Copland's *The Crisis in Australian Finance*—were all reviewed in 1931. In May of that year, an East African romance was found wanting in comparison to 'the dozen or so excellent Australian novels produced recently'. In the overall account, though, there are probably more books reviewed from New York than from Australia, and not just because of the limitations of the local publishing industry. These new, imported books were the books modern young Australians wanted to know about.

Although modernism scarcely rates a mention (*Wheels*, the Oxford anthology, was described as '100 parts of balderdash'), the review section was always contemporary, praising a psychoanalytic study of Ibsen for example (April 1922) and noting in its early years the latest, controversial books such as A.S.M. Hutchinson's *If Winter Comes*, the 'suppressed eroticism' of Robert Keable's *Simon Called Peter*, and daring Americans such as Floyd Dell and Joseph Hergesheimer.[17] Located still within a journalistic sphere, the emphasis was on the newsworthy. Reviews were presented more as book news than reflective criticism and were never more than three paragraphs long. Like the review pages of the *Bulletin*, they often seem to address two audiences at once: on the one hand, fellow 'ordinary' readers, addressed more or less as equals, informing them of the latest new books and book news; on the other hand, those already engaged in the business of books and writing, fellow members of the freelance, journalist, 'bookish' and sometimes bohemian communities (no doubt this was something for ordinary readers to keep up with, too, at once entertaining and informative). Neither audience had a close or necessary connection to the honest, patriotic citizens addressed elsewhere in the magazine.

In the magazine's early years, much of the reviewing was handled by L.L. Woolacott, a journalist, playwright, and later editor of the *Triad*.[18] Woolacott seems to have been behind the magazine's surprising interest in American writing and the 'new sexuality' of contemporary literature. All the new American generation figured, from the Exquisites to the Realists.[19] H.L. Mencken, the iconoclastic, anti-Puritan satirist, was celebrated; so too the radical *Liberator* and *Masses* magazines (March, April 1922). In Woolacott's hands the philosophy of the reviews pages was often vitalist, keen to celebrate the natural expression of sexuality and to expose Sham and Respectability: 'all great literature is licentious, namely, *unrestrained, exceeding the limits of law, morality and propriety*' (April 1922). Although these vitalist themes gave the review pages much of their energy, they are strange tastes to find in a populist, nationalist magazine. That they *are* found there tells us more about the diverse journalistic and literary world in which *Aussie* existed than about its readers' tastes or its own editorial platform. In the same issue as Ernst Toller's radical *Masses and Man* was described as 'one of the greatest of all modern plays', an essay on Australian art stated that 'it may be taken for granted, that in the end, the bush spirit is going to dominate this land: it is prepotent, dissolving all the imported "isms" by its easy tolerance' (August 1924). The books pages were scarcely manifesto-driven.

Of course vitalism could be thoroughly conservative: anti-feminist, because women were to be natural; anti-modernist, because the modern city stifled natural creativity; and 'masculinist', because manliness was where the vital energies were to be found. Books were praised for being 'clean, yet virile', and showing 'vigour and sanity' (February 1922). Hergesheimer's *Linda Condon* was described as 'a compelling story of a woman poisoned (or inspired?) by ultra-modernism and of an artist who was also a man' (March 1922). *Aussie*'s editorial pages of April 1923 contained an extraordinary article on 'Literature, the Feminist Movement and Nationality':

> At the present time the literature of England and America is being absorbed in vast masses by the Australian people, who are assimilating the ideas and sentiments

which are necessitated by the conditions prevailing in crowded, if not over-crowded, countries, but are, or should be, alien to Australian circumstances …

A very great deal of the imported books with which Australian homes are flooded, are prophets of the feminist movement; and the main objection to the flood is that it threatens to extinguish the home fires that it is necessary to keep burning if Australia is to reach a safe nationhood.

'The feminist movement is the subconscious effort of human society to prevent the tragedy of overcrowding'; or, in more straightforward terms, 'The feminist revolt means the production of fewer babies'. The role of an Australian literature, by contrast, was to express the national needs of an under-populated country and thereby, it seems, boost baby production. But this eugenicist discourse has little to do with the variety of books and opinions welcomed onto *Aussie*'s own review pages.

THE AUSSIE WOMAN

For *Aussie*, as for many of its contemporaries, the 'modern girl' was the focus of its understanding of post-war modernity. In the late twenties 'Phyllis Phlapper' became a regular columnist, and in April 1929 there was a special Flapper Number. *Aussie* could, with qualifications, celebrate her coming into being, as the symbol of the emerging generation. An essay on 'the Aussie girl of 1920' expressed a characteristic mix of curiosity, appreciation and unease. She was 'strangely restless and self-assertive … in the mood to criticise … eager for the gratification of her own personal ambitions and desires [and] eager for new experiences' (December 1920). This 'difficult, but interesting and inevitable girl', it was hoped, might be replaced with Miss Aussie of 1921, 'perhaps a happier, more normal and tolerant type'. Miss 1923 seemed to combine the best of both girls:

> She is credited with being a symbol of the downfall of the race, and she has to chuckle merrily to herself, knowing full well that she is really far wiser than her sister of yesterday …
>
> A girl [in 1923] must be interesting, a good listener, a good dancer, a good sport, and a good bridge player. She must have good looks and that elusive quality called charm. She must be able to see a joke and tell a risky story with a dash that carries it off …

The modern girl is brave, she is bright, she is loveable, and she is great fun. What more can the world demand? (September 1923)

The modern girl, the 'Dancing Flapper' (July 1923), even the 'Efficient Woman' (April 1928), symbolised both the best and worst of modernity: on one side, a new-found freedom from Victorian moralism, a new naturalness and practicality, and the rejection of old hypocrisies; on the other, an unnatural departure from womanly functions.

On the positive side, the idea of the young, self-reliant modern woman fitted neatly with the magazine's sense of its own contemporaneity as the voice of a young, modern, self-reliant nation. The spirit of jazz could be the spirit of optimism— 'Spring is the flapper of the year … *Aussie* is exceedingly grateful to Spring, with her jazz, her music and laughter' (August 1923). Modern fashions, like modern manners, were 'natural', healthy and sensible. *Aussie* supported the 'common sense of the modern woman' which had 'eliminated what she considers unnecessary garments to the point when unpleasant people say the Law ought to interfere' (July 1924). A 'motor smash would not appal her, and a fall at a fence should merely be the signal to brush the mud off her garments' (September 1923). In such arguments *Aussie* was anti-wowser and anti-Victorian, as its special Mrs Grundy Number of May 1929, immediately following the Flapper Number, made clear. In this mood, *Aussie* was happy to identify itself with the modern girl who had 'a plan for earning her own living, played sport, and wore clothes that were simple, graceful and serviceable', for she had 'studied hygiene in studying dress' (September 1923). In the spirit of self-reliance, the magazine promoted articles on the virtues of the bed-sitting room for independent girls (June 1926) and the need for every girl to have a 'training that will fit them to be independent'. Brilliant girls could become 'lady doctors and lawyers'; clever, practical girls might consider nursing; attractive girls might turn to the stage; there was journalism and photography for the artistic girl, secretarial work, and 'positions in libraries [for] girls who are fond of books'; otherwise domestic service was always open (July 1924). 'Any girl who is earning her own living, no matter in what sphere, is able to hold her head high among her fellows and say, "I am independent. If I never marry, I shall still have a life of happy usefulness"'.

On the negative side, the girl 'with the courage to be her own natural self [was] a rarity' compared to the mob of fashion followers, and the

Dancing Flapper was the epitome of the unnatural modern city and 'over-civilisation'. She had no conversation, 'no views on anything but dress and dancing'; and she 'admits, in her eighteenth year, that love is a snare and a delusion' (July 1923). This author suggests, more than half seriously, that the cause of the problem is 'the city flat'; the flapper, 'this artificially delightful little creation', lived 'in a totally artificial atmosphere'. Even her food was 'prepared, preserved, and cooked until it has lost all the freshness with which Nature endowed it'. The new woman was inevitably linked to modern American culture: to the '"modern woman" novels from America' (June 1926), to jazz music, and to the 'foolish feminity (sic) of the average Yankee film [which] probably causes more domestic trouble than anything else in modern times' (March 1923). In a poem from January 1925, the new women were 'Synthetic Women':

> [Lanterns] cast reflections on the restless feet
> Of modern women moving to the beat
> Of barbarous tom-tom and snatch of song
> That makes the zest of jazz more keen and strong.
> Sydney! In silks arrayed,
> Jazz-fond as Paris and the older world …

Yet even here the restless energy and glamour is attractive. As 'Polly Phone' puts it, in the same issue, 'Jazz! Jazz!/The only thing a girl has'! This was the spirit, too, of *Aussie*'s myriad flapper cartoons, admiring, celebrating, trivialising and disciplining the flapper's freedoms simultaneously— 'Whirled Without End' (October 1928).

Nonetheless, the rhetoric of hygiene and nature was always to hand with its own disciplinary imperatives to counter modernity's excesses: 'it is more than fashionable to have nerves—it is a kind of DSO of modernity, the outward and visible sign of a super-civilised state' (April 1930). What was both energising and unnerving (in some sense literally) was the simultaneous sexualisation and public-ness of the modern girl. This was the age of 'youth insurgent; youth tumultuous; youth triumphant'; of 'undress, Elinor Glyn, bedroom plays, exotic movies, jazz, cigarette-smoking, and all-night parties'; of 'Freud, Wells and Shaw' (October 1924). The modern female body seemed to be both over-sexed and under-sexed: 'There is a difference between rounded slenderness and thin flat-chestedness which looks as if it had come to earth via a gas-pipe and collected a lot of foreign coloring and barbarous ornamentation on the way' (July 1923). An advertisement for the Juno Culture Company offered the new woman new ways to become 'plump and pleasing' (January 1925).

A similar, if less indulgent, ambivalence can be seen in the magazine's responses to feminism. In October 1921, *Aussie* printed Gertrude Lawson's argument that ideas regarding women's domestic duties remained 'old-fashioned'. The article offered a utopian 'vision of perfection' based on the municipal kitchen 'where one big power does away with all domestic worry ... where all this individual work is brought under one head and executed under the control of skilled men, whose knowledge of engineering and chemistry would cut the work down to a fraction of what it is now'. There was a dignified defence of spinsters: 'Since no sneer attaches to the bachelor ... why should he and his benedict brothers have the effrontery to sneer and carp at spinsters?' (November 1920). In May 1921, 'Adi Marie' argued that women's greatest 'industrial enemy' in the war for equality was not man but 'her parasitical sister, who is an insidious foe because she hugs her age-long chains'. On the other hand, a 'mere mother' wrote to assert that 'the more feminist a woman becomes the less feminine she is'; women's real business 'is the raising of a next generation of men and women who are Men and Women. Everything then will be automatically righted' (February 1922).

Editorially, the magazine was predictably serious about the role of women in securing 'the future of Australia' (November 1928). Less predictably, Jago could tie this to female emancipation:

'Female emancipation' is the catch phrase, and, when one looks back on the social conditions of less than twenty years ago, the phrase has everything to commend it

...

The old idea—the old man's idea—that women needed only protection and not freedom is happily gone to the discards, like many other fool platitude since 1914. She needs, and has a right to, freedom to accomplish all of which she may be capable. Nothing is unsuitable to a woman which she has the ability to achieve, and it is up to this advanced social and political land, Australia, to remove all the unfair barriers which have hitherto kept her going aimlessly round in a circle instead of marching onward, stride for stride with her menfolk, to the ultimate peak of the Commonwealth's destiny.

As the last phrase suggests, the containing rhetoric was still national efficiency. Freedom thus brought with it 'a multitude of obligations to the citizen'. Australian womanhood would acknowledge these for the sake of 'our young, eager and prideful nation in the South Pacific'.

For 'The Aussie Woman' it was Dulcie Deamer who drew this moral, surprisingly perhaps given her reputation as the 'Queen of Bohemia'. Deamer was the lead writer for 'The Aussie Woman' from early 1927 until the magazine's close. As in her later work for the *Australian Woman's Mirror*, Deamer's writings for *Aussie* were unconventional and she shared the public rather than merely domestic interests of *Aussie*'s women's pages. They were often, in Sharyn Pearce's terms, 'deliberately worldly, cynical and iconoclastic'.[20] In this vein, Deamer reassures her readers that 'Love is as uncomfortable as a tram accident, as an over-ripe lobster, as wet feet and a hot head, as the position of the Irish gentleman between his two pigs when they both started in opposite directions' (April 1928). But she also 'held an implacably conservative view of the nature of sexual politics', one that could fit neatly alongside Jago's patriotic nationalism no less than the anti-feminist vitalism of the Lindsay circle.[21]

In 'When Country Came to Town', Deamer finds 'Dad, and Mum, and Sarah, and the twins ... the most Real People in any city' compared to the 'smart and modern ... human ants' who live there (August 1929). In 'Half-Forgotten Pride', she acknowledges the drudgery of domestic life for the young mother that sometimes causes her to wonder, 'What is the use?' (March 1927). According to the present-day standards of 'individual and personal gratification' there is no use. But, Deamer argues, there is a deeper purpose. Children are 'the little living "bricks" ... of which the living structure of a nation—your nation—is to be built up'. The young mother is not just a 'bungalow worker' but 'an architect, a sort of consecrated artist-artisan': 'Every bungalow-worker with Willie and Beryl leaving marmalade on her door-handles is an Australian nation-builder, and of no mean nation either, for it earned its newer title at Gallipoli'.

POPULAR MODERNITY

Over its decade-long appearance, *Aussie*'s overt nationalism was absorbed into the less rigorous popular sentiments which elsewhere the magazine reflected and returned with interest to its readers as entertainment, literary matter and public comment. As such, *Aussie* mediated for its readers, women as well as men, the acceleration of social change after the war: the sexualisation and 'productivisation' of young women; the technologisation and commodification of sentimental culture; the rise of mass politics or, differently, the bureaucratisation of political life; and the consumerisation of the city, in this 'age of mechanism and sensation, of the surface rather than of the soul'.[22]

Below the level of the nation, as it were, *Aussie* could thoroughly enjoy the changes and challenges of contemporary urban life. The magazine aligned itself with those forces of modernity it could recognise as progressive, scientific, efficient, vital and natural. It accommodated more threatening changes largely through its humorous trivialisation of them, which amounted to saying that they were ephemeral and superficial, nothing that a good dose of cheerfulness or 'cleanliness' wouldn't fix. There was a containing rhetoric on hand to moderate their effects, to instruct and discipline readers, or to reveal the universal wisdom concealed beneath the flurry of contemporary fads. Nonetheless, the anxieties that modernity generated, the new complexity and massification, the speed and dynamism of change, and, not least, the instability of gender boundaries, recurred either as threat or comedy in each issue, however cheerfully and efficiently *Aussie* despatched them.

To read the magazine (and its contemporaries) in this way is to read beyond its editorial platform, beyond its ideological coherence in so far as that can be derived, even in a sense beyond its contents, to consider its situation within a busy, modernising, competitive urban print marketplace. *Aussie*'s ambivalence towards the modern was characteristic of the bohemian journalistic milieu in which the magazine was centred and, in a different way, of the liberalism to which it was connected through its interest in national efficiency. But it cannot be understood simply at the level of rhetoric or textual content, for its rhetorical ambivalence was also determined by what we might call a structural ambivalence, that produced by the imperfect match between the magazine's platform—where, for example, women were reproductive nation-builders—and its actual institutional setting—where women were in fact freelance journalists, artists, bohemians, lawyers, actors, librarians and secretaries, 'new women' of one sort or another. In slightly different terms, there was a mismatch, too, between its platform and its actual marketplace, where men and women were consumers as well as citizens. Its writers and readers 'were poised on the cusp of the local and the global, the national and the cosmopolitan'.[23] Even as the national was subject to increasing discipline, its boundaries were being rapidly dissolved and reshaped by newly fashionable transnational print and visual cultural forms. It is precisely these ambiguities that suggest why *Aussie* demands to be brought into our cultural history alongside its better-known competitors in the print culture of the 1920s and 1930s.

'SCREAMERS IN BEDLAM'
Vision 1923–24

And then there was *Vision*.

Vision was the first magazine in Australia to launch itself into the world with something like a modernist manifesto. This was despite its aggressive denunciation of modernist art. The Foreword to the first issue, in May 1923, proclaimed a Renaissance of the Imagination in the name of gaiety, fantasy, beauty and vitality of emotion. *Vision* would be the voice of youth, and youth was 'any condition of mind which is vital, which ascends'. Against the primitivism, jaded nerves and 'locomotor ataxia' of the modernist, *Vision* would build the 'undying and ever youthful body of Imagination'. It would 'vindicate the youthfulness of Australia, not by being modern, but by being alive'.[1]

The argument was anti-modernist, rudely and relentlessly. It was anti-Flaubert, anti-Dada, anti-Matisse, Shaw, Picasso, Satie, Epstein, even Ornstein—the Russian-American composer and 'futurist pianist' Leo Ornstein, known, one imagines, to very few Australians in 1923.[2] And yet the form in which the magazine's spirit of revolt was asserted in the first issue, and in the Forewords to each subsequent issue, was the modernist form of the manifesto. The style is militant, excessive, paradoxical, reiterative— anything but genteel. 'We would seek to be as young as Aristophanes, not as mentally frozen and impotent—*i.e.*, as old—as Bernard Shaw' (I). Like the great modernist manifestos, communist, futurist or surrealist, the *Vision* Forewords seek not only to describe but to evoke or *manifest* the 'vision' upon which the magazine is founded.[3] And again like the great modernist manifestos, this is a vision of the present world spiralling into decay and self-destruction. Crisis is evoked through dramatic polarizations, between energy and decadence, life and death. The magazine announces an 'onslaught', an 'attack'. *Vision* spoke as if at a pivotal moment, the moment its own speaking manifested, the turning point between the old world and the new. It had come to announce that 'the old world is dead' (II).

> When Picasso hung a geometrical pattern in gold paint in the last Autumn Salon, or Satie put typewriters in the orchestra of 'Parade', they were both as old as any other form of Egyptianism. Beethoven's Seventh Symphony is still as young as the dawn. If then we are to vindicate the possession of Youth, we must do so by responding to all other expressions of Youth, and by rejecting all that is hieroglyphic, or weary and depressed. If Australia alone in the world is doing this—and we see no evidence for any other conclusion—then the Renaissance must begin from here, and both the onslaught of expression and the analytic attack must begin from here also. (I)

No less than the formalist and programmatic innovations of modernist art, the *Vision* program to leap over or blast through the chaos and decay of the present was a 'violent rejection of the society which had begotten the 1914–18 war'.[4] In Norman Lindsay's words, 'The age of Queen Victoria the Good ended in the bloodiest and most destructive war this earth has seen.'[5] Christianity and 'humanitarian ethics' (II) together had been exposed as fraudulent, dangerous lies, part of the disease not the cure. It was an 'axiom of thought' that 'the generation which produced the War is utterly damned' for the war 'was only a surface expression of a devitalisation that went far deeper than political causes or all the laws of the belly stated by Marx' (II). That was the modernist, avant-garde insight. *Vision* shared the modernists' sense of a profound crisis in civilisation; and in its loudly advertised rejection of despair, it shared their despair at what that civilisation had become.

This modernity is present in the Forewords to each of *Vision*'s four issues and in some of its critical pieces, mostly by Jack Lindsay. Apart from a very few of its poems, *this* is where the magazine's energy is to be found, in its anti-modernist polemic, its programmatic manifestos. Here it can gather the force to dismiss in a gesture 'the whole preposterous system of moral and social stultification and repression that is Man's civilisation' (III). In such rhetoric, at the very height of its anti-modernism, *Vision*'s language most nearly resembles the language of the modernist avant-garde. Elsewhere its verse and fiction, like Norman Lindsay's illustrations, are merely pre-modern: gay, death-haunted songs or a melodramatic blustering rhetoric, no less haunted. They are seldom more than whimsical or wistful, gothic or fantastic, like Hugh McCrae's 'Pale priests and jewelled castle-boys/As thin as winter wind'.[6] There is a real pathos in the gap between *Vision*'s polemic and its performance, recalling Peter Bürger's remark that for the avant-garde movements of the early twentieth century, 'the attempt to do away with the distance between art and life still had all the pathos of historical progressiveness on its side'.[7] The same pathos is present in *Vision*'s attempt to do away with history altogether.

The *Vision* manifestos suggest why, despite its anti-modernism, the magazine should be taken not as a symptom of Australia's conservatism or backwardness, but as a sign of Australian modernity. It is a characteristic of the modern work of art that it appears together with a discourse about the work, with an in-built or adjacent manifesto to announce its newness, its break with the past, its leap beyond the present.[8] In terms of the magazine form, the manifesto is not a secondary performance but a primary, perhaps *the* primary, performance which 'energises' the rest of the contents. Regardless of how far individual contributors such as Kenneth Slessor or Louis Lavater shared the manifesto's program, in the magazine their works become part of a single 'manifestation'. *Vision* is the first Australian magazine in which the poetry is driven by an explicit program (despite its abhorrence for abstraction); or rather this is the claim the magazine wants to make. *Vision* was itself about bringing the program into being, partly by assertion, partly by attraction, trying it on, testing it out, however far the actual poetry fell short. This was especially so for Jack Lindsay as he sought to work out his own aesthetic in relation to Norman's charismatic manifesto, *Creative Effort* (1920), on the one side, and, on the other, the range of modernisms—Symbolist, Imagist, and Sitwellian—with which he was also engaged.[9]

Vision can be understood as modern less for the ideas it expressed than for the way it expressed them or, better, for its mode of apprehending how ideas existed in the world. The summoning of a moment of crisis from which the magazine speaks, its declaration of a program to banish the old world in a stroke, its grasp of ideas as weapons in a struggle over the future of civilisation, its violent rejection of pieties and progress, its sheer impatience—all of these summon the 'desperate pace and frantic rhythm' of capitalist modernity.[10] Ideas are grasped, not as part of the evolutionary progress of civilisation or as the civilising accomplishments acquired by the educated man or woman, but as conflictual, matters of life and death, antagonistic ways of being in the world. With Darwin, Marx, Nietzsche and Freud, the simple evolutionary discourse of civilisation had fractured into an unprecedented multiplicity of 'isms'. Art had fractured too, first with naturalism and symbolism, but then spectacularly, all at once, with Cubism, Futurism, Vorticism, Imagism, and Dada. This is the vortex into which *Vision* pitched itself—in a way that no other Australian magazine had done—even as it sought to transcend the 'devitalisation' it discovered on every side. It rejected humanism, and in this sense we might say it shared modernism's rejection of modernity.[11] In Humphrey McQueen's words, *Vision* 'was up-to-date in a way that almost no other local publication had managed. Its contributors scoured the cultural presses of the world in search of decadence to attack. The cadavers of literature, music, art and science were dissected with amused horror.'[12]

More than any other magazine, *Vision* also invented itself as the expression of a movement or 'school', again a characteristic of the historical avant-garde and modernist movements. The formation of magazines and movements was a typical expression of the modernist desire to alter the relationship of art to thought, and art to life, which forms itself more or less explicitly into an aesthetic or political program. The point can be made about *Vision*, even though it rejected the very notion of schools (for it did so 'programmatically'); and even though such a movement scarcely existed beyond the pages of the magazine or beyond the pen of Jack Lindsay. For the magazine itself stands as the movement, its collective manifestation, representing that mobilisation of ideas and art that attempts to do away all at once with the distance between art and life which marks its modernity.

II

The story of *Vision*'s founding has been told many times, for it is deeply embedded in the multiple legends of the Lindsay family which have their own life in Australian cultural memory. The magazine was conceived in late 1922 or early 1923, and it appeared in four numbers between May 1923 and February 1924.[13] Calling itself, rather staidly, *A Literary Quarterly*, the magazine was edited by Jack Lindsay, Frank Johnson and Kenneth Slessor, supported from the clouds of Springwood by Norman Lindsay. Each issue was a solid fifty pages or more, illustrated by Norman's centaurs, satyrs, fauns and mermaids. Each opened with a blast from its Foreword, followed by ten or so poems, a number of short prose fictions, a couple of critical essays or reviews and some interesting occasional features—poems by Wyatt, translations from Heine and Catullus, fillers quoting approved sentiments by Blake, Nietzsche and others, and, in 'Screamers in Bedlam', quotations from local and overseas contemporaries whose apparent nonsense required only the briefest editorial annotation. There was also a healthy number of advertisements, sometimes with an irony that was, it seems, not obvious at the time—the Essex car advertised under the single heading 'BEAUTY!' alongside advertisements for such modern gadgets as the very realist Kodak or the modern vacuum cleaner in the hands of a thoroughly modern and bourgeois young woman. This was not quite the Hellenic world that *Vision* meant to celebrate. More seriously it indicates something of the ambivalence of *Vision*'s institutional position: on one side, its desire to transcend (or simply blast through) the literary mainstream and its marketplace, and on the other, more realistically, its desire to be a serious, commercially sustainable literary quarterly (it claimed to offer 'the highest payment for published work'). The world of bohemian journalism shared a similar kind of ambivalence—modern, professional and freed from the world of genteel letters, a profession, calling or trade that still allowed forms of creativity and originality to survive the need to make a living, but one no less tied to the rhythms of the market.

The magazine also had a pre-history. Jack Lindsay had moved from Brisbane to Sydney in June 1921. In late 1919, after their first contact for many years, Norman had sent Jack some etchings, a copy of *Thus Spake Zarathustra*, and finally a manuscript version of *Creative Effort*, the major statement of his aesthetic and philosophical program. Jack's own intellectual development had been wide ranging and dynamic—Plato, Greek and Elizabethan poetry, Blake, Keats, Shelley, Symbolism. He had already discovered for himself a romantic model of the self-creating intelligence; his own intelligence was ripe in its intensity and hunger for hearing Norman's self-creating manifesto. Norman's ideas focused Jack's desire to commit himself to the 'deep most creative tasks of art':

the desire to grasp and develop the inner struggle of poets like Blake and Shelley, Keats and Rossetti, and to transport into an Australian sphere their intensities of imagery, their power to concentrate a profound moment of experience in a poetic symbol ... What Norman's theory and method offered was a means whereby one aspect of poetic activity, the sensuous image, could, it seemed, be mastered.[14]

He was at least responding to the most productive parts of *Creative Effort* and, defined in this way, the task was a necessary 'modernising' imperative. But *Vision* suggests that in taking on the project of the sensuous image, Jack embraced much more than a question of technique (and, in a sense, much less). For the sensuous image was the hinge on which the whole of Norman's idealist, transcendent program depended. No less important, the potency of Norman's prose style carried its own message—its urgency, its startling antitheses and reversals, its deliberate flouting of decorums—which would re-appear in *Vision*'s manifestos.

Creative Effort was almost three hundred pages of Lindsay pronouncements, 'repetitive, rhetorical, paranoid, elitist, racist and utterly infuriating; but energetic and powerful in places despite these things'.[15] The uncompromising form is a token of the author's (and the ideal reader's) membership of the elite whose existence it asserts, the few great individual artists and thinkers who exist outside mere earth-bound time, outside the mere Existence which consumes the great mass of society. Beyond the realm of Existence is the universal realm of Life, the realm of 'all that goes beyond the body, the impulse that we vaguely call the mind, the soul, the intellectual process'.[16] If Life and Existence, mind and body, are opposed, the sensuous body nevertheless, through sexual experience, was the vehicle through which a glimpse of the eternal might be achieved—or at least it might for some, those whose pursuit or possession of Mind, Beauty and Passion transcended merely physical, ephemeral experience (sex was an attitude as much as an act). It was given to only a very few individuals, this power to discover within themselves and to express the existence of Mind, Lindsay's capitalized name for the eternal life force, the ideal realm beyond time.

The function of Art was to give such glimpses of the eternal energies of Mind, Beauty and Passion more permanent expression in the Image. Making art, like making love, was the highest expression of both individuality and universality.[17] Neither had anything to do with society, morality or history, except as these were inevitably hostile to creative effort. Art had no responsibilities except its duty to itself to become more conscious, for the 'highest intellect is that which is able to manifest the deepest perception of itself'.[18] This was an eternal struggle against the entanglements of time, history and human brutality, an heroic undertaking fit for giants only (and only male giants at that)—Shakespeare, Beethoven, Plato, Praxiteles, Keats, Rabelais, Rubens, Byron. This made of Art the highest calling, 'a calling, not merely a trade'; a matter of 'holy' laughter and holy anger, or at least high disdain.[19]

There has been some debate about the exact degrees of Nietzschean or neo-Platonic influence in *Creative Effort*.[20] The important point for the present is that whatever the influence of Platonic—and later idealist or romantic—ideas, the *energy* of the polemic derives from Nietzsche, from the model he provided of a 'unique and complete rupture with dominant modes of thinking and writing'.[21] Nietzsche provided the modernity of Lindsay's thinking, and the limits of its modernity. Perhaps the strongest effect of all is of Lindsay's auto-didacticism, forcing old or merely conventional ideas into a form that could seem strikingly original and utterly contemporary. As John Docker puts it, *Creative Effort* 'offered a mode of thinking which *dramatised* the problems and tensions the artist faced'.[22]

Despite Lindsay's emphasis on the sheer individualism of true creative effort, his manifesto was also a call to action. It was a call to others to bend their creative energies to the task of renaissance; its energy was designed to energise. In 1921, quite in the mode of Ezra Pound, Norman had attempted to colonise Sydney Ure Smith's quality art magazine, *Art in Australia*. Ure Smith, a Lindsay supporter, was receptive to the idea of broadening the magazine's scope beyond the visual arts, and a literary supplement had been contemplated as early as 1917. Lindsay's own interest, of course, was more narrowly focused. His idea was, first, for a new journal, *Literature in Australia*; if not that, then at least for *Art in Australia* to become the literary vehicle for stimulating creative effort in Australia, the medium for his own message to be iterated and reiterated. The literary section should be called 'Vision' and should be edited by Jack.[23]

Art in Australia did alter its presentation for the first two numbers of 1922 (February and May), but Ure Smith clearly had his own agenda which was not quite Norman's. The format was enlarged, the price lowered in an attempt to reach a larger audience, and the magazine announced a new interest in 'literary contributions', together with articles on architecture and music. Against Norman's advice Ure Smith retained Bertram Stevens as his co-editor, and then appointed Leon Gellert for the second number, after Stevens's death. Although there was no separate literary supplement, the contents did now carry the modest title 'Literary Contents, Etc'. Poems by Slessor, Gellert and Hugh McCrae were published in the first issue, but Norman was loudest with a sixteen page essay called 'The Inevitable Future'. No essay half as long had previously been published in *Art in Australia*.[24]

Lindsay was still writing at the altitude he had attained in *Creative Effort*. He offered nothing less than a theory through which the collective mind of 'the earth' could grasp a higher morality for civilisation. The war prompts him to look backwards and forwards, with some startling prophecies of nuclear and chemical warfare (even solar and tide power!) and of coming war between America and Japan. Lindsay does sometimes write as if he comes from another planet. America had a vital role to play in the impending struggle between East and West, even if it represented 'the lowest depth of moribund earth morality to-day' (36). The point of the history, though, was less to explain the present than to discover the eternal: 'Commercialism is the spirit of man on earth to-day, and war is only one of its effects. But at least the war of 1914 has robbed us of any further ignorance of man. He stands before us starkly revealed in eternal primitivism' (22). The bedrock of Lindsay's theory is that the condition of Man or mind or civilisation is fundamentally static. There is no evolution, no human progress, only the savage and the civilized in Man 'always striving against each other, always remaining—statically side by side on earth' (25). The problem of the present is that savagery is dominant because of the devitalisation of the civilised: 'the whole outburst of modern savagery, with commercialism as its creed, and war as one of its effects, is due to the inertia, cowardice, and feebleness of the civilized mind today. The civilized mind is a sick organism, depleted of mental energy exactly as a physical organism becomes shattered by disease' (31).

Reformist talk about education or humanitarianism was, for Lindsay, just as much a symptom of this devitalisation as was modern scepticism. So too in art: realism and impressionism were devitalised, amounting to little more than 'the dismal repetition of facts' rather than the 'inner vision of creative power ... the very nature of Earth Actuality' (31). Aestheticism was only another facet of the same limited 'objective vision', the only difference being that it arranged the facts tastefully instead of accepting their crude disorder. Vital civilisation, by contrast, depended upon the creative mind which 'generates ideas, defines form, and analyses passion':

> By defining form, beauty comes into being.
>
> By the analysis of passion, man comes to self-knowledge.
>
> By the generation of ideas, man is able to balance cause and effect; divine an intention in life, and perceive the dual nature of his being between mind and matter. (31)

By this process, the 'Educable Mind' could be stimulated by the 'Creative Mind' towards useful programs for social organisation. Lindsay's project enjoined upon the west a 'mission of earth civilisation', for the creative mind originated with the Greeks and therefore 'has its tradition only in the West' (37). In this mission, Australia had a special role because primitivism in the arts had not yet arisen and there were some in Australia still prepared to 'face the simple truths of life without arousing the instant attack of puritanism and neurotic shame' (38).

The new format of *Art in Australia* was not popular with its regular readers, and no doubt, for some, neither were Lindsay polemics. Jack followed Norman in the May issue with an essay on 'Two Directions in Modern Poetry', interesting for its extended attack on Pound as a merely intellectual poet driven by no sensuous or spiritual necessity; Walter De la Mare is preferred for although he was not a 'vital mind' he had truly sought Beauty.[25] *Art in Australia* had not previously hitched itself to a single program as overt or 'offensive' as that of the Lindsays, despite Norman's ubiquity in the magazine's early numbers. His essay 'A Modern Malady' had appeared in the very first issue in 1916. Prophetically, in this essay, his remedy for the 'theological' malady of proliferating artistic creeds was 'a little more light heartedness'.[26]

After the May 1922 number, the earlier format was resumed. But if the failure of the *Art in Australia* venture confirmed Norman in his isolated genius, the idea of a magazine would not disappear. It was in one sense an inevitable consequence of the kind of argument he had announced, which called for a public manifestation of its truth—a movement, a magazine, a manifesto. There was all the difference in the world between an article and a few poems in *Art in Australia* and a whole journal dedicated not only to arguing but to enacting the renaissance. There was an 'absolute necessity' for a magazine 'which would say all the obvious things that had never been said before'.[27] Despite Lindsay's disdain of mere reformers, the point of the argument, after all, was to transform the world—or at least to tell it loudly why it was incapable of transformation.

The 'will-o'-the-wisp periodical', in Jack Lindsay's words, took more definite shape in discussions later in 1922 with Johnson, an assistant in Dymock's bookshop 'who made something of a club out of his corner of the shop'.[28] In the same year Jack had met Slessor, then working at the Sydney *Sun*; and outside the great fact of Norman, Slessor's verse seemed the best evidence yet of an Australian renaissance. Slessor shared the Lindsays' distaste for contemporary literary decadence, whether primitive or genteel, and he became involved in the planning towards *Vision* late in January 1923. Johnson offered to look after finances. The 'magazine was plotted in sessions at Mockbell's Castlereagh Street café over coffee laced with rum'; Robert Fitzgerald insisted that they 'establish a new school of poets to be called the Pre-Kiplingites'.[29] All was set for *Vision* to appear in the May-time, appropriately the traditional European time of renewal and re-birth.[30]

III

For all its vehement anti-modernism, *Vision* was no respecter of tradition. The word is never employed positively in the magazine. It could be as fiercely anti-bourgeois as any of the avant-garde magazines. It had no respect for history. In the *Vision* program the vitality of true art, true passion or spirit, lives in an eternal present, in a 'youthfulness that affirms the eternality of all things' (I). The universal qualities it celebrates are not the 'time-honoured' verities of nineteenth-century belles-lettres, those slowly-evolving qualities which will reveal themselves to the steady view. *Vision* suggests an action more like 'blasting through' the overlays of rotten history to the luminous energies buried within. Again this is a gesture characteristic of avant-garde modernism.

Dispersed across the pages of *Vision* we can find more than one kind of parallel to the near-contemporary work of literary modernists such as Pound and T.S. Eliot. Like them, *Vision* developed a poetic of the 'concrete image' to break once and for all with the mellifluous sweet nothings published as verse in the newspapers and magazines which surrounded them. It reprinted the sensuous, intelligent poetry of Thomas Wyatt as a 'revaluation of the Image'. It argued, too, that 'part of the battle must be fought by the *analysis* of creative thought ... by a vast revaluation and analysis' (I)— asserting the necessity of intellectual effort and critical intelligence in the act of creation. Like Pound, *Vision* returned to classical Greece and Rome for images that could restore health and sane energy to poetry; like Eliot, it celebrated the Elizabethans over and above the Augustans and Romantics. Like the modernist critics, Norman and Jack attacked the 'Shelley myth', and in terms Pound, Eliot and Leavis would have endorsed: 'The only sensation which [Shelley] really knows is the dizzy speed of this collapse of overwhelming emotion'.[31] Pound's lists of necessary writers—Homer, Sappho, Catullus, Villon, Dante, Marlowe, Shakespeare and Heine, but not Milton or Wordsworth—are almost identical to *Vision*'s (the exception is Dante). But while Pound could add Stendhal, Flaubert, Yeats, Joyce, Eliot, William Carlos Williams and Wyndham Lewis, *Vision* found it hard to add any names later than Byron.

At the same time, the historical perspective of a 'modern tradition' was scarcely available in 1923; Edmund Wilson's *Axel's Castle*, for example, first appeared only in 1931 and F.R. Leavis's *New Bearings in English Poetry* in 1932. The names and styles of Eliot, Pound and Joyce competed with a whole host of others—the Sitwells, e.e. cummings, Robert Graves, Aldous Huxley, to mention only some of those noted in *Vision* itself, alongside many names which have fallen altogether from view. There was a contemporary proliferation of styles, schools and sensations many of which, no doubt, were as fake or foolish as *Vision* could find them. There were plenty of examples to hand of 'glutinous chatter about Chelsea artists—or reports from passionate spinsters on their souls—or studies in the rectangular nude by futurist tradesmen ... or the album-cleverness of young ladies and gentlemen who write *vers libre*'.[32] More significant is the magazine's rejection, not of particular schools or movements, but of schools or movements *per se*. The shorthand for modernism was Cubism or Futurism, and the break up—or break down—of Art into so many 'isms' was at one with modernism's break-up of form and surface. This sense of endlessly proliferating discourses, of 'screamers in bedlam', against which one single eternal or universal principle must be held, was a common feature of resistance to modernism; less common was *Vision*'s militancy, its refusal to retreat into tradition or convention, at least in its own view.

But despite their rejection of the sentimental or morbid sweetness of contemporary versifying, and despite the understanding which they also shared with modernism that this sickly poetry was symptomatic of a sickly state of civilisation, the *Vision* aesthetic could not break through to something new—or, for that to matter, to something old. Its poetic universe was still defined by the nineteenth-century religion of poetry and its quests for individual spiritual development and eternal beauty. Its ultimate goal was still, always, *transcendence*—transcendence via Beauty, Passion and vitality in Art, 'Passion … transfigured by Beauty and Beauty vitalized by Passion' (Foreword, III). More than anything else, this language signals its distance from contemporary modernisms.

The vision and its mechanisms were scarcely new. But in noting its high romantic, neo-Platonic or Nietzschean conventionality we are only noting the most obvious thing about the magazine's aesthetic. The interesting point is not *Vision*'s reactionary program but the magazine's powerful and *attractive* sense of its own contemporaneity. Locally it drew writers towards it—Fitzgerald, McCrae, Dorothea Mackellar, Vivian Crockett, Adrian Lawlor, Dulcie Deamer—by saying something new or saying something in a new way or saying it *here* for the first time. It attracted readers, and struck reviewers as different and new. How, then, did *Vision* function as a program for the present? What did it show, in its poetry above all, towards a renaissance in Art that could prefigure a renaissance in Life?

Like the English-language modernists, *Vision* ranged across the whole of European civilisation seeking masters and precursors. Its poetry is full of scenes of past times and imitations of past modes in which it seeks to find, or to which it seeks to *give*, a sensuous present-ness and vitality. It reacted, no less than Eliot and Pound, against the archaising sensibility, the 'mahogany feel' of late-Victorian or Edwardian verse.[33] The past, for *Vision*, was typically loud, vivid and crowded, lusty and bright, not swathed in mists or damp with sentiment. Indeed it left any nostalgic sense of history behind in its conjuring of moments of eternity and of the eternally youthful Minds of the great artists, who existed somewhere that could not be described by words such as 'tradition' or 'the past'.

But at this point we arrive at something like the opposite of what Eliot and Pound understood about history and tradition, that the individual poet speaks or can learn to speak, here and now, a contemporary language that carries within it the history of European civilisation. This materiality of language, of accumulated language, defined the present-ness and modernity of history, for the past was no longer remote. It made the renovation of poetic diction the modernists' first, 'historic' task, even before 1914. Once the accumulation of sentiment, eloquence and moralism had been seen through, the form and structure of art, its existence as language or line, of word and concrete image, could be grasped and redeployed. For Hugh Kenner this sense of history—'from which the romance of time travel is excluded'—is linked to cubist collage principles of composition.[34] As in the modernist poem or novel, so in the cubist picture, a new form is defined by the juxtaposition and superimposition of forms, lines or phrases drawn simultaneously from the history of artistic languages and from the contemporaneity of everyday life. There was of course *Vision*'s emphasis on the concrete or sensuous image, and thus on renovating poetic language; and, unlike most of their local contemporaries, the *Vision* poets could think of poetry as indeed something to think with. But the search for the sensuous image or sensuous rhythm *alone* led more often than not to a poetry of surface effects and surface drama.

Europe could not be present to the writers of *Vision* as it was for their modernist contemporaries; despite Jack Lindsay's voracious reading, their frame of reference was more narrowly English or else historically remote, Renaissance Europe or earlier. And because what mattered in the past was eternal, because history was merely accidental, neither history nor tradition arose directly as problems of literary form or structure. Europe could be dismissed *as* history, as cause and effect of all the present rottenness. Paradoxically, this meant that 'the romance of time travel' could *not* be excluded from the magazine's poetry. Scenes of Life are imagined almost anywhere but in the present. The sensuous image is almost always a lost image or event, to be recovered. Thus the archaising sensibility returns to haunt the gaiety and fantasy which the magazine so desperately asserts: 'Some spirit of the air/Defeated hath Despair' (McCrae).[35] Most interestingly, in Slessor's verse, it reveals a bleak nothingness just where the Eternal should be.

By pitching their verse beyond history, the *Vision* poets also pitched it beyond the present. The poetry of youthful renaissance is peopled with witches, fairies, 'easy maids' and 'pistol-boys', pirates and wenches, huntsmen, country lovers, 'Plump cherubim with blown cheeks', highwaymen, harlots, masquers, 'hulking centaurs' and 'naughty satyrs'.[36] There are some more or less accomplished imitations of Elizabethan song and blank-verse drama— Jack Lindsay's 'The Death of Marlowe' and Slessor's 'Man of Sentiment'— accomplished but perhaps also pointless. The sentiment of a lost world overwhelms any renascent vitality. Hence the gothic notes, even stronger in the prose fiction. Despite some virtuoso performances, some startling images and rhythmic complexities especially in poems by Slessor and Lindsay, the effect is closest to costume drama:

Fans clap and sword-knots dance, the Court sweeps down,
The Countess hurries with grass in her powdered hair,
The Duchess with a King's arm round her waist—[37]

More than once the poetic imagination seems to draw its images from the new 'moving pictures' rather than from the great poets and artists of the past.[38]

Dorothea Mackellar's first poem in *Vision* is called 'Fancy Dress'; she understood where the poem belonged. In a brilliant perception, Peter Kirkpatrick has seen fancy dress as the key note of Sydney's 'Bohemian twenties'.[39] Drawing together the remarkable Artists' Balls, the exotic performance life-styles of inner-city bohemia, the glamour and novelty of the movies, the fantasy worlds of Norman Lindsay's art, and, not least, the poetic bravura of *Vision*, the theme of fancy dress describes both a specific milieu, that of Sydney bohemianism, and a widespread reaction to post-war cultural changes. It describes both a celebration of change, of new freedoms in dress, manners, morals, incomes and identities; and an escape from change, from the disorientation of a society still in the shadow of war and revolution. It was a celebration and an evasion of modernity, perhaps both at once. Fancy dress, for Kirkpatrick, like fantasy in the arts, provided 'the illusion of transformation', transformation into pastoral, 'period', carnivalesque or jazz modes as the spirit moved.[40] Fancy dress or costume drama provided a weak form of the transcendence which the *Vision* poetics proclaimed.

Perhaps it is not paradoxical, then, that despite the manifestos, despite Jack Lindsay's dialectical intelligence and Slessor's brittle gloom and glamour, *Vision*'s poetry amounts to little more than a collection of *light verse*. Its Passion is more often 'delight'. Norman's illustrations are the visual equivalent, almost drawings for a children's book, for there was an awful chasm between his rhetoric and his art. At this place, at this point in time, the art of transcendence had come to mean a forced superficiality—surface at all costs! Only in Slessor could this generate an interesting problem for poetry—for getting things said, for finding what moved beneath the surfaces—which would eventually become a question of technique. Elsewhere, the poetry extends certain minor strands of romanticism to their extremes (but short of breaking-point). It is, in this sense, itself a form of decadence. But again, the 'failure' of the poetry suggests not simply *Vision*'s provinciality or mere conservatism, but, on the contrary, its contemporaneity and 'internationalism', its urgent response to the moment, its newness for its contemporary readers. 'Australia has its first quarterly worthy of the adjective "literary"', claimed the *Sydney Daily Mail*.[41] The 'scenery' of the poetry was new. Its language was bright, different, more vivid. So was its energy, which could seem to offer something vital, optimistic and worldly that shook *Vision* clear of 'magazine verse' and modernist despair. But could it do more than repeat its initial gesture?

IV

We have already heard the sound of *Vision*'s opening manifesto. Its logic is relentless in dividing civilisation in two: on one side, Beauty, Youth (and Australia); on the other, modernism, realism (and France—'the pestilence of Zola', 'the locomotor ataxia of Flaubert'). The typical attributes of modernism were primitivism and 'complex superficiality'. Formal experimentation was taken as a sign of mere intellectualism, despair, fear of life, or 'civilised savagery'. 'For the first time in history', the Foreword proclaims, 'Primitivism in the Arts has been expressed by a deliberate intellectual choice.'

The role of Australia in this modernist equation is revealing. The second issue announces: '*Vision* is Australia's only answer to the literature of Europe ... *Vision* will not discuss any topics of parochial or ephemeral appeal ... *Vision* will not concern itself with dying stockmen or the great Australian bush ... *Vision* invites and publishes contributions unaffected by the demand for local colour, but will not consider free verse'.[42] There is scarcely a place for Australian references in the poetry or fiction, unless we count 'the Milky Way' in Slessor's poem 'January 18, 1922' and references to the harbour, explicitly once, an echo elsewhere. Besides Norman's discussion of 'The Sex Synonym in Art', which sees *Ulysses* as an expression of Disgust for Life ('a slovenly mass of mental matter petrified in type matter'), the major critical essay in the first number is Jack's 'Australian Poetry and Nationalism'. Here nationalism is seen as the inevitable product of the rising popular or peasant element in Art worldwide. The situation is worse in Australia because, as a young country, it has had belatedly to go through the folk stage of culture to 'give the people some root in the soil'.[43] If nationalism exists necessarily as 'part of the people's process towards consciousness', this 'educative work' can be best be done by 'the ordinary novel' (31). It has nothing to do with Art—the model for which, in *Vision*, is always poetry, the highest of artistic forms. A genuine Australian literature depends not upon local colour but upon 'the endless search for the image of beauty' (and so on): 'A poem in a medieval setting like the Eve of Saint Agnes, or Romeo and Juliet, ... can do this as no poem set in Sydney can ... There is something in the realistic atmosphere of the actual conditions that surround one that stultifies the free and *concrete* movement of emotion' (34).

The emphasis on 'setting' is revealing of *Vision*'s fatal attraction towards costume drama. Lindsay goes near to contradicting himself through his discomfort with the 'realistic atmosphere of the actual conditions surrounding one', as if the 'gods' cannot be summoned in local terms after all, surely a failure of *Vision*'s own logic of eternal recurrence. For Lindsay, in direct contrast to Eliot and Joyce, 'Romeo can no more exit into a backyard in Sydney than he could into one in London' (31). Was Lindsay thinking of Tiresias, or Hamlet and Odysseus in Dublin?

At the same time, *Vision* was more Australianist than it knew. Its images of a youthful, sunlit Australian-led renaissance accords with a widespread imagining of Australia's difference from the old world. Notions of the young, virile nation had reached one moment of apotheosis in late-nineteenth century images of the bush, and after the Great War the conservative pastoral version of this Australia, 'young, white, happy and wholesome', that came to be accepted as the true image of the nation.[44] The contrast was not primarily with wilder or gloomier images of Australia, as it had been in the nineteenth century, but now, more urgently, with the decadence of Europe. The more that was known about modernism in the arts, the more the diagnosis appeared sound. Modernism was 'foreign' in every sense, foreign to Art, Place and Race. The war provided whatever further confirmation was needed. On the one hand, the Digger had proved the Australian virtues to the world. Australian youthfulness and virility, it appeared, had achieved what the old world had been unable to manage on its own. On the other hand, the war and modernism were symptoms of the one disease, the exhaustion, the mental inertia, the 'physical tiredness' and 'jaded nerves' of Europe. The emphasis on the physical is not accidental, for physical health, energy and virility were the bases on which notions of racial hygiene and cultural vitality were founded (*Vision*'s first number includes an advertisement for the Langridge School of Physical Culture). The concerns were anxious ones, because the very bearers of the nation's meaning, the Diggers, were also those likely to be affected by 'neurasthenia', the modern disease.[45] Contemporary ideas about spiritualism, mesmerism, electricity and x-rays, eurhythmics, eugenics, physical culture, psychoanalysis and modern physics can often be understood in relation to one another, and all in relation to art, as theories about the same kind of thing: physical, spiritual and racial fitness in the face of modernity. Norman Lindsay firmly believed in the physiological effects and causes of art, at least for those with the appropriate highly-developed 'nerve tissue'.[46]

It was a mainstream view, not merely a quirk of *Vision*, that Art should express youthful vitality, and that Australia had already shown the way or held the line, or at least held promise for the future. Divisions might arise over just where healthy vitality was to be found—was it in farming or in sex?—but pastoralist and vitalist positions could in practice overlap. The argument might be nationalist, focused on the 'vision splendid of the sunlit planes extended'; but then again it might not, for it could take the form of faith in Australia's capacity to revivify European civilisation. Young Australia, at the point of crisis which *Vision* claimed as its own, held the best promise for civilisation's next vital epoch.

It is exactly at this post-war moment that the Foreword to *Vision*'s second number positions itself: 'We stand for the younger generation: those who had experience in the war and yet had sufficient courage to survive its mental effect of horror'. The war is portrayed as the result of two deadly forces: 'the bludgeon of English morality [and] the dissecting-knife of French rationality'. Both have 'ended in Primitivism, in the proclaiming of Chaos as the governing principle of Modernity'. On the side of the damned are ranged Macauley, Ruskin, Arnold, Botticelli, Epstein, Dante, Milton, Michelangelo, Shelley, Swinburne, Raphael—Haters of Life and dealers in abstraction. On the other side, with Apollo and Aphrodite, are Nietzsche, Rubens, Praxiteles, Keats, and *Vision*. Jack Lindsay's engagement with the French account of modernity leads, in a later essay in the same number, to the conclusion—or in this case, the opening sentence—that 'The French mind has devastated Europe'.[47] When it comes to modernity, he is nothing if not inclusive:

> Baudelaire and Huysman, with their depth of horror and disgust; Verlaine, with his abysmal self pity; the primitives seeking flat or lumpy forms, de Chavannes, Matisse, Gaugin, Cezanne, Van Gogh; the depressed Flaubert, and Zola, 'the delight to stink'; the de Goncourts, Remy de Gourmont, Anatole France, all sceptical, barren and tired; Debussy, or the revolt from the power of Wagner; Satie and the Dadaists, or childish uproar. (39)

'We can say with justice, that without Paris, Modernism could never have got the hold it has' (39).

In the same number, Norman introduces a new home for true Art and true Artists, the realm of 'Hyperborea'. The old arguments are replayed in a new shorthand—Hyperboreans, now, versus mere Man: 'Hyperborea is a place where Man is not'.[48] Before a poem or a painting, the Hyperborean will be revealed: 'Word, phrase, and image, form, rhythm and emotion, each in turn will be absorbed into the substance of his mind' (15). As for Man:

> We have only to turn to his actions in the mass; his collective impulses expressed in his commercial greeds; his activity in manufacturing implements of destruction, his last war, and the war he is preparing for, to realise that this animal, for all his rituals in religion, his conventions in sociology, his prattle of humanitarianism, and all the surface effects of civilisation in city streets and civil life, is just as savage and dangerous as he was a million years ago. (17)

In the face of such powerful *modern* disgust, it is as if Norman is drawn, irresistibly, to the light and comic. He returns to Hyperborea in the following number, to Hyperborea as costume drama with a vengeance, full of 'good fellows and gay girls, of poets, painters, and musicians, spendthrifts, and libertines; in short, all who make gallantry, gaiety, ribaldry and loose-living the industrious pastimes of their leisure'.[49] The bohemian basis of his philosophy—or at least its very local anti-suburbanism—was never made clearer. Mere 'Man's Art', for Norman, is 'an Art pallid with dwelling in the gloom of suburban back parlours' (16). Still, his best or worst energy is reserved for his modernist enemies:

> One was a French Vers Librist, one was an Intellectual Bolshevist from Patagonia, one was a Bulgarian Atrocitist carrying an image of a corpse modelled in dough, and another, I think, was a lady Futurist from Chelsea, draped in alternate streaks of pink, puce, purple, and the colour of toads, and they all settled down in that part of the bog labelled America.[50]

Oddly (but in other ways unsurprisingly) there's something of Huxley's or Lewis's satire in such writing. Few Australian critics could write as vividly about modernism.

In Jack's words, between 'pastoral contentment and the passionate consciousness of high mind, there stretches the Hell of Suburbia'.[51] We can take 'suburbia' not only as shorthand for puritanism, philistinism or commercial values, but as synecdochal of modernity more broadly. As mere savagery or mere sociology, the 'facts' of modernity had nothing to do with Art. What is significant about *Vision*, though, is how far it has to travel in order to keep this modernity at bay—not just into the past but beyond history altogether. Thus the characteristic scale of its romantic, time-travelling poetry and fiction—desperate jollity and period 'charm'; pastoral innocence or gothic melodrama; and, strangest of all, the persistent note of darkness, loss and 'wistful regret'.[52] Fitzgerald caught the note that haunts *Vision*'s affirmation of Beauty and Joy: 'the rose is shattered by that wind's wrath/And blown out in the cold, blackening west'.[53]

Was *Vision* a freak, then, or truly of its place and time? The question is simple and misleading, for the place and time of the magazine's appearance can be grasped in many different dimensions. It was as often well reviewed as criticised—it is hard to know whether the visionaries were more delighted by the *Daily Mail*'s judgement that it was Australia's first literary quarterly or by the *Age* finding an excess of 'satyriasis and nymphomania'.[54] The printers could barely keep up with the demand for the magazine's first number, and by November 1923 the editors could claim that '*Vision* has attained a circulation higher than that of any other quarterly of its class in Australia'.[55] Its very disdain for a mass audience had its own attraction for a self-selecting readership, telling them they were different: 'Can we lend you a pair of spectacles? That depends. We may not like you. *Vision* will not lend spectacles to anyone'.[56] The audience *Vision* addressed, ideally, was the creative few whose effort would achieve the renaissance; more modestly, as the *Daily Telegraph* noted, it offered writers 'who do not wish to conform to the demands of local colour a better chance to do original work'.[57] As Kirkpatrick suggests, the magazine's 'modern' sexual morality also made it attractive 'to a liberal young readership'.[58] Nor should we underestimate the appeal to this readership of its pure (and sexual) commitment to Art, which in itself could appear to be liberating.

But the purity of its initial gesture could not be repeated indefinitely.[59] After the initial success, sales had fallen, and by Number Four it was already beginning to look like 'just' a literary magazine. *Vision*'s claim to be the only Australian magazine with a 'definite literary standard' could be read as a modernising gesture, announcing its break with the present, but perhaps it also signalled its distance from the avant-garde. If Number Five had appeared as planned this trend would have been confirmed. Johnson's idea was for a more popular, expanded format and more frequent numbers; ironically, perhaps even something closer to *Art in Australia*.[60] But the finance did not come through. In any case, perhaps, as a 'manifestation', *Vision* had served its purpose, in its time and place.

V

More than any other Australian magazine until the Depression years, *Vision* grasped its moment as a moment of crisis, a crisis in western civilisation that expressed itself both in war and modernism, in art and society (in commercialism, puritanism, suburbanism). As such, this self-destructive turn in culture was simultaneously local and international. *Vision* grasped— or glimpsed—that the relationship between art and civilisation was central to the diagnosis of crisis and perhaps to its remedy as well. It mobilised art, here in the name of the 'legionaries of the new Roman effort to reconstruct earth' (Foreword, IV). This militancy enabled *Vision* to appear new and utterly contemporary to its readers, not least because of the way it could make modernism seem merely ephemeral, a moment in the recent past, the last gasp of the old.

John Tregenza has offered an extended comparison of *Vision* and the literary scene of the English 1890s, the era of Wilde, Beardsley and Dowson. He reads poems by Slessor and Fitzgerald alongside Dowson to argue that 'they were in much the same poetic situation in Sydney in the nineteen twenties as Dowson in London during the nineties'. They did not write like Eliot because 'they did not know his world'. In particular:

> They had not experienced the disillusion and bitterness of the post-war years in
> Europe, nor did they know at first hand the quality of life in a large industrial city.
> They rightly refused to assume a tired cynicism which they did not genuinely feel ...
> The life they did know—the respectably dull life of Sydney—oppressed them just as
> Victorian London had oppressed the poetic coteries of the eighteen nineties.[61]

But Tregenza underestimates how far the disillusion of the post-war years could be imported, or rather, how it was local and immediate. The war was omnipresent on the home front, and its political and social after-effects were by no means worked out by 1923.[62] More immediately, of course, *Vision* was 'after' modernism, and however remote its local context was from the modernist vortex, this fact makes its 1920s fundamentally different from London's 1890s. The disillusion and bitterness which it might read in modernism, the experiments in form, the manifestos and movements, were central in defining its sense of its own occasion. The *Vision* reaction was more urgent than Tregenza allows. And yet the comparison does have its point. The respectably dull life of Sydney could be understood as a symptom on the same plane as the war or modernism, another symptom of cultural devitalisation. One way or another, culture—poetry—seemed locally to be in the hands of the respectably dull. There were no Australian modernist schools and movements against which to launch the *Vision* campaign, but the refusal of modernism (and French rationality or objectivism) could be joined with the refusal of (English and local) moralism.

Thus the double image of Australia for *Vision*. On one hand Australia was still Victorian, even more so than Victorian London, and the modernising effects of suburbanisation only intensified its worst aspects. On the other hand, the country had escaped the worst savageries of modernism. It was, in this sense, outside time, and so the perfect setting for *Vision*'s new 'Hellenic world of strong and free spirits' (Foreword, IV). Despite its horror of gum-leaf verse, it is to Australian nature rather than culture that *Vision* finally turns, not overtly in its imagery but in its evocation of youth and vitality.

Tregenza's point about the city raises another dimension of *Vision*'s time and place. If Sydney was not quite London, it was unmistakeably a modern city. It was stratified by class, stimulated by commerce. If it was respectably dull, it also had the energy of urban concentration and popular consumption. It could spawn its own bohemia, concentrated in the inner-city but also, uniquely perhaps, in reach of the Arcadian harbour and romantic ocean. *Vision* proudly reprinted the *Bulletin*'s comment that it was 'as naked as Manly Beach' (the mixture of sensuous pleasure and innocence is just right).[63] Besides its cafes, pubs and restaurants, the ecology that supported Sydney bohemianism and hence *Vision* itself was the booming newspaper and magazine scene, which, together with commercial art, provided both permanent and freelance employment.[64] Although Sydney had had a bohemian culture from the late-nineteenth century, the new bohemianism was a distinctly post-war phenomenon. Kirkpatrick sees the 'cult of youth and sexuality' which arose in the twenties as a reaction to the war, not so much to the horror of war, perhaps, as to the sense of an old world which had irrevocably passed.[65] The new world meant new social and sexual freedoms—the figure of the flapper was its readiest shorthand—and it found its reflections and rhythms in the new forms of popular commercial culture, in Hollywood and jazz.[66] This was a city culture; motor cars and apartment blocks were part of its landscape. We might say, then, that Tregenza also underestimates Sydney's modernity.

Tregenza describes *Vision* as a 'decided step forward in the evolution of Australian poetry' despite the limited success of its poetic output. The metaphor of evolution is unhelpful, for we cannot think of Australian poetry or culture as a single organism. But we can rescue the point through another marker of the magazine's modernity. More than other Australian magazines of its time, *Vision* apprehended the growing modernist separation between popular and high art forms, even as it sought to leap backwards into a future beyond such separations.[67] *Vision* was a new kind of publication, not only because of its manifestos, but also because it suggested a new sense of art's autonomy, one that exceeded even its own romantic vision. The consequences would be worked out in the careers of Slessor, Fitzgerald and Jack Lindsay.

PARIS, MOSCOW, MELBOURNE

During the time of the historical avant-garde movements, the attempt
to do away with the distance between art and life still had all the pathos
of historical progressiveness on its side.

(Peter Bürger, *Theory of the Avant-Garde*)

In August 1931 a little magazine from Melbourne announced that 'Ezra Pound, in a letter to the Editors, has granted *Stream* the Australian rights of publishing any of his new work. A selection of Mr Pound's recent writings will be presented shortly.'[1] Unfortunately *Stream* did not survive long enough to enter the Poundian archive and we do not know how Pound came to hear about it. Nevertheless, even the editors' brief announcement in what was only the second issue of the magazine suggests something to us about Pound's relentless imperialism across the face of the literary globe but also something about the international reach of modernism itself.

Stream is the most remarkable of a small number of magazines published in Australia in the first half of the 1930s. These magazines show a sudden—if delayed—moment of accession to contemporary debates about modernism and the avant-garde. It was a condition of Australia's postcolonial situation that the avant-garde and the modernist 'arrived' together and all at once.[2] The avant-garde moment in Australia was also a post-Depression moment, deeply marked by the severe local effects of the Wall Street crash. In addition, in a cultural situation in which the mainstream literary and artistic institutions were bourgeois and commercial rather than high aesthetic—that is, despite some bohemian journalistic circles, there was no real aesthetic elite separate from establishment or commercial realms—the avant-garde moment involved a high degree of politicisation. The target of avant-garde critique was the commercial 'prostitution' of art rather than its aesthetic detachment from the everyday, although the two could be discovered as identical in cause and effect.

The apparently rival claims of radical avant-garde and radical proletarian art formed a crux of debate; they were sometimes bitterly opposed and sometimes difficult to distinguish as they identified a common enemy. In September 1931, *Stream* announced a major symposium on the question of 'Paris or Moscow?' for a future issue which sadly never appeared. For a brief but exciting moment in certain Australian—or at least certain Melbournian—intellectual circles, this seemed to be the most important question of all.

The first magazine that took up some of these dramatic questions—and took them up dramatically—was *Strife* (1930). The name, of course, is indicative. The magazine was designed to cause trouble and it did; its sole issue was seized by police at a demonstration of unemployed marching on Parliament House in Melbourne. This was the height of the Depression and the magazine was produced in part to raise funds for unemployment relief. The two young editors, Judah Waten and Herbert McClintock, not yet the novelist and painter they would respectively become, were arrested for vagrancy.[3]

No doubt the contents of the magazine would have astounded the unemployed and police alike. On the inside front cover, it presented its manifesto:

STRIFE!

STRIFE is another force added to the world-wide movement to uproot the existing social and economic order of chaotic and tragic individualism!

INSTITUTIONS that represent this must be destroyed, and, on the newly-turned soil of free human aspiration, a nobler edifice erected.

ALL WHO DENY THIS MECHANISM of Progress are our enemies; all who await impatiently the new dawn our comrades! All who accept the permanence of the present regime, whether as protagonists or complacent nay-sayers and futilists, are our foes. All who believe in the permanence and validity of conscious and creative liberating energy, our blood brothers and friends!

STRIFE is an organ of the new culture, destructive and constructive, a culture plowing deep into the roots of life, and, as such, contemns and rejects all manifestations in form and content of the social disorder we oppose.

STRIFE affirms the validity of materialism in its widest sense. It affirms that, as the future belongs to the people, the new form and content must be a proletarian form and content!

APPEAL

On this broad basis we appeal to the people of Australia, both industrial and intellectual workers, whose revolt we embody, to further our aims. The columns of *STRIFE* are wide open to all who feel and can express forcefully and really this SPIRIT OF REVOLT.

The sinews of war, in the form of cash contributions, small or great, are urgently needed. We are confident that the advance guard of the NEW AUSTRALIA will not be niggardly in providing this publication, its first and most vital medium of expression, with the means of carrying its CAUSE a step further on its march through the long and stressful hours that herald the COMING DAWN. The attack has already sounded! Forward.

With a formality that seems out of place the manifesto is signed 'The Board of Editors', although Waten is almost certainly its author. This was a largely unprecedented kind of writing and an unprecedented (anti-)aesthetic stance for Australia.[4] And of course *Strife* wanted to announce itself as unprecedented. The magazine as a whole is an uneven mixture of attitudes: bohemian, libertarian, communist, proletarian, anarchist, and avant-garde. As Charles Merewether has suggested, there are similarities in its manifesto to Marinetti's 1909 *Futurist Manifesto*, among others, although *Strife* proclaims a collective rather than an individualist revolution; closer models might be the Russian futurist Left Front of Arts (LEF) and constructivist groups of the 1920s.[5] But the similarities have as much to do with genre— the genre of the manifesto—as with any ideological convergence. Indeed, the production of a magazine and a manifesto *before* any 'literary' work as such is utterly characteristic of the avant-garde moment. The manifesto itself becomes a primary form of the avant-garde work.[6]

The main burden of *Strife*'s radical stance is anti-capitalist, driven by the sense of a revolutionary content, as it were, rather than by a more purely avant-gardiste revolution of form: it proclaimed an extreme realism rather than extreme formalism. And yet we can see how the radical re-vision of art through the reformulation of its proper content can lead to an attitude and a set of practices similar to those which stem from the radical remaking of artistic form. Soviet art of the 1920s provides many dramatic examples of these overlaps and of oppositions that keep turning into each other. A more direct influence in Australia was the American magazine *New Masses* and the work of its editor Mike Gold, inspired by the way 'the Kremlin had transmuted "vouchers, daybooks and index cards" into poetry'.[7] The appropriate category to describe *Strife*, then, might be 'left avant-garde' or better 'proletarian avant-garde'.

Some of the arguments from Peter Bürger's *Theory of the Avant-Garde* enable us to claim *Strife* as an 'avant-gardiste manifestation', and as the first such manifestation in the literary field in Australia, albeit sudden, belated and ephemeral as I have suggested.[8] Bürger argues that what is distinctive to the avant-garde is its critique of art as an institution. The avant-gardiste critique no longer takes place within the institution of art—for example, as criticism of previous art schools—but attacks the institution itself from its margins.[9] Thus we find *Strife* celebrating its own marginality (even from 'the people' it claims to represent). Even more pertinent, the avant-garde movement or gesture is defined by its attack on the concept of art as autonomous, and by its desire to 'reintegrate art into the praxis of life'.[10] The manifesto form itself is one expression of this desire: its object is to transform not just art but life as well, such that the very distinction between art and life stops making sense.

At the level of the text, Bürger argues, the avant-gardiste critique is directed against the organic work of art, an attack carried through via the principle of montage.[11] This is one possible description of the magazine itself. *Strife* is a very long way from the decorative and decorous format of the conventional art magazine or literary periodical, although in comparison with something like Wyndham Lewis's *Blast* it is conventional typographically. But any unity which can be posited for the diverse materials collected in the magazine—articles, notices, appeals, graphics, verse, manifestos—is at best strategic and occasional. In Bürger's terms, it is a 'manifestation' rather than a 'work'.[12]

What is most interesting is that where *Strife* does seem to participate in the historical moment of the avant-garde is precisely where 'modern' art and revolutionary communism are forced together: where it goes beyond the call for a newly politicised content in the work of art to the call for a new kind of art altogether. The magazine is never 'modernist' in, say, a

Poundian or a surrealist sense but its extreme anti-formalism draws it to repeat certain gestures of the avant-garde.

Earlier bohemian magazines in Australia, in particular *Vision*, had criticised art in its present condition but had done so in the name of Art. In *Strife* the critique throughout is directed at the level of the institution; in Bürger's terms, at the 'productive and distributive apparatus ... and the ideas about art' rather than the content of individual works or the practices of particular schools.[13] When the manifesto declares that 'the new form and content must be a proletarian form and content', the range of reference is ambiguous: is it literature, art, or every institution of social and political life that must be revolutionised?

It is on these grounds that *Strife* also announces its own radical break with the past. Past and future, old world and new, bourgeois and proletarian are radically polarised in the characteristic rhetoric of the modernist manifesto, 'not only describing but evoking and enacting the desperate and frantic rhythm that capitalism imparts to every facet of modern life'.[14] Or in the language of *Strife*: 'Rotten at the core, and torn asunder by the crisis of over-production ... [capitalism] is being driven on and on by the law of its nature to its final crash and destruction'.[15] The 'conscious and creative liberty' thus released leads not simply to the destruction of art but to the liberating—or forcing—of aesthetic creativity into the praxis of everyday life. Thus *Strife* announces itself as 'an organ of the new culture, *destructive and constructive*'.

We can in such claims note similarities between the proletarian and the avant-gardiste projects: art as sheer 'fact' meets art as sheer 'construction' as both explode organic form. This complex pattern of overlaps is just as likely to find itself expressed in discourse *about* art as in the actual practice of art. Both forms celebrate a kind of destructive and constructive energy, often summed up in the image of the machine. This image is generated by the project of a radical break with the past. What could better express the revolt against the organic work of art? This is the message from dadaist automatic writing, futurism's speed-obsession, constructivist 'factography', or the avant-garde and proletarianist fascination with cinema and photography (in Aleksander Rodchenko's words, 'Art has no place in modern life ... Photograph and be photographed!').[16]

Writing itself was to become machine-like and thereby also more creative: the writer as typewriter, camera-eye or engineer. *Strife* expresses this image of the writer as machine, with all the impersonality of a radio, a diagram or a headline, but also with their modernity:

> The proletarian writer will tell us why wars are made. They (sic) will tell us about the international competition for oil, coal, steel, markets! He will state facts. He will condemn; he will annihilate.[17]

Is this a description of art or not? The answer is yes—and no. But this is precisely the point, just as the dadaist work refuses both to be and not to be a work of art. For *Strife* the revolution of the world does not mean just a new content for the work of art. The revolution is of such scope that the very principles of the work of art are revolutionised until they are scarcely recognisable. And as such, the revolution of art becomes part of the revolution of everyday life.

The closer the magazine's writing approaches this point, the more likely it is to approach the rhetoric of the manifesto:

> Facts are the new literature. The proletarian writers will break with the sickly plots, tremulous love chirpings, ecstasies, sex triangles, and individual heroisms of the writers of the past. He will work with facts. He will not worry too much about form; he will transcend the antiquated forms of the past, to create a new form based on facts.
>
> Utility and social theory will create a beauty of form in the proletarian masterpieces of the future. In Soviet Russia this is already true. The works of the American proletarian writers, Gold, Dos Passos, Charles Yale Harrison, Paul Peters, and others herald the growth of the new revolutionary literature.
>
> STRIFE is unique. We will confound the fainthearts and sceptics. We believe that the present conditions of our life can produce men who can give us masterpieces. Masterpieces are made from periods of great social activity.
>
> The capitalist world has to be changed. We will contribute to the change.
>
> STRIFE announces the birth of a new full-blooded fighting literature. To Hell with futility, hypocrisy, and sex obsession. Hey, there! Make way for the voice of the despised.[18]

What might such a new literature of facts look like? The list of American proletarian writers suggests one model. Dos Passos, Gold and the American *New Masses* were particularly important for the small group around *Strife*. But even the Soviet Five Year Plan can be made to support an aesthetic experience:

> A fascinating book has been compiled by the State Economic Planning Commission, and adopted by the Soviet Government. Published in England … under the title of 'The Soviet Union Looks Ahead: The Five-Year Plan for Economic Construction.'
>
> Every line in this magnificent book breathes of the mass enthusiasm for socialist construction; of mass creative effort.
>
> Unlike most books of figures and tables, it is quite as exciting to read as it is important. It is of supreme importance, because it represents the concrete working programme of a socialist planned economy, without the aid of capitalists. It is exciting because it represents a picture that forms a pattern to the eye, because it is conceived as a whole and a picture of a moving situation, a process of creation and growth …
>
> The tremendous growth of socialist economy in Russia has not only confounded the sceptics, but has sounded the death knell of capitalist society. The U.S.S.R. is the beacon light of the communist world revolution.[19]

What else is being described here but a new literature of facts, a new beauty of form which unites utility and social theory, transgresses the institutional boundaries of art, and returns the aesthetic to the praxis of everyday life? The same set of impulses produced constructivist industrial design and the 'modernist' photographs of the Dnieper dam and other examples of 'socialist construction' in the Soviet Union, so popular in the West in the 1930s in magazines like *USSR in Construction*.[20] But we might also wonder whether there is only a thin line, after all, dividing the 'left avant-gardism' of *Strife* from what would soon become socialist realism, as the assemblage of facts swells to encompass the whole world.

However simplistic and absurdly disconnected from the authors' immediate situation, the combination of attitudes expressed in *Strife* is familiar from the history of avant-garde artistic debates in the Soviet Union and then America and Europe in the 1920s and 1930s. But their appearance in Australia in 1930—the contemporaneity of this one-off manifestation—is extraordinary. None of the individuals involved in the magazine had a literary or artistic reputation (almost by definition). The contributors were a mix of young journalists and graphic artists, bohemian drinkers and talkers, students, and immigrant communists. There were parallel relationships in their institutional locations: the journalists were marginal in relation to literature, the commercial artists in relation to fine art, the students in relation to the academy, the communists in relation to party politics. The literary institutions against which they were arguing were either narrowly parochial, middlebrow or Anglophile. *Vision's* response to modernism might have been one distant rival, however it is unlikely that it was remembered in detail, if at all, although it would have been difficult to ignore Norman Lindsay. Contemporaries like Katharine Susannah Prichard or the Palmers did not come into view, positively or negatively, except through a brief mention of the 'art theatre movement' and then only to be dismissed as divorced from mass society. What enabled *Strife* to achieve its momentary coherence was its 'revolutionary' sense of internationalism, political in origin but bringing with it an utterly new sense of modernity, of revolutionary developments in all aspects of life and art.

But the magazine was also without a sustaining context. Not only were its arguments unlikely, they involved both a stunning misrecognition (alongside a half-formed recognition) of the modernity of the local present. *Strife* could not form the basis of a movement or even become a lasting irritant. There was scarcely an antagonist—whether high modernist or traditionalist—to be galvanised into action and to force positions to be staked out and defended, and literary culture probably failed even to notice its brief existence. Local critics discussed the latest bestsellers from London or were just discovering the powerful charms of defining an Australian nationalist tradition. There was little density in either mainstream or oppositional institutions. So *Strife* did not survive beyond its memorable first issue; but then again, perhaps as a 'manifestation', it could not be repeated.

Six months after *Strife*, Melbourne also saw the first publication of *Stream* (1931).[21] There seem to be no direct connections between the two although there were overlaps in the circles from which contributors and readers might be drawn. Across the history of new and especially modernist magazines in Australia, each publication has had to reinvent modernism anew and to argue, as if for the first time, a connection between modernism and its own local time and place. The existence of a modernist 'tradition' could scarcely be assumed, and even where it can be invoked its local relevance needs to be articulated and reclaimed. This was still the case in the 1980s for a magazine such as *Scripsi*. How much more the case, then, in the early 1930s.

What is remarkable about *Stream* is its unapologetic and un-anxious assumption of the simultaneity of the modernist project wherever it occurred—Paris, Moscow or Melbourne ('a place teeming with modern activities'):

> *STREAM* ... is a medium of international art expression.
>
> *STREAM* is universal in outlook, and does not definitely ally itself with any particular art movement of the day: it seeks, in short, only what is vital and genuine in contemporary art, literature and thought ...
>
> *STREAM* has no geographical prejudices: by Australian art it means no more than art that is created in Australia: and its evaluation of such works will depend entirely upon the degree of sincerity and vitality that informs them.[22]

Stream manifests this form of internationalism in the range of materials and contributors it includes, but more importantly in its format and style: above all, in a regular feature called 'Montages', significantly enough, extending over several pages in each issue. 'Montages' comprises paragraphs of news about contemporary 'art, literature and thought' drawn from an extraordinary range of magazines from France, Italy, Germany and the Soviet Union. It calls attention to Luigi Pirandello, the Soviet VOKS (Society for Cultural Relations with Foreign Countries), Charlie Chaplin, T.S. Eliot, Theodore Dreiser, and revolutionary Soviet directors Sergei Eisenstein, Ilya Trauberg and Vsevolod Pudowkin. The column works to suggest that all this is of immediate and pressing relevance to readers here and now in Australia—not exotic so much as irresistibly modern. Elsewhere the magazine reprints pieces by Basil Bunting, Fernand Léger, Robert McAlmon and Spanish author Azorin, alongside its local contributors.

Stream situates itself in a fluid modernist tradition which embraces symbolism, post-impressionism, surrealism, Eliot and Pound, Huxley and Lawrence, Proust and Rémy de Gourmont whose 'Credo' it published:

A writer's capital crime is conformity, imitativeness, submission to rules and precepts. A writer's work should not only be a reflection, but the magnified reflection of his personality . . . his only excuse is to be original. He should say things not yet said, and say them in a form not yet formulated. He should create his own aesthetics, and we should admit as many aesthetics as there are original minds, judging them according to what they are not.[23]

Although *Stream* celebrates the artist's individuality, it is also alive to the radical democracy of modernity (present, perversely, even here in de Gourmont) wherein every person could be an artist and the materials of the everyday, from the city streets to dreams, could provide the materials for their art. Nevertheless it is still surprising on the evidence of the magazine's first number (July 1931) that proletarianism ever becomes an issue. It does so as early as the second number in August. Proletarian art here is understood not so much in terms of its politics but in terms of its modernity. Mass or collective forms are seen as one expression of modernity, but one only, alongside symbolic-mythic forms, surrealism, or Pound's 'classicism'. All are held in opposition to the bourgeois orthodoxies.

So an article on Eliot and symbolism is discovered side by side with another on Joyce and surrealism, a review of the English proletarian novel *Hunger and Love*, and, by the third issue, a piece on Soviet literature by Zinovy Lvovsky (around the 'classic' Five-Year Plan novel, Fedor Panferov's *Brousski*). Quotations from German left-wing author Ernst Glaeser writing in the French magazine *Bifur* ('The writer should be acquainted with the great laws of economics ... He should know modern man [and] the economic laws which control him') are set beside a declaration from the French *Union des artistes modernes*: 'our modern architects and decorators point to locomotives and airplanes, dynamos and Chicago wheat silos, and say: There are our masters and models'.[24] The complete break with the past declared in such a statement confronts Pound's high-modernist classical 'Credo':

Mr Eliot, who is at times an excellent poet and who has arrived at the supreme Eminence among English critics largely through disguising himself as a corpse, once asked, in the course of an amiable article, what 'I believe'.

Having a strong disbelief in abstract and general statement as a means of conveying one's thoughts to others, I have for a number of years answered such questions by telling the inquirer to read Confucius and Ovid. This can do no harm to the intelligent and the unintelligent may be damned.

Given the material means I would replace the Statue of Venus on the cliffs of Terracina. I would erect a temple to Artemis in Park Lane. I believe that a light from Eleusis persisted throughout the middle ages and set beauty in the song of Provence and of Italy.

I believe that post-war 'returns to Christianity' (and its various sub-divisions) have been merely the *gran' rifute* and, in general, signs of fatigue.

I do not expect science (mathematics, biology, etc) to lead us back to the unwarrantable assumptions of theologians.

I do not expect the machine to dominate the human consciousness that created it.[25]

To point to this mix of materials is not by any means to accuse *Stream* of incoherence. On the contrary, its coherence is created out of the montage of positions through which it establishes an ongoing debate with itself around the question of modernism. These are the terms of the debate which it spells out in the projected feature on 'Paris or Moscow':

PARIS OR MOSCOW   SYMPOSIUM

Stream announces for publication shortly a symposium on a subject of the first importance: the possibilities and claims of the two rival aesthetics indicated by the above title. Is individualist literature doomed? Is the collectivist idea capable of supplanting it? The question cannot be discussed without reference to the creative process itself. Is this process, as we see it manifested in masterpieces of the past, constant in art? Or can it be changed or radically modified by external life forces? It is possible to come to conclusions on this matter which shall be quite detached from current political considerations. The symposium, to which many writers will contribute, will therefore be non-political.[26]

We can distinguish *Stream* from the earlier *Strife* even in the terms in which it announces its interest in proletarian realism. The concern here is to be 'non-political'. Despite the avant-gardism of many of its contributions,

Stream situates itself ultimately within the realm of the aesthetic. Proletarian realism can be seen as a 'rival', but as a rival on the same plane, a rival aesthetic. Issues such as individualist versus collectivist practice, the 'creative process' versus 'external life forces', are to be concluded within the domain of art and outside politics. As thoroughly modern, the magazine is as interested in the cinema as it is in painting and poetry, but this represents an extension and 'modernisation' of the aesthetic rather than its dissolution.

Strife announces itself as a provocation, as disruption and 'strife'. What is remarkable about *Stream*, on the other hand, is precisely its utterly confident and convincing assumption of its place within a modernist main 'stream'— an extraordinary leap of the imagination given its local situation and likely audience. Again those behind the magazine were figures on the fringes of the literary and artistic establishment: young journalists, worker artists and writers, commercial artists, students, young professors, communists, a bookshop owner, and so on. Again there was scarcely any chance of it provoking a dialogue, even less a confrontation, between modernists and traditionalists, or between radical and conservative modernists, in the larger cultural sphere. *Stream* had to conduct the latter debate within its own pages, and could only do so for three issues. The groups were fragile and temporary, and there were few middle-range publications between the little magazines and the commercial reviews or establishment newspapers in which a debate could be sustained. It was only in the late-1930s and 1940s that a major series of debates around the question of modernity would begin to overturn the whole organisation of art in its institutions, its practices and discourses, and even then much more successfully in the realm of painting than in literature.

Two other magazines can be mentioned quickly (and again their titles are significant): *Proletariat* (1932–34) and *Masses* (1932).[27] *Proletariat* was published from within the Melbourne University Labor Club, a group of students, young academics, and non-university radicals which included a number formerly associated with *Stream* (Alwyn Lee, Jack Maugham and Cyril Pearl, plus Guido Baracchi, Winston Rhodes, Ralph Gibson, Esmonde Higgins, and Geoffrey Sawer). The primary interests of the magazine were contemporary history and Marxism as a radical intellectual practice, indeed Marxism *as* contemporary history. As an intellectual mode, this is precisely what 'proletarianism', more so even than 'communism', signified in this period. Literature enters as a subsection of this larger concern, as one of the areas of revolutionary change in contemporary history but not necessarily its advance guard. American proletarian writing or the 'new realism' is once again a major reference point, as a movement more modern than modernism in the Marxist reading of historical development:

> This new school of writers is a reaction against the introspective literature of our time ... Individual problems, the personal experiences of separate egos may be of value at other times, but the living human experience of the workers is chiefly of another sort. Therefore Proletarian Art attempts to give vivid representations of social passions. The aim of such a literature is to reflect the forces conflicting in a revolutionary period, to look at life from the point of view of the masses ...
>
> [H]owever crude it may be, however horrible, here is something thrown into artistic form by the volcanic energy of a mind that knows what it is to be but a fragment of that nameless, formless thing which cries: 'The Masses count, not men'
> ...
>
> [H]ere we have writers whose aim is to place the stamp of proletarian ideals on the culture of the world. We may resist them if we will, welcome them if we can, but if we ignore them we will do no service either to reality or art, which is the expression of that reality.[28]

One of the major categories of understanding throughout *Proletariat* is that of the 'mass' or 'masses'. In Australia as elsewhere in the period, the term signified the sudden irruption into bourgeois history of 'mass forces' and 'mass consciousness'. It meant history perceived as class struggle and as energy, as revolution, as 'destruction and construction'. This was the set of ideas—more than any utopian hopes for the future brotherhood of man—behind the radicalisation of so many individuals both in the universities and beyond in the 1930s. It was also the discourse, taken as a threat or a promise, that led to the formation of new kinds of writers' and artists' groups, and to the publication of their magazines and manifestos.

Masses, then, was almost inevitable as the name of a magazine (as indeed was *Proletariat*). *Masses* was the publication of the Workers' Art Club, its slogan 'Art as a Weapon'. Again names of contributors and editors from the previous magazines reappear—Lee, Maugham, Lockhart, Gibson, Youssevitch—suggesting just how fluid the boundaries were between modernist and left-wing projects, and how small were the cultural networks. Like *Strife*, *Masses* was committed to experimental forms of realist writing—reportage, the documentary or cinematic novel, the prose sketch, even the manifesto—but modernity is not quite the issue any longer, despite the magazine's internationalist, proletarian basis. The claims of realism are no longer so radically anti-formalist, and thus, as the apparent paradox works itself out, less likely to resemble the claims of the avant-garde:

Art is the product of a consciousness that is socially created. Again, if art influences the individual (i.e., if it is anything at all) it plays a socially organizing role. This is a platitude; but its implications are revolutionary ...

The naked class alignment of current bourgeois art (in films, novels, magazine stories etc.) should be clear enough even to people not accustomed to Marxian criticism ...

Proletarian art gives expression not only to the essential humanity which can only derive from the social class, the workers, but to the actual field of antagonism between the working-class and the anti-social ruling class. The communist works to make complete and effective the social consciousness of the workers, and so for the struggle against capitalism; the proletarian artist strives to give expression to the spiritual renascence which has its roots in that struggle ... [T]he working class carries the germs of an all-embracing civilization within it.[29]

For all its revolutionary élan, the descriptions of the role of art here recall nothing so much as the conventional terms of aesthetics ('spiritual renascence', 'all-embracing civilization'). As Bürger suggests, the avant-gardiste provocation, because of its very nature, cannot be repeated indefinitely. It will turn to either aesthetics or politics, or shuttle between the two.

It would be the early 1940s and in the midst of a world war before any comparable modernist and/or radical magazines appeared again in Australia, with *Angry Penguins* (1940–46), *A Comment* (1940–47), *Barjai* (1943–47) and *Australian New Writing* (1943–46).[30] My brief account of four ephemeral Australian magazines from the early 1930s suggests something of the conditions under which an avant-garde moment could occur in a postcolonial situation. It was unlikely that the institutions of art would produce such a development in the course of their own evolution: if this was heading anywhere it was towards one or other version of a national tradition. What was needed was a political or social catalyst, in this case the Depression, which was at once immediate and of 'mass' significance, at once local and international, in its effects. The issue was not so much poverty or hardship experienced directly by writers and intellectuals. Rather it was the radical effect of this 'crisis' in forcing a reconceptualisation of history, society and art as a sudden break with the bourgeois past and the unprecedented simultaneity of changes in 'modern' life, and in every aspect of life. This was the kind of perception that the Depression produced, and which also opened up new ways of perceiving Soviet society as modern—indeed as the future.[31]

Such a political catalyst, then, helped create the sense of internationalism and simultaneous modernity which defines the cultural politics I have described through the little magazines. In one direction this could lead to something very like avant-gardiste manifestations; in another, to extreme forms of proletarian realism that resembled nothing so much as the projects of the avant-garde, and which repeated battles already fought in the Soviet Union, Western Europe and America. Elsewhere perspectives were opened up onto what could be understood as a modernist tradition. Elsewhere again we find the first hints of a popular (nationalist) tradition or an extreme anti-modernist socialist realism. Perhaps this array is just what we should expect as the result of the sudden forcing together of radical aesthetic and revolutionary political categories.

The magazines also saw the first signs of a whole new generation of artists, writers and intellectuals. There was no smooth passage from these marginal sites into the artistic mainstream. On the contrary, there are many lost or delayed or damaged careers to be noted among those involved. Some went on to become respected novelists or painters; others became noted professors or journalists (literary critic and contributing editor for *Time* magazine in the case of Alwyn Lee); many disappeared from sight altogether. But what we see is a clear generational 'break' acting as a spur to the production of art and of new kinds of talk about art. The critique of art tends to come, through these figures, not altogether from outside but from the margins of the established institutions—from 'new' journalism, commercial graphic art, and a 'new' articulate political theory. The magazine form itself is again significant here: it enabled things not only to be said, but also to be presented, in format, graphics and typography, in ways scarcely available in other formats, especially through the juxtaposition of stories, politics and artwork. In addition, the very techniques of these marginal areas were the ones initially mobilised by the radical writers and artists: reportage and the prose sketch rather than the fully-worked short story, the cartoon and the print block rather than the easel painting, the manifesto rather than the formal essay. The literature and the art-work were themselves typically *magazine-like* in structure and address.

It is still necessary to insist in Australia—and no doubt elsewhere—that Australia has a 'modernist history' irreducible to the mere importation of European or American modernism; and also to insist that modernism was not invented out of the void by the last generation laying claim to it. These magazines exist because the issues became important in distinctive ways in Australia at a particular time. It is significant, I think, that although the magazines all disappeared largely without trace, the middle and later 1930s saw a major and again relatively sudden increase in the production of Australian fiction, a body of fiction whose concerns recall those of the earlier magazines and whose modernity is again generated by the crossover of new aesthetic and new political concepts.

THE MYSTERY OF THE
MISSING MIDDLEBROW

My interest in this essay is to drive the historical concept of the 'middlebrow' through Australian literary history from the 1920s, when the concept and the characteristic forms of middlebrow culture emerged in Britain and America, into the present time. Reading the Australian history against those of its more powerful cultural relations I want to locate when, if ever, the institutions characteristic of middlebrow culture and taste came into being in Australia; if not, why not; and if so, whether they took distinctive local forms. Despite substantial work on the historical formation of middlebrow culture in Britain and America no comparable Australian studies have yet been published, although work on patronage and the formation of taste in the art world has gone some of the way.[1] The high modern, the postmodern and the popular have been researched into centre field but not the mundane, respectable middlebrow.

I have been tempted at different times by the two extreme conclusions: to argue on the one hand that Australia has *never* had a middlebrow culture; and on the other that it has never had anything *but* the middlebrow. Both extremes contain a thread of truth but like most things to do with the middlebrow the answer lies somewhere in between.

It is remarkable how much of our professional reading of literary and other cultural forms is still structured through the spectacular opposition between high culture and low or popular or mass culture, even as we empty the oppositions of fixed value or positive essence. The good reason for this is that the institutions of culture and hence cultural value are still pervasively organised through some such hierarchy, although as John Frow, for one, has argued the high-low opposition scarcely captures the contemporary organisation of the cultural field.[2] The not-so-good reason might be that the opposition dramatises our modes of cultural engagement through a form of hyperbole—thus the cultural studies habit of turning popular culture into a kind of vernacular avant-garde in order to mobilise it against the high—or middle—brow.

While the terminology of high and low might still have a point in describing the institutional structuring of culture, its effect in cultural studies has been to produce an excluded middle. To shift the metaphor from hierarchies to spatial organisation, neither literary criticism nor cultural studies have had much to say about that broad domain of culture which is neither auratically high nor assertively low—the vast middle where high culture values are folded into the commodity form of quality entertainment or discerning lifestyle choice. This describes much of television on both commercial and public broadcasting, much of commercial theatre (think of Andrew Lloyd Weber), and much of the literature that goes under the heading of 'good books', the books we find in the 'good book stores'. We should take such familiar terms seriously. If literature is what gets taught, this category of 'good books' mostly won't get taught, either as literature or popular culture, thus it has largely slipped by the attention of literary history.[3]

THE HISTORICAL MIDDLEBROW

The term 'middlebrow' names but does not explain this in-between space. To make it do more we need to turn to its history and in particular the emergence and deployment of the institutions which established, governed and maintained middlebrow forms and tastes. Historians on both sides of the Atlantic have identified the 1920s as the decade in which the middlebrow was named and its characteristic institutions established. Here the concept of overdetermination sounds like a form of understatement: changes in publishing, bookselling, consumption and reading practices, the emergence of new cultural media and new critical institutions, ideological responses to the First World War, urbanisation, professionalisation and shifts in class relations might all be cited in order to explain the emergence of middlebrow culture.

Both American and British historians have identified, first, a rapid expansion of the reading public in the last quarter of the nineteenth century and, second, a reorganisation of the book trade.[4] The latter saw the abandonment of expensive 'triple-deckers' (three-volume novels produced largely for the circulating libraries) followed by the rapid proliferation of cheaper single-volume novels. There was an initial acceleration in production in the late-nineteenth century through to the war and then a second in the 1920s. There were more new books, larger print runs of first editions, and a significant expansion in the circulation of books supported by the growth of the commercial lending libraries. Fiction moved to the centre of the publishing and bookselling industries which were re-organised around the category of the bestseller, exactly the territory of the middlebrow (the cheaper forms of popular genre fiction such as romances or westerns tend to sell serially rather than spectacularly; that is, they depend upon recurrent volume and turnover from 'bestselling authors' rather than the bestselling individual title).[5]

Distinctions between high and low fiction were already well-established before the end of the century, and were manifest in what were virtually two separate publishing industries and markets. However the idea of the middlebrow depended not just upon the existence of a hierarchy of values scaled between high and low, but more specifically upon the contemporaneous emergence of artistic and intellectual modernism, on one side, and the new media and technologies of 'mass commercial culture' on the other. It emerged from the distinctively modern segmentation of cultures which became visible or, better, institutionalised in the first three decades of the twentieth century.

Middlebrow culture was named most insistently in relation to the novel and to changes in the 'fiction industry' institutionalised in the 1920s around the growth of mid-range fiction, the rise of the literary bestseller, and the emergence of a new class of readers comprising an expanded *literary* reading public. These developments produced change across the whole field of cultural production—in authorship, especially in ways being a novelist might be conceived as a profession, a career, even a trade; in the commodity function of the book; and in the distribution of literary value and reading competencies.

These were the new structures that produced the 'literary phrenology' of highbrow, middlebrow and lowbrow, ubiquitous terms from the 1920s to the 1960s.[6] 'Middlebrow', of course, is no more a fixed, objective historical category than its companion terms 'high' and 'low'. Like those terms, it is an artefact of a specific historical period and a product of cultural transformation. 'Highbrow' and 'lowbrow' emerged in the USA in the late-nineteenth century and then a little later, early in the next century, in Britain. While the terms could be used neutrally to describe different tastes or sectors of the cultural market, increasingly they become pejorative (or were asserted positively in defiant opposition to the accusation of being high or low). Out of this charged opposition, the idea of the 'middlebrow' emerges, almost inevitably, in the 1920s. As Stefan Collini has argued, the dynamic of the language of brows 'was driven by the notion of the "highbrow" ... [It] took the arrival of the third term "middlebrow" to transform what had been a rather sporadic and one-sided pattern of name-calling into a fully-developed "battle of the brows".'[7] The terms in opposition emerged to name what was new about divisions in the field of culture in the twenties and to stake out territory in an early form of culture war. They expressed an apprehension not just of divergent tastes but of antagonistic taste cultures, organised hierarchically, and mapping more or less neatly onto social class. All three terms were almost always terms of abuse and (in order to be so) were routinely feminised as the pansy highbrow, the sentimental, domestic middlebrow, and the all-consuming lowbrow in the image of the female consumer.

'Highbrow' named the middlebrow judgement on modernism. Whether it saw cubism, futurism, nihilism, narcissism or intellectualism as the problem, the point was that the middlebrow, in its own estimation, had no 'isms' (it was even nervous about realism if that looked too much like a theory). The 'middlebrow', in turn, named elite culture's apprehension of the new commercial modes of cultural production and dissemination (or at least the apprehensions of its 'modernising fraction'), apprehensions expressed most forcefully in F.R. Leavis's *Mass Civilisation and Minority Culture* and Q.D. Leavis's *Fiction and the Reading Public*.[8] While the mass culture critiques of the Leavises, among others, are well-known, it is sometimes forgotten that their intellectual and professional anxieties were provoked as much by the rise of middlebrow culture as of low-popular forms. Virginia Woolf, famously, saw the highbrow and the lowbrow as natural allies against the middlebrow, with its version of 'what they have the impudence to call real humanity—this mixture of geniality and sentiment stuck together with a sticky slime of calf's-foot jelly'.[9] The contemporary force of such arguments has been over-ridden by subsequent debates conducted only in terms of the high culture/mass culture stand-off. The point, of course, is not to redeem the Leavis position but to restore the distinctive presence of the middlebrow to cultural history. It represented a division—or rather multiplication—at the *quality* end of the market, a horizontal proliferation of literary value rather than its vertical restriction. The problem, in other words, was not just the expansion of popular culture but the spread of bestsellerdom upwards and the increasingly mass consumption of what at least looked like high culture, the *faux bon*.[10]

Middlebrow culture can be identified with a distinctive range of institutions which emerged in the 1920s and 1930s and disappeared or declined in significance around the 1960s: subscriber Book Clubs (most famously the Book-of-the-Month Club in the USA), book societies, bestseller lists, commercial book magazines for a broad public, radio book programs, books on how to read books, and World's Classics, Greatest Books or Outline series. These institutions were committed to expanding the circulation of culture and 'education' through culture, but also, indeed as a corollary, to certifying standards via panels of experts, lists of greatest books, book-of-the-month selections, and how-to-read manuals. While middlebrow culture was characteristically generous in its understanding of good books, it carefully policed the boundaries of taste and worthiness, against the vulgar at one end and modernist abstraction or pessimism at the other.

The middlebrow in every respect was a product of modernity. Middlebrow institutions typically reproduced high culture values and forms—such as good writing, good music or serious talk—but reconfigured them through new media and new forms of consumption, broadening their markets and multiplying their utility. Significantly, the first recorded use of the term 'middlebrow', from *Punch* in 1925, refers not to literature but to radio, to the BBC's 'claim to have discovered a new type, the middlebrow ... people who are hoping that some day they will get used to the stuff they ought to like'.[11] This ironic definition captures both the disciplinary and aspirational dimensions of middlebrow taste as well as its distinctive modernity.

The First World War plays a central role in the British story, largely absent from the American case. Rosa Maria Bracco sees middlebrow culture as managing, through containment, the threats of urban modernity— massification and atomised subjectivity, the rupture of tradition and authority, the expansion of commercialisation itself. Thus, she argues, the theme of individualism dominates the English middlebrow novel of the twenties, while tradition and 'English character' dominate the novels of the thirties. She emphasises the fiction's middle-class conservatism and thus its residual nature.[12] More recent work has, by contrast, examined middlebrow fiction's more positive engagement with modernism, indeed its own modernity.[13]

American accounts have focused less on texts and more on the complex institutional history of middlebrow culture, ranged across publishing, marketing, journalism, and academia. In this history, the middlebrow is revealed as emergent rather than residual. Janice Radway thus describes the Book-of-the-Month Club as a 'characteristically *modern* cultural institution'.[14] Middlebrow culture, she argues, provided new forms of cultural capital for an emerging professional-managerial class. For this aspiring class, set apart from labour by their educational or professional success, middlebrow culture repeated the lesson that culture was linked to social and personal distinction and that this could be acquired not just through inherited cultural capital but through discerning consumption of more or less interchangeable commodities (a book a month). It assured readers that commerce and culture were not intrinsically opposed, that expert or specialist opinion could be turned to the interests of general culture, and that modernity and individuality progressed along the same trajectory. The Book-of-the-Month Club, Radway suggests, did not just commodify individual books, it commodified and offered for consumption 'culture' itself. What it valued in and transmitted through the experience of good books or good reading were affective qualities of empathy and identification in a manner Radway labels 'personalism'.[15]

The dense institutional history of the American universities was also critical in the formation of American middlebrow culture and marks one of the clearest differences for the Australian case. On the one hand, the universities produced the authoritative figures of middlebrow culture. Joan Shelley Rubin traces a line of continuity extending from the 'genteel tradition' to the early-twentieth century cultural generalists—those in the universities opposed to the increase of academic specialisation—and then to the leading middlebrow spokespersons who were university literature professors, like Henry Seidel Canby from Yale, as often as they were journalists or entrepreneurs.[16] On the other hand, the university produced the fiercest critics of the middlebrow for its commercialisation and standardisation of culture. The complexity of this history can be indicated by the story of the Great Books curriculum, introduced at Columbia University in 1920. If those promoting the program were committed to the eternal values of the 'best that has been thought and said' the course also suggested that these values could be acquired by the general reader and that there was utility in so doing. The famous Harvard Classics collection of handsomely-bound but affordable classics, the 'Five-Foot Shelf of Books', had similar objectives. The collection was 'guaranteed' by the Harvard name (and selected by its President, Charles W. Eliot) but also sold with the famous guarantee that they could be consumed, and hence culture acquired, by a program of fifteen minutes reading per day.[17]

Perhaps the key point is that in all its literary functions middlebrow culture was *reader*-oriented. It shifted the point of culture from the intrinsic values of the text to the pleasures and utility of reading. Thus, while it drew on the aura of literary authority offered by the academy, it explicitly defined itself against academic specialisation. The ideal middlebrow subject was the 'serious general reader': that is, not the idle or undiscriminating consumer and not the professional critic or specialist. The category of literature was still privileged but rather than a single, restricted scale of values the world of good books was understood as broad and diverse. Middlebrow culture thus multiplied the field of worthwhile literature, but it managed this potentially unmanageable proliferation by its own proliferation of guides to reading, lists of the ten best, expert selections and so on. Ironically, a whole array of new critical and certifying practices were instituted to assure readers that the newly-formatted classics or the new good books could speak directly to them without any (specialist) mediation.

AN AUSTRALIAN MIDDLEBROW

My own interest in the middlebrow was first prompted by the study of a wide range of Australian magazines from the 1920s. What I encountered there was a sense of the literary that would not resolve itself neatly into the framework of 'high' and 'low'. Perhaps, then, 'middlebrow' was the term I needed to describe the mixing of literary levels and modes of evaluation the magazines embodied. Ultimately I decided it was not appropriate, at least not for the early twenties, for although the hierarchy of literary evaluation was already routine, as in A.G. Stephens's frequent distinctions between 'craft' and 'Art', the term was anachronistic because the dichotomy between high modernism and modern mass cultures was as yet hardly present in Australia. Instead what I was encountering were the residues of an earlier form of literary journalism, the 'new journalism' of the 1880s and 1890s. What can be observed over the course of the decade, however, is a re-organisation of the print economy such that by the 1930s classifying culture by the level of its brow often seemed to make best sense of emerging divisions across the field; or, equally significant, it was something one had urgently to resist or confront.

The twenties saw the progressive disappearance of key magazines characteristic of late-nineteenth century print culture: general commercial magazines, produced by independent journalist-editors, such as the *Bookfellow* (1899–1925), the *Triad* (1915–27) and the *Lone Hand* (1907–21). Here a broad commitment to culture was embedded in practical familiarity with the business of writing and publishing and hence with the heterogeneity of print culture, when print had the field pretty much to itself. Rather than highbrow or lowbrow, their readership was conceived as a *public*, a notion as inclusive as the market itself, and 'public affairs' meant literature and theatre as well as business or politics. These magazines shared with the commercial theatre—which they reviewed relentlessly—its sense of a heterogeneous audience, its orientation to urban markets, and its expectation that culture and entertainment could be found together on the same stage or page.

To trace changes over the decade, let me take the *Triad* as my first example, for it pitched itself 'higher' than its contemporaries. It had, in its own words, a 'modest belief' that its readers were 'a little above the average' (May 1922). Its moving spirit, journalist Frank Morton, gave Arnoldian culture a vitalist twist.[18] The magazine could use 'profoundly intellectual' as a term of praise (August 1922) and it welcomed the new American realism and *vers libre*. At the same time it happily reviewed books on golf and cowboy romances, and, in a somewhat ironic spirit, published a special Mary Pickford number. Pickford claimed to be an avid reader of the magazine (April 1922).

My interest is in what happens in the mid-twenties, after Morton's death, as the magazine tries with increasing desperation to reinvent itself in relation to what were changed cultural circumstances—as it tries to reinvent itself as more Australian, more jazz age, more popular, more modern. In the process, the language of brows became unavoidable. In May 1925 the new editor, L.L. Woolacott, explained changes in the magazine: 'The Old *Triad*, rightly or wrongly, was dubbed High-brow. The New *Triad* is neither High-brow nor Low-brow. It is Broad-brow.' The public did not want endless tripe, as the 'experts' kept saying, but 'neither do they care for caviar, except in very small portions. The *Triad* menu henceforth is neither tripe nor caviar, but a properly balanced diet, from soup to sweets.'

But the Broad-brow was a trick the magazine rarely pulled off. It was as if, quite suddenly, the relationship between being popular and being modern, between being cultured and being commercial—or, slightly differently, between literature and journalism—had become problematic (and the problems would prove fatal as the magazine ceased in 1927). The segmentation of cultures had, by this time, become actually-structuring for both producers and consumers, as the visibility of modernism's break with the nineteenth century, its division of culture, became unavoidable. The *public* which the earlier magazines had addressed was also in the process of being segmented and 'massified' simultaneously—segmented as journalism became more specialised and professionalised (literary and art criticism would later follow); and 'massified' through the new forms of urban entertainment. Above all, the spectacular rise of the cinema worked to transform that earlier sense of a knowable public into the apprehension of an unknowable 'mass'. In the process, culture, entertainment and public-ness were disarticulated. The *Triad*, interestingly, began reviewing films alongside theatre as if they were much the same thing, but by the mid-twenties they had been apportioned to different realms.

A similar process can be observed in the declining fortunes of the *Lone Hand*. Initially a quality general commercial magazine, in the early twenties it sought to reinvent itself as popular and national through strident 'Australianism' (its term). As H.M. Green wrote, 'there were obvious efforts to brighten and popularise [the *Lone Hand*] by the introduction of new and striking features ... [It] assumed the characteristics of light, cheap journalism, which did not however prevent it from becoming dull'.[19] Perhaps editor Walter Jago half-understood his dilemma when he announced in February 1921, in his final editorial, that the *Lone Hand* 'dies ... slaughtered on the altar of Charlie Chaplinism'.

By way of contrast, middlebrow culture was first given substantial form locally in the art world, specifically in Sydney Ure Smith's magazines *Art in Australia* (1916–42) and the *Home* (1920–42). Both were new *kinds* of magazine, the former focused on contemporary painting, etching, sculpture and other artistic forms, the latter on modern design, fashion and society news. *Art in Australia* has too readily been dismissed as conservative; the *Home* too readily celebrated as modernist. While the former advanced local pastoral impressionism in painting, it understood this style in the context of contemporary art movements (especially from Britain);[20] and while the latter was about the only journal at the time receptive to modernist art and design, its embracing discourse was good taste. Both magazines addressed an audience possessed of good taste and the means to purchase it; both aimed to increase the *circulation* of good taste. *Art in Australia* was established expressly to broaden the 'picture-buying public', while the *Home* was an up-market consumer lifestyle magazine. Both were contemporary in focus but drew the line at the '*ultra*-modern'.[21] It makes historical sense that the middlebrow should emerge in this milieu, first because the art commodity was more clearly linked to social status than was literature, second because modernism was literally more visible in art movements than in literature, especially via cubism and futurism. The commercial challenge to high art values was not popular illustration per se but mass *advertising*. It is no accident that Ure Smith ran Sydney's artiest advertising agency.[22] These were upmarket magazines however, appealing to both old money and, as Radway suggests for the United States, to an emerging professional managerial class. Studies of the British middlebrow have emphasised, rather, the lower-middle class—the emerging 'clerks'—as the crucial aspirational audience for middlebrow culture, and this seems closer to the Australian situation.[23]

More generally, while the middlebrow beckoned, it had not yet found local institutional form. The emerging segmentation of values and markets can certainly be observed, as indicated, but while the new magazines of the late twenties *were* more specialised or more frankly consumerist, most periodicals were still characterised by the promiscuity of their literary values—as writers of all levels appeared together—rather than by their stricter organisation of taste. Often this was their only virtue.

Even with a busy print culture, then, Australia in the twenties lacked the density of institutions, particularly the institutions of high culture, through which and against which the middlebrow formed in America and Britain. There was no equivalent to the depth or modernity of the American universities which could generate both middlebrow culture and its enemies (the Australian universities were just establishing their first Chairs of English literature). Although the 1920s saw rapid urbanisation and a shift in the balance of power from pastoralism to manufacturing, the professionalisation of the new middle class was less advanced. There were few institutions of high literary culture—no literary quarterlies, no local avant-garde, no independent intelligentsia. There was little 'higher journalism', and only a small, dispersed book publishing industry. The largest publisher, Angus & Robertson, depended for its survival upon reprints of popular (middlebrow) bestsellers from overseas. Middlebrow publications from Britain and America such as *John O'London's* or the American *Vanity Fair* were available in Australia, but this in itself could inhibit the development of Australian equivalents.

Indeed middlebrow culture was largely an imported phenomenon, a crucial fact in its different dynamics in Australia. Reading the Australian magazines reveals a book culture—say in the pages of the *Bulletin*—made up very largely of the products of mainstream contemporary English (and American) publishing. Although this is unsurprising—these were obviously the books going to land on editorial desks—Australian criticism has not much considered the point except negatively. The issue is not simply cultural imperialism or the cultural cringe, for the local book culture so takes for granted its contemporaneity with London publishing that the notion of 'imperial domination' seems to miss the point. Editors and reviewers certainly encouraged Australian books wherever they could, but there is little sense of opposition between English and Australian, or that the English middlebrow wasn't the appropriate range for local readers.

The distinctive forms of mid-century middlebrow culture in Australia begin to emerge more clearly in the 1930s. What we observe, and this is the key point I think for defining the nature of the Australian middlebrow, is a process that might be characterised as the middlebrow absorbing the national—or the national absorbing the middlebrow. Rather than *radical* nationalism, or anti-radical nationalism for that matter, I would now want to argue for an Australian cultural history written around middlebrow nationalism. And middlebrow rather than merely popular, for the term captures something that 'popular' misses about the cultural aspirations, for example, of those writers and readers who created the local bestsellers of the 1930s and 1940s, from Frank Clune to Ernestine Hill—the kinds of virtuous citizenship and 'nationed' modernity these books offered.

MIDDLEBROW MODERNITY

In the first half of the twenties, then, we see the residues of an earlier form of literary journalism rather than modern forms of mass or middlebrow culture. By the end of the decade and into the thirties the space of the middlebrow was emerging, not just in relation to high culture, but also in relation to the idea of national culture. Magazines of book news and reviews such as *All About Books* (1928–38) and *Desiderata* (1929–39) mediated between market and cultural imperatives, between modernist and popular reading, and between national and imported 'books of the month'.[24] The national middlebrow reaches its peak in the late 1940s with a significant thickening in the institutional context, both in the professional-commercial and the high aesthetic corners of the cultural field: booksellers' and publishers' associations had formed; radio had become a major cultural medium, not least for books and drama; the circulating library network was booming; avant-garde or radical 'little magazines' had appeared; and with the Jindyworobaks, the first modern-ish literary movement in Australia had been established.

The crisis of war produced a range of manifesto-driven magazines such as *Angry Penguins* (1940–46), *A Comment* (1940–47), *Design* (1940), *Meanjin* (1940–), and *Venture* (second series, 1939–40). All were launched in 1939–40; all were expressly distanced from the market and mere entertainment; all privileged *poetry* rather than fiction as a sign of their seriousness; all were, in a word, highbrow. At stake for each magazine was not mere 'cultivation' but the intellectual and psychic well-being of individual, nation and civilisation, in a distinctly modern equation. For Max Harris, founding editor of *Angry Penguins*, 'Poetry … must be in large measure intellectual'. Announcing his magazine's critical distance from the middlebrow he proclaimed: 'this is not an easy book. It is not intended to be entertaining' (2, 1941). In best modernist style, *Angry Penguins* published three poems called 'Poem' in its first number. *A Comment*, in its opening number, announced proudly: 'Our public is practically nonexistent' (1, 1940). *Meanjin's* first two issues were 'Traditionalist' and 'Criticism' numbers, again in a distinctly post-Eliot equation. James Picot wrote that the Australian poet 'live(s) in the world of Lenin and Hitler and Einstein and Freud and Whitehead ... International affairs, propaganda, emigration, psychology, the challenge of Freud to the individual and of New Economics to the society—these cannot be kept out of Poetry' (February 1941). Even the conservative Catholic *Design* understood itself to be 'among those magazines of which Mr T.S. Eliot spoke when he referred to little publications keeping alive some flame of right thought and sense, of culture at a time of the breaking of nations' (April 1940). In *Venture*, the Jindyworobaks claimed to 'stand for a *precise* cultural movement' (April 1939); the adjective is utterly modern.

In short, the figure of the intellectual and the serious writer was dramatically divorced from that of the literary journalist, popular novelist or commercial writer. The modern was divorced from the merely contemporary. Typically the new little magazines launched themselves as if into a cultural void, as if no other magazines existed, despite the busy print culture that surrounded them. That was precisely the point: to claim the modern, the serious and the permanent over and against the bright, noisy ephemera of book talk and mass entertainment in the newspapers and commercial magazines.

I have not included *Southerly* in my list of new little magazines, despite its 1939 launch. What is surprising about the early *Southerly*, at least from this point in time, is its proximity still to the journalistic and commercial magazine world around it; perhaps, too, that its supporting body, the English Association, might be described as typically middlebrow. *Southerly* was not yet primarily a journal of academic criticism. Its editor, R.G. Howarth, explained that the journal would not be 'merely popular' and that it could be cautiously modern (September 1939). In response to a demand that it should open its pages to 'experimentalists, "futurists" and the like', Howarth replied that *Southerly* was indeed open to 'modern experiment'—provided it stayed within the bounds of 'ordinary decency' (July 1940). One cannot imagine Harris or C.B. Christesen, editor of *Meanjin*, offering their readers anything so middlebrow as 'pleasure and mental profit' as Howarth did (1, 1946). The academy, in short, was in this period often more comfortably middlebrow than the literary intelligentsia on its fringes. At the same time,

Southerly was perhaps the first magazine in Australia to promote literary scholarship and to use the term 'criticism' in the full modern sense, to distinguish its practices from the middlebrow book talk happening in its commercial contemporaries (and indeed at times still in its own pages).

The important point for my purposes and the dimension that has been left out of Australian literary history is that alongside an emerging modernist high culture we also find a thickening of the middlebrow in a range of new commercial magazines with a serious interest in books, culture, taste, and entertainment—and in boosting their Australian production and consumption. *Pertinent* (1940–47), for example, was a commercial literary magazine launched with the highest of aims, the general diffusion of culture to save 'universal mankind' from self-destruction. But editor Leon Batt assured readers that '*Pertinent* won't be highbrow … it is to be the voice of, and for, the common man and woman' (July 1940), by which he meant the middle class consumer not the proletariat. The first issue ranged from elite to popular, across Norman Lindsay, Vance Palmer, Lennie Lower and F.J. Thwaites. By December 1946, under a new editor, the boundaries around the middlebrow were even sharper: 'Art and writing of the surrealist type, arty crafty, pedantic or introspective, will not be welcome … nor will the pornographic or the cheap and tawdry'. Sydney Ure Smith's new monthly, *Australia: National Journal* (1939–47), was a middle-range version of the *Home*, focused as much on entertainment as taste. Its values can be suggested by quoting a book review from its August 1946 number in which the reviewer 'longs for the day when an Australian author will write a novel about Sydney or Melbourne which is as neat and sophisticated as a recent novel about Montreal … a city of strong charm, inhabited by civilised and cultured people'. For its own sophisticated, cultured readers each issue carried social and cultural 'Roundabouts' from Sydney, London, Melbourne and Brisbane alongside literary stories (by Ruth Park, D'Arcy Niland, Beatrice Grimshaw, Eleanor Dark, Marjorie Barnard or Myra Morris), elegant 'light' essays and modern verse, art reproductions, and double-page photo-features on new Hollywood films which were also presented as charming and sophisticated.

Although the institutional structures were still piecemeal compared to the rich American context, their range and diversity needs to be taken seriously. Representing quality radio, for example, the *ABC Weekly* (1939–

59) was both program guide and cultural review. It carried short stories by 'serious' and popular Australian authors plus regular departments on World Affairs (Rupert Lockwood), Australiana (Frank Clune), Film (John Hinde), Drama (Leslie Rees), Women (Ernestine Hill) and Books (Florence James and Vance Palmer). Again the list of names extends across the middle range from popular to high. Perhaps because of a sensitivity to the charge that 'culture on the wireless' was too highbrow, too middlebrow or too lowbrow (all three accusations were made) the magazine closely followed contemporary outbreaks of the highbrow-lowbrow debate which occurred regularly in the thirties and forties. Although newsier and more celebrity-focused, the commercial radio magazine, the *Listener-In* (1925–55), also carried a weekly books feature, by a Miss J.G. Swain, presenter of a weekly radio program called *Living Authors*. A Book of the Week selection usually appeared on the Women's Page. Again, book talk in such places was intensely reader-oriented and feminised; and it was managed through the trope of direct communication with 'living authors' (even those long dead).[25]

It is not surprising, then, that the new women's paper, the *Australian Women's Weekly* (1933–), soon to become the country's largest circulation magazine, also featured reader-oriented chat about good books, good reading and the highbrow-lowbrow debate. A worried stenographer wrote to the *Weekly* with perfect middlebrow pitch: 'I like biographies, best-sellers, history and travel books and most of the classics, but the girls I have come in contact with cannot be bothered with any of these, and, if they read at all, just read light fiction' (20 July 1940). As Patrick Buckridge has argued, in the *Women's Weekly* 'Good books and good reading [were] defined mainly by negation ...: they are what "light fiction" is not ... Good books could also be defined ... as the books that should be owned and kept in the home'.[26] Like its American sisters, the *Women's Weekly* carried advice on books as interior decoration.

Across the gender divide, *Man: The Australian Magazine for Men* (1936–74) defined itself in the 1930s and 1940s as 'both highbrow and lowbrow'.[27] It was proud of its 'quality' both in appearance and contents and of its commitment to Australian writers. It combined popular fiction, risqué cartoons, 'art' photography and 'expert' articles for the general reader. Contributors included anthropologist A.P. Elkin, educator and critic George Mackaness, and novelists Ernestine Hill and Vance Palmer.

Ion Idriess edited an 'Australasiana' department. *Man* claimed not only to entertain, but also to address 'the reader who likes to read serious ideas and reflect upon them' (December 1946). Its implied audience was modern, urban, sophisticated and national. In Richard White's curious but intriguing phrase, this was 'the nationalism of P.R. Stephensen and the middlebrow which asserted that Australian enterprise could produce a magazine as glossy and with as many cartoons as magazines overseas'; *Man* 'wanted a new, unselfconscious national literature that could, like any other commodity, be "as good as" the English or American equivalent'.[28]

Without pushing the point too far, I also find it interesting to think of the popular geographical magazine *Walkabout* (1934–74) alongside *Man* within the category of the middlebrow. It shares a similar life span and in many ways was addressed to the same readership as *Man*, if not quite to their same capacities. It addressed a general audience and most articles were written by freelance generalists rather than scientific experts: Henrietta Drake-Brockman, Ernestine Hill again, R.H. Croll, Tarlton Rayment, J.K. Ewers and Mary Durack. Here, I think, nationalism did provide a kind of upward mobility through culture, although the culture the magazine offered was based on picturesque natural science, pioneering history and stories of contemporary industrial development rather than literature or interior decoration. The writing nevertheless carried the traces of the literary essay. By combining popular writing and picturesque photography with specialist articles and ethnographic illustrations, all in an attractive large format, *Walkabout* upgraded 'Australiana' into a serious but still entertaining business, bringing the vast continent and its unique natural and human history—this was how the magazine presented its interests—into the possession of its mainly urban readers.

The second half of the 1940s, the moment of post-war reconstruction, represents a high point for the national middlebrow. The period is marked by the local appearance of typical middlebrow institutions—book societies, book-of-the-month selections, radio book shows, commercial book reviews, and so forth. This was also a period when the magazines were full of talk about the need for a quality national theatre which would include drama, ballet, opera and orchestral music, an idea symptomatic of the merging of national and middlebrow and of the final disappearance of that busy early-twenties world of literary journalism and commercial theatre. Australian book culture was also more woman-centred than before or since—perhaps until the very recent past—while the weakness of the universities meant a prominent role for schoolmasters like A.A. Phillips and the lesser-known J.O. Anchen, Senior Inspector of Schools in Victoria and author of *The Australian Novel*. In fine middlebrow fashion, Anchen's critical survey supplied readers with a list of '50 first-class books' plus a recommended top ten which mixed highbrow and popular, Christina Stead and Arthur Upfield, without anxiety.[29]

One way of understanding post-war reconstruction is as an imperative towards the widest-possible diffusion of culture in general and *national* culture in particular. Government was to be re-purposed to intervene in civil society; culture meant both social improvement and democratic community. Class mobility could be understood in these civic-cultural terms rather than more starkly in terms of income or job status. Culture, democracy and nation came together to express an aspiration which was future-oriented, even when it invoked pioneering traditions. Whatever its language, and it could be liberal-conservative or socialist, the scope of this aspiration was likely in practice to be middlebrow.

The new post-war institutions included an Australian Book Society, formed in 1946 as a 'rallying place for all book lovers who wish to see Australian writing of all kinds ... given its full place and prominence as our OWN expression of literature'.[30] Its executive featured well-known academics, serious novelists, and enthusiastic book lovers including Mary Gilmore, J.V. Duhig, Walter Murdoch, George Mackaness and Marjorie Barnard. The Society launched the journal *Australian Books* (1946–48), a magazine of book news rather than literary criticism. Each issue published a monthly Australian book selection (with Barnard a prominent judge). A more professional but otherwise very similar magazine from the same year was the monthly *Australasian Book News and Library Journal* (1946–48); it, too, featured an Australian book of the month.

Also in 1946, the ABC launched a seriously middlebrow monthly entitled *Talk* (1946–47): like its model, the BBC's *Listener*, its aim was 'to continue the technique which radio at its best should employ, of presenting really worthwhile material in an attractive, popular and easily-assimilated form'.[31] *Talk* consisted largely of the texts of ABC radio talks delivered by prominent authors, scientists, journalists, historians and so forth, drawing on their field of expertise but addressing a general, educated audience. Here we start to see the cross-over between university specialists and generalist media characteristic of the US middlebrow. Professor of Botany at Sydney University Eric Ashby, for example, argued the case for a distinctively Australian and suspiciously middlebrow version of the highbrow:

> The lowbrow in Australia already gets a pretty fair deal; and quite rightly, for he is the backbone of the country ... But the highbrow, who is the nerves of the country, does not get such a fair deal ... Of course, there are highbrows and highbrows. I do not mean the pansy sort who have none of the Australian vigour ... and who live in a cloud of European ideas ... I mean men who put into words, music and colour our way of life.[32]

In the mid-late forties we can point to a relatively dense middlebrow culture in the mainstream magazines: in the *Australian Women's Weekly*, *Australia: National Journal*, *Pertinent*, the *Bulletin*, *Australia's Progress* (1945–46), *Australian Books*, the *Australian Book News*, *Talk*, and *View* (later *Focus*, 1946–48), among others. Symptomatic of the new segmentation between modernist and middlebrow cultures however, what might have looked like real success for Australian book culture, looked to Harris like the worst kind of cultural debasement. Modern art had been reduced by these magazines to the merely fashionable and journalistic; they were 'a nasty endemic rash on the body aesthetic'. In *Australia: National Journal*, 'literary standards ... became reoriented to fit the cultural demands of the modern urban community'; *View* was 'intellectually mendicant, aiming to offend none and please all'; the left-wing *Progress* was the worst of all, 'the most dismaying product of this cultural popularising ... By necessity and the nature of the medium, the literature as literature will be reactionary and debased.'[33] Harris, by contrast, thought black American jazz the most authentic modern art form.

If black American jazz was an unusual taste in mid-century Australia, the local presence of contemporary American literary culture was surprisingly pervasive. In 1940, Angus & Robertson reprinted Mortimer Adler's middlebrow classic, *How to Read a Book*, with a foreword by Walter Murdoch—Australia's equivalent perhaps to Henry Seidel Canby, who left Yale for literary journalism and the Book-of-the-Month Club.

Murdoch remained a professor but most of his writing life was passed in the newspapers and magazines, turning scholarship into intelligent, charming book chat. Richard Wright's *Native Son*, a controversial Book-of-the-Month Club selection in the USA, was also reprinted by Angus & Robertson in the same year. American professors featured regularly in the pages of the *ABC Weekly*, while the Harvard Classics set was available from local agents after the war. In April 1946, Mr E. Ogilvy-Brown of Elwood, 'special representative of the Harvard Classics in Victoria', placed an advertisement in *View*, the Melbourne 'journal of opinion'. It was headed 'An Appeal to Intellectuals', and asked readers: 'Do you desire to increase your intellectual stature? Would you take pleasure in doubling or trebling your earning capacity?' Recommending Charles Eliot's program of fifteen minutes reading per day, the advertisement adds, 'No intelligent person can do this, with devotion, for 365 days and fail to be transformed'.

Henry Seidel Canby himself toured Australia in 1945 at the invitation of the University of Melbourne. He lectured around the country and addressed the Australian Book Society at a literary luncheon in Sydney. In the following year, Melbourne University Press published a short book based on his talks, *A New Land Speaking: An Essay on the Importance of a National Literature*. Canby's message, though, was less nationalist than middlebrow: 'What every writer needs most of all in such new nations as Australia is a public eager to read and able to write intelligently. For its instruction, the best books should flow in from everywhere. As a slogan, "buy Australian books" is of little use to the native writer, until his public has listened to the sounder appeal of "buy books."'[34]

Another candidate for the title of Australian Canby is George Mackaness, Vice-President, with Murdoch, of the Australian Book Society. Writing in *Australian Books* in 1946, Mackaness defined literature as first and foremost a matter of 'public interest, public opinion and public education'.[35] Literature depended upon the support of the writer, the publisher and the reader, but *not* the critic, who was 'but an excrescence, almost a parasite upon the body literary'. Nonetheless, Mackaness felt the lack of a 'real critical journal'. There were newspaper book pages and 'half a dozen small cultural magazines', but it was precisely the authoritative middlebrow that was lacking. Mackaness's models were predominantly American: 'we need an authoritative monthly journal, a *Fortnightly*, a *Munsey*, an *Atlantic*, a *Harpers*, to which we could look for guidance in our reading'. This is a fascinating moment in the history of the Australian middlebrow, suggesting a modern, urban, middle-class and modestly cosmopolitan nationalism rather than nostalgia for bushy blokes.

In this large middle ground of Australian literary culture, the national comes to perform precisely the same role as the middlebrow in drawing boundaries before mass-commercial culture on one side and modernist culture on the other. Like the middlebrow, a *modern* national culture offered to reunite individuality, class aspiration and democratic community, and to mediate between modernity, populism and tradition. Nor was this just a matter for amateur 'book lovers'. Most of Australia's serious writers (their term), especially those in the middlebrow's own field of the novel, were located institutionally right on the cusp of high and middle. By necessity, given the relative thinness of high cultural institutions, the careers of writers such as Palmer and Barnard were mostly lived in the range of the middlebrow. But this was also a necessity turned into a virtue. Hence their deeply ambiguous sense of the reading public, of modernism, of writing as craft or profession, and of themselves as literary intellectuals.

Even as they distinguished themselves from the writers of commercial bestsellers, these mid-century writers shared middlebrow culture's commitment to realist form and intimate communication between writer and reader (something, to their anguish, that popular commercial writers seemed to manage much more successfully). They shared the middlebrow's fear of the mass and hence its emphasis on discriminating quality and taste; and despite their commitment to a serious and modern Australian culture, they shared its unease about modernism, abstraction and elitism. Despite their commitment to serious intellectual engagement, they shared the middlebrow suspicion of highbrow attitudes and specialisation. They were committed to disseminating culture to the general reader, although the class nature of this reader was mostly blurred through being conceived in national terms.

The habitus of these mid-century writers can be suggested through the notion of 'craft'. This was an important category for earlier literary journalists such as Stephens; but in its modern, heightened sense it could distinguish the serious writer or artist from the mere entertainer, the professional from the mere amateur. As such the notion of craft became a key term in mid-century modernism, indicating that distinguishing concern of the serious modern for *form* as well as for story or sentiment. It connects writers such as Eleanor Dark, Barnard and Palmer to the modernist artists and designers of the thirties and forties (also a woman-centred modernity).[36] At the same time, the idea of craft could be used to draw the line at 'ultra'-modernism, so often seen as the dislocation of form or more simply its sheer absence. Significantly 'craft' was a term that criticism, later, would have little use for. A.A. Phillips, in certain ways an exemplary middlebrow critic, was perhaps the last to give it a central place in his critical vocabulary in the late forties-early fifties and he did so consciously against the academics.

MIDDLEBROW AND HIGH POP

The mid to late 1940s was the last period before the professionalisation of Australian criticism, a process I now see as having killed off the mid-range middlebrow magazines, none of which survived into the 1950s. It is more than accidental, too, that the decline of the national middlebrow coincides with the rise of Robert Menzies's rather different dream of urban modernity. Class mobility was reconfigured away from cultural aspiration towards household consumption. Middlebrow culture was disarticulated from the national, while modernism was tucked away as an academic tradition. Australian literary history was recast in the image of Patrick White, the least middlebrow of writers. Most of the book clubs and circulating libraries disappeared, so too the vein of mid-list Australian bestsellers. And then, of course, there was television.

The general reader, if never entirely absent, was an increasingly abstract notion in the presence of literature. Just when an independent, modern intelligentsia had announced its split from mere literary journalism, the expansion of the academy split the field again. *Meanjin* went academic; Max Harris went into bookselling and journalism. By the 1960s, the typical cultural magazine was the serious, more or less specialised, critical quarterly.

To conclude, however, it is not the decline of the middlebrow I want to emphasise but its contemporary resurgence. If the *term* has faded (or if it did fade, only to make a comeback in recent years) this is not because the middlebrow function disappeared. On the contrary, contemporary book culture is characterised by its ever-wider dispersal through the diffusion of modernist forms into 'high pop' and the reconfiguring of cultural consumption into mainstream markets.[37] Hence the collapsing utility of the distinctions the term helped articulate.

There were a number of remarkable developments in Australian book culture in the 1990s. First, the regularity of local bestsellers among *literary* novelists—Peter Carey, Tim Winton, Murray Bail, Helen Garner and David Malouf; second, their international success; and, third, the unprecedented popularity of new literary genres, especially books of essays, memoirs and cross-over forms shuttling between essay, memoir and fiction, through writers such as Robert Dessaix, Drusilla Modjeska and Inga Clendinnen. The essay has a prominence it has not had since Murdoch's reign between the wars. There is now an annual *Best Australian Essays* and a *Quarterly Essay* series. Publishers are searching high and low for the next bestseller in the newly-defined 'creative non-fiction' market. These developments are supported by a mature publishing industry, integrated more than ever before into international markets. Finally, there has been a boom in the new institutions of book culture—in literary festivals and prizes, even literary breakfasts; in author celebrity; in reading groups, today's version, perhaps, of the book clubs; in literary bestseller lists, ubiquitous in the quality newspapers and now with internet ordering links (a middlebrow entrepreneur's dream); and in the proliferation of 'good book stores' in the inner city and professional suburbs, stores that offer contemporary Australian and international literary fiction, alongside boutique histories and biographies, lifestyle, travel and gourmet titles, good music (jazz, classics and world, but not pop), and good coffee.[38]

Modjeska and Dessaix were particularly significant in altering the nature of Australian book culture. What they and their publishers managed was to make intensely aesthetic, self-reflexive, morally-serious books into desirable commodities. In the process, both authors acquired a heightened public presence as *writers*, in the fullest sense of the term. As Peter Craven, our Murdoch or Canby for today, said of Dessaix: he has 'proved himself to be someone whose signature mattered more than the thing they signed'.[39] Modjeska's *The Orchard* sparked off a series of new books with art-house design, books pitched at serious readers who were, at the same time, life-style consumers (with the emphasis both on *life* and *style*).

This is an international trend, and Australian books now gain part of their meaning by the ease with which they enter this cosmopolitan marketplace (or at least look as if they do). To quote from a review by Andrew Reimer of Nick Jose's *The Red Thread*, an Australian novel about China published in San Francisco: 'Everything—the *trompe-l'oeil* dust jacket, the typeface, the artwork and the quality of the paper—contributes to a sense of restrained sensuousness, luxury tempered by elegance and good taste.'[40] Reimer's high cultural sense of good taste meshes seamlessly with the new consumer culture of good books. A similar taste for serious literary fiction and boutique history marks the reading groups which have grown extraordinarily over the last ten years or so across Australia (as they have elsewhere in the English-speaking world). Reading groups favour quality bestsellers, whether Carey or Malouf, or 'good books' such as *Eucalyptus*, *The Reader*, *Memoirs of a Geisha* or *The Map that Changed the World*. No less remarkable has been the success of ABC Radio's *Australia Talks Books*, a radio talk-back book club with an estimated 50,000 listeners across the country, and the 'One Book, One Brisbane' scheme which imagines the whole of Brisbane city as one great reading group, all reading, say, *The True Story of the Kelly Gang* simultaneously—'getting our whole city alive with reading a good book,' as the Lord Mayor said. Or the lifestyle book magazine *Good Reading: The Magazine for Book Lovers*, launched in 2001. On sale in book stores and newsagents, this looks like a lifestyle magazine—like *Better Homes and Gardens* or *Gourmet Living*—which is just what it is. It features celebrity readers, reviews of literary fiction and genre fiction, articles on cooking, gardening and art, author interviews, book news, and a monthly feature reporting on a reading group from somewhere around Australia. The *Australian Author* described *Good Reading* as 'targeted at the mid-range rather than the literary market' and 'sure to be a hit with members of the hundreds of book clubs that are such a unique feature of the Australian book scene.'[41] In thorough middlebrow style, the magazine's title embraces both the popular notion of a 'good read' and the more demanding notion that reading is good for you.

As this magazine suggests, while the new book cultures are still privileged forms of consumption they do not simply reproduce old cultural capital. Instead, even when nostalgic for literary presence, they manifest the redistribution of cultural capital consequent upon expanded tertiary education, media pervasion, and globalised culture markets. In this sense, the new book cultures cannot be seen simply as a reproduction of mid-century middlebrow culture. Literature's role is more specialised, although part of the reason for its rebirth is the promise it still holds of 'general culture'. Further, there are both class and generational splits dividing the contemporary book culture(s) I have been describing. For the moment, though, we might focus on the 'top end' of this new phenomenon, its 'power consumers', those within and around the *new* professional-managerial classes. These readers have been variously named as the 'new class', as 'cultural omnivores' or as 'neo-consumers'—who, apparently, constitute 24 per cent of First World populations but who possess more than half the discretionary spending and 'have a huge appetite for books'.[42]

While accepting, as Jim Collins argues, that 'it is a serious mistake to conceive of the current popularisation of elite cultural pleasures as simply the most recent incarnation of middlebrow aesthetics', it is revealing nevertheless to analyse the new book cultures through the concept of the middlebrow.[43] To do so highlights their contemporary reconfiguration of high and low. Good books in the present proclaim their distance from commercial media, at one end, and from the new *academy* (rather than 'high culture') at the other. At its least benign, this opposition means a new manifestation of the culture wars, produced this time by anxieties at the postmodern blurring of boundaries between popular and modern, cultured and commercial, which has elsewhere provoked new creativities. While the university has in large part produced the reading and writing subjects of contemporary book culture, the good reading of good books seems to many of its citizens to be precisely what the academy has abandoned.

The new niche function for literary reading among the array of lifestyle, media and entertainment choices, I think, is to provide two primary experiences. First, ethical seriousness. Reading is being deployed for exercises in self-fashioning in which class privilege is rendered as a form of social conscience. While this has parallels in certain forms of cinema, music or theatre, books are still peculiarly suited to the practice of therapeutic interiority (thus in the good book stores the new fiction sits alongside the new lifestyle guides on sex, *feng shui* or gourmet cuisine). Second, and perhaps something newer, the new good books offer readers not just cultivation or taste, but a kind of cultural cosmopolitanism. And what the good book stores tell us, in turn, is that this cosmopolitan style can be fashioned through discerning consumption. The internationalism of quality bestsellers—the latest Anglo-Indian, Chinese, Latin American or Australian good novel—is one of the most distinctive features of contemporary book culture and one of its most distinctive sites, of course, is the airport book store. Airport book stores now stock much more than 'airport novels'. They are full of serious, desirable, up-market, middlebrow good reading.

Cosmopolitanism is thus the new form of class mobility that culture offers or reflects back to the general reader in the era of globalised culture markets. Australian fiction now appears within this cosmopolitan array much more forcefully than in any *national* ordering. Mostly that task is left to the academics.

'SOME MEANS OF LEARNING OF THE BEST NEW BOOKS'
All About Books and the Modern Reader

We launch this Journal on a sea already overcrowded with journals, magazines and daily and weekly papers of all kinds, to say nothing of a superabundance of books published each month—this is just the trouble. As very ordinary members of the great public, we have found much difficulty in sifting the grains of wheat out of so much chaff, and many in our circle of social and business friends are in the same predicament. We like reading, and welcome with open arms anyone who can tell us of a good book.

If we could only find some means of getting recommendations of the best new books without having to read long, critical reviews, and search two or three papers for even this information, it would be a great boon. We read mainly for recreation, and want some means of learning of the best new books—some summary that will enable us to decide quickly if a book is the kind that will give us the pleasure and recreation or the information we desire …

We intend to give information rather than criticism. We lay no claim to literary distinction. We do not even desire to be original. But we do aim to keep you advised of the best new books and what leading reviewers think of them, to give you interesting information about books and authors, to let you know of the books that are attracting worldwide attention and, perhaps, bring to your notice older good books you may have overlooked.[1]

This was a novel way for a new books magazine to make its claims on readers' interests: by downplaying literariness and originality. But from its launch in December 1928, *All About Books*—or to give it its full title, *All About Books for Australian and New Zealand Readers*—was a new kind of magazine, and in some respects not a literary magazine at all. It was interested in books before literature, and in readers before criticism.

The journal's Introduction sets up the themes of my own essay, through four interconnected points. The first is that distinctive sense of an overcrowded print economy, especially a 'superabundance' of new books. While this sensation of drowning in a sea of print has a longer history, it is characteristic of 1920s–30s modernity, and was instrumental in generating new institutions, like *All About Books* itself, for mediating between new books and new readers. Second, this sense of the contemporary marketplace produces a distinctive temporality. *All About Books* is geared almost entirely to the books and authors of the moment rather than to the past or tradition, and to up-to-date *news* about books, delivered 'quickly' and efficiently.[2] Thirdly, this temporality produces a particular attitude to criticism, suggested by the distinction drawn between 'criticism' and 'information'. It is not that the magazine rejects evaluation; on the contrary, its whole purpose is to know the *best* new books. But for the most part this task is not organised around notions of tradition or permanence. The editorial desires a very different relationship to books, one based upon forms of utility answering to specific needs, 'the pleasure and recreation or the information we desire', rather than the universal ends of 'literary distinction'. As an article celebrating the modern phenomenon of pocket editions put it: 'Civilisation comes to us to-day in exquisite fragments suitable for shelf, suitcase or car, purposely designed to meet the fleeting needs of the modern race of nomads'.[3]

This relationship to books is manifest, finally, in the primary orientation of the magazine towards readers. It offered book news to readers and consumers, not criticism addressed to the culture. The first issue of *All About Books* included a paragraph from C.E.M. Joad's *The Future of Leisure*, on reading as 'the most satisfactory of all the ways of spending leisure' (10). It announced a competition for the best reader's letter on 'The Book I Most Enjoyed Reading This Year'. The first reviews page was called 'Novels I Think You Would Like to Read'. Written by Stella Macfarlane, its first question, one that echoes throughout the magazine, was 'What book, but recently published, will appeal to a variety of tastes?' (the answer was Warwick Deeping's bestseller *Old Pybus*). The editors themselves write as readers, indeed 'very ordinary' readers: 'We like reading ... We read mainly for recreation'. And when Nettie Palmer, then among Australia's best-known literary critics, began writing regularly for the magazine in June 1929, she did so under the heading 'A Reader's Notebook'.[4]

While it would be too much to claim that *All About Books* invented a new kind of Australian reader, the magazine can be used to explore a set of relationships between Australian readers and contemporary books that emerged in the 1920s, and which might be measured in terms of its distance from the modes of colonial readership prevalent in the nineteenth century. If colonial reading takes its bearings from and seeks to affirm a relationship to British or European literary traditions, 'modern' reading takes its bearings from the contemporary book and the contemporary book market, and with little sense of colonial displacement. Rather than the shift from a dependent to an 'independent' culture (the binary itself breaks down), what I'm describing is a new relationship to books as commodities, often new kinds of books as new kinds of commodities.

The shifts in 'book culture' that can be observed over this period are the result of structural changes in the British (and American) book trade, and consequently in Australian publishing and bookselling; and in the class location and social function of books and reading. *All About Books* is one local manifestation of these changes in the dissemination and circulation of books, which, historians have suggested, accelerated in the 1890s and culminated in the 1920s–30s.[5] The rapid expansion of publishing and of the reading public, and the restructuring of much of the book trade around the bestseller or popular non-fiction title, meant a rapid 'contemporisation' of books and reading.[6] Book culture was significantly reorganised around the category of the *new* (the book of the week or the month); even the classics, repackaged for modern readers, functioned as new kinds of commodities. Institutions built around the tasks of 'keeping up' with and discerning the best of the new books proliferated as fast as the new books themselves. These effects were no less, and possibly even more, intense in Australia because of the fact that local book cultures were constituted overwhelmingly by the dissemination of imported books and book talk.

Certainly, there is a recurrent perception in the 1920s of being in the midst of a new commercial and cultural phenomenon, not just more books, but more new books, and new kinds of readers or reading occasions. As *All About Book*'s introduction to its readers suggests, the prospect was at once energising and unsettling.

While there were specific class resonances in the magazine, as suggested by the reference in the Introduction to 'our circle of social and business friends', its primary interest was to maximise the occasions of book consumption, to bring publishers, booksellers and book-buyers together as efficiently as possible. In its first issue, a substantial 44 pages, it offered brief reviews of more than 100 new books, from Virginia Woolf's *Orlando* to Sax Rohmer's *She Who Sleeps* to Esme Wingfield-Stratford's *The History of British Civilisation*.[7] It printed more than thirty multi-title publishers' advertisements; initiated short newsy pieces on contemporary authors, with photographs; and boasted the new 'technology' of the bestseller list.[8] As is clear again today, author celebrity is a characteristic of a reader-oriented book culture. In another contemporary echo, the magazine promoted schemes for book clubs and reading groups in order to expand the commerce between books and readers.[9]

II

Rather than a single discourse of value, *All About Books* manifests the tensions and divergent energies that characterised the book culture of its moment, especially in its conceptions of readers and of the role of critics. These dynamics are best understood by reading the magazine, not as a falling short of full literary status, but as a distinctive manifestation of contemporary middlebrow cultural dispositions, the product of new relationships between 'consumerist modernisation' and literary value.[10]

Although launched as a monthly magazine with its own numbering and subscription price, *All About Books* also appeared as a supplement within the trade magazine *The Booksellers, Stationers and Fancy Goods Journal*.[11] This was unusual company for a literary paper. Founder and editor of both journals was D.W. Thorpe, and Thorpe's background was in neither journalism nor letters but in the stationery and newsagent trade and then bookselling from the 1920s. While never a shopkeeper or bookseller, Thorpe made himself a professional agent for the bookselling business. As such he was representative of the new generation of professionals committed to 'modern business methods' who emerged in the 1920s, centrally in retailing and marketing, but also in psychology, management, domestic science, and other fields of 'scientific' cultural reform.[12] Although he had little formal training, Thorpe was, in his own words, 'a passionate advocate of orderly trading and trade co-operation'.[13] He was President of the Wholesale and Manufacturing Stationers' Association and, most importantly, in 1925, he became secretary of the newly-formed Australian Booksellers' Association, a position he held until 1949.

In short, *All About Books* emerged from the world of commodity culture rather than literary culture. As such, it was unlikely to be hostile to the effects of the market and likely to be predisposed towards the interests of consumers. (It is almost certainly no accident that the magazine was launched in time for Christmas.) *All About Books* addressed modern men and women constituted as readers and book-buyers by their relationship to the contemporary marketplace rather than to literature; hence its interest in 'information' before criticism. More accurately, 'literature' was part of what circulated and produced value in the marketplace, and here there was a role for the critic.

Whether the abundance of new books was a sign of cultural vitality or the ultimate victory of sordid commerce was one of the decade's recurrent themes, in Britain producing the popular book paper *John O'London's Weekly* (1919–54) and F.R. Leavis's *Mass Civilisation and Minority Culture* (1930) for example, at its beginning and end respectively.[14] Certainly *All About Books* evokes the sense of being surrounded by readers in a busy marketplace, one configured by the latest bestsellers and popular general knowledge titles, the repackaged classics and 'world's greatest books' series (such as Dent's Everyman's Library), and by the book of the month clubs, radio book shows, and other emerging institutions of a consumer-oriented book culture. And yet what marks its contemporaneity is its sense, not just of abundance, but of excess or '*super*abundance'. Thorpe's literary values might have matched his modern business principles in suggesting that, while the market had to be encouraged, its rapid proliferation also needed to be guided, organised and *made reliable* for buyers and sellers alike. Building a market and building a culture might not be so very different after all, not as different as criticism was wont to suggest—for the critic, too, had a role in regulating the market.

The middlebrow can be defined by its mediations between the scales, not just of 'high' and 'low', but of consumption and criticism, ephemerality and permanence, recreation and cultivation—between incommensurate temporalities and structures of value—managed primarily through the flimsy but overdetermined notion of 'good books'.[15] Emerging between high modernism and urban popular culture, middlebrow institutions were typically invested in maximising the occasions for cultural consumption while simultaneously certifying 'quality': multiplying the categories of good books and good reading, while at the same time, in a relentlessly contemporary market where tradition might be no guide at all, ordering that proliferation through discerning the 'best', and reassuring 'very ordinary' consumers that the best was within their reach. Thus the combination of imperative and pleasure characteristically expressed in the idea of 'good books': 'books which you not only SHOULD read, but will also enjoy reading'.[16]

If the category of 'good books' could mediate between the values of cultivation and consumption, the very indeterminacy of the term left all the work of discrimination still to be done. For the book trade agent and the ordinary reader, no less than for the literary professional, there was a sense that the sheer volume of new books made it increasingly difficult to discern the best—harder to inform oneself authoritatively, but also, because of the shifting cultural meanings of reading and owning books, ever more necessary that one should be so informed (and so distinguished from the 'mere' consumer). For the *critic*, in more predictable terms, the contemporary situation might be dramatised by the urgency of the need to discriminate, in Nettie Palmer's words, 'between what is significant and germinating, and what is merely commercial ephemera'. The phrase is from a letter of 1930 in which Palmer accuses Thorpe, as editor, of 'a steady habit of confusing literature with bookselling'. Elsewhere, Palmer welcomed the magazine 'with its bluntly utilitarian aims', as 'a sort of sutler to the literary army's advance'.[17]

On the scales of both 'literature' and 'bookselling', then, there was an interest in discerning the best new books; and although, as Palmer's comments indicate, these different scales of value could be contradictory, in the commercial institutions of book culture they were also thoroughly entwined, each balancing different *kinds* against different *values*, each seeking an informed reading public. If, today, we are liable to read such 'confusion' in terms of anxiety—and for those committed to good books, there was always something potentially unsettling about the abundance of new books— perhaps what is more telling is the degree to which competing discourses of value are allowed to sit 'un-anxiously' together in *All About Books*.

The division in the magazine's interests became explicit on its sixth anniversary, in January 1934:

> Honest and capable reviews by qualified critics are necessary for the good of our
> nation, but, unfortunately, it is not what the general public wants … Knowing this,
> we have endeavoured to serve a dual purpose. Qualified critics such as Mrs Palmer
> and Professor Cowling give critical reviews regularly, whilst other reviewers,
> engaged for their ability to 'sort' books into different classes, give summaries of
> different types of novels.[18]

When framed by the nation, criticism was a necessary public good. When framed by the market (more transnational than national), the task was different, merely informing rather than forming public taste. Thus, on the one hand, the magazine made a feature of its authoritative critics, Nettie Palmer and George Cowling, Professor of English at the University of Melbourne. On the other, its pages were filled with brief, more or less anonymous reviews which claimed no more authority than that of a fellow reader. Although most named reviewers were regulars, my sense is that they were not known as literary commentators, certainly not as 'critics'.

Over the bulk of its review-filled pages, then, *All About Books* was cheerfully agnostic about where good reading might be found: '"A good book" may fitly describe any type of book from a novel by Charles Garvice, Arnold Bennett, Warwick Deeping, or Tolstoi to a scientific treatise on snakes. It all depends upon the taste, mental condition, humour and education of the reader, and the purpose for which it is required'.[19] 'Good books' could extend to an 80-volume library of psychology, philosophy and science for the lay reader, new from publishers Kegan Paul, and reviewed as news. Psychoanalysis, here, sounds like a prescription for middlebrow reading: it allows 'the individual to integrate his own personality for the purpose of an effective life'; it is 'so intensely personal in its appeal, and so practical in its application, that few readers can afford to ignore it'.[20]

More strongly, the magazine was committed to the democratisation of taste (and the broadening of consumption) produced by the expanding marketplace: 'We are ... convinced that no particular class or profession contains a monopoly of the literary inclined. The professions and higher classes of society are frequently disappointing as readers, whilst one is being continually surprised by the interest in good books shown by those of the "working" classes'.[21] Good readers could be found across all social classes, just as good books could be found across the whole field of literature. This generated, not a single vertical scale of literary value, but a horizontal multiplication of types of books and of readers. Thus there is little sense of anxiety in *All About Books* about 'lowbrow' fiction. Its reviewers do, however, repeatedly take their bearings from the 'highbrow', sometimes happily recommending books for highbrow readers as simply one class of reader among others, but more often defining their own tastes against the highbrow, and with a symptomatic mix of self-assurance and defensiveness. So in December 1937 (the subject is again Warwick Deeping): 'Some "highbrows" accuse him of sentimentality, but, as one reviewer put it, "let them produce something half as entertaining"'; and in March 1933, via J.B. Priestley: 'don't be either a highbrow or a lowbrow. Be a man. Be a broadbrow ... And if you find yourself liking what a great many other of your fellow-creatures like, own up to it and take your place alongside them'. The *All About Books* reviewer adds, 'whilst this will have little effect on the unconvertible highbrow, it certainly does give us poor ordinary people a feeling that we are not such worms after all'.[22] The magazine's reviewers were thus happy to multiply the categories of taste to get a neat fit between product and consumer, but also to affirm their own tastes *against* literary expertise. There were books for 'literary connoisseurs' and books for 'business men', historical romances that 'appeal to some in all classes of readers', and, the privileged category, 'books of wide appeal and not lacking in literary merit'. There were 'novels of distinction for discriminating readers', novels for the 'feminine habitué of ... lending libraries' and novels for 'those who take their fiction slightly more intensely'.[23] The utility and pleasure of good books could be multiplied in almost every direction.

But this kind of product endorsement co-existed with a desire to produce *better* readers, or at least more readers for better books. Similarly, there was a recurrent interest in discerning among the contemporary flood of titles those books with 'permanent value'.[24] This concern was generated by the anxious sense that more and more books could devalue 'good books' to the level of disposable commodities. Discerning permanent value perhaps operated only as a higher form of product endorsement—here was a title you could safely buy for your personal library—but it approached the scale of criticism and the Arnoldian task of elevating taste. In this form, the goal was to *restrict* rather than multiply the categories of good books. *All About Books* embraced all these aims: to produce more readers and sell more books; to produce better readers (and sell more *good* books); and to produce an Australian book culture based on 'sound literary judgement'.[25] This has some odd but symptomatic effects: new books with permanent value are discerned *month after month* as the two different temporalities are brought together. In one discourse, different tastes were just a matter of taste; in the other, taste was everything, a question of culture. The former takes its bearings from readers' tastes (in this sense *everyone* had taste), the latter from the critic's taste, something much rarer, to be cultivated.

III

Middlebrow institutions constantly affirmed that 'good books' were not the province of highbrow culture alone (indeed the highbrow was likely to mistake artifice or pretence for quality), and equally that good popular books could be distinguished from the bad. In making these affirmations, middlebrow book culture called upon forms of literary expertise—the established critic, the university professor—to mediate between notions of the best and the affirmation of reader preferences, indeed as far as possible to align the two. But the context was one of heightened ambivalence over the cultural authority of the critic in an increasingly segregated book culture. If, on the one hand, the superabundance of books meant an ever greater demand for critical guidance, on the other the increased public access to books and book talk undermined older forms of literary authority.[26] Similarly, the expansion of the marketplace multiplied the occasions for critical influence, and yet, it seemed, simultaneously reduced them by its vulgar commodification of culture.

The modern critic emerged through the splitting of 'serious criticism' from the 'book chat' (the title of Thorpe's earlier attempt at a book magazine) proliferating in contemporary publications and radio shows—indeed, in *All*

About Books itself. There was a recurrent complaint, still heard, that what we lacked was *real* criticism. In Vance Palmer's words, from the Melbourne *Age* in 1935:

> Our main lack in the literary field is a lively and intelligent criticism. There are columns of gossip about books and authors, but little sense of values ... The criticism of music, painting, even the drama, is taken seriously and done by experts, but when it comes to literature people believe that one person's opinion about a book is as good as another's, one vote, one value.[27]

If this was a call for expertise, the role of the critic was nonetheless also distinguished in the name of general culture from *other* forms of modern specialisation—the academic or the highbrow. This ambivalent positioning of literary expertise between specialisation and general culture marks the careers of both university and independent literary professionals as various as Walter Murdoch, George Mackaness, Frederick Macartney, the Palmers and George Cowling.

What is striking about *All About Books* is the extent to which it both exemplifies the kinds of 'gossip' Palmer deplores, and yet shares his desire for 'lively and intelligent criticism'. Rubin describes a contemporary distinction, often adversarial, between reviewing and criticism, between treating books as 'news' or as 'literature'.[28] In these terms, both Cowling and Nettie Palmer take on the critic's task of evaluating works on the scale of 'permanence', but in qualified form. While Palmer is always concerned to discriminate the significant from the merely ephemeral, the value she invokes is not that of literature per se, but of an emerging continuity in Australian literature, a 'certain unity of outlook', the 'hint of cumulative force in our literature'.[29] She adopts a form of national anxiety, the furthest thing from most of the paper's reviewers:

> Dorothy Cottrell has been greatly praised, and will be praised again: she has thus been given the freedom of the popular book world. Anxious onlookers can only hope she will be able to use that freedom some day to write a careful, sound book ... drawing on her large fortune of intimate bush knowledge and youthful vitality. Meanwhile 'Earth Battle' beats many a popular throb-novel at its own game. We merely ask, from her, something different and better.[30]

Palmer invokes a collective reading community rather than a marketplace of so many readers and tastes (evoked in her wonderful phrase, 'the freedom of the popular book world'). Nonetheless, she shared the magazine's generous sense of good or useful books, for, in her case, the cumulative force of Australian expression could be found broadly, in essays on the lyrebird or memoirs of bush life as well as in serious fiction. She encouraged good Australian books of all kinds, even as she restricted the terms on which their value might be discerned. She was concerned to create a broad Australian reading and book-buying public, not a minority culture. And she was enthusiastic rather than snooty about the new phenomena of book clubs, precisely because they spread good books more broadly.[31]

Cowling is an even more revealing case. He began writing for *All About Books* in early 1931 and continued until its close in 1938, mainly reviewing contemporary English fiction. Cowling is best remembered for his article in the Melbourne *Age*, following Vance Palmer's, in which he argued that 'from a literary point of view Australia lacks the richness of age and tradition.[32] Cowling, in short, is remembered as an Anglophile conservative and literary traditionalist. So he is, although his sense of contemporary books and market imperatives is not quite what we might expect. In the *Age* article he argues that the novel should attract Australian writers 'because it is now definitely a trade'. Australian writers should 'provide novels of school life, boys novels of adventure, feminine novels of character, dramatic stories, detective novels and thrillers'. On one level this is simply patronising: Australian literature can only aspire to the lower levels of literary form. But it also expresses a pragmatic, contemporary sense of the marketplace. In *All About Books*, Cowling happily reviews English bestsellers on a monthly basis, recommending the best, but embracing much of the popular middle ground.

As Professor of English, Cowling was a professional reader. Yet despite his own formal training in Shakespeare and language studies he was, like the American professors who ran the middlebrow journals and the Book-of-the-Month Club, a cultural generalist.[33] As a number of his reviews reveal, the emerging forms of academic specialisation in criticism were thoroughly foreign to his tastes. It was the very conventionality of his literary vocabulary—his belief that good literature required sincere emotion, unity of purpose, sympathetic characters and a good story—that enabled him to embrace the new bestsellers, to find in them plenty of examples of the great and nearly great, or at least of the charming and delightful. By the same token it enables him to draw the line at highbrow modernism. Of an Ethel Mannin novel he writes, 'It is very provocative, and "crowded with culture" of the highbrow sort that is now talked, according to Miss Mannin, in the Café Francais, London'.[34]

Cowling was an ideal figure of middlebrow cultural authority, bringing his authoritative status to bear in guiding readers as to where quality could be found across contemporary fiction and essays, but dissolving that authority in a familiar 'readerly' manner, as a reader writing for readers not as a critic for critics. On the one hand, this rendered the commercial book world consonant with literary quality for new book consumers; on the other, it reassured readers as to the irrelevance of the highbrow and modernist. Arnold Bennett emerges as Cowling's hero, and like Bennett he is happy for authors to be successful in the marketplace: 'I should like to see Australian literary men sailing their own yachts, managing repertory theatres, travelling *de luxe*, filling the stalls at the theatres in immaculate evening dress, and collecting books, pictures and bric-à-brac'.[35] While he claims the authority to describe the 'books everyone should read', he also recommends the month's best detective novel.

Indeed, Cowling is happy to side with bestsellerdom against academic criticism. Reviewing an American history of the novel, he parts company with its authors over their preference for what we would now see as a modernist tradition.

I should naturally hesitate to say that sales alone proclaim the excellence of an author, but I should certainly take them into account …

Has the novel ceased to be a good story, well told, and become a jig-saw puzzle or a cross-word? Personally I do not believe it … I can assure the authors that the reading public is not attracted by the symbolism, the word-making and word-playing of Mr Joyce. It prefers a good story by J.B. Priestley, Brett-Young, or A.P. Herbert, who … like E.C. Booth, is not even mentioned. Personally I refuse to believe this academic rubbish. Dorothy Richardson and James Joyce are not 'big noises'. They are 'noises off'. A few critics chirp about them, but the vast reading public goes its way undisturbed.[36]

He also criticises the book for ignoring detective stories and thrillers. Perhaps most tellingly, Cowling concludes that 'contemporary literature can only be reviewed' (i.e., not criticised). By the late 1930s his reviews page had the impeccably middlebrow title: 'All Sorts of Reading For Everybody'.

IV

Rather than genteel or specialist reading, *All About Books* encouraged a form of discerning consumption in which individuals took responsibility for their own 're-creation'. At one end was what Captain C.H. Peters, bookseller and ABC radio book show host, called 'reading with a purpose': 'Even the ardent reader must know discipline. A comfortable chair, by the fireside, light falling over the left shoulder, *a card for notes*, a soft sharpened pencil; and away upon a magic carpet'.[37] At the other end was reading for 'pleasure', probably the most frequent term of recommendation in the magazine. But this was purposeful not idle pleasure, hence the key term 'recreation'. As an article quoted from *John O'London's* explained, 'there are two kinds of recreational literature. The one kind gives you real recreation—that is, new mental health—the other gives you mere relaxation—that is, mere mental rest'. The former cannot 'be enjoyed without effort'; the latter is 'cheap in every sense', although admirable 'for people who have got influenza'.[38] Typically, the hierarchies of value are weak and scarcely literary, but the work of distinction is pervasive nonetheless.

At the same time, the discourse of self-improvement characteristic of the earnest working-class reader is scarcely present in the magazine. While there is an emphasis on teaching new habits of reading and book-buying, there is little sense of a reading 'curriculum' as is characteristic of working-class self-education.[39] Its readers, we might say, were *already* readers and book-buyers. What *All About Books* offers is less self-education than a kind of social 'ease' around books and authors, an up-to-date familiarity acquired more through shared enthusiasm than critical pedagogy, a kind of guidance that was at once personalised and 'personalising' even as it drew a 'circle' of class distinction.[40]

This emphasis is also manifested in the magazine's insistence on owning books, not just reading them: 'Own the books you most wish to read. Have them in your library, carry them in your pocket'; '*Castle Gay* is a book for one's own library shelf; it is too good a piece of work to read and pass by'.[41]

The building of a personal library, too, meant taking responsibility for one's own recreation and culture. Palmer shared these encouragements.[42] Indeed the serious reader is precisely the reader who will buy books for *re*-reading, for a personal library or thoughtful gifts, one way of building a 'reading nation'. Consumers like this were not irrelevant to the building of a national culture, however threatening the market appeared in other contexts.

All About Books took its bearings from its contemporary situation: an accelerating book market configured by an ever increasing number of new fiction and popular non-fiction titles, and a new sense of readers as modern consumers who would take responsibility for their recreation no less than for their education or cultivation. Thus it multiplied the categories of taste and classes of readers, expanding but also ordering the categories of good books. In doing so, it occupied the cultural space best described by the term 'middlebrow' (rather than 'popular'): invoking quality but distributing it much more widely than the canons of literary value; constantly ranking and recommending the 'best' while drawing a clear line before the highbrow. National culture had a relatively low profile in this market orientation towards the contemporary, although it did carry its own imperatives and responsibilities for the critic and serious reader. It is tempting to say that the magazine combines two forms of address, one organised around pleasurable and informative reading addressed to readers as modern consumers, the other organised around 'culture', criticism and the nation, and addressed to readers as modern citizens. By the time of *All About Books*, these two discourses were already largely irreconcilable, but in the absence of densely-formed local intellectual networks in the universities or higher journalism they could still inhabit the same publication.

REALISM, DOCUMENTARY, SOCIALIST REALISM
Fiction and Social Crisis
1930–60

THE ART OF CRISIS

'Facts are the new literature.' This bold assertion comes from *Strife*, a one-off magazine published by Judah Waten and other young bohemians in 1930.[1] *Strife*'s literary manifesto expressed a radical impulse towards documentary writing, a break with all prior traditions, and a sense of the present as a moment of crisis:

> *STRIFE* is another force added to the world-wide movement to uproot the existing social and economic order of chaotic and tragic individualism! The proletarian writer will break with the sickly plots ... sex triangles, and individual heroisms of the past. He will work with facts.

The stand of the avant-garde *Strife* is extreme, but its linking of an artistic break from bourgeois fiction and a compelling sense of social crisis is shared by a wide range of fiction and commentary from the early 1930s to the early 1950s. The sense of social crisis was a distinctive response to the Depression, international fascism, and the threat of world war. Fascism particularly affected writers, being perceived as the very antithesis of culture.[2] These successive movements of history are linked in numerous writings as symptoms of the one disease: capitalism. From M. Barnard Eldershaw's *Tomorrow and Tomorrow* (1947):

> The whole world was sick. The war was not an accident but the expression of a deep and terrible distemper, erupting from within … [W]ithin society the cracks widened and competition hardened and increased, competitive living, competitive loving, competitive suffering and death.[3]

For many writers the historical sequence of Depression, fascism and war meant a profound disturbance in their sense of social relations. Society becomes an arena not just for the play of individual motives but of momentous historical forces and class divisions, of 'mass villains, mass victims [and] an awakened mass consciousness'.[4] Contemporary social upheavals are represented not just as local disorders but, in the words of the magazine *Australian New Writing* (1943–46), as an apocalyptic 'crisis in the history of civilisation … a clash of two irreconcilable ideologies: fascist against democratic, barbaric against civilised, hysterical brutality against reason'.[5]

This notion of crisis was itself symptomatic of a crisis in liberal humanism whose traditional terms seemed inadequate to comprehend such massive social change. Mass social forms and ideologies seemed to threaten human nature as a source of value and continuity. For a number of writers this ideological crisis produced a serious involvement with communism—if not the Communist Party—or with socialist and populist ideas, often as a form of cultural nationalism. Frank Dalby Davison wrote in 1942: 'national unity, to which we are now trusting so much, is the stronger for having been confirmed in our nascent literature'.[6] For all the writers considered here, the period meant heightened debate over cultural meanings and a reformulation of the relations between fiction and society, individuals and society, and, not least, writers and society.

In order to engage with this new social reality—at once individual and historical—works of fiction were forced into formal experiment. Conventional plots and characterisation were transformed as texts were opened up to 'facts', political rhetoric, and utopian discourses. Such expanded forms of fiction in Australia include novels of large scope like *Tomorrow and Tomorrow*, Eleanor Dark's *The Little Company* (1945) and Frank Hardy's *Power Without Glory* (1950). The claim by *Strife* to a 'new form based on facts' suggests that more modest kinds of documentary fiction should also be included in this mapping of new forms.

The genres of documentary developed in the 1930s were not simply modes of recording contemporary experience. Style and subject-matter were politically motivated as writers attempted to represent forcefully, in literary discourse, facts and attitudes which they believed literature had conventionally excluded or falsified:

> London, 25 November—The late Mr Harry Bellingham Howard Smith, shipping director, who died in Australia, left estate in England and the Commonwealth valued at £1,077,012—*News item.*
>
> From the bowels of the tourist ships the firemen can sometimes hear the laughter of the passengers and the slip, slip of their feet dancing on the deck above them.
>
> Each passenger pays £35 for a trip round the islands. The firemen are paid £2 per week.
>
> For four hours at a time they stand half naked before roaring furnaces shovelling in the coal that drives the mighty engines. The sweat that's wrung from out their blackened bodies leaves streaks of cleanness on their hides.
>
> From where they work the firemen can sometimes hear the laughter of the passengers and the slip, slip of their dancing on the deck above them.[7]

Texts such as this, by Alan Marshall, need to be seen as contesting the claims of well-made fiction to reflect reality. Marshall's sketch, typically, challenges any clear-cut distinction between the aesthetic and the documentary. By forgoing certain aesthetic effects while emphasising others, the text assures that it is read neither as 'mere' fiction nor 'mere' documentary. This ambivalent status is characteristic of documentary and socially critical fiction, which both claims and disclaims art in order to establish its own truth.

In the 1930s and 1940s Marshall and John Morrison published sketches of proletarian life in left-wing journals. It could be argued that these link back to the sketches of Henry Lawson and the *Bulletin*, but any similarities are due more to a common marginal position in relation to the cultural establishment than to a continuous Australian literary tradition. The significant influences were contemporary and international: Ernest Hemingway, John Dos Passos, Sherwood Anderson, *New Masses*, and new kinds of writers' and artists' organisations. In Australia, Workers' Art Clubs began in 1931; a Writers' League was established in 1935, amalgamating in 1938 with the Fellowship of Australian Writers; and by the mid-1930s New Theatre groups were operating.[8] The prose sketches can be compared to the graphic art and theatre of the period (Betty Roland, for example, published scripts in the *Communist Review*, 1937–38, with titles such as 'The Miners Speak' and 'Workers, Beware!').[9] In these three areas, documentary and didactic modes overlap in highly stylised work.

The prose sketches show a range of techniques for creating effects of immediacy, including the use of short sentences, a compressed time-span, present tense and second-person narration (this is in contrast to the yarning narrators of Marshall and Morrison's later, better-known stories). Morrison repeatedly begins his waterfront sketches with an abrupt statement of time and place: 'The Compound Mid-winter. Eight o'clock Friday morning'.[10] Similar bold effects are present in descriptions of the new subject of work in Kylie Tennant's *The Battlers* (1941) and Jean Devanny's *Sugar Heaven* (1936):

> Each man took his place at the head of a row of cane; the left hand grasped the thick stick; the broad-bladed short-handled knife was wielded to sever the stalk on a level with the ground. No time for waste motion. Another stroke with the knife severed the top; two downward motions cleaned the trash from the stalk. The fifth motion heaped the sticks ...
>
> Cut low! Cut lower! Cut right into the ground! It's every last vestige of sugar content harvested or the 'sack' ... Big Boss Ratoon needs a clean stump to spring from! And Big Boss Sugar Baron hears the sweet chink of gold emanate from the clean fields![11]

The effect of rapid notation, the unfinished quality of the sketches, their very fragmentation and plotlessness, operate to signal the writing's 'authenticity'. The formal disruptions and excesses of style—both overstatement and understatement—are techniques by which radical documentary marks out its difference from bourgeois fiction. Such a difference is doubly marked in Marshall's *How Beautiful Are Thy Feet* (1949) by a division in the text between italicised passages and the main narrative. The former are the site of a shifting didactic, 'camera eye' or collective voice:

> *The Factory snarls as it eats ... it rears its head above the damp of narrow streets ...*
> *above the swamp of houses ... it is a dinosaur ... it is Tyrannosaurus Rex ... it is*
> *destruction ... its talons are steel ... its entrails are machines ... its mouth is a door ...* [12]

The bulk of the narrative is more conventional except that again the narrative focus is highly mobile. The text is a collage of short scenes or sketches. One effect of this is to transform the presence of character, to register an altered sense of the relation between social forces and subjectivity. As Humphrey McQueen remarks, 'Marshall challenged all the canons of Australian literature and bourgeois individualism by making a boot factory the protagonist of a novel.'[13] The characters are only voices or gestures; but rather than just a reduction of individuals to types, the novel deliberately produces a *multiplication* of types. Characters no longer represent mere subjectivity, but are sites where social forces and ideologies play out their effects.

In incorporating a range of characters the novel is not simply attempting to be faithful to reality. Its sheer abundance of voices and plots opens up the narrative to those contemporary social facts conventionally excluded from fiction. First, work itself becomes a primary subject. Second, the novel's multiple voices generate an excess of erotic energy, spilling over the bounds of sentimental romance, an erotic force juxtaposed with the sheer facts of work. The conventional marriage plot is displaced by multiple plots; and like many novels of the period *How Beautiful Are Thy Feet* includes the story of an abortion, representing symptomatically the contemporary crisis in social relations. Third, in dialogues throughout the text, the novel incorporates political discourses beyond liberalism, including communism, fascism, Social Credit, even eugenics. Here too, there is a kind of excess beyond the needs of documentary or plot, expanding the fiction towards history.

In reclaiming this writing we can underline not the naturalness of its discourse but its modernity. Though less intellectually wrought, Marshall's novel bears comparison with, say, Christina Stead's *Seven Poor Men of Sydney* (1934) or Dark's *The Little Company*. Major novels of the 1930s and 1940s can be productively read, not as reflections of life or as organic unities, but as narratives which mediate between the explanatory, evocative or persuasive powers of different literary and non-literary languages: documentary, traditional realism, political theory, utopianism, even romance. The tension between these competing claims, as each novel situates itself in relation to other fiction, other fact, and other propaganda, generates the distinctive and diverse forms of the period. Their diversity argues against the view of social realist writing expressed in Patrick White's historically momentous phrase describing Australian fiction as 'dun-coloured ... journalistic realism'.[14] To stress diversity is also to resist the pressure towards homogeneity inherent in national literary histories especially when focused on prose fiction, seen by H.M. Green, for example, as 'that part of [literature] which most clearly reflects the national life'.[15]

REVOLUTIONARY ROMANTICISM

The tensions within realism are extreme in works with a positive revolutionary message which forces the text to engage directly with political rhetoric. Both Devanny's *Sugar Heaven* and J.M. Harcourt's *Upsurge* (1934) have a documentary base: the former records a canecutters' strike, the latter conditions for relief workers during the Depression. The documentary, though, is part of a larger political design revealed through communist characters and stories of politicisation. However, the politics of each text lie beyond plot, in the relationships between political and erotic themes and in the different rhetorical models which each narrative incorporates. This entails thinking of propaganda, not as the bits of political rhetoric insufficiently made over into art, but as an available narrative strategy.

Both novels signal their break with 'mere' fiction. The language of sentiment is displaced in the narrative by the language of politics. In *Upsurge*, magistrate Riddle's disquiet at the disintegration of 'modesty' is reinterpreted by his communist friend Graham. In the exchange, the narrative anticipates, as it must, the charge of propaganda:

> 'The morality of a civilization,' said Graham, 'is an ethical reflection of the economic organisation of that civilization ... '
>
> The magistrate shook his head irritably ... 'You attempt to solve every problem you encounter by reference to Karl Marx. His theories dominate your whole outlook.'

'Marx made the obvious discovery that the first task of the human species is earning a living,' Graham observed, 'and that that task is sufficiently important to colour all our other activities, our art, morality, philosophy, religion.'[16]

The significance of Graham's language is not that it announces a correct political line but that it provides an alternative rhetorical mode, another way of understanding, beyond the individual and the ethical. From this point on the two narrative scales are read off against each other.

Graham, a chemist, embodies the scientific appeal of Marxism (though given the text's frequent images of explosives perhaps his profession has a dual significance). By contrast, Theodora Luddon is politicised through industrial experience. The story of betrayal by conventional union leaders, presented here, is a recurrent theme in radical fiction—from Katharine Susannah Prichard's *Working Bullocks* (1926) to Dorothy Hewett's *Bobbin Up* (1959)—indicating the narrative's own break with convention. Another character, Peter Groom, is moved from despair to political enthusiasm by the power of agitational rhetoric. Groom's 'reckless elation' (262) is combined with Graham's logic and Luddon's experience, and through Groom and Luddon the novel enacts the shift from individual to mass consciousness. At a demonstration they are together 'borne along by the irresistible current of the crowd' (274). Finally there is the working-class communist Steve Riley who embodies communism as the force of history, revolutionary 'upsurge', itself. His extreme character is a means of representing the violent disruptions to the bourgeois order of a 'new ideology ... a new consciousness' (69). This new consciousness is shown also to be a characteristic of certain illegal texts:

Between novels by Henri Barbusse, Romain Rolland, John Dos Passos, Jack London, Upton Sinclair, were sandwiched such works as the 'Capital' of Karl Marx, the 'Socialism' of Engels, the 'State and Revolution' of Lenin, the 'Communist Programme' of Bucharin. The mantel was loaded with the literature of class-war and revolution! (52)

This list—even the sandwiching of revolutionary doctrine between fiction—provides models against which *Upsurge* itself can be read. Part of the novel's challenge to the bourgeois order is a challenge to the order of its fiction. The novel provides frequent models—allusions to other texts, narrative styles or ways of reading—in order to proclaim its own status as a new kind of fiction. For example, Riddle witnesses a didactic, highly stylised political play. It is 'weird and unreal' but disturbing precisely because of its unreality: 'Was that extraordinary play a true representation of the facts? … His mind was still troubled by the bizarre fantasy he had witnessed' (217, 222). The play justifies the novel's own departures from illusionism, implying that the stylisations of propaganda and theory in the text's own 'bizarre fantasy' of revolutionary upsurge are a true representation of 'facts' that could not otherwise be represented. A contemporary comment on *Upsurge* might be truer than it intends, describing the novel as 'quite in the modern vein of realism at any price'.[17]

In *Sugar Heaven* characters are also associated, beyond personality, with alternative narrative genres and political options. Hefty represents physical vitality, like 'the blood in the stalks' of the cane, but he is 'only a militant' (14, 270). Bill is able to talk theoretically, but is less 'clean' (a key figure in the novel). Eileen is 'militant and clever', but 'fluent, without discipline or restraint' (144, 95), embodying the erotic and political desires, distributed elsewhere throughout the text, whose organisation would have revolutionary potential. The communists provide figures of discipline and restraint. Hendry, the communist leader, is one of the novel's many figures of transformation: once 'rough', now 'clear and … philosophical' (134).

The central story is Dulcie's transformation from self-consciousness to class-consciousness. Like *Upsurge*, the text figuratively links erotic and political desire in enacting this transformation. Dulcie's conventional morality entails an 'instinctual allegiance to conventional political forms' (55); these are linked in turn to conventional *literary* forms. Dulcie 'had fed voraciously on paper-backed editions of the early Victorians' until, significantly, 'crisis conditions had … dried up the fount of her literary digest' (12). In response to the 'exotic infringements' of the physical vitality and politics of the canefields, Dulcie's 'self-sufficiency' is transformed (15, 11):

> Here was drama! Here was colour! The great Painter, Life, was at work upon the hitherto dull canvas of her existence. The colours were impure, the brushstrokes heavy, but like a Goya canvas they projected intense and mordant life. (55)

Dulcie had kept herself 'clean' in conventional terms, through repression; 'hate and desire' (36) intermingle in her subsequent violent transformation: 'She felt herself changing, not subtly nor delicately, but violently, in leaps; a development in keeping with the lush tropical growth' (123). Ultimately, both sexual and political passion are cleansed and cleansing. Dulcie reflects: 'The strike has washed all sorts of impurities out of me' (300).

The reference to Goya in the quotation above is also significant, for the images describe one of the novel's own styles, a vitalist mode that links natural beauty, sexual desire, and even industrial militancy. The intense, subversive emotions of this mode are juxtaposed with the reasoned discourse of communism. Out of the 'impure' rhetorical styles of desire and 'revolutionary hysteria' (227) the narrative attempts its own transformations, at times neither 'subtly nor delicately'. Its documentary modes, though shading into the register of propaganda, are anti-utopian. Nonetheless the novel rises to an 'epic' pitch (Devanny's term), characteristic of attempts to express 'the spirit of the war of the classes ... its immensity, its dramatic force, its terrific fervor'.[18] At these moments the novel does not so much 'lapse' into propaganda, in Drusilla Modjeska's phrase, as launch into it.[19] Dulcie's first apprehension of class consciousness is a moment of 'sublime reason' born out of 'emotional tumult' (140–41); and the utopian moments are given in visionary and *sensuous* language, envisioning 'expanded joys and vibrant life' (271). The mode here is that of 'revolutionary romanticism'.

Katharine Susannah Prichard claimed *Upsurge* as 'Australia's first truly proletarian novel'. Jean Devanny wrote of *Sugar Heaven* as 'the first really proletarian novel in Australia'.[20] Both claims are made in the context of the doctrine of socialist realism. In the words of A. A. Zhdanov, at the 1934 First All-Union Congress of Soviet Writers:

> The truthfulness and historical exactitude of the artistic image must be linked with the task of ideological transformation ...
>
> Romanticism is not alien to our literature, a literature standing firmly on a materialist basis, but ours is a romanticism of a new type, revolutionary romanticism.[21]

Both *Upsurge* and *Sugar Heaven* can be understood as revolutionary romanticism. However they represent arguments towards, rather than applications of, socialist realism. In the attempt to construct a narrative that shows historical veracity, artistic conviction, and revolutionary optimism, the novels are relentlessly self-reflexive, making explicit their work on often incommensurate discourses.

The history of socialist realism in Australia is complex, as the diversity of novels by Prichard, Devanny, Harcourt, Waten, Hewett, and Hardy suggests. First, until the late 1940s socialist realism was only one option—or an array of options within itself—for radical artists. The history of socialist realism cannot be separated from those of literary nationalism and populism. The possible models for a socially committed realism were diverse, from Lawson to Gorky, from Dickens to *New Masses*, and only in the Cold War years did the Communist Party of Australia give socialist realism a full policy weighting.[22] Second, whatever its policy functions, socialist realism *did* offer a coherent theory of the relations between fiction, fact, and political doctrine, and between intellectuals and society. If it is crude perhaps this is only because it makes explicit the contradictions that are present in all realist aesthetics.

What did occur in the 1940s and 1950s in the interaction between Communist Party policy, socialist realist theory and nationalism was the favouring of more orthodox modes of literary realism. Writers positioned themselves less on the radical margins, as they had in the 1930s, and more at the centre of a tradition. *Bobbin Up*, which resembles the novels already discussed more than its own contemporaries, was criticised in the communist press for its 'naturalism' and 'concentration on the unusual or sensational ... [a] pre-occupation with anatomical description of woman (sic), an overstressing of physical relations'.[23] Over the same period the New Theatre turned towards more classic and illusionist drama, and to nationalist and popular themes.

KATHARINE SUSANNAH PRICHARD

Prichard's career is instructive. *Working Bullocks* and *Intimate Strangers* (1937) share thematic and structural qualities with *Upsurge* and *Sugar Heaven*: the displacement of romance by desire, the transformation of self-consciousness into class-consciousness, and mixed rhetorical strategies for incorporating a revolutionary perspective into a faithful picture of a non-revolutionary society. Patrick Buckridge has demonstrated the juxtaposition in *Working Bullocks* of three narrative options for political fiction: romance, a folk tradition, and a propagandist mode.[24] Each has its own powers of representation and transformation yet none is sufficient in itself, and the novel proceeds by a juxtaposition of rhetorical styles and the values each represents. There are also parallels with *Upsurge* and *Sugar Heaven* in the way that political purpose is 'disseminated through the entire text as a form of desire'.[25] In *Working Bullocks*, the rhetoric of the central socialist character, Mark Smith, is represented simultaneously as common sense and fantasy, fact and art, inspiration and seduction; it is alternately factual, theoretical, and agitational. But despite its authority, his is an alien discourse to the worker community ('such talk had never been heard').[26] This sense of foreignness is characteristic of Prichard's fiction. Not only political discourse, but also passion, in certain novels, is represented as alien, powerful and exotic, and *therefore* able to transform common sense. It is often represented by foreigners or wanderers, characters who are both insiders and outsiders, like Tony Maretti in *Intimate Strangers* and Nadya Owen in *Golden Miles* (1948). Jack Lindsay has remarked of *Intimate Strangers*: 'we feel the socialist viewpoint as something strange, almost foreign and exotic, set over against normal Australian life'.[27] However this is not simply an ideological problem; it is also a narrative problem and its solution.

Prichard's writings reveal a commitment not only to political purpose but to a liberal humanist tradition stressing organic form which held that great art was beyond propagandist rhetoric. The message, in other words, must be both concealed and revealed. *Intimate Strangers*, from its title on, produces a pattern of associated images of strangeness or foreignness through the main characters: Tony, his mother, Guido, Jerome, Prospero, even Elodie ('Elodie had her roots in mixed blood, Slav instincts', 17). These characters and associated images provide the novel's critique of bourgeois institutions, acting to defamiliarise them. The foreign characters also provide the novel's intellectual framework—and it *is* a novel of ideas in its treatment of romance, not a domestic drama with a factitious political ending. The narrative does not simply contrast false romance with the realities of sexual and economic exploitation. Like *Working Bullocks*, the predominant mode of the novel itself is romantic: its task, then, is to split romance, to separate sentiment from sensuousness, false utopias from true, and the false promises of art from its true transformative capacities. In

Elodie, Prichard mediates between the familiar and the foreign, and her music provides the narrative's self-reflexive models. Only Beethoven is adequate to her 'passion and despair' (98). This music, contrasted to 'blithe, sentimental ditties' (111), recalls Mark Smith's rhetoric:

> Chords ... crashed with a proud violence. The lyric at its core, rising triumphantly, soared and dominated with its wild sweet song. The dark turbulent floods of destiny might carry it away ... but defiant in defeat, it could still sing on, inviolate, immortal. (98)

This language also prefigures Tony's political speech, in a scene where Elodie and the working-class audience are transformed by a 'dazzling vision' (294). The text appropriates the very imagery of romance that would seem to belong to the wandering sailor Jerome: the 'struggle of the working people' is transformed from a 'pitiful, hopeless resistance' to a 'magnificent adventure, as magnificent ... as the adventure of Columbus embarking to discover a new world' (294–95).

In the goldfields trilogy—*The Roaring Nineties* (1946), *Golden Miles* (1948) and *Winged Seeds* (1950)—the prominent foreigners, who are also women, again introduce a radical intellectual framework and history; plus, as Sneja Gunew has argued, a sexual politics which is pushed to the fringes by the more explicit critique of capitalism.[28] There is a different ordering of genres and discourses in the later novels which shows the more direct influence of socialist realism. Further, whereas *Intimate Strangers* is Prichard's novel of the 1930s 'crisis of modernity', these are cold war novels. They are without the sense of crisis which characterises much 1930s and 1940s fiction. Instead they provide a long historical perspective, less apocalyptic than evolutionary.

The form of the trilogy might be described as the yarn expanded into saga, or documentary expanded into social history. Its governing rhetorical mode is matter-of-factness, represented in sober speech, ordinariness, and hard facts (the novels *are* prepared to risk their organic form for the sake of the inclusion of documentary material). Through the central figure of Sally Gough the texts seek to turn political rhetoric into experience, to merge nature, common sense and doctrine. One of the novels' triumphs is the linking of Sally and Kalgoorla, for the Aboriginal woman represents the most alien but also the most immediate political experience. Sally's function in the narrative alongside the wise old miner Dinny, its other 'commentator', indicates the novels' populist vision and in particular the manner in which such populism precludes, for the most part, writing about 'the nexus between sexuality, the unconscious and nature'.[29] As this populist, matter-of-fact mode is itself inadequate to produce either a narrative or political resolution, the foreign characters and discourses (Chris Crowe's utopian mumblings, Pat and Pam's exotic modernism) act as supplements in the text, meeting a lack in its dominant genre. In this respect the trilogy s formal inventiveness, as well as its realist orthodoxy, needs to be emphasised.

SOCIAL REALISM

In Australian criticism since the 1940s, the term 'social realism' has overlapped with 'socialist realism'. But while the latter is derived from an explicit theory, the former is rather the result of a *lack* of theory, although the term was frequently deployed. The difficulty is that its meaning appears to be self-evident, concealing assumptions about the ways in which art reflects life. It becomes a way of not talking about language and politics, for it conceals the variety of realist solutions to the problem of relating artistic form and political or documentary purpose.

The ambiguous status of Kylie Tennant's work in the Australian canon is symptomatic of ambiguities in the concept. Her novels have been described as examples of 'social realism' and 'the sociological novel'.[30] Perhaps they do resemble sociology in concentrating on a group of characters primarily in their social relations. However the social realism of her novels is anything but self-evident. Documentary and low-life modes—comic types, multiple characters and episodes, and picaresque structures—are mixed and reclaimed for a new kind of popular narrative.

We can see this process in *Tiburon* (1935), in its description of the play 'The Mackoniculls of Kilmuckie'.[31] This episode has been used as an example of Tennant's lack of 'art'—although praised for its humour, the scene has been criticised for its irrelevance.[32] The play itself is a terrible mishmash of music hall and melodrama. Yet it is a success, and not merely because of the vulgarity of its audience. The reader joins in the carnival, as the play's sentimental conventions are constantly subverted by breaches of artistic decorum which make a low comedy out of what would otherwise have been high melodrama. This play can be compared with another, a modernist 'little theatre' play which contrasts unfavourably with the sheer excess of 'The Mackoniculls of Kilmuckie'—'the heroine … had done nothing but lie on a green satin couch uttering aphoristic and charming words while the players fell in love with her' (275). We can read *Tiburon* itself through this contrast, as redeeming the artifice of certain popular forms by its own comedy and excess, while subverting the artifice of other sentimental and highbrow forms.

Subversive qualities are found in the most unlikely places: in one character's stubbornness or vulgarity or in another's sentimental verse. But the comic perspective of the narrator allows vulgarity to express originality, and sentimentality to express a desire for beauty, both in opposition to the power of convention and class. What have been seen as Tennant's strong working-class sympathies might be seen more broadly as a principle of resistance to institutionalised power which finds its figures in the dispossessed and the misfits (not simply the proletariat). Again there is a sense of fiction being opened up to what it had previously excluded, as the novel breaks down distinctions between the documentary and the aesthetic. *Tiburon* shifts the conventions of the realist novel to allow its so-called subplots to crowd onto centre-stage.

Brian Matthews has analysed the documentary aspects of *The Battlers* and shown how the novel's descriptions can be 'intensely ideological'.[33] A strong protest is implied throughout Tennant's fiction against a social and ethical system which produces a dispossessed class and then blames it for being dispossessed. This protest is also expressed in a satirical mode aimed at utopian or idealist systems of thought—from institutionalised charity to eugenics—which are exposed as self-perpetuating systems of power. Communists, clergymen and capitalists all become targets, while in the economy of the novels 'the battlers' can become figures of rebellion or independence, less because of their virtues than their outcast status (which is linked in *The Battlers* with the 'real Australia'). All utopian and institutionalised systems are comically subverted, including those of art itself.

Tennant's 'social realism' cannot be seen simply, in Adrian Mitchell's terms, as reproducing 'the unruly manner of documentary' or 'the false realism, the factitiousness, of the popular fiction of the period'.[34] In these criticisms, her work is caught between the demand for an art that is true to life and the demand for an overriding formal unity. Tennant's fiction is calculated to violate expectations of organic form. On one hand it is structured so as to create the artistic *illusion* of 'the unruly manner of documentary'. On the other, like Furphy's *Such is Life*, the move beyond conventional plot means that the narratives comically exploit their own unavoidable 'factitiousness'; that is, their mediations between different formal (and ideological) options.

LIVING IN HISTORY

Many novels of the period could bear the epigraph Prichard gave to *Intimate Strangers*: 'The international chaos, the social chaos, the ethical and spiritual chaos, are aspects of one and the same disorder.' This understanding motivates Eleanor Dark's *Waterway* (1938) and *The Little Company*, and M. Barnard Eldershaw's *Tomorrow and Tomorrow*. The dynamic of these novels, however, is less the struggle between capitalist and working-class than a humanist struggle between optimism and despair, a crisis of faith in human nature. For Gilbert Massey in *The Little Company*: 'This, finally, was the issue which split the world in two, split nations, split parties, split friendships and families—do you believe in human beings, or don't you?'[35]

The interior monologue, the primary mode of Dark's novels, provides a means of linking the 'international chaos' and the 'ethical chaos', registering the pressure of social upheaval on the individual psyche, and showing character itself as a complex of ethical, political and spiritual discourses. The novels expand 'inwardly' as each character's memories and reflections are unfolded. Characters are shown to be 'living in history', as Marty puts it in *The Little Company* (38), as history is compressed into critical moments in individual lives. The effect of compression and expansion in *Tomorrow and Tomorrow* is even more remarkable: on a single day in the twenty-fourth century Knarf reads out his vast historical novel of Australia. The novel's futuristic fiction is its means of comprehending an apocalyptic present. It is dated 1940–42, and the crisis it expresses, of civilisation collapsing from within, is close to that expressed in *The Little Company*, set in 1941–42; close also to Vance Palmer's 'Battle', in the 1942 'Crisis' issue of *Meanjin*.[36]

Waterway is also apocalyptic, in its double climax. A march of unemployed gets entangled with a society wedding, with violent consequences which arise less from political consciousness than from a 'return of the repressed' in the organism of society. Then a ferry carrying many of the novel's main characters is sunk in a collision. This is a disturbing scene, because although it cannot be turned into any simple allegory it nevertheless fully dramatises the novel's sense of social and ethical chaos: 'a happening so monstrous and cataclysmic and yet so utterly formless.'[37] This phrase expresses what Dark shares with the more explicitly political writers, but also what distinguishes her liberal humanist view.

The source of the novel's power, as with *The Little Company*, is its ability to signify disorder simultaneously on different levels—in the psyche, in society, and in nature. The novel's framing character, Oliver Denning, provides the underlying structural and thematic figures of the narrative:

> It seemed a very fair slice of time, this barely recordable blink in humanity's
> existence! And, crossing your own life, it held many other lives, touching, running
> parallel for a little while, closely woven, breaking away, so that you could never …
> study a life solely your own, but always a life thrumming and alive with contacts,
> reacting to them in harmony and discord like the strings of a violin. (13)

The figures of harmony and discord link relations between the conscious and unconscious in the human organism, relations between individuals and classes in the social organism, and finally the relations between civilisation and nature. A sense of Australian history as the story of civilisation in discord and harmony with its environment—the subject of Dark's *The Timeless Land* (1941)—provides *Waterway* with its final resolution. The discord of 'turbulent human life' is displaced by the image of harmony between the 'eternal' and 'its people'.

The Little Company engages more directly than *Waterway* with contemporary history and political, specifically communist, doctrine. It is also more intensely self-reflexive, one aspect of what Modjeska describes as its 'dialectical' structure.[38] Rather than a single, authoritative viewpoint the novel provides a series of dialogues between different ideologies and different ways of seeing, from communism to moralism. The novel positions itself in the midst of crisis, between the old order and the new, a moment represented by the writer's block which both the central characters, novelists Gilbert and Marty, suffer. The harmonies possible in Gilbert's early novels are fractured by a new historical awareness, beyond mere fiction: 'Characters … which he would once have regarded as mere fictional material could no longer be regarded as such when they had become manifestations of a social disorder'.[39] For both, a new kind of fiction is projected, linking an individual story with mass historical change; for Gilbert, optimistically, it would be 'the old but always new story of the dynamic of humanity … expressed in terms of one obscure life' (241).

In *Tomorrow and Tomorrow* social crisis is comprehended in similar terms: 'the microcosm of the individual reflected the macrocosm of society' (317). Like *The Little Company*, its politics lie in reflections on its own status as historical fiction. Two notions of history are contrasted in Knarf, the novelist, and Ord, an archaeologist, contrasting humanist and materialist ideologies, the very crisis for liberal intellectuals in the 1930s and 1940s. Knarf and his son swing the debate towards humanism and 'liberty', but the narrative's own historical excursions suggest that liberal humanism 'needs' the explanatory power of a materialist system. The novel, indeed, leaves open the question as to which mode is the utopian one.[40] Like Dark's novels, *Tomorrow and Tomorrow* finally looks beyond politics to the land itself to maintain faith in human nature, concluding: 'The earth remains.'

POST-WAR REALISM

In the post-war period, a diverse range of realist fiction appeared from such writers as Vance Palmer, Leonard Mann, Donald Stuart, Gavin Casey, and F.B. Vickers. Some of the most striking novels of the period, however, are identifiably communist novels: Prichard's trilogy, Frank Hardy's *Power Without Glory*, Ralph de Boissiere's *Crown Jewel* (1952), Judah Waten's *The Unbending* (1954), and Dorothy Hewett's *Bobbin Up*. In these we see a continuation of themes and structural effects already noted: the desire to expand the scale of fiction to invoke vast historical movements; the foregrounding of conventionally excluded subjects; and the juxtaposition of documentary, novelistic, and political discourses.

Both *Power Without Glory* and *The Unbending* reveal divisions between a documentary mode which tends towards chronicle and historical specificity, and a self-consciously literary mode which tends towards plot and universal significance. Critics have frequently rescued *Power Without Glory* from itself, as it were, by reading it as a study of power, universalising its story against the grain of the novel's historical specificity and class analysis.[41] The narrative frequently turns to a 'history voice', directed at a contemporary audience and breaking down the effect of aesthetic autonomy. It can be contrasted in this respect with Dal Stivens's *Jimmy Brockett* (1951), a fable of corruption that yet makes no claim to a specific history, one that the reader *shares* (the claim *Power Without Glory* makes). However, *Power Without Glory* also shares the aspirations of its critics towards the traditionally perceived universal qualities of literature, especially in the ethical language of its characterisation of John West, the central figure representing power and corruption. The novel cannot fuse its two modes, but their juxtaposition has its own narrative and political force in creating a tension between moral and historical perspectives.

The Unbending draws together documentary and a more classic realist form. On one level the novel's realism is characterised by its scepticism towards rhetoric: its prose is unadorned, in characters reticence is preferred to fluency, and story-telling itself is shown to be dangerously seductive and utopian. At the same time, the novel includes the rhetoric of radical propaganda in speeches and quotations from documents, again less to lay down a correct political line than to include perspectives that realist novelistic discourse could not otherwise include. The novel juxtaposes utopian images (including images of revolution) with alternative political perspectives, in a longer historical view. Throughout, foreigners are figuratively linked with the working-class, especially with the radical International Workers of the World (the 'Wobblies'). We see both migrant Hannah Kochansky and labourer George Feathers gaining *speech* in opposition to dominant religious and patriotic languages that would otherwise silence them. In concentrating on these marginal groups, the novel offers an alternative history of class conflict: the Wobblies, not the Anzacs, provide the initiating moment of a modern national history. As A.D. Hope recognised, in an appreciative critique, the novel desires classic realist form, but also to go beyond 'bourgeois' realism.[42] It remains divided, but its effectiveness is due in part to the way it is forced to highlight divisions between different rhetorical styles.

Bobbin Up, by contrast, recalls earlier radical fiction because of its narrative focus on 'myriad lives woven and interwoven' (67) and a collage-like juxtaposition of scenes.[43] The novel's formal inventiveness is again an aspect of foregrounding conventionally excluded subjects: politics, the everyday lives and dreams of an inner-city working class, especially women, and, above all, desire. The novel is rich in different voices, sensuous and rhythmic, contrasting with the neutral prose of other post-war realist writers:

'My heart was achin' that night at Harry's … plentya booze and the jazz, the jazz …' hot and sweet and restless, dust and sweat and sand and sea, shuffling feet and moths sizzling against the fairy lights … 'Another day older and deeper in debt'. (38)

The novel targets sentimental romance, linked here with consumer society. Against which, as Veronica Brady has suggested, there is 'a letting loose of desire in general and in particular of the desires of young women—normally taboo in patriarchal society'.[44] It could be argued that most of the male social realist writers cut themselves off from this most powerful fictional language for representing social crisis and *political* desire. The erotic and the unconscious were marginalised as inessential to the political, as 'merely subjective'. *Bobbin Up*, as Brady suggests, is able to show 'lively, defiant, sensuous young men and women fighting to take possession of themselves, their bodies, their desires, their hopes in a world intent on alienating them'.

All the novels mentioned can be placed in a broad category of realism. This discussion has argued for their diversity and, indeed, their modernity. In the face of successive social crises which appear to redefine history and reality itself, the forms of realist representation are constantly reinvented. A desire to expand and even violate the limits of fiction distinguishes each of these texts—few of which until recently have received sustained critical attention.

'CURRENT HISTORY LOOKS APOCALYPTIC'
Barnard Eldershaw, Utopia and the Literary Intellectual

'It is certainly the fate of every Utopia to be more or less misread.'[1] So claimed H.G. Wells, speaking not about the simplicity of the reading public, but about the complexities of the utopian genre. In this essay I want to read M. Barnard Eldershaw's *Tomorrow and Tomorrow and Tomorrow* as a utopian novel, or to misread it, perhaps, in terms of a utopian discourse that the novel itself disavows.

A primary effect of reading *Tomorrow and Tomorrow* through its utopian frame is to foreground questions of genre, questions which have been only furtively present in its critical reception to date. But my concern is not to reclaim the novel from any scandalous misreadings. The text sanctions the broadly nationalist and realist perspectives through which it has been read, and, in itself, privileges the *novel* as a form over the utopia. Further, its utopian frame has always been recognised, if only as a necessary contrivance, a mere container, or as weak prophecy. My modest claim is that there are other ways of reading the utopian genre, and thus of reading this novel's relationship to it. Less modestly, my argument is not just about a single novel but about a specific ideology of the novel current in mid-twentieth century Australia, a specific formation of literary intellectuals, and a discourse on culture which I will describe as utopian.

H.G. Wells, writer of utopias, appears in *Tomorrow and Tomorrow* as God. More precisely, in the delirious dreams of a fictional character, God takes on the features of Wells, then George Bernard Shaw, then Winston Churchill with a Hitler moustache.[2] Utopian rationalist becomes Fabian becomes conservative demagogue then fascist dictator. The character who dreams is himself a utopian, 'possessed of millennial longings', desiring universal happiness and 'peace without socialism'. But God, as H.G. Wells, offers only 'the Law of Cause and Effect'. This unlikely scene, in short, speaks of rationality, materialism, community, social change and historical process, terms which serve equally to define the utopian terrain and the faultlines of mid-century liberalism. In summoning the name of Wells, the episode also summons a potential generic referent. Finally, the character's delirium invites us into what is a distinctive 'period' sense of social crisis, the sense that 'current history looks apocalyptic' (in Marjorie Barnard's eloquent phrase).[3]

Jill Roe has argued that *Tomorrow and Tomorrow* 'is neither utopian nor anti-utopian'.[4] My claim is that if this is the case it is so only because the novel is *both* utopian and anti-utopian. *Tomorrow and Tomorrow* can be situated thematically on the utopian terrain; that is, it can be read productively through a grid of categories which thematise the key questions for late-nineteenth and twentieth century utopian thinking: the nature of true community; the application of reason and science to social institutions and ethical questions; the centralised, cooperative reorganisation of production and distribution; and the recasting of work and leisure. Similarly, we can plot a characteristic utopian critique of capitalism in the novel's thematisation of alienated labour, competition, production for profit, and mass consumption. From the many possible examples I choose an obvious one from the words of the novel's twentieth-fourth century novelist, Knarf:

Civilisation was loaded with an insufferable burden, the wrong sort of plenty … Competition from being a means become an end. Man building his life in repetitive images from bargain sale to war, from competitive breadwinning to competitive nationalism. (90)

To say that *Tomorrow and Tomorrow* articulates these themes is scarcely contentious; to say they constitute its primary discourse, and to refer this to utopianism, is probably more so. Still, to make even the former claim is to defer expressive or nationalist readings. But thematics here are only weak generic markers. We need to travel further into the utopian terrain.

While it cannot be maintained that *Tomorrow and Tomorrow* is purely a literary utopia, or a pure dystopia, it can be argued that utopias are generically impure. Literary utopias have been described in recent genre theory as threshold or boundary texts, 'taxonomically ambiguous' works, 'designed to resonate between opposing genres and interpretations'.[5] As well as playing tricks with the boundaries between fact and fiction—in order to claim, for example, that the incredible future is simple and real while the real present is simply incredible; or, as in the case of *Tomorrow and Tomorrow*, to claim that fiction is history and history fiction—utopias typically combine didactic and novelistic modes of narrative with satire, essay and allegory, often without much attempt at a (realist) synthesis. Bakhtin tells us that we should not assume the novel form's homogeneity or naturalism either; but the hierarchy of discourses and the techniques of composition are differently ordered between the novel and the utopia, and the fact that we hesitate in certain cases between the two categories helps make the point.

A utopian reading of *Tomorrow and Tomorrow*, then, will not be surprised to find generic faultlines (in one sense it will produce them). But previous readings of the novel, or at least readings within the domain of literary criticism, have instead synthesised as much as possible of its narrative into a realist novelistic discourse, thus rendering its portrayal of a twenty-fourth century society as at best 'necessary machinery', at worst mere fantasy. For H.M. Green:

> The picture of the Depression … make[s] the book; but the other part is by
> contrast unconvincing, though it provides a suitable background and the necessary
> machinery: the people of Knarf's world … are not much more than abstract figures
> in a fantastic film.[6]

(The final reference is intriguing: is Green thinking of Charlie Chaplin or Fritz Lang, appropriate genre references after all?) Green is responding to the text's own centralising of realist fictional modes, but he does not see the curious status this accords the novel's futuristic tale, as at once necessary and extraneous; he does not consider the work as one 'designed to resonate between opposing genres and interpretations'.

Readings of the novel from outside the domain of literary criticism, reading it as history, politics or sociology, have been no more comfortable with its generic mix: '*Tomorrow and Tomorrow* is a hard book to write about because one is never quite sure whether the authors expect their anticipation of social and political events to be regarded as accurate prognostication or not'.[7] While responding to the novel's discourse on history and politics in ways that the literary critics find difficult, the 'non-literary' commentators have also sought a kind of historical coherence that the novel cannot provide (but cannot avoid intimating or imitating).

To say that *Tomorrow and Tomorrow* is *not* utopian, I take it, is to say that the novel does not offer its future society as blueprint, prophecy or 'nostalgia for the future'. This is clearly the case. To say that the novel is not *anti*-utopian is to say that it does not reject all projects for imagining better communal forms. This is also the case, although less clearly. Before turning to the novel directly, I want to insert some remarks about the genre of utopian fiction, first to suggest that *Tomorrow and Tomorrow* is less *unlike* a utopian fiction than it has looked; second, to suggest the discursive space that utopias occupy.

Critics have recently argued that modern utopian fictions ask to be read not as blueprints but as critique. This is scarcely a remarkable observation, though a necessary one given the bad critical press that utopian fictions have generally received, as bad novels or bad politics. More important is the argument that the utopia's critical dimension is a function of its very fictionality. Utopian fictions depend less on converting readers to a program than on 'defamiliarisation', placing the reader in a dialectical situation 'on the very boundary between an unacceptable social reality and an impossible utopian dream'.[8] In Darko Suvin's words, 'utopia is … a method rather than a state, it cannot be realised or not realised—it can only be applied'.[9] Such readings turn utopian fictions from closed didactic forms into open dialogic ones, with particular attention to their characteristically weak framing devices. Elsewhere, critics have underlined the modern utopian fiction's generic proximity to satire rather than pastoral, hence its concern with reason. The utopian project envisions what Raymond Williams calls a 'willed transformation'; it is humanist and *historical*. Thus modern utopias (and dystopias) are characteristically set not in another place but in another time: they represent 'our familiar country transformed by specific historical change'.[10] Emergent tendencies within contemporary society are taken as foundational of a total social transformation.

These perspectives illuminate the method of *Tomorrow and Tomorrow* and situate it discursively. Its future society is one of ordered simplicity, rationally planned production and distribution, and a 'world federation of economic non-national states "each composed of a number of cells or communes"' (223). The function of such descriptions as a critique of capitalism is clear: the future society is without class divisions, war, over-production, profit, exploitation and competition. Crucially, these utopian themes also allow the novel to talk explicitly at the level of structure and system, and to incorporate abstract modes of historical explanation. To read this part of the novel in a generic sense as utopian is not to be committed to taking its future society as blueprint or prophecy.

It is not contradictory to go on to suggest that a dystopian perspective prevails in the novel. *Tomorrow and Tomorrow* is written mid-way between Aldous Huxley's *Brave New World* and George Orwell's *1984*. Like them it shows a technocratic society managed by a specialist elite; the practice of eugenics; a lack of creative, useful labour; a reduced, impotent future literature; and a rebellion against utopian well-being (including the characteristic dystopian scene in which a 'ruler' explains the bases of the new society to the leading rebel). The key generic point here is that dystopias emerge 'within the structures' of utopian fiction, characteristically as inversions of utopian themes.[11] Like utopias, dystopias represent our familiar country transformed by specific historical change; no less than utopias, they function as critiques of the present. In *Tomorrow and Tomorrow*, for example, the technocratic future depends as much for its recognition on contemporary practices in capitalist society as on any possible future socialism.

Dystopias and utopias, then, are more like each other generically than either is like the realist novel, so perhaps it is not surprising after all to find the two modes together in the one fiction. Indeed we can speak of the utopian bases of dystopian critique, and I will be doing so later in relation to Barnard Eldershaw's novel. These genre relations have a specific history. Dystopias represent the utopian agenda rewritten under the twin pressures of, first, the contemporary success and failure of capitalism (mass consumption on one side, Depression on the other); and, second, the contemporary success and failure of socialism (achieved revolution on one side, totalitarianism on the other). Fascism provided a further axis. Was it the antithesis or the logical extension of capitalism—or of socialism? Versions of all three political futures, capitalist, socialist and fascist, could give rise to dystopian images of state bureaucracy. To sum up, we might say that dystopias represent a resistance to all those aspects of contemporary 'mass' society and discourses about society which disturbed liberal notions of the primacy of the individual.

To re-read *Tomorrow and Tomorrow* in terms of the utopian genre is not to say that it *is* a utopia, but rather to activate a set of relationships between genres. Generic definitions involve a series of like/unlike statements. As Anne Freadman has written, 'what we do with genres is not to know them inherently, but to know—"tell", or enact—the differences *between them*'.[12] Our critical practice, then, might be to split the novel into its array of narrative and rhetorical modes rather than attempt to synthesise them. Our primary axis will be the ways in which utopian fiction is like/unlike the novel. Modern utopian fictions have depended on being read as 'not novels'—read adjacent to and against bourgeois realism—although they must equally signal their likeness/unlikeness to other non-fictional prose forms including political theory, propaganda and history. Utopian fiction partly reproduces, partly violates novelistic decorum, violating in the degree of abstraction or didacticism it seeks to make explicit. It draws on our novel reading competencies but only in order to draw us to quite un-novelistic ends. Dystopias might be said to reverse this procedure.

Tomorrow and Tomorrow multiplies such differences through its structure of frames and inversions. The futuristic name of Knarf as an 'artificial' inversion of Frank (a good word for realism?) is itself a generic marker. The novel needs its utopian supplement in order to get outside novelistic discourse—to find an abstract or totalising language—but it also needs to subsume 'mere' utopianism in order to make its claim on history, that is as more than 'mere' fiction. Thus the novel within the novel comes to frame its own frame. But this internal novel, the story of the twentieth century, is itself fragmented by its realist burden to incorporate 'the whole story'. It thus produces its own supplements, like the 'starving poet of King's Cross', one among a range of characters who say what the internal novel cannot say in its own voice. Indeed much of the complexity of *Tomorrow and Tomorrow* arises from the way that within it novelistic discourse is both one mode among others and an over-arching, totalising mode. At the same time, utopianism is discovered not simply as the text's superstructure but at the heart of the internal realist historical novel as well.

A generic grid for the reading of *Tomorrow and Tomorrow* also suggests the conditions of possibility for its writing and the discursive constraints generating its distinctive mix of forms. Utopianism, I would argue, becomes an irresistible option in so far as it mediates between a novelistic language that is primarily ethical, a liberal language of universal principles, and a materialist political-historical language. At the manifest level, for example, it can be seen that the novel's future society is not wishful or wistful dreaming but an elaboration of materialism, in various senses of the term, including a political one. Less manifestly, the novel can be read as an extended dialogue with communism; not with Marxist philosophy as such, but with certain historical scenarios. Sid Warren, the novel's revolutionary, never articulates theory but instead signifies the force of historical inevitability, 'apocalypse now'.

The urgent sense of present social crisis defined a significant group of literary intellectuals in Australia in the 1930s and 1940s. While, on one level, this was a considered and historicised response to the manifest problems of contemporary politics and social relations, the sense of crisis was also generated by the very terms within which liberalism conceived of politics, society and the individual. The crisis is grasped in terms of a breakdown of social consensus, a division between individuals and between nations, and, in what is in many ways the fundamental dialectic, a division between the intellectuals (the 'little company') and the people. Instead of consensus and community there is the massifying impetus of modern society. This contemporary social history is perceived, in evolutionary terms, as an inevitable result of the logic of capitalism. Such a history produces a sense that the crisis is *total*, not the result of bad management but of a system fundamentally rotten from its ethics to its economics. This in turn gives rise to projections of total change, 'the death of the old world and the birth of the new'. Hence the apocalyptic look of 'current history'. Diagnosis and cure are never far from the realms of utopian thinking.

Liberalism discovers a crisis in its categories of historical and social explanation, above all within its central modes of relating individual to society, and it is most sensitive to these challenges to its own certainties along those borders where it meets materialist history and politics. One of the symptomatic expressions of this crisis was the image of an excess of discourses or an 'orgy of ideologies' (138), as ethical, political and historical languages appeared increasingly fragmented and disparate. As Marjorie Barnard put it, retrospectively:

> There was a confusion of ideologies and we sought among them for some sort of intellectual salvation.
>
> … I was, and remain, a 19th century liberal. This philosophy had passed into my blood and bones and now I found it inadequate. I read and pondered and could find nothing between Christian pacifism and communism that offered me the intellectual support I needed to face the ominous future. To be eclectic in a vacuum was no help at all.[13]

But discourse abhors a vacuum. It is in the gap between pacifism and communism that a utopian discourse arises, to mediate between universal ends and historical means. It is also in this gap between idealism and materialism that the form of the novel is re-defined as a particular mode of knowledge or technique for knowing. Barnard continues, in the article quoted above: 'I transmuted my doubts from the intellectual to the creative sphere and I found a quite illogical release in stating the whole problem … in a novel instead of in an ideology, creatively instead of politically.'

For Marjorie Barnard and Flora Eldershaw, for Eleanor Dark, Vance and Nettie Palmer and others, who together define a distinct formation of literary intellectuals, the novel came to be not just one art form among others, but art's privileged mode. It was the novel alone that could contain, could both include and order, an uncontrollable excess of ideologies. It was the novel's very project to synthesise the disparate ethical, historical and political knowledge of the present. Above other literary forms and modes of knowledge, the novel could reconnect the individual and the social, the humanist and the materialist, by speaking of both at once. So the great insight of the period's major novels is that expressed in *Tomorrow and Tomorrow*: 'The microcosm of the individual reflected the macrocosm of society' (317).

But each insight brings its own blindness. What was enabling in this conceit was a political sense of culture, acted out for example in the formation and activities of the Fellowship of Australian Writers.[14] What was disabling we might call a cultural sense of politics. In this mode the work of art, the novel, comes to stand as an ideal model of human society itself. The novel stands for the culture, culture for the totality of social relations.

It was precisely around a specific discourse on culture that this formation of literary intellectuals could define itself in a shifting, burgeoning intellectual field comprising journalists, academics, economists, administrators, communist and liberal commentators, and, of course, other novelists. The problem in the 1930s and 1940s for these intellectuals was not how to create an Australian literature out of nothing or how to initiate Australian writing in a cultural desert, although this was often how it was expressed. It was less a problem of absence than of abundance, of the multiplication of print, in newspapers, commercial magazines, popular novels (Ion Idriess, Frederick Thwaites, Frank Clune), and also the cinema.[15] The central task in the project of defining the role of the (literary) intellectual in such a context was that of carving out a space for the 'serious novel': the novel that was historical without being mere history, political without being mere politics, and, first and last, fiction but not mere fiction—art but not mere artistry.

There are a number of careers parallel to Barnard Eldershaw's—Dark's, for example, through *Waterway* to *The Little Company*. What needs to be stressed is the newness and contingency of such novels rather than their connection to any established local tradition. Such an expanded conception of the novel and the novelist had to become possible, and it would not remain possible for long. It is fascinating in this respect to find Barnard, already author of nine books, writing to Nettie Palmer in 1941: 'I'm going to write a book—for the first time in my life, a book. And it's going to be called *Tomorrow and Tomorrow and Tomorrow*.'[16] But if this was, in a special sense, Barnard's first book, it was also her last novel. As if fiction were no longer adequate to the task or because its demands were impossibly totalising, her subsequent books were all works of history.[17]

The totalising conception of the novel was indeed both its success and its failure, a dialectic present in *Tomorrow and Tomorrow* at the level of its form, and also self-reflexively in recurrent dialogues about the relations between history and fiction, especially between the characters Knarf and Ord. The ambiguous modernism of *Tomorrow and Tomorrow* itself—its contemporaneity, its nostalgia for nineteenth century realism, its willingness to experiment—is expressed in the conception of the novel that emerges in these dialogues: the novel as both a provisional, open-ended form, and as organic form. The 'antique form of the novel' (its antiquity in the twenty-fourth century is its newness in the twentieth) is described by Ord as:

> the typical form of the period; large, rich, confused, intricate, it needs an elastic, free, inclusive form … The novel is the organ of becoming, the voice of a world in flux … The novel was a mouth, sucking avidly at life. A Protean form for an age out of control … The enormous clash and upheaval was reflected in chaotic literature. The surge of novels—what was that but an attempt to get the chaos of circumstances into some sort of shape, using every method of attack, every ingenuity. A natural organic reaction. (79–81)[18]

The novel, so conceived, becomes impossible by its very ambition, as always the deferral of a larger organic whole. As a consequence, the attempt to tell the whole story is dispersed into the piecemeal narratives of history. The complex formal structure of *Tomorrow and Tomorrow* expresses just such a dispersal, as indeed does Barnard's subsequent career as a writer. The only possible place of recuperation is the realm of culture, but like the novel form itself, 'culture' promises a totality that is always deferred, always there but never quite there, and so prone to states of crisis.

Culture in its fullest sense for these writers signified community: a shared ethos, a collective history, and close identification between readers and writers. It is populist and consensual, although (therefore) always ambiguous as to the role of the intellectual who is at once communal spokesperson and isolated conscience, an ambiguity represented in Knarf's self-absorption even as he speaks for the whole of a collective Australian history. This very ambiguity generates an organic notion of culture (or the literature which stands in for it), defined in all-embracing terms against technology, modernity, and institutions. Dymphna Cusack wrote:

Cultural deficiency is a revelation of the fact that our whole basic life has failed. The whole principle of an industrialised community is against the development of the artist. There seems to be no place for him. Our values are wrong. They are turning to his regimentation, his standardisation …

It is necessary that the State should exist for man's fullest development … It is only by clinging to truth and liberty that we can have any hope of building a world in which men and women can become full human beings, and in which culture can come again into its full heritage.[19]

Bracketing off nationalist imperatives for the moment enables us to see that the project of culture in this sense is to reconcile divisions within the individual and society which are invoked as symptomatic of industrial/technological civilisation (to reclaim 'full human beings'), and it is by speaking in the name of this project that the literary intellectuals defined a distinctive 'culture' of their own. This discourse did provide a kind of politics and a kind of aesthetics. Most importantly, it provided, or prompted, a history. Yet it is centrally an ethical language which has as its *telos* the formation of the 'exemplary persona' of the literary intellectual. Hence the choice of authors as protagonists in *Tomorrow and Tomorrow* and *The Little Company*; hence the ethical vocabulary of the Palmers' literary criticism; hence Christesen's beautifully utopian description of Vance Palmer:

The poet, the man who sees the whole while others are fumbling round with the parts, has a vision of Australia as it will be some day, a land of noble buildings, of craftsmen and creators, of farmers and pastoralists, 'weaving a natural poetry into their lives', a land leading the world in the tradition of the brotherhood of man.[20]

The organic text can be expressed in the figure of the organic intellectual, who in turn can stand as a figure of the organic community.

At this late stage, let me distinguish between two primary forms of utopianism, the aesthetic and the programmatic. The former proposes a dialectical model of personal and social progress from division to wholeness, to the complete development of individual and society. In the realm of the individual, divisions between, say, the sensuous and the rational are diagnosed and reconciliation is offered in the sphere of culture.

In the social realm, the central division is discovered in the diagnosis of alienated labour, and reconciliation is projected in a sphere of communally-organised production which, in William Morris's terms, will 'win back Art again to our daily labour'.[21] We might quote from the concluding sections of Frank Dalby Davison's 1938 booklet *While Freedom Lives* (Davison later repudiated this work but it stands nevertheless as a *locus classicus* of the 'crisis-reading' of contemporary society):

> That we are at the birth of a new age there can be no doubt ... The new age promises to be better than any humanity has known. With competitive nationalism abolished the basis of intercourse between races would be mutual consideration, as it is between well-bred individuals.
>
> The application of science to industry ensures the practicability of the Greek concept of life in which men, freed from want and uncertainty and too-exacting toil, would have time to cultivate themselves. It is very possible, in the age that draws close to us, that the question, 'What does he do?' will not apply to what a man does for a living, his duty to the State, but to the activities and pursuits of his leisure.
>
> ... [I]n the future the individual will be liberated, set free to be himself, through harmonious relationship to society ...
>
> What has been noted here about the possibilities of the new age is not utopianism.[22]

Davison's projections are, as it were, protected against utopianism because they are based on the 'inevitable', evolutionary processes of history rather than on a willed plan or program. But this is precisely their aesthetic utopian character. The emphasis of aesthetic utopianism is not on rational social planning, but on growth, process, reconciliation and the fully developed human being. Programmatic utopianism, by contrast, emphasises institutional reordering as the basis of social harmony. It takes the form of an all-embracing scheme for the reorganisation of social space and an exhaustive program of social regulation, typically founded on a new philosophical, economic or ethical principle which promises to purge existing society of its contradictions and rebuild it according to a single rational plan.[23]

My argument, in these terms, is that *Tomorrow and Tomorrow* resists certain materialist and systemic forms of sociological thinking, or at least resists their programmatic utopian claims to completeness, but does so from an aesthetic utopian or 'culturalist' position. 'Economic determinism,' says Knarf, 'never explained more than half the process' (91).[24] At the same time, precisely because of the organicism of this position, the novel aspires to the systemic and abstract dimension of programmatic and materialist explanation. But the foundation of the novel's own social critique is equally singular, its multiple images of alienation generated by the single aesthetic utopian dialectic of complete development. This is expressed at the individual and social levels in images of self-formation or self-determination. Apparent ambiguities in the novel can be resolved in terms of this utopian dialectic. For example, the ambiguity of the novel's attitudes to reason—such that the twentieth century is (on the whole) criticised as irrational, the twenty-fourth century as over-rational—is precisely the effect of the dialectic of complete development and its ideal of reconciliation in the realm of culture.

On one level, there is an alternative and counter-utopian theme in the novel, embedded in a set of figurative links around images of 'the earth', connoting the instinctual or pre-social (and 'pre-utopian'). The novel's descriptions of Aboriginal life, for instance, are less utopian than Arcadian, appropriately set in a 'timeless landscape'. The question of true community, which is one form of complete development, is conceived in the novel in terms partly of the relationship between individual and society, partly that between nature or environment and civilisation. These two modes of understanding produce two different inflections of organicism. One is historicist and utopian, circling round figures of co-operative, self-determining forms of social organisation and non-alienated labour. The other is 'universalist', possibly Arcadian, and finds its imagery in nature. The former offers projections of individual and communal perfectibility; the latter is sceptical of any *social* formation when measured against nature. But both provide a fund of images—pastoral or utopian—of reconciliation, wholeness and harmony (or their loss), images projected into the past or the future, in which the individual can stand for the communal and *vice versa*.

The negative representations of both present and future society are predicated upon the ideal of wholeness. Capitalism is figured in terms of division at the level of society and individual. We can see this in one of the novel's key sites, the city. Knarf's novel begins with an urban crowd scene: 'It was all without pattern or direction; no common purpose or thought held the crowd together, an infinite crisscross of destinies, in the mass illegible and insignificant' (45). This antithesis of true community signifies modern capitalist society as *mass* society, and the novel shares the full burden of this concept with contemporaneous liberal social theory in its totalising critique of the present in terms of alienated labour, mass culture, bureaucratisation, and so on. The city itself is figured as a vast machine, a product of the division of reason and the technological from other human faculties. Through the alternative inflection of organicism, the city is seen as a force of nature evolving out of control towards its own destruction, representing on this side the unbalanced dominance of the irrational.

In the twenty-fourth century we have the Centre, 'so compact where once a great city sprawled' (14). The critique of the system is dominant here, but the underlying models are the same as support the critique of twentieth century capitalism. The divisions of individual and society now extend the diagnosis in terms of specialisation and standardisation, the dominance of the rational and technological, and the lack of self-fulfilling labour or self-determination. Perhaps the key character is Sfax ('facts'): 'specialised brains, no imagination, specialised stupidity' (228). Again the one-sided, alienated individual stands for the one-sided, alienating society.

These linked aspects of the novel's future society disclose the utopian bases of dystopian critique. But we do not need to rely on dystopian inversions to discover positive utopian signs in the novel. These are dispersed throughout the text, and moored to a range of unequal characters; but as the utopian framework of the narrative teaches us that this is not primarily a novel about personality, we enter these various dialogues, characters and images into a larger conceptual framework. The central character of Knarf's novel contrasts the alienations of city life to an earlier experience within a (failed) rural co-operative. Other characters, particularly members of the (failed) Peace Party, provide images of self-determining communities and self-creating labour: 'co-operative efforts of all kinds—men and women working in small groups in their own world' (173); 'the division of government among the people ... co-operating in small bunches for local welfare ... Everyone working, not only in some industry or other, not merely for his daily bread, but at the construction of life' (298). These positive images survive their local failures in the novel. The ideals of true community (which are also ideals of 'independence', of self-formation as well as self-determination) are overtaken by the apocalyptic force of current history, just as the Peace Party is overtaken by the revolutionary movement, but they remain as key points of reference in the novel's larger argument—resonating, for example, in the dystopianism of its future society.

Such utopian imagery of true community can be linked to liberal 'social consensus' theory which envisions a society without class and made without class struggle: 'Changes come so slowly. Like a range of mountains raised out of grains of sand fused together, each grain a living man' (175). Knarf himself envisages change as 'a slow organic growth'. He adds: '[T]he very thing you have to break through is the idea that the whole of life can be tabulated and docketed and served in a machine' (454). Knarf can also insist that 'utopia [is] a scientific possibility' (239) and that 'the road is open to the principle of liberty as never before' (455). But what the novel cannot envisage, through any of its speakers, is a political theory or a set of institutions through which social re-organisation might be articulated. We do not need to commit ourselves to a Marxist dialectic of class in order to identify this absence as utopian; we might point, instead, to the lack of any engagement with the governmental. There is nothing in the novel between the irresistible force of history, which amongst much else consigns the University to its dustbin, and 'a slow organic growth'— or rather, it is between these two perspectives that the discourses of utopianism become irresistible, even when impossible.

To the objection that *Tomorrow and Tomorrow* is only a novel after all, I would reply that that is exactly my point. It is precisely the choice of novel-writing, in this context, and thus the place of novels within a generic or discursive field, that is significant. What novels cannot easily say without becoming un-novel-like is as revealing in this respect as what novels habitually say. The transformations of form in this particular novel, most overtly through its utopian structures, reveal an 'ideology of the novel' which, I've been suggesting, is to be understood in terms of a specific discourse on culture, a discourse which reproduces the features of aesthetic utopianism.

Thus the final site of utopian images in *Tomorrow and Tomorrow* is the figure of the novelist or novel writing. The artwork is the pre-eminent mode of non-alienated, self-creating labour: at once individual and communal, a product of the highest civilisation yet transcending the merely rational or programmatic to unite intellect and senses. This mode of reconciliation simultaneously describes the aesthetic domain of the novel form and the ethical domain of the novelist (the figure of the literary intellectual). It produces the great inclusiveness and 'historical imagination' of *Tomorrow and Tomorrow*, even as it seals the novel's withdrawal from politics and makes it the last of its kind. After the war, after Reconstruction, the voice of culture could no longer speak confidently as the voice of politics; politics was happening elsewhere and the realm of culture appeared increasingly fragmented. Literary criticism would continue to take the literature for the culture, and culture for society. But increasingly, for the literary intellectual, self-formation was a professional not a cultural responsibility.

COMMUNISM AND CARNIVAL
Ralph de Boissiere's
Crown Jewel and its
Australian Context

The Australasian Book Society (ABS) was established in Melbourne in 1952 by a small group of left-leaning writers, unionists and literary supporters. It was inspired in part by the success of Frank Hardy's scandalous novel of Labor betrayal, *Power Without Glory*, which in 1950 had been published independently—and printed secretly—outside the commercial publishing networks. Many of those involved were communists but although the ABS came to operate in accord with Communist Party cultural politics it was never simply a Party front nor did it publish only communist writers or communist texts. For the most part it operated under a broader notion of 'progressive', nationalist or democratic literature.[1]

The objectives of the ABS were literary, nationalist and left-wing, a triad which would produce spectacular internal conflicts especially in the company's early years. For some, its primary purpose was to publish books with a 'progressive social content' which would be unlikely to find a commercial publisher; more narrowly this could be taken as an imperative to publish books for 'worker readers'. For others, literary nationalism rather than working-class realism was paramount, the primary purpose of the ABS being to sustain and expand Australian literature itself, which it was felt was largely being ignored by commercial publishing. Of course the two perspectives converged where the authentic Australian literary tradition was understood to be naturally democratic, realist and vernacular. Literary nationalism, in general, was more prominent than communism in the company's practices and publications.

In this context, one of the intriguing facts in the history of Australian literary nationalism is that the first book published by the ABS was Ralph de Boissiere's 'Trinidadian' novel *Crown Jewel*.[2] (It was paired, for ABS members, with Frank Hardy's *Journey Into the Future*, a late example of the utopian genre of the writer's journey to the Soviet Union.)[3] De Boissiere's novel tells the story of the struggles of Trinidad workers and unemployed against white colonial capitalism in the second half of the 1930s. It was a striking choice for an organisation established to further the publication of Australian books in the progressive democratic tradition of the national literature then claimed by the left.

As Jack Beasley explains, the first selection panel for the ABS list was 'literary' in its qualifications—fiction writers Leonard Mann and Alan Marshall and critic A.A. Phillips. *Crown Jewel* was selected 'for its rather considerable merits, and also because no suitable manuscript of Australian life was available'. Beasley reports that response to the book was positive and 'did not seem to be affected very much by its being a story of people in a strange, far away land'.[4] De Boissiere himself was working part-time for the ABS in this period, addressing meetings in suburban homes and at factories in order to build ABS membership. With its membership base, the ABS could commit to larger print runs than was usual for commercial publishers, especially for a first novel. Three thousand copies of *Crown Jewel* were printed.

In what ways might we consider *Crown Jewel* an 'Australian' novel? In what ways does its provenance or perspectives mark it out as different within its Australian context? De Boissiere was born in Trinidad in 1907 to a middle-class 'creole' family. He began publishing stories in the late 1920s in the emerging local literary magazines, *Trinidad* and the more famous *Beacon*, associated with C.L.R. James, Albert Gomes and Alfred Mendes. In Allan Gardiner's terms, these stories

> have a spaciousness of social context that promises the detailed evocation of Trinidadian society to come in *Crown Jewel*. Although they are still limited to the viewpoint that de Boissiere knew personally, that of relatively well-off creoles,

increasingly they came to measure the impact made on such people of the poverty of the mainly Black, lower sections of Trinidadian colonial society.[5]

De Boissiere began writing the first version of a Trinidadian novel around 1935. According to Gardiner this 'began life as a comedy of manners in which the perspective is again that of the well-off'.[6] But the industrial and political unrest in Trinidad in the late 1930s, particularly strikes in the oil industry and their effects on the political organisation of the Trinidadian working class, profoundly influenced de Boissiere's politics and hence his writing. He recalled, 'When the Trinidad uprising took place in 1937 I knew I was writing the wrong book, that I was writing about nothing'.[7] Already, by this time, he was associated with the Negro Welfare Cultural and Social Association, the militant working-class 'Negro Welfare' of *Crown Jewel*.

The novel was then rewritten and completed during the war, the period of American military 'occupation' of Trinidad which drastically altered social attitudes and broke the hold of British colonialism. De Boissiere recalls a friend sending the manuscript to Knopf in the USA around 1943 where it was promptly rejected with the comment: 'this is a thesis, not a novel'.[8] He left Trinidad for the USA in 1947 to take a course in motor mechanics offered to West Indians, and then, responding to a government advertisement for automobile factory employees in Victoria, migrated with his family to Australia, in December 1947. He worked for a year at the General Motors automobile manufacturing plant in Melbourne before returning to clerical work in order to have time to write. He soon began attending meetings of the Fellowship of Australian Writers in Melbourne, and after encountering Frank Hardy he joined the left-wing Realist Writers' Group. He joined the Communist Party of Australia (CPA) in 1951.

The Realist Writers comprised communist and left-leaning writers or would-be writers committed to realism and literature's role in social change. Members included Hardy, Eric Lambert, Walter Kaufmann, John Morrison, Bill Wannan, David Martin and Judah Waten, to mention only the better known. The sense of the newness and expanding strength of this contemporary realist project should not be under-estimated, allied as it was to a post-war optimism about progressive social change and emergent cultural nationalism, all of which could be seen to fall naturally within the project of communism too. Something of this enthusiasm can be seen in an editorial from the *Realist Writer* in March 1953 reporting on the previous year's activities:

> Frank Hardy—*Journey into the Future* completed and published; *Power Without Glory* translated and sold overseas in scores of thousands … Ralph de Boissiere—*Crown Jewel* published here and accepted for translation in Polish and German; *The Invaders* [i.e., *Rum and Coca-Cola*] completed; Eric Lambert—*The Veterans* completed; *The Twenty Thousand Thieves* published in three editions in Great Britain; Judah Waten—*Alien Son* published, sold and reprinted, and a novel completed under Commonwealth Literary Fund grant; Walter Kaufmann—*Voices in the Storm* completed (now printing); Nance McMillan—play *Christmas Bridge* completed and played in Sydney, Melbourne and London; Laurie Collinson—play *Traitor Silence* completed; David Martin—with regular publication of verse in working-class press, emerged as the most widely-read contemporary poet in Australia.[9]

This was the context that led to the formation of the ABS and the Realist Writers, a rich and productive context for de Boissiere's rewritten but still unpublished novel. What complicates the picture is that these enthusiasms and achievements coincided with an increased focus among communist writers (and Party officials) on the literary theory of socialist realism.

C.B. Christesen, editor of *Meanjin*, assisted de Boissiere in sending his manuscript to large publishers in London and the USA. At the same time, between 1949 and early 1952, de Boissiere began to rewrite *Crown Jewel* yet again, under the influence, in his own terms, of his contacts with the Australian working class:

> two years in this country had a remarkable effect. You step out of very small, enclosed areas … and you get into a much more developed country where you have a working class which is very experienced over a number of years. You gain a different outlook on life and on your own people. You see possibilities you couldn't see under Crown colony rule, which is based on slavery, on generation upon generation of blacks growing into slavery.[10]

'The effect,' he wrote elsewhere, 'was to give me a heightened appreciation of what West Indian workers were capable of achieving, a clearer realisation of our strengths and weaknesses.'[11] The earlier manuscripts are not available to be compared with the published novel so it is difficult to know exactly what changes were produced by de Boissiere's experience of the Australian working class, or perhaps more precisely his experience of the CPA, the ABS and the Realist Writers. Certainly, de Boissiere was consciously searching for a way to make his writing more fully Marxist; and publication by an independent left-wing Australian publisher rather than a mainstream London house meant thinking of the novel and its readers in a different way.

It is tempting, but almost certainly over-simplifying, to suggest that an original emphasis on the politics of race and British colonialism, arising from de Boissiere's Trinidadian experience, was subordinated to the story of class conflict in the later version. The representation of class and in particular the necessity for militant working-class organisation seems too fundamental to the novel's structure—and to de Boissiere's own historical experience—to be a late innovation; and in any case the politics of race and colonialism remain pervasive in the novel, never separated from the perspectives of class. What we might suggest is that de Boissiere's Australian (and in fact distinctively Melbourne) experience confirmed a particular historical perspective on these class struggles, and made central to the novel the specifically communist theme of the struggle between a reformist 'labour' party (The Workers' Party) and a militant working-class organisation (the Negro Welfare). This was the central theme of Australian communist attempts to 'do' socialist realism, embodied in a series of historical novels in the 1940s and 1950s.[12]

De Boissiere's representation of the 1930s industrial and political struggles allows no positive role for bourgeois nationalist independence or anti-colonial politics. It is in this sense explicitly *not* a nationalist or perhaps even a 'postcolonial' novel. Gardiner argues that the 1952 version of *Crown Jewel* was thereby at odds with the CPA's adherence to Stalin's 'stages' theory of decolonisation, in which a first stage of support for nationalist movements would be followed by the struggle for working-class power.[13] The idea of nationalism, interestingly, is wholly absent from *Crown Jewel*, and while colonialism is the problem it is so primarily as a manifestation of capitalism. Independence is fleetingly mentioned, but the key historical and political issue for the novel is the emergence of militant trade union organisation. In this emphasis, I would argue, the novel was closer to the prevailing local understanding of the communist or socialist realist novel than Gardiner's doctrinal point might suggest.

Certainly at this very moment in the early 1950s the CPA was taking an increasingly close interest in 'cultural matters'. As I have argued elsewhere, it was only in this period after the war that literature and, in particular, the theory of socialist realism, began to carry a serious policy burden in the Party.[14] Only in the fifties was the theory consistently named and defined. Nonetheless, what socialist realism meant in the actual practice of writing was less clear. The historical novel, as Susan Lever has suggested, was one Australian interpretation of how the theory could be put into practice.[15] Hardy's 'Author's Note' to *Power Without Glory* suggests another: showing 'men and women alive in an environment that is peculiarly Australian yet universal, typical of the stage of social history in which we find ourselves'.[16] For de Boissiere himself—*after* the publication of his two Trinidad novels—the 'socialist realist method' meant:

> The depiction of real life and not the fevered dreams of the author's bewildered,
> unhappy mind; the use of the typical to portray reality; the use of the dialectical
> approach in the portrayal of situations and characters; and a humanist attitude
> throughout our work.[17]

What separated socialist realists from the great realist writers of the past was 'the understanding of the objective laws operating in society, or if you like, the contradictions in society' which enabled the socialist writer to show 'the new inevitably rising to take the place of what is old and worn-out'.

Socialist realist theory, then, set broad boundaries by prescribing realist priorities in subject matter and plot, proscribing 'formalism' and 'subjectivism', and promoting 'typicality' and 'positive heroes' (characters and situations which exemplified the true progress of history). The primary task of fiction was to portray the essential characteristics of 'our time'. As a broad policy orientation it seemed clear—realism with a socialist tendency. As a theoretical framework, although abstract enough to bear endless reiteration, it could provide a coherent set of objectives or principles. In practice, however, for the writer confronting the blank sheet of paper, or in de Boissiere's case the always-rewritable manuscript, the issue of how to write a socialist or communist novel was still very much an open question, and it is important to see the debates and 'experiments' that socialist realism occasioned as *productive* of writing and ideas, not merely as ideologically stifling and aesthetically toxic. Socialist realism spoke to needs and aspirations; it articulated a conceptual and historical dimension to the literary. It was precisely this issue of what social(ist) realism might mean, engaged as it was with the question of the nature of the Australian realist tradition, that led to the formation of new writers' groups, new magazines and new publishers.

Indeed, de Boissiere's novel was *early* rather than late in the Australian experience of socialist or communist fiction. While he could involve himself in a lively literary and political milieu which was engaged in the very issues that he had himself been struggling with, there was scarcely a canon of works to 'inherit'. A significant number of Australian writers were associated with communism as Party members, as associates on various cultural and political causes, or through a shared general commitment to the idea of a democratic national tradition; but the explicitly socialist novel was a rare thing. In the early 1950s there was only a handful of local models. Katharine Susannah Prichard's *Working Bullocks* had been published in 1926 and *Intimate Strangers* in 1937. The former had been received as a major achievement by literary nationalists at the time but appears to have largely disappeared from view until its republication in 1957. At this crucial moment in local cold war cultural politics, it soon assumed the role of the great forerunner of Australian socialist realism because of its representation of the 'typical' hero. *Intimate Strangers* never assumed that role, being always compromised by its bourgeois setting.

Closer in time were Prichard's Goldfields Trilogy (1946–50) and Hardy's *Power Without Glory*. These were more typical of post-war socialist fiction than the 'revolutionary romanticism' of earlier radical writing. Both aspired to the qualities of classical realism in its historical, indeed *epochal* mode; even Hardy, whose model was Balzac although his effects were sometimes closer to those of popular fiction.[18] Whereas radical fiction from the 1930s focused on the immediate crisis in contemporary capitalism, the post-war novels took a long historical perspective. While they might still be structured around moments of crisis, these were now historical and seen through the epochal story of the rise of socialism, unionism, class consciousness and eventually, inevitably, communism.

This was the movement of history that the socialist realist category of 'typicality' existed to express and which made the communist novel more than classical realism alone.

In one sense, then, there was only one story for socialist realism to tell—the inevitability of socialism—although its settings and occasions were multiple (Eureka, the rise of Labor, the Depression, or indeed industrial action on Trinidad's oilfields). Closer to the bone of the fiction itself, there were two stories: first, the inevitable betrayal of the workers' interests by social reformist 'labour' parties; and second, the emergence of working-class class consciousness, often expressed as the transition from fatalistic despair to self-conscious purpose or, in the political register, as the need for organisation and discipline over and above political militancy. Strangely perhaps, although it does make sense in terms of the historical trajectory just described, the communist novel seemed happiest in the 'pre-communist' period. Both Prichard's and Hardy's work mostly *pre-figure* the emergence of communist parties or genuine working-class organisations. The story of industrial action is usually the story of a failed strike. The rest, as it were, was up to history.

To this extent, *Crown Jewel* might be seen as an Australian novel (or at least an Australian communist novel). The structuring of his 'pre-communist' story around the two principal themes indicated above might well be what de Boissiere learnt from his Australian milieu, although these were almost inevitable themes in any attempt to turn the narrative of Marxism into the narrative structures of the realist novel. *Crown Jewel* also shares with these slightly earlier Australian novels the incorporation of documentary elements into the fictional texture and the use of a large cast of characters to represent both social density and, more importantly, a range of class and political identities and thus the dynamic of history. At the same time *Crown Jewel* stands apart from the bulk of post-war Australian social or socialist realist fiction—including de Boissiere's own later 'Australian' novel, *No Saddles for Kangaroos*—in a number of crucial ways.

First, as suggested, the novel shows a sensitivity to—more than that, an absolute lived understanding of—the fine calibrations of race and colour as these both confirm and cut across the boundaries of class. This is brilliantly managed in the opening sections of the novel which introduce many of the principal characters. It begins in Dollard and Company's lumber yard where we are first introduced to two clerks, the creole Andre de Coudray, 'descendant of a count and a Negro slave' (430), and Joe Elias, son of a wealthy Syrian merchant. Andre reflects on missing out on a promotion to an imported Englishman; Joe's friends 'were almost all Negroes' (3). Soon after we meet the black worker Jacob, 'always ready to agree with those more powerful than he'; another clerk, the Venezuelan Popito Luna; and Dollard himself, Trinidad-born but English-educated, his wealth based on land as well as commerce (first cocoa, then oil). In the space of a few pages, the calibrations of race, colour and class are shown in their everydayness and interiority, and generalised as the structure of colonial society:

> In the mind of Trinidad 'Society' our people are graded somewhat as follows: first the whites, then the Portuguese, Chinese and Indians; then sundry nationalities, newcomers who have not yet gained an important place in the island's economic life, such as Syrians, Lebanese, East Europeans, Greeks; and last of all, the Negroes. Yet the blacks form the great bulk of the population. They and the Indians are the principal beasts of burden – the Negroes on the oilfields and the cocoa estates, the Indians in the sugar belt.
>
> Andre knew it was an unwritten law that black men must be workers, white men must rule black men, and Englishmen must have the best jobs. Therefore, if one had not the good fortune to be English, one must be white; and if one could not be white, then one must not mix with those more coloured than oneself. But this was what Andre had begun to do ...
>
> About his colour he had always had a sense of guilt that affected him like a spiritual paralysis. A stranger might not guess that Andre was coloured, but a West Indian could always tell. (3)

Class is lived in the modality of race.[19] The narrative shifts easily between the perspectives of history, politics and caste and the domestic and intimate. The novel is memorable for its physical detail, of cooking and making and doing; and for its range of 'accents', hence its range of individuals. We enter Joe's family, Andre's, Luna's; we enter the stories of mothers, daughters, prostitutes, servants, lovers, husbands and neighbours; we move across improvident or desperate poverty, petit-bourgeois aspiration, middle-class snobbery and white governing-class superiority. It is as if the situation of colonial capitalism, at once blatant and blind in its hierarchies of exploitation, enables de Boissiere to present both the structure of the society and the *dynamism* in the structure—the movement, the faultlines, across the hierarchies of class and caste. This is not a quality one would associate with much Australian social or socialist realist fiction.

What makes the novel much more than a thesis is the way in which it shows colonial society involving, and depending upon, the interaction of the different classes and castes. It is interesting to read de Boissiere on what he learnt from pre-revolutionary Russian literature in contrast to Dickens:

> Reading Dickens, I saw the rich and poor just as God had arranged it ... In the Russian pre-revolution novels, however, I found us all mixed up. We were all searching, tormenting others, ourselves tormented by the search for truth. Some were crushed, others rolled over and over in the dust by change. The intelligence stifled in the vast and backward countryside and the sleeping towns ... It was strange that I could find in the work of these writers echoes of my own tiny country where seldom were we out of sight of one another.[20]

Within the strict hierarchies of de Boissiere's Trinidad, too, the classes and races are 'all mixed up' (although we might note that his Chinese are always sly, calculating merchants). White superiority is implicated with black labour and depends upon maintaining shadings of colour and racial registers in between. As the novel shows, and as postcolonial theory has confirmed, white identity depends upon its construction of less-than-fully-civilised others, especially by mobilising race and colour differences even as colonial society multiplies hybridity. De Boissiere has a particular interest in border-line or border-crossing cases, those not quite white enough, such as Andre, Joe or Popito, and those who struggle against their class status: both the positive heroes such as Andre, Le Maitre, leader of the Negro Welfare, Cassie, the black servant girl who becomes a political leader, or Elena Henriques, a poor Venezuelan who comes to identify proudly with colour; and the negative exemplars, Joe, whose desire for a Socialist party turns into self-serving ambition, or Boisson, of French heritage, leader of the quiescent Workers' Party.

Andre and Joe in many ways carry the thematic burden of the narrative. Both are positioned on the racial and class faultline, not-quite-white-enough, certainly not English enough, middle class through old and new money respectively, but excluded from the 'natural' governing class. Although the political message is not subtle, as Andre goes one way and Joe the other, it is buried or embedded in the novel's larger, dispersed multiplicity of narrative lines. Something similar might be said about the other main thematic contrast, between Le Maitre, the heroic representative of the real workers' party, the party for the working class 'in itself', whose message is *organisation*, and Boisson, whose Workers' Party can only tell the working class to accept its lot. Le Maitre's heroic portrait—a type of the socialist realist positive hero—is tempered by the representation of his erotic desire for Cassie which he has learn to express on her terms. These themes are also played out at a psychological level in the recurrent contrast in characters' attitudes and speech between fatalism and purpose, or detachment and commitment. If the English governing upper classes remain cartoon-like in their one-dimensional vanity—except for the Governor himself, a sympathetic figure sacked for his sympathies—perhaps, as Salman Rushdie suggests in a review of the 1981 reprint of the novel, this is because 'colonial whites frequently are mere cartoons of human beings'![21]

Second, *Crown Jewel* is unusual, at least among the fiction of de Boissiere's male contemporaries, in the prominence it gives to its female characters. Moreover, they are 'erotic' rather than merely sentimental figures. In this the novel shares more with the radical fiction of the 1930s than the socialist realist 1950s, with the exception, perhaps, of Dorothy Hewett's *Bobbin Up* (1959). The female characters are not just the sentimental objects of desire for the male revolutionary whose attainment coincides with and completes the hero's political education. This plot, a common device of communist fiction, *is* present in *Crown Jewel*, as the wavering Andre turns from his upper-class English lover to Elena Henriques. True love coincides with true politics. But Elena has already been given her own life in the novel, a story independent of Andre's; she has, as it were, her own narrative energy. (At the same time, the sentimental romance plot is explicitly deflected in the Le Maitre-Cassie story. Although political integrity is sometimes associated with 'manhood' in the novel, there is no sense that this has any priority over femaleness.) Although Andre is with us at the very beginning and end of the novel, his story, as suggested, disappears and reappears as only one thread in its much broader social canvas and political meaning. Thus the novel ends in a relatively low key, its various narrative threads held in suspension: the strike a mixed success, Le Maitre in prison, Cassie not with her own child but one adopted from a comrade's family, Mrs Henriques, still as generous, impractical and poor as at the outset, and so on.

This dispersed narrative structure has some similarities to de Boissiere's Australian contemporaries. Both Prichard and Hardy evoked history though a large cast of characters whose stories are pursued longitudinally, creating a sense of history that almost inevitably produced *sequels*—completed in Prichard's trilogy, planned in Hardy's announcement in the Author's Note to *Power Without Glory* of 'a series of novels, planned to give a picture of the mainstreams of Australian life in the 20th century'. De Boissiere published *Rum and Coca Cola* in 1956 and later wrote a third, still-unpublished novel about Trinidad. The relatively low-key, unresolved ending, in other words, is less a failure of plot than an imperative of historical meaning. The characters shrink back into history, into a larger story that exceeds the novel's bounds, even as they emerge *into* history through their political commitments. This has a specifically communist meaning, too, as the relative failure or at best provisional success of the immediate politics (of the strike, the organisation) prefigures the historical need and inevitably of communism and a Communist Party. But this is the story that can scarcely be told in the Australian communist novel. It can only be prefigured, 'led up to', shadowed in the margins. De Boissiere's own *No Saddles for Kangaroos* is one of the rare Australian novels with a contemporary setting in which communism plays an explicit role.

Where *Crown Jewel* differs from most of its Australian contemporaries, and where again it recalls some of the earlier 1930s radical fiction, is in its focus on a critical moment, the months that shook the world of Trinidad and colonial rule, in 1936–37. This gives it its remarkable sense of contemporaneity, its close-up feel for the domestic and physical details of its characters' existence, even as it moves outwards to broader social perspectives throughout the story. One of the novel's strengths is thus a dynamic of structure and perspective between *compression*, its focus on a critical moment which changes the political and personal lives of its central characters forever, and *extension*, its historical story, which has both a pre-history in British colonialism and slavery (the novel begins with a panoramic parable-style account of Trinidad from Columbus to 1935) and a continuation beyond its characters' lives, into the future both of Trinidad and of the working class everywhere.

If *Crown Jewel* does carry the message of its Australian communist contemporaries—what we might call the theme of *discipline*—this is entangled, energised, complemented and contradicted by what we might call the theme of *carnival*. I do not want to invoke stereotypes of 'colorful Caribbeans'—de Boissiere's novel will not allow that—nor am I invoking a strictly Bakhtinian sense of the term. I'm referring, instead, to the presence the novel itself gives to pleasure, joy and 'poetry' (the word is recurrent), to its crowdedness and its comedy. These are not secondary to political struggle but as much a part of its meaning as a wage increase or the right to form a union. The principle of carnival, in this sense, is within but cannot be contained by the political struggle of the story or by the ideological frame of the narrative. *Crown Jewel* largely resists the literary critic's habitual desire to separate the 'political' story from the 'human' story.

Although reviewed positively, the *Crown Jewel* of 1952 made little impression on Australian literature outside the circle of realist writers and ABS readers. Perhaps this was simply a question of its subject matter or a result of being published by a small independent left-wing house; or perhaps it was because the critical establishment, whether in its nationalist or 'seriously literary' modes, could not read the book. It did enter the networks of translation and publication in the communist countries. More significantly, perhaps, it slowly made its way into the field of 'Commonwealth literature', especially after its 1981 re-release (a revised text yet again). As Louis James wrote:

> The discovery of this novel written in the 'forties ... gives the student of Caribbean writing a curious sensation. In many respects the tone, the style, is that of an earlier period. Yet it is a new voice, a new piece of the jigsaw which, when set in place, significantly changes the picture one knew before. If this novel had been published, what other writing would it have made possible? Would it have changed the direction of young writers in the way *In the Castle of My Skin* influenced a whole generation? We will never know. Meanwhile, *Crown Jewel* earns a place in Caribbean literature as a work of historical importance published out of its time.[22]

From an Australian perspective, *Crown Jewel* is one of the very few Australian novels before the 1990s to have become part of world literature.

O'GRADY, JOHN
SEE 'CULOTTA, NINO'
Popular Authorship, Duplicity and Celebrity

There are two kinds of hoaxes. The first works only so long as it remains undiscovered. Blow the hoaxer's cover and the hoax collapses. The second, by contrast, depends upon being discovered. Only when the hoaxer's cover is blown will the point of the hoax be revealed. Most scientific hoaxes— or 'fraud' to use the stronger term—belong in the first category. Literary instances are rare and usually involve obscurer psychological impulses that stretch the limits of the term (Paul Radley, Demidenko/Darville).[1] Examples of the second kind, however, are 'core business' for the arts and humanities, from the Ern Malley affair to Sokal and *Social Text*. In these cases, the hoaxers might well blow their own cover, for that is the point, to make the hoax *news*. At its strongest, the hoax in this mode can be understood as a form of satire, exposing modishness, pretension, bias or sheer ignorance from the standpoint of some more traditional or universal system of values. The strategic fraud is perpetrated to expose a larger fraudulence. In this essay I want to consider John O'Grady's invention of 'Nino Culotta' in *They're a Weird Mob* (1957) as a variant of the second kind of hoax, in this case more bluff than fraud. I am less interested in the original and originating duplicity for its own sake than in the sequence of textual and institutional effects it set in train.

Where contemporary criticism has considered *They're a Weird Mob*—and criticism is sparse—O'Grady's deployment of the Culotta figure is understood as a more or less offensive form of 'passing' or speaking for the other: white Australian deploys migrant voice to make a disciplinary case for assimilation. There have been both reductive and sophisticated versions of this critique. For Janis Wilton and Richard Bosworth, O'Grady is an 'emblematic writer of assimilationist Australia.'[2] Bob Hodge and Vijay Mishra recover a more complex text in which O'Grady's 'pseudo-European' is confronted by 'an equally alien pseudo-Australian, whose otherness must equally be appropriated and spoken for'. This point speaks to the doubleness or duplicity that I want to explore from a different perspective in this essay—'O'Grady becoming Culotta looking at O'Grady looking at Culotta'. Nonetheless, the burden of their argument is O'Grady's 'reconciliation between the new migrant and the old Australian', which they describe properly as more 'ideological feat' than sociological fact.[3]

There have also been recuperative readings. While acknowledging the novel's assimilationist and disciplinary dimensions, Ruth Brown, in the irresistibly titled 'From Nino Culotta to Simon During', argues that *They're a Weird Mob* offers a remarkable, non-patronising image of the Australian suburb as a place offering both communal and aesthetic fulfilment—remarkable, that is, in the history of images of suburbia in Australian literature.[4] This conclusion adds an important dimension to the challenging task of explaining the book's extraordinary popularity—'entirely unpredicted by publishers at the time, and only speculatively explicable even in hindsight', as Patrick Buckridge has put it.[5] Perhaps the most sophisticated cultural history of the novel is Lindsay Barrett's reading of it alongside a range of other texts from the late-1950s and early-1960s in terms of a newly-dominant structure of meaning around the Australian male, centred in the figure of the 'self-made man', the free enterprise 'common man' in a nation of self-made men.[6]

The point of the present essay is neither to condemn the novel again for its 'passing' nor, by discovering some hidden subversiveness, to redeem it from critical readings of its ideological performance. Its assimilationism is foundational and pervasive, although not as one dimensional in its historical effects as the novel's closing exhortation to 'new Australians' would suggest. I want instead to approach the novel from a different perspective, setting aside ideology critique for the moment and focusing rather on questions of authorship and the marketplace.

The ironies of O'Grady's subjection to his subject, Nino Culotta, was already something of a journalistic stand-by in the mid-1960s, having been teased out perceptively by John Hetherington in his portrait of O'Grady as 'Nino Culotta's Prisoner', one in his series of mini-biographies of Australian authors.[7] Hetherington concluded: 'Precisely where John O'Grady will take Nino Culotta—or, perhaps more accurately, where Nino Culotta will take John O'Grady—in the unspecified future is impossible to forecast. It appears certain, however, that, wherever they go, it will be together, for they are now inseparably linked.' Taking up Hetherington's cue, I want to examine this doubleness as an institutional effect, as an effect of the way authorship circulates at the popular end of the literary marketplace, and therefore as in some ways less idiosyncratic than it first appears. The fate of *They're a Weird Mob* and of O'Grady's public career were determined as much by the structures of the literary marketplace, the publishing industry and contemporary book culture—which they then helped to re-structure— as by biographical or ideological factors. This perspective alters how we might understand Nino Culotta as an 'authored hoax'.

There is nothing in the archival record or in historical circumstance to suggest that O'Grady's use of a pseudonym was to gain financial or intellectual or other advantage by misrepresenting his ethnicity. The Ure Smith company knew the author's identity from the outset; its correspondence and contract were with John O'Grady.[8] Nonetheless, the pseudonym was clearly more than an innocent *nom de plume*, for the hoax was elaborately built into the material book itself. There were no signs of the author on the book, and when the question of authorship arose, booksellers, reviewers and readers were deliberately kept in the dark— but, no less deliberately, only for a time, the first month or so, as the book made its initial impact. Certainly, both author and publisher came to see the hoax as a smart marketing opportunity, and improvised a publicity campaign with a kind of inspired amateurism that in some ways matched the novel's own. Booksellers were contacted in a direct, personal fashion, small print-runs kept them constantly fearing they would run out of stock, and trade advertisements adopted a 'Weird Mob' vernacular.[9] Problems arose of course following the book's extraordinary success, with requests for biographical information and author interviews, and even an invitation for Nino to appear at Melbourne's Moomba celebrations.[10] Sam Ure Smith strategically withheld and then 'broke' the story, about two months after the novel's first release.[11]

Thus if signing the book Nino Culotta was a hoax, it was a hoax with built-in obsolescence, always designed to fail. For if the point of the novel depends (or appears to depend) upon the reader being taken in and reading the text as the true voice of an Italian migrant, at a second and more permanent level the joke just gets better when we can read the *performance* of this Italian voice. Hence the brazenness of its fraud—hidden in full view—as the novel begins: 'Who the hell's Nino Culotta? That's what you asked yourself when you first picked up this book, wasn't it? Well I'm Nino Culotta.'[12] An older meaning of the word 'hoax', perhaps, is revived by O'Grady's strategies: a hoax as an 'amusing or mischievous fabrication or fiction'; or as a verb, 'contriving wonderful stories for the publick' (1808).[13]

In other words, in addition to its celebratory, comic presentation of Australian English and 'weird' Australian customs, the novel depends, not upon passing itself off as the authentic voice of an Italian migrant, but rather upon this passing being seen through; only then can the comic performance be fully appreciated. Thus, far from denting the book's popularity, the revelation of O'Grady's 'wog drag' appears, from the sales figures and the subsequent history of book and author, to have doubled the comic effect.[14]

The ideological effect of this doubleness, of course, might only have been to double the force of its assimilating trajectory. Irish-Australians imitating Italians was one thing; the reverse equation, one guesses, was scarcely imaginable as a popular literary strategy in the assimilationist fifties. But the effects on O'Grady's name as an author, his signature and his celebrity, were less predictable than an ideological reading by itself can suggest. As Hetherington anticipated, O'Grady's whole career as author and popular celebrity, in private and in public, would be inflected by the doubleness—the frank duplicity—of his writing self.

This duplicity was acknowledged by a *mise en abyme* in the text of *They're a Weird Mob*. One of the book's best but largely-forgotten jokes is that 'Nino Culotta' was only the pseudonym of the story's 'real' Italian author. The novel's opening continues:

My father had me baptised Giovanni—John—well Giovannino is like Johnny, and Nino is an easier way of saying it. Or a lazier way, if you like. The Culotta family is not famous for doing anything the hard way. It is not famous for doing anything. Because as far as I know it doesn't exist. Not in my family anyway. My family name is something quite different, but I can't use it here. Because this little book is about Australians, and if they knew who wrote it, some of them might put bricks through my windows.

In a similar vein, similar in its layering of comic deception and transparently fake claims to authenticity, the conventional authorial disclaimer at the start of the book, signed 'N.C.', is reworked to read: 'Anyone who thinks he recognises himself in these pages, probably does'. If this is a weak literary joke, it might nonetheless have appealed to the 'non-readers' or non-regular buyers of fiction who, the book's unprecedented sales would suggest, made up a large part of O'Grady's 'fan base'. And given the book's subject matter, *recognition* was the most apposite mode of consumption it could recommend to these (and other) potential readers.

The Author's note on the inside of the back dust jacket continues the play with publishing conventions:

> Nino Culotta is in Samoa at the present time, busy writing his second book. So we wrote to him and said, 'Nino, we must have a photograph of you because novels always have a picture of the author on the jacket.'
>
> Well, here it is; but, of course, it doesn't help much.

The photograph was a rear view of a large male figure (O'Grady in fact) in singlet, shorts and work boots, seated on a kerosene tin, with no facial features visible—'bum on a kero tin' in O'Grady's succinct description (he *would* later produce a book on Australian dunnies).[15] Again the comedy was at once puerile and carefully gauged as a populist joke at the expense of literary decorum.

It is worth recalling the novel's extraordinary popular success because this is critical in understanding the functions of authorial identity it set in train. *They're a Weird Mob* first appeared in November 1957, published by Ure Smith in Sydney. It is the book that Beatrice Davis of Angus & Robertson 'most famously turned down'.[16] The text was illustrated by the well-known cartoonist 'Wep' (William Pidgeon) and it appears that the book's distinctive illustrations became almost as recognisable as its pseudonymous author's name; indeed the illustrations probably played a significant role in giving that name a 'physical' presence. Certainly, the cover illustration of Nino, palms up-turned and shoulders shrugged in an expression of bafflement, was frequently used in publicity for this and subsequent books and became part of the branding of the O'Grady/Culotta name.

They're a Weird Mob was O'Grady's first book, but he was by no means an unpublished or unpractised author, although that would become part of his persona. He had already published stories and verse in the Bulletin and the Australian Journal and written one-act plays for the Sydney Repertory Theatre. His war-time diaries and note-books, full of projects and sketches, indicate an inveterate writer, although perhaps also a writer in search of an authorial identity.[17]

Interestingly, there was a model close to hand. O'Grady's brother Frank had published three novels by the time They're a Weird Mob appeared—The Golden Valley (1955), Goonoo Goonoo (1956) and Hanging Rock (1957)—all published by the London firm of Cassell. These were pioneering sagas set in western New South Wales. On the evidence of O'Grady's correspondence, however, Frank represented an entirely negative model, a kind of literariness and respectability against which O'Grady's own persona would be formed. Just before They're a Weird Mob was accepted by Ure Smith, O'Grady wrote to his son in Sydney, from Samoa where he was employed as New Zealand Government pharmacist, that he had just received his brother's third novel, Hanging Rock, but that he was 'shirking' the task of having to read it, as Frank would want a 'crit.': 'A delicate job, disguising real opinion under platitudes'.[18] Later, after the appearance of his own book, he wrote:

> Why do all these budding novelists make their characters speak like somebody out of Scott, and Dickens or Ethel M. Dell. (That brother of mine please note.)
>
> My mother writes that she has read my 'book'. It is terrible. All that swearing! … Why don't you write decent books like Frank?[19]

Frank, by contrast, dedicated Hanging Rock to their mother. Family legend has it that O'Grady began writing They're a Weird Mob at the Oatley

Hotel, Sydney, as the result of a £10 bet with his brother.[20] Perhaps in more than one sense being Nino Culotta was a way of not being frank.

Although Ure Smith had no track record in publishing fiction (John O'Grady Jnr had chosen them at random from the telephone book), *They're a Weird Mob* was an immediate bestseller. The first print run of 6000 hardback copies sold out in less than six weeks. By April 1958, the novel had already been reprinted eight times and had sold 74,000 copies.[21] The book trade magazine, *Ideas*, noted that it had set 'a record for all time for sales of a new book' (December 1958).[22] By mid-1959 sales had topped 200,000, and 500,000 a decade later. The book continued to be reprinted throughout the 1960s, indeed to the mid-1990s, with paperback editions from 1964. It stayed near the top of the bestseller lists for more than two years, outselling overseas blockbusters such as *Peyton Place* and *Doctor Zhivago* as well as Nevil Shute's international bestseller *On the Beach*. English and American editions were produced, the former with a three-page glossary (neither sold well). By the time of O'Grady's death in 1981, *Weird Mob* was in its 47th impression with sales approaching the one million mark.

In sum, *They're a Weird Mob* sold more copies, more quickly, and over a longer time than any other novel published in Australia, at least until Colleen McCullough or Bryce Courtenay.[23] But what does this kind of first-book success do to a writer's career and authorial identity, especially when it is managed via a pseudonymous first-person narrator? O'Grady was self-consciously a popular writer, although also 'self-conscious', as I have suggested, in the sense that he gauged his claims to authorship and authenticity knowingly against those of the literary. He made repeated, if often jokey and conventional claims for the greater authenticity of his books compared to those with literary pretensions. When interviewed for the National Library of Australia by Hazel de Berg, O'Grady claimed he was 'incapable of writing fiction'.[24] On learning that *They're a Weird Mob* had been entered in the Miles Franklin award, he wrote that, had he known, he would have opposed this 'on the grounds that "entertainment" is seldom considered to be "art" (I can't understand *Voss* either, any more than I can understand Salvador Dali)'.[25] The claims are both proud and defensive.

In some ways pop celebrity provides a better model than authorship for understanding the trajectory of O'Grady's career. O'Grady's success almost immediately turned into celebrity. There were celebrity features in the *Australasian Post, Australian Home Beautiful, Walkabout* and *Women's Weekly*; an advertising contract with the NSW Milk Board (which O'Grady jeopardised by announcing on TV's *Meet the* Press that he never touched the stuff); a request from the Divine Word Missionaries of Marburg, Queensland, to write for their publication *The Word*; regular television appearances and newspaper columns; a celebrity recipe—for spaghetti marinara—in the *Sunday Sun*; and photo-features in *Il Progresso*, a magazine for Italian migrants to Australia, in which an Italian translation of *They're a Weird Mob* also appeared.[26] O'Grady was probably Australia's first writer-celebrity since C.J. Dennis (Lennie Lower's fame was more local, while *My Brother Jack* did not appear until 1964). According to the *Oxford Companion to Australian Literature*, O'Grady was 'occasionally described as the Rolf Harris of Australian literature'—a comparison not without its point although I have not found any such reference myself.

O'Grady's pop celebrity brings us back to the question of hoaxing. Hoaxes in the cultural domain matter most where authorship and originality matter most, where the signature of the author guarantees the artefact's uniqueness and value. Hoaxes matter in an economy of scarcity. This is generally not the case in the mass market (except in corners of fandom). Here a form of *brand identification* matters most, where the guarantee is less that the object is unique or original than that this particular object belongs to this kind, this series, this line of objects. As John Frow argues, in the mass cultural market the signature is 'corporatised' and operates more as a brand name.[27] The cultural economy of scarcity is thus defined against an economy of repetition and reproducibility. In the latter, the full-blown meaning of the literary or artistic hoax scarcely makes sense, although 'imitations' will always be possible. Of course, this distinction is as much a cultural artefact and institutional contingency as the distinction between high and popular culture upon which it depends. The oppositions between the 'high' and the 'popular' are reproduced within every sphere and microsphere of the cultural marketplace; and, as Frow has argued, in the contemporary marketplace the fundamental similarity between 'signature' and 'brand' in facilitating the commercial exchange of objects has been revealed.

Nonetheless, we can still describe different economies at work: for my purposes, and for want of better terms, the 'literary' and the 'popular'. Literature is a complex example because of the reproducibility of *all* its products, high as well as low (and by exactly the same technologies). But of course publishing formats, marketing strategies, bookstore arrangements and the critical habitus itself work precisely to create at least the resemblance of scarcity—or rather of preciousness and value—for 'serious fiction'. If Mills and Boon is an extreme example of a brand name at the other end of the scale, there is also a sense in which the names of best-selling authors such as Tom Clancy, Frederick Forsyth and Stephen King operate as much as a guarantee of 'reproducibility' as of 'originality'. Mass market publishing, like popular cinema, loves a sequel or seriality in any form, and thus we have seen 'Jane Austen' shift from signature to brand name.

More immediately, we can see *They're a Weird Mob* as situated on the cusp between the two economies. The novel was reviewed in the cultural quarterlies as well as in the newspapers.[28] It was thus considered seriously as an applicant for entry into 'Australian literature', as a work of Australian fiction, even if for the critics by and large it passed the test only in a qualified form. On the other hand, by 1964 when it was released in paperback, the book was re-located, 'repackaged' primarily as a popular work of humour and Australiana—less 'literature' than 'entertainment'. It was released in a new 'Humorbooks' series which its own success had initiated, as were a number of other O'Grady/Culotta titles. They were given standardised or 'branded' covers, and O'Grady's own writing took on the logic of seriality by reinventing Nino Culotta, and following *Gone Fishin'* (1962) with *Gone Troppo* (1968) and *Gone Gougin'* (1978). Both 'Nino Culotta' and 'John O'Grady'—and indeed the phrase 'They're a Weird Mob'—came to function as brand names, getting attached, by O'Grady and/or his publishers, to all sorts of projects as a kind of corporate rather than individual signature. For the remainder of this essay I want to trace how these effects were played out across O'Grady's career, and then to position the 'weird mob' phenomenon alongside other popular successes.

Whatever the point of the original hoax, its effect was to enter O'Grady's writing career—and public celebrity—into the logic of the mass market; or rather into an ambivalent shifting back and forth between systems, between a writerly, embodied authorial presence (signed John O'Grady) and a public persona (branded 'John O'Grady' or 'Nino Culotta') in which the *performance* rather than embodiment mattered. On one level, of course, Nino Culotta was simply a comic creation, like Harry van der Sluys performing Mo or Barry Humphries performing Edna Everage. We do not mistake the act for embodiment, or not for long (for there *is* a certain pleasure, after all, in making the mistake). The extra difficulty for O'Grady as an *author*, perhaps, was the degree to which being an author still implied 'finding one's own voice'.

To put it another way, the question posed for O'Grady by his success was how to keep performing his writing self, how to make the originary author coincide with the public authorial presence. With this success based on his performance of wog drag, the question was not just what to write next but *who* to write. While still in Samoa in 1957–58, he resisted the idea of a sequel. He rejected his own idea of taking Nino and his wife back to Italy, and thought the idea of 'Nino goes bush', suggested by his son, would 'be a bit of a flop' once it became known that Nino was 'a fake'. If there was to be a sequel, O'Grady's preference was for Nino to turn up in Samoa.[29] At the same time, even as Nino was being set aside, we see him increasingly begin to take on a life of his own as a persona, a way of seeing, a figure O'Grady as author has to negotiate. While working on a manuscript with neighbours in Samoa, O'Grady wrote to Sam Ure Smith that 'further work by Nino will have to wait'; but in the same letter, considering the offer of a column in the *Daily Telegraph*, he wondered, 'Would Nino's wanderings in NZ and Samoa, presented in column-narrative form, for collection later into book form, be of any use?'[30]

On one side, Nino could appear as O'Grady's most valuable literary property. On the other, it was as if he defeated O'Grady's efforts to be fully present to himself as author. As early as February 1958, he was trying to kill off Culotta and absorb him back into O'Grady. He wrote to his son:

> Have started work on what could easily be another winner. *Not* Nino Culotta. I have had Mr Culotta. I am heartily tired of Mr Culotta. There will be no sequel. There will be no 'Cop this Lot' … Mr Culotta has had his day. Let him die. He is now O'Grady and finished anyway.[31]

He rejected an offer from Frank Packer for Nino Culotta to write for the *Weekend* magazine ('Culotta does not write again until he is ready … I have no interest in Culotta any more'); and in June 1960 he delivered a funeral oration for Nino in the bar of the Toongabbie Hotel.[32] But the announcement of Culotta's death was premature. Indeed such a gesture only breathed new life into Nino. If Nino had to be killed off for O'Grady to live, it was just as true that O'Grady could not let him die, in so far as he had become a necessary part of the O'Grady writing or speaking position.

Even in the new non-Culotta work mentioned in the letter above, what we might call the Culotta effect seems to have been a necessary device for the story-telling, a story-telling that again involves whiteness passing as other:

> It will be written in the first person—difficult but rewarding—putting myself into the mind of a someone entirely different to Nino ... a Samoan ... No Samoan has ever written a book; no Samoan has ever given *his* side of the white man-brown man problem. One is going to do so now. There will be no bitterness, no smart cracks—whimsicality, good intentions gone wrong, misunderstandings, and an earnest desire to learn the white man's strange character and habits ... They don't regard me as white. So I'm going to put forward their point of view, gained through long study and personal contact.

As with Nino Culotta, whiteness is both normative and estranged in this kind of narrative compulsion towards passing ('One is going to do so now'!). Something more than simply inventing a character is involved, for the narrative duplicity is fundamental to the conception of the tale, linking the story to a comic form of colour instability, providing its motivation, becoming the *point* not merely the method of the fiction. O'Grady's books would provide a neat example for Jennifer Rutherford's Lacanian analysis of the aggression present duplicitously within the Australian 'good neighbour'.[33] They both ridicule and affirm white superiority, welcoming (some) others into the enlarged circle of representability by making whiteness comic and relative while affirming its capacity to contain and comprehend, indeed to overcome, all difference.

As it turned out, *No Kava for Johnny*, as the new work would be called, had to wait for the Culotta sequel after all. Sam Ure Smith had urged a sequel and pushed the idea of having Nino take 'the weird mob' overseas—a kind of '*They're a Weird Mob*' in reverse'.[34] He guaranteed publication if O'Grady were to undertake a trip to Italy to research the book (which was canny publicity too; on his return the press were waiting dockside to meet the author of *They're a Weird Mob*; one of the news stories was O'Grady's meeting with a real Nino Culotta on board ship).[35] Although while in Italy O'Grady had wanted to remove Nino altogether from the story and write it instead as 'pure fact written by O'Grady',[36] the manuscript was completed in May 1960 and published in June that year as *Cop this Lot* by Nino Culotta. It also sold well—150,000 copies within a year. Nino's 'exposure' did little to effect the success of his performance.

O'Grady had seen the comic potential of Nino's duplicity. Reprising the opening of his first novel, *Cop this Lot* begins with a page and a half in Nino's best, ill-tempered comic mode, explaining how some character called John Patrick O'Grady had pinched the manuscript of *They're a Weird Mob* from the garbage can, and even pinched his pseudonym (which he translates as 'big backside'):

> Who the hell's Nino Culotta? You will say this is an easy question to answer. Nino Culotta is John Patrick O'Grady. So I will ask another question. Who the hell is John Patrick O'Grady? And how can he be Nino Culotta when not even I, Nino Culotta, am Nino Culotta?

Doubling the doubleness becomes central to the performance, and the prefatory material becomes a highlight of the books. The joke, at this level, is at the 'fraudulent' nature of fiction in general and *realist* fiction in particular, a populist version of Ross Chambers's point that realism depends upon a disguise which must be penetrable.[37] The writerly work must disguise or deny its artifice in order for the work to make its claim on reality, but it must also let that artifice be seen in order for the work to make its claim to art. The point, in O'Grady's hands, is not poststructuralist or postmodernist *avant la lettre* for at base it depends upon a clear distinction between 'fact' and 'fiction'.[38] But this *is* the nature of the joke, the claim to authenticity of a work of fiction. By the same token, the joke is also about the nature of authorship, about the gap between the self and the signature, about the ways in which the author can never be identical with his or her own text but simultaneously can never escape the identity those texts create. Obviously this is not what the books are 'about'; the social comedy that follows works in a simpler register. But their comic edge is never far from this original scene of Nino's creation.

Significantly, when *No Kava for Johnny* did appear in the following year, 1961, the Culotta effect was prominent. The book appeared under O'Grady's own name but the story is narrated by—and presented as written by—a very Nino-ish Samoan, Ioane Papatiso (John the Baptist). With pop culture logic, the novel was promoted as 'the Weird Mob of Samoa' and, like the previous two novels, was illustrated by Wep. It sold reasonably well—50,000 copies by 1970—'but modestly by comparison with *They're a Weird Mob* and *Cop this Lot*'.[39] Again the Foreword has O'Grady, this time in his 'own' voice, working the same vein of humour around authorial authenticity:

This is the story of Ioane Papatiso, Polynesian, as told by himself. My publisher doesn't believe this. He says Ioane didn't write it. He says I did. He says I'm to take full responsibility for it. He insists. We had a long argument, and at the end of it he said, 'Look, you got away with being Nino Culotta for a while, but you've got no show of being Ioane Papatiso. You're the wrong shape, wrong age and wrong colour … Your name goes on the book as the author, and that's final.'

… Anyway, whether I wrote the story or whether Ioane wrote it doesn't matter. What matters is that in all essentials it is a true story. Ioane was my constant companion during nearly three years spent in his islands, and I am proud of his friendship. He's a great little bloke.

The character William Neil—Uiliama—is myself, slightly disguised by being given red hair, which I don't have. I don't have much of any kind of hair. Except on my chin. I'm not quite sure why this disguise was adopted, except that it was Ioane's idea …

I don't care what my publisher says. I say this is Ioane's story. So I'll shut up and let him tell it.

Much of the opening chapter of the novel is about Ioane's name, or rather the sequence of names he has, from Pepe to 'Ioane, Husband of Pigs', before he can claim his own (which is, of course, already someone else's). The story of the novel, although respectful towards Samoan customs, is ultimately a modernising one.

O'Grady published two further Nino Culotta novels. According to Hetherington, he first tried to write *Gone Fishin'* (1962) as O'Grady, but when this proved unsuccessful he reluctantly agreed to Ure Smith's request to resurrect Nino. The ventriloquising worked again, as the book had sold

100,000 copies by 1970. Fishing, of course, was tailor-made for O'Grady's bluffing. The Foreword, signed N.C., again plays transparent tricks on its reader:

> It has been said to me many times that I should never believe anything told to me by a fisherman. But all the fisherman I have met have been as truthful as I am myself. Anyone who thinks that fisherman are not truthful will probably not believe this story. He will say it is fiction. And I will not deny this, because every man is entitled to his opinion. But every fisherman will recognise the truth in it, even if he does not recognise himself in it. I am sure no fisherman would ever accuse another fisherman of telling lies.

In a manner that signals the text's *lack* of autonomy, this 'circumtextual' apparatus becomes essential to the fiction's claims on the reader and the ways these books might enter readers' lives. These were not books for the study, perhaps not even for the armchair, but tales that might circulate like jokes or gossip, rather than like artefacts. To put it another way, they were the kinds of books non-readers might read.

Gone Troppo (1968) promised a repeat performance but was signed O'Grady. *Gone Gougin'* (1975), though, was Nino's. Described, inevitably, as 'the Weird Mob in the opal fields', it is narrated by Nino Culotta, whose name is on the spine and front cover, although this time the name of the author, John O'Grady, appeared in brackets on the title page following Nino's.[40] By contrast, O'Grady's best-selling picture book on Australian toilets, *Ladies and Gentlemen* (1966), reversed this relationship by having John O'Grady on the cover, followed by 'Nino Culotta' in brackets and 'Narrated by Nino Culotta' on the title page.

Over the two decades following the success of *They're a Weird Mob*, O'Grady became Ure Smith's most prolific author, publishing a book a year on average from 1960 to 1977. Sixteen were under his own name, but only two of his novels (*No Kava* and *Gone Troppo*, both of which operate still under the sign of Nino). The Culotta effect was revived for *Are You Irish or Normal?* (1970), by 'Sean O'Grada', and *It's Your Shout Mate!* (1972), narrated by 'James McIntosh', a visiting Englishman reporting on Australia's 'alcoholic ways'. If, for a while, *They're a Weird Mob* made O'Grady a popular expert on all things Italian and migrant, its more lasting effect was to make him a popular expert on all things Australian (and male). The book had exposed a rich vein of material for Ure Smith and other publishers, a line of popular, humorous books about Australian English and Australian customs. O'Grady himself contributed *Aussie English* (1965) and *Aussie Etiket* (1971). In early 1966, *Aussie English* and another pseudonymous work, Afferbeck Lauder's *Let Stalk Strine*, both published by Ure Smith, were one and two on the Australian bestseller list. Like an early Paul Hogan, this popular Australianness became no less an act of performance and ventriloquising than O'Grady's 'non-Australian' characters. He became something of a house author for Ure Smith, his name or Nino's being attached to a wide range of projects—fiction, Australiana, photography books, novelty books, even other people's books—in a manner that illustrates Frow's initial argument, that the brand name functions as a corporate rather than a personal signature.[41]

Nino Culotta thus became the most important property that O'Grady possessed as an author (alongside all that the 'Weird Mob' label had accumulated). Like all property, it had to be husbanded, protected, but also exploited, if its returns were to be realised. Nino had to be reproducible— and O'Grady makes this part of the joke—but that reproducibility had to be managed, for it was always in danger of multiplying beyond its creator's control. From the outset, *They're A Weird Mob* began to reproduce itself in ways that made rights in the property crucial. In 1958 it was serialised in the *Sporting Globe* in Melbourne and in a number of papers in other cities; it was adapted for radio by the ABC, with John Meillon as Nino, and then, in 1959, by Melbourne's 3XY.[42] As early as January 1958, there were plans for a musical (starring Mario Lanza according to Frank Devine). '*Please! Please no! Please no Musical!*' O'Grady wrote from Samoa.[43] A song was written and released on record in July 1959, with music and lyrics by George Dasey and arrangement by Graeme Bell; the Elizabethan Theatre Trust expressed interest in a stage adaptation; Cedric Flower and Alan Seymour, author of *One Day of the Year*, wrote a stage play that Ure Smith sent on to John McCallum at J.C. Williamson's, who would later invest in the film version. Film rights were sought from the earliest months, and indeed were purchased in 1958 by Gregory Peck, no less, who had read the book whilst filming *On the Beach* in Melbourne. (O'Grady wanted Burt Lancaster to play Nino.) Chips Rafferty then expressed interest in the screen rights, but they were eventually sold on to British producer and director Michael Powell. At least three versions of the script were produced before the film was released and the success of the novel relived in 1966.[44]

If the story and its narrator never left O'Grady alone for long, neither could he leave them long alone. In addition to the series of books already described, O'Grady began his own stage play of They're a Weird Mob while still in Samoa; later he decided that someone else should do the dramaturgy. He signed postcards 'Nino'. He worked on dialogue for a daily or weekly cartoon series based on the book, although from the drafts that remain in O'Grady's papers it appears that this was to feature only the Aussie workmates, not Nino himself. Indeed in one form or another, O'Grady kept trying to write the story of the weird mob without Nino, but apart from the Australiana books either couldn't do it or couldn't make it interesting to anyone else. In 1967 he toured Vietnam as part of a 'Weird Mob Show' which does seem to have lost all trace of the Italian angle and to have been pure Australiana.[45]

Thus the text's 'afterlife', its sequels and remakes, and the cultural resonance its duplicity left behind have far exceeded the artefact itself. This is how the book sits (at the time of writing) in a glass cabinet in the National Museum of Australia, as a cultural icon—'inside a fifties style kitchen in a section called "Suburbia: Way of Life".[46] But Nino Culotta and They're a Weird Mob also bear comparison, in this respect, with Steele Rudd and On Our Selection. Both were first books which because of their spectacular bestselling success virtually 'wrote' the rest of their authors' careers. In both, the pseudonymous narrator came more or less to obliterate the name of the author, to reproduce itself in ways that could only partially be controlled by its creator. (C.J. Dennis and The Sentimental Bloke could also be considered in the equation; Dennis was often known, simply, as 'the Sentimental Bloke'.) Both books were pitched at a local, popular market, although both authors carefully measured their relationship to literary fiction; both are comedies of national character; both drew on vernacular language and returned it with interest to their readers, so much so they entered the vernacular themselves. Both were remarkable bestsellers with a multiplying afterlife that extended way beyond the original text into other print, radio, visual, musical, theatrical and cinematic offspring. Both bound their authors to a series of returns to the original scene of their success, producing a kind of repetition compulsion, partly driven by the industry and the marketplace, partly by the individual and institutional structures of popular authorship.

The original 'hoax' thus entered O'Grady/Culotta into the serial logic of the popular market. The novel's extraordinary success intensified these effects of reproducibility, but they were not in themselves unprecedented. The duplicity of authorship became a kind of running gag, the comedian's 'tag' or catch-cry, thereby generating further repetitions. Interestingly the *Oxford Companion to Australian Literature* reverts to language that we might use more commonly of a stand-up comedian than an author, when it notes that O'Grady 'had a keen ear for the Australian idiom ... but he overworked his material'. The Culotta effect was not a device that O'Grady could simply put away at will. It continued to shape his writing self precisely because of the way it *displaced* the autobiographical voice; because of the value it (re)produced in the popular culture marketplace; and because its jokes about fiction and truth-telling were endlessly repeatable. One of O'Grady's least successful books was his attempt at straight autobiography, *There was a Kid* (1977). O'Grady himself would probably have enjoyed the irony of 'his' index entry in the *Penguin New Literary History* of 1988: 'O'Grady, John *see* "Culotta, Nino"'.

THE WIDE BROWN LAND
ON THE SILVER SCREEN

LANDSCAPE AND NATION

The signs are that there has been a shift in representations of the Australian land and landscape, in particular those landscapes which most fully signify the nation. I'm thinking of the images of land and landscape which circulate through cinema, television, advertising and tourism. We need to be wary of the notion of 'shift' just as we need to be wary of taking a handful of images as signifying the national culture or psyche (as if there were one). Representations circulating in the public and popular cultural spheres do not shift evenly or once and for all. New meanings are teased out of old images in new combinations, while the old meanings are almost always still available. We will find realignments and accretions in the repertoire but seldom simple evolution or substitution. Nonetheless, as the whole field of representations is reordered, the old meanings are less and less likely to mean just what they always did. My emphasis will be on what is new, indeed what is largely unprecedented, in the contemporary repertoire of land and landscape representations. To take one significant example, the Australian Bicentenary was more remarkable for the new forms of national celebration it invented than for the old forms which it revived.[1]

The land has long been a source of non-Aboriginal images of a distinctive Australian identity, first as the site of difference, a source of exotica and antipodean inversion through flora and fauna, later as the *conquest* of difference, the stage or page on which the progress of civilisation was played out through the heroics of explorer journeys, or rather their heroic narratives. Most famously and persistently the land was summoned to play its part in settlement myths of men and women 'made for' the land, less by birthright than by having lived, worked, suffered, and died there. 'The Man from Snowy River' is a household name today not just because of rural nostalgia or media commodification, but because he provides a telling myth of unique fittedness to the land which can thereby serve as a myth of national belonging. Like Clancy and many others, he has no name except a place name. These stories are still powerful, still capable of calling forth strong identifications, not least because they do define something of a distinctive past the material effects of which can still be seen on the contemporary environment.

Despite the persistence of the bush myth my argument is to point to other relationships between land and nation which have emerged since the late-1980s and which in many respects have left the old bush mythery a long way behind. A great deal of the critical energy expended on debunking the bush legend is already obsolete, lagging way behind popular culture's self-critique. Even at its starkest, the bush signifies a populated landscape, one worked into a *pastoral* economy of money and meanings. What I want to emphasise is the degree to which, despite its ubiquity, this populated and storied landscape, the landscape as resource, is no longer the most potent image of the land for the purposes of eliciting national identifications. Of much greater significance in recent years, of greater signifying power in terms of the nation, have been images of 'unpopulated' landscapes: above all, wilderness and desert. (At least these landscapes *look like* they're unpopulated, a point to which I'll return). It is clearly the 'red centre' or 'wide brown' landscape that now most fully signifies the nation; and since *Crocodile Dundee* (1986), the Kakadu-style wilderness as well. We might say that in relation to Sydney and Melbourne at least, there has been a shift north and west in the landscapes of deep national belonging. These landscapes, I want to argue, perform their 'nationing' in a way that has little to do with the old bush imagery although the transition from one to the other might be virtually seamless.

I make this point even in the face of such evidence as the Winton Waltzing Matilda Centre and the Longreach Stockman's Hall of Fame. It is true that 'the Outback is back in', as the Longreach tourist officer told me. At the same time and in a sense in the same modernising trajectory, the bush myth in its various manifestations—parched or pastoral, solitary or matey—is more than ever vulnerable to critical and parodic treatment even if in mostly affectionate ways. One of the many things *Crocodile Dundee* showed was that it can now scarcely be represented in other than critical and parodic ways (except perhaps in mining publicity). There is some distance between *The Man from Snowy River* (1982) and *Crocodile Dundee*, even before we reach *The Adventures of Priscilla, Queen of the Desert* (1994). *Crocodile Dundee* is an irresistible example for the way it combines the old and the new. Dundee is the bushman, if you must, but his habitat is wilderness, not the bush; it is outside the pastoral economy. Interestingly it is also something less than the epic landscapes traversed by heroes from Voss in *Voss* (1957) to Archie and Frank in *Gallipoli* (1981).

As these references remind us, the pastoral myths never had the field to themselves. Myths of the centre, the empty, inscrutable, impenetrable, unpossessable desert space, form their own tradition from Charles Sturt to Mad Max to corporate advertising. Here are other stories of national belonging, sublime rather than pastoral, where the land is a mythic space, beyond culture and history, always threatening to defeat meaning while promising some ultimate meaning. It is a space for heroic individuals, the white men who traverse it or become it; but as Ross Gibson has shown, these are heroes of a rather distinctive kind, hence their distinctive potential for national meanings: 'the laconic "minimalist" hero hews a path for himself, communing with the spirit of the land, reading its messages, jotting down hints for survival ... The land is habitable, but only by a very special breed of people.'[2] While both *Dundee* and the later *Mad Max* movies recycle bits of these myths they do so in a knowing, relaxed and revisionary manner— *hence* their success in the 1980s. The old myths could no longer work fully seriously, either for authors or audiences.

ANCIENT AND MODERN

Despite all appearances to the contrary, I would also argue that the representation of the land in *Crocodile Dundee* is remarkable for the way it repeats scarcely any of the familiar tropes of Australian landscape, those for example in the period and scenery films which preceded it. The film works hard at achieving the casual air of Dundee's belonging, not least in its knowing winks to its Australian audience—who know, unlike the Yanks, just how seriously to take Mick Dundee (not very) and just how seriously to take the landscape (very, but in an unstated, understated way). If the tourist image is one thing the film provides for its Australian and international audiences, another and more important effect, available to its Australian audience alone, is that of *sharing a secret*. Its self-knowing 'at-homeness'—in what was in 1986 scarcely a familiar landscape—is in its own way unprecedented; it is not, of course, politically innocent.

Every landscape tells a history (as *Crocodile Dundee* also knows). In the new landscapes of wilderness and desert, history works in the opposite direction to earlier pastoral landscapes and is of another order altogether. In the place of a landscape of bush or pioneer settlement that leads forward narratively into the present with the force of both evolution and destiny, there is instead an ancient and primeval landscape that leads backwards into the *pre*historic past. As the voice-over put it in the bicentennial show-piece program, *Australia Live*, Australia is 'the oldest earth on earth'.

National advertisers, of course, are among the first to understand and underwrite such new meanings. Beers, cars, mining and petrol are no longer associated just with the history of (white) human achievement but more richly with the 'history' that has 'always been there' in the land. This is now the site of national meaning and, what is new, this 'timelessness' is now an unavoidable part of the meaning of Australian *modernity*. Thus we have images of the very latest 4x4 vehicle dominating the red centre but also, somehow, sharing its spirit. Perhaps 1988 represents a key moment in the deployment of this type of imagery which can suddenly render the bush or pioneer legends strangely ephemeral. Here we have nation-making at its strongest, giving one of the newest nations on earth an unexpected depth and centredness in the oldest earth on earth. In the primeval landscape it is as if time and place become one, and uniquely 'our' time and place, our history *and* our present. Of course, the word 'our' has to appear in quotation marks, for the social function of such representation is richly, unavoidably ambiguous.

Shifts in technology have been crucial in this process, especially in television and telecommunications. Tele-communication has not only multiplied the number and the presence of national images, so that they are now pervasive rather than occasional, it has also altered the manner in which different and even contradictory ways of representing the nation are present alongside each other. The typical effect of tele-communication is *simultaneity* rather than history or distance. Primeval and modern, desert and metropolis, black and white, immigrant and indigenous exist simultaneously in tele-communication time in the one space in the present. There are no more frontiers; we can see the frontier as a colonialist metaphor which makes less and less sense of Australia's 'postcoloniality'. If this seems postmodern too, its politics might nevertheless be deeply nationalist.

The key word I have not yet spoken is 'Aboriginal'. For of course the desert and wilderness landscapes I've referred to are not unpopulated. To put my central point more accurately, the landscapes that now work with the full power of nationing are *Aboriginal* landscapes; Aboriginal landscapes made available, as it were for the first time, to all Australians.[3] This is what is unprecedented and politically ambiguous. Again *Crocodile Dundee* is a key transition site, both producing this Aboriginality and removing it from any contemporary politics of possession and dispossession.

A critical posture towards such activities of aesthetic appropriation and cultural assimilation is absolutely necessary. It might well be that the last thing you'd expect to find in these 'Aboriginal' landscapes is the representation of contemporary Aborigines. But it is no less plausible to read the signs optimistically. Defining the nation in terms of landscapes that simultaneously signify Aboriginality and national belonging also represents a shift in attitudes to place (if not necessarily to Aboriginal politics) among non-Aboriginal Australians, a shift we can represent as a moment of 'decolonialisation', a move towards new ways of seeing and identifying with non-European landscapes, to ways of seeing just ever so slightly at a tangent to European frames. Such ways of seeing might even be called *ecological* (in a cultural as well as environmental sense). Ancientness no longer exists in the past but is discovered in our here and now.

As such, this discourse expresses an original, powerful and dangerous myth of non-Aboriginal belonging: original because of its leap beyond European and North American ways of knowing Australia; dangerous in that it both recognises and effaces the distinctive nature of Indigenous claims to land. Still, its terms are remote from earlier models of national independence which found their bearings through difference from the mother country and the disappearance of Aboriginal Australia. Now the 'mother country' is the nation here and now and takes its bearings in part at least from its *proximity* to Aboriginal Australia. Aboriginal sovereignty becomes an unavoidable meaning in the force-field of national representations and must always be negotiated, one way or the other.

'Australia's history is 40,000 years long'. This was another powerful theme in 1988 and its rhetorical achievements are remarkable. The depth of an Aboriginal past is made available, once again for the first time, to all Australians, as the history of post-invasion settlement is merged, more or less seamlessly, into Aboriginal time. Again the ambiguous politics are obvious, and the Aboriginal counter-slogan 'White Australia has a Black History' made the point unforgettably. For the equation is unequal: no dispossession is entailed for the majority culture; quite the reverse, even if an adjustment of perspective is required. Still, there are positive effects, for the place of Aborigines in the national history can no longer be represented in terms of its timeless or childlike prehistory. If the nation's past is pushed backwards, so that here too one of the newest societies on earth is given one of the oldest histories, in the same process Aboriginal time is pushed forward into the present. Its meanings and force are contemporary. The effects are complex: Aboriginal culture in both its traditional and hybrid contemporary forms is rendered at once ancient and modern.[4]

We needn't just be cynical when a Western Desert dot painting is offered as a prize on *Sale of the Century*; or when a Walpiri painting is set beside the new BMW. For this latter promotion, paintings were commissioned from Ken Done, Esther Mahlangu from Transvaal, and Michael Jagamara Nelson on the theme 'Impressions of Mobility', as was a CD from James Morrison.[5] The choices are telling, the associative links rich with potential meanings: contemporary Sydney—brash, ocker, camp, cosmopolitan—linked to an Aboriginality at once contemporary and traditional, and both linked to contemporary/traditional African art in a move that might be seen to parallel the notion of World Music.

Despite everything else we might say about this globalising commercialism, mightn't we also say that it opens up the possibility of new ways of recognising culturally distinct Aboriginal modes of understanding? Nor is this negligible in the process of recognising Aboriginal sovereignty. As non-Aboriginal Australians come to identify bits and pieces of Aboriginal culture as *their* culture (and of course it can only ever be 'bits and pieces') there is every chance that this appropriation also means negotiation; some chance, at least, of a more subtle appreciation of cultural difference. If, today, forms of Aboriginal culture can be celebrated as Australian culture, then this is not just something done to Aborigines but also something Aborigines have done to the rest of Australian culture through the sheer power and political savvy of contemporary artists and performers.

Obviously European desires for the exotic, the authentic or the primitive are threaded through every dimension of these representations of land and Aboriginality and the transactions are always likely to be unbalanced. But again I think there's more at stake than mere repetition or appropriation. In the new rhetoric of Aboriginal Australia a nexus has been established between Aboriginality and Australian modernity that is unprecedented and which will not be easily broken.

THE FAMILIAR EXOTIC

This is a good moment to bring *Priscilla* into the spotlight. The argument about this film could be twisted in a number of ways: either that it overturns the old Australian legends by its high camp journey into the centre or that it confirms them because the only women who make it are really white men after all. (That isn't quite true, of course, for there's a successful white businesswomen and a transsexual at the film's centre.) Or it might be that the desert is still the forbidding but alluring place that demands to be conquered by white men even if they can only go there in disguise. Doubtless the film calls up all the layered meanings which the culture has already attached, variously and vicariously, to masculinity, Aboriginality, land, journeys into the centre, being lost in the desert, and so on.

My interest is more in the way the film plays with notions of the exotic and the familiar. For a start, it relies as much on the *familiarity* of gay, transsexual, cross-dressing Sydney as on its otherness. The famous Oscar-winning thong dress makes my point. It's not hard for the straight, soberly-dressed viewer to think 'this is ours'; to assume a viewing position the Mardi Gras has already helped license. If anything seems strange or threatening, at least for an urban audience, it's the country towns where the characters stop. But the film isn't just managing a simple reversal of exotic and familiar nor a cute paralleling of exotic with exotic (although it milks both possibilities for all they're worth). I think it invents a more original sort of hybridisation. Take the drink-till-you-drop contest between transsexual Bernadette, played by Englishmen Terence Stamp, and a tough-talking, blue-singletted local *woman*; the combination of traits twists almost every national legend imaginable not least because there is, as we say, something 'very Australian' about it.

What of the landscape? The 'red centre' landscape, of course, is there in all its sublime spaciousness (it is often accompanied by operatic music), but it is no longer there as the mythic or mysterious centre which must be pierced, the forbidding other against which identity (masculine and national) will be registered or else the self dissolved. The effects are interesting: if the land is still in one sense the ultimate destination it is also already familiar. Rather than signifying a mythic home or an epic homelessness, the meanings of this landscape might best be described as 'homely'. The journey isn't only to the red centre but also to an international resort, to a wife and son, and to a few varieties of love. Not that the land is tamed or domesticated. The sublime dimensions are still there; the land maintains its otherness even as it appears as just the right place for the main characters' drag queen dramatics. They comment on the space that 'never ends' and decide to turn for 'home', but the desert landscapes have been more than anything else welcoming to them. And perhaps it is this combination of the land's otherness together with a sense of intimate relation to it that can be called ecological.

To risk the paradox, the landscape represents a uniquely familiar kind of otherness where exotic and familiar, primeval and modern, traditional and trashy, Aboriginal and Abba are put into plausible, unpredictable, low-key relationships to each other (low-key despite the high camp). Beyond the running gag of incongruity, of men in dresses in the desert, or, in the film's language, cocks in frocks on rocks, the extremes of nature and culture which these juxtapositions invoke neither clash nor synthesise. A bit like *Crocodile Dundee*, *Priscilla* shares a secret with its Australian audience in which 'flaunting' can become a kind of intimacy. There are no momentous resolutions, only a few resolving moments.

In this scenario the meeting between the three white characters and Aboriginal characters in the desert is a key moment which the film handles in an original manner. Although the Aborigines might 'loom up out of the desert' as they do in so many previous narratives, here they're also located in the contemporary world where bad pop songs can be good fun: the racial and ethnic difference does not do work as a difference in time. After all, who's anachronistic, who's dancing to pop songs two or more decades past their prime? The Aborigines in this scene also maintain a kind of privacy. We might have expected that the exoticness or otherworldliness of our three heroes would function in the film as a key giving them access to this private Aboriginal world. But it doesn't. Nor does the scene present us with a neat figure of fusion where all differences dissolve away. This is why I'm drawn to the word 'hybrid': the exotic and familiar on both sides are performed together, before our eyes, but so are the differences that the various characters inhabit. And the song they perform together is 'I Will Survive'! (This might all be contrasted to the other scene of exotica that the film cannot manage with originality: the Filipina wife.)

What's also interesting is that the Aborigines do not participate in the film's uplifting humanist trajectory in which the different characters' individual natures emerge from beneath their costumes and conventions. This could be read as yet another case of Aborigines being disappeared by white narrative procedures in time for an individualising and socialising *dénouement*. But the humanist convention of the 'good Aborigine' shown as an individual ('just like us!') isn't necessarily much better than sheer absence. I think the film's choices are right. As I said, the Aborigines retain a sense of privacy (and privacy rather than 'mystery'). If they like Abba too we can't automatically think 'just like us'.

If we were searching for precursors for *Priscilla* we might find one, in a surprising place perhaps, in *Voss*. While in one dimension the novel participates in the epic mythic-centre landscapes described earlier, in another dimension it also prefigures many of the features of *Priscilla*. Its own journey into the centre is nothing if not high camp, it has a rich comedy of representation in which its imagery (and syntax) is thoroughly excessive, and it shares *Priscilla*'s unexpected homeliness in Laura Trevelyan's final manifestation at the novel's conclusion. Perhaps too, although with a little less confidence, we might see White's treatment of his novel's Aboriginal characters—as homely and altogether 'other'—as a prefiguring of the later film.

Priscilla understands at least some of the ways in which Australia means Abba *and* Aboriginality: both insights are significant and their connection quite remarkable. The way that the film shows its central characters both out of place and at home almost wherever they are makes it one of the most interesting statements of 'belonging' that Australian culture has yet produced. This is so, not least because what gets left out is precisely rural or pastoral Australia. The film is both post-*Crocodile Dundee* and post-*Mad Max 3: Beyond Thunderdome* (1985) in the meanings available to it—sharing something of the former's casual insidership and something of the latter's reconstituted community (the beautiful ending of *Beyond Thunderdome*)—but going further than either. Like both the earlier films it flaunts its 'positive unoriginality', in Meaghan Morris's term.[6] It is also, despite everything, a film without nostalgia. Each of the three films mentioned, in fact, can be understood as a 'theorising' of the complex relations between foreign and indigenous, national and international, which define Australian culture. *Priscilla* also suggests why the European dreaming films such as Werner Herzog's *Where the Green Ants Dream* (1984) seem so deeply unoriginal, in a much less positive sense. The myth of the last frontier and the empty centre has just about reached its use-by date for its Australian consumers.

THE NATURE OF TELEVISION

Television has also played a crucial role in defining the imagined community of the Australian nation. As a condition of its postcoloniality, identifying with the nation's human history and community in Australia has always been incomplete without an identification simultaneously with its land and landscape. As Tom Griffiths has written, 'Europeans ... often turned to the natural environment rather than the uncertain human past for temporal depth ... it was the disciplines of natural science rather than history that first offered them a meaningful, but sometimes disturbing, landscape narrative'.[7] For more than fifty years, Australian-made television series and documentaries have been the most familiar media for the vast majority of Australians through which the Australian landscape has become known, inhabited, and in Graeme Turner's shorthand, 'made national'.[8] Natural science and national history have worked side by side giving popular meanings to each other, to the nation, and to our sense of 'Australian television'. My interest here is in the changing nature of the nature in programs from the 1960s to the 1990s.

Again we need to be wary of the disposition within cultural studies to read textual variations as symptomatic of profound shifts in the culture itself.[9] In the limited field of landscape/nature series on Australian television, earlier styles and modes are not so much displaced as consolidated, gathered-in to new styles and genres. They become part of the generic field, still present as interpretive and compositional tools for both producer and consumer. In the realm of landscape, above all perhaps, it is easy to point to the recycling of earlier images, especially through everything the mythology of the bush has represented, and it has often represented everything. But in television, no less than cinema, there has been something of a revolution in what is sayable and 'see-able' in Australian landscape and nature. I will propose a history in four phases or four genres of landscape/nature programs (and here my emphasis will be on landscape rather than fauna): the Antipodean, the Adventurist, the Ecological and the Aboriginal.

THE ANTIPODEAN

The 'Antipodean' phase is in a sense the pre-history of my history. It refers to the store of 'nature' and 'landscape' documentaries made on film in the decades before the introduction of television and during its early years. According to my research at the National Film and Sound Archives, these documentaries and newsreels were massively dominated by the popular furry animals—kangaroos, wallabies, wombats, koalas, platypus—plus emus and kookaburras. Wedge-tailed eagles, bower birds and fairy penguins made a few appearances. This was still pretty much what Australian nature meant in primary and secondary schools in the 1960s.

The animals and birds which starred in these films were presented less in the terms of ecology or natural science than as oddities, exotica, *antipodea*. The interesting point is that this was the case even to their primary Australian audience. There is a 1932 Efftee production, or as they called it an 'Australian Marvelogue', with the characteristic title, *Nature's Little Jokes*. There is another called *Aussioddities* (1938). These were the familiar exotica that reassured the nation of its distinctiveness; but it was a weak distinctiveness, in effect held under the reassuring colonial gaze that rendered both observer and observed antipodean. Hence the characteristically comic tone of these films, also common in newsreels. They were a belated, comic version of the earliest settlers' responses to Australia's apparently contrary nature, and perhaps this repetition manifested in part the local film culture's relationship to Hollywood and the British film industry just as the earlier responses had manifested a colonial relationship to the imperial centre.

At the same time, natural science and natural history movements had a rapidly expanding influence in the early years of the century, an influence that would eventually help generate a different understanding of the uniqueness of Australian flora and fauna. Griffiths's account of the early, amateur nature writers from the 1880s to the 1930s shows clearly the English sources of their delight in natural observation and their 'desire to cultivate popular sentiment in the land and its inhabitants'. Their activities belonged to the pastoral mode, and as a consequence their chief focus appears to have been on birds and plants, particularly in the 'soft' landscapes around Melbourne's Dandenongs. But their emphasis on observation and recording—before the professionalisation of the sciences in the 1930s—encouraged detailed knowledge of native flora and fauna in an intimate, humanised relationship. In the first decade of the twentieth century, state schools in Victoria were scheduled with Arbor Day, Bird Day and Wattle Day in order to promote this close identification between a natural and a national heritage.[10]

But an interest in native flora and fauna, even an activist interest, was not necessarily anti-English or anti-imperial. Discovering a local heritage, at once natural and historical, was as much a way of maintaining continuity with the English past and imperial present as of defining a new orientation, a new way of seeing. Despite its serious scientific interest in native fauna, even the establishment of such an institution as the Healesville Sanctuary— officially opened in 1934—represented something of the antipodean construction of what we might call the 'national natural', at least in its popular, public mode. Its star attraction in the 1930s, drawing crowds of thousands, was Splash the platypus, who lived four years in captivity, then a record. He was later stuffed for the Institute of Anatomy in Canberra, at the heart or head of the nation.[11] Thus the novelty items of Australian nature were preserved in sanctuaries (the choice of word is an interesting one—like nature 'reserves' or Aboriginal 'reservations' it suggests an imperial drawing of boundaries). Australian fauna was on show for the visitors' recreation and weekend education but with only a casual relationship to the rest of their Australian lives. Such places in the present, by contrast, will tend to have an *exemplary* relationship to the life of the Australian citizen.

The National Film and Sound Archives reveal little evidence of the landscape itself as the subject of these early films and newsreels, although there was a 1955 documentary called *A Sunburnt Country*. The landscape was there in feature films, of course, firmly in its pastoral guise, as in *The Overlanders* (1946). But as far as Australian television is concerned it appears that it was not until the mid-1960s and early 1970s that a new kind of interest in traversing, capturing, reproducing and viewing the landscape emerged.

THE ADVENTURIST

In the early 1960s Australian television schedules included the occasional locally-made nature documentary series, for example *Australiana* on TCN-9 and a one-off ABC program called *Creatures of the Dawn* which featured the 'stars' of the Healesville Sanctuary.[12] By 1963 the ABC had begun to sponsor wildlife or Australiana documentaries specifically made for television: for example, *Australian Wildlife* (1963), a five-part series devised by the naturalist Graham Pizzey featuring penguins, possums, seals, platypus, ant-eaters, water-birds and the Mallee; and a series of fifteen-minute fillers, *Around the Bush*, featuring naturalist Vincent Serventy (1968). Unlike the earlier films, these were made or presented by professional naturalists and their mode was natural history. Channel Nine screened *Nature Walkabout* on and off throughout the second half of the sixties, usually at odd hours of the morning. Otherwise we had the American *Wild Kingdom* for a decade or more on Ten. What is interesting here, perhaps, is how different its formulas were from those which operate in the Australian-made programs, especially the most popular and critically-acclaimed. The vast stage of nature, featuring the 'universal' animals (lions, tigers, birds of prey) and relentless apple-pie moralising ('But he'll return next year, a happier and a wiser beaver') proved inappropriate for local knowledges in Australia.

The naturalist documentaries were one important if sporadic line of development in the sixties, and while they still tended to concentrate on the high-profile, photogenic creatures, their broad natural history focus worked towards dissolving the merely antipodean framework of perception which had governed the earlier films. These documentaries took their points of reference wholly from the local. This point recalls an argument mounted in other contexts by Albert Moran and Tom O'Regan, that television has been at least as important a force for 'Australianisation' as for any purported 'Americanisation'.[13] I would argue that television's nationing effects have in fact been far more significant than any 'un-nationing' that its load of American and British imports might have achieved.

This nationing effect can be seen especially clearly in the changes in landscape/nature television in the 1970s. The naturalist programs did not disappear—*Wild Australia* began in the early 1970s—but neither did they prosper until the boom following the high-rating BBC program *Life on*

Earth (1979) in the 1980s. The genre that flourished instead was both old and new. The Leyland Brothers produced their first documentary in 1963, *Down the Darling*; in 1966 it was *Wheels Across the Wilderness*. By the 1980s they had their own series and had produced almost 300 television programs. To their spectacular story we can add a number of others. The ABC's *A Big Country* moved to prime time in 1969. *Rolf Harris's Walkabout* began on the ABC in February 1970, again in prime time. This series, described as a 'safari from Darwin to Sydney ... to discover outback Australia' featured Rolf and his family travelling around in 4x4 vehicles with the naturalists Vincent Serventy and, interestingly, Harry Butler. It was shot in colour, thus making the most of its settings—Uluru, Arnhem Land, jungle and desert, 'native flora and fauna, and the Aboriginals and white people who live in the outback'. *Peach's Australia* began in 1975, once more on ABC prime time evening television. It featured visits to people and places across the continent, not least pilgrimages to historic sites and historic routes—across the Nullarbor, for example, in the steps of Ernest Giles. Commercial television also screened occasional documentaries by the adventurer Jack Absalom.

The reasons for this new development were at once technological and cultural: the introduction of colour television in 1975; the development of corporate advertising using the national landscape; television ratings which, by the late 1960s, showed a clear market for local product; increases in accessibility for tourism; and a resurgent political and cultural nationalism (which television helped create).[14] These structural changes, however, do not explain the particular form that these programs took. The dominant mode of television documentaries in the period was what I have called 'adventurist'; not altogether accurate perhaps but the play on words was difficult to resist. Rather than animal or natural history documentaries, the new series were dominated by landscape and travel. From the domestic sphere of the cute, bizarre marsupials, we move to a genre in which the central trope is the sheer *size* of the country itself. The central strategy is coverage, moving across the country from north to south, from east to west, and from present to past. If the country is (once again) rendered unknown, it is no longer unknowable.

There were elements of the travelogue or the tourist itinerary in these series, forerunners perhaps of lifestyle programs such as Bill Peach's

Holiday on the ABC and Nine's *Getaway*. But far more significant I think is the way that the bulk of these early programs replay the nineteenth-century tropes of exploration. Although their locations are often in unique and spectacular areas—the red centre, the outback, the wilderness—the focus of the narrative is generally upon the journey itself: the emphasis is on *distance* rather than destination. The narrative point is the story of human survival, human resourcefulness, adventure and indeed conquest, rather than 'natural wonders'. The most popular narrative ploy was indeed to trace the steps of the explorers, down the Darling, up the Murray, across the top, into the desert.

Griffiths has traced the popularisation of the inland to the 1920s, when 'writers and artists journeyed to the centre and celebrated it for a largely urban audience'. In the 1930s particularly, Frank Clune, George Farwell, Ion Idriess, R.H. Croll and Ernestine Hill pursued this task of popularising, making the inland at once familiar and other. *Walkabout* magazine began publication in 1934. The 'red heart began to replace the golden summers' of the pastoral mode as a more modern symbol of Australia; the imagery of the Centre also supported the sense of a pilgrimage, thereby giving new life to the old images of exploration just when the 'heroic' age of exploration could be pronounced dead.[15] Many of these texts were still circulating in the 1960s, but the genre was ripe for reappropriation in the age of the four-wheel drive, the caravan and the colour television.[16]

With the Leyland Brothers and Jack Absalom, at least, we are clearly in the presence of modern bushmen and explorers, bits of larrikins too, making tracks for us into the wilderness, battling the perils of flood, fire, drought, snakes and crocs, *modernising* these images of national representation through the resources of the new medium. They re-enacted for the first TV generation the processes of exploration, settlement and frontier-marking that literary narratives had once performed. But the medium made a difference, of course, so that it was not a matter of mere repetition. For television inevitably meant a peculiar kind of domestication and a commodification of the landscape at the point of consumption. The explorer-filmmaker-narrator was a familiar travelling companion, and the landscape unfolded before him with a certain ease despite its dangers (they were to my knowledge all male). Local knowledge was a key trope, for if the sublime emerged from time to time, the overall effects were low-key, yarning rather than epic. We might say that these were familiar landscapes we had never seen before.

These were neither trivial nor necessarily undesirable effects; they contained all the ambiguous politics of new mythologies of belonging to a unique continent, a unique nation, now with its own time and place. While the notion of the 'centre' always had the potential to disturb neat borderlines, the notions of 'outback' and 'inland' were firmly based on the cultural boundaries of European settlement, as was the notion of the journey inland being simultaneously a journey back in time. The new television programs were as often journeys to the north and north-west as they were journeys to the centre. They emphasised remoteness and distance, but their Australian nature, their landscape, was no longer exotic or antipodean, no longer colonial in *this* sense, although it took another act of colonisation to banish the earlier colonial images. The stories they told were settlement myths after all, even when the land traversed was not fit for a white man (as they used to say). Their domain was the nation's frontiers. This was the key to their nationing effects, for as they worked to extend the nation's boundaries they worked to define its core.

THE ECOLOGICAL

Many aspects of the 'adventurist' genre are still with us—some of the programs are still with us. Nevertheless I want to define a new phase by referring to Harry Butler's *In the Wild*, shown on ABC TV in 1978 and 1979. Butler himself is clearly a type of the modern bushman and the success of the program depended on his ability to keep being this despite all his scientific knowledge and green rhetoric. His natural habitat was remote Australia. But the originality of his programs can be marked by their distance from the earlier narratives of exploration or settlement. And despite their continuities with the natural history series, they *felt* very new when they were first shown. What *In the Wild* managed to achieve, I want to argue, was an *ecological* perspective in which, for the first time, the land itself became the primary subject, the landscape *as* ecology. The programs, in short, presented a quite new relationship between the human and the natural world, a relationship that was, then and there, distinctively Australian. This was no small achievement, if largely accidental or, perhaps, overdetermined.

As a consequence of its ecological perspective, the effects of the program tended to be small-scale—ants, insects, lizards, small rodents, anything that lived under a rock or in a hollow tree, animals and plants, animate and inanimate drawn together into the one relationship. Here the notion of 'environment' was more important than notions of 'outback', and the landscape was for the most part a non-human, unpopulated one. The word 'wilderness' was prominent. Harry Butler was clearly at home in the landscapes he visited, but the viewer was made conscious that he was indeed a visitor and was required to watch his manners, obeying rules of appropriate environmental behaviour that were not of his own making. 'Nature must have its way, and its laws must be obeyed.'[17]

Butler himself located the program explicitly *after* the earlier genres: 'Too many of us have grown up with the idea that the only interesting native animals are the funny or cuddly ones like the koala. That's fine if you're running a souvenir shop, but it's not much good when you're watching an infinity of evolution on the brink of extinction.' His rhetoric over the two series turns more and more on the notion of 'a delicate balance', the ecological 'balance of nature', the 'need to save *all* the ingredients of any area to preserve particular beauties ... the uglies, unloved and hated reptiles, and creepy-crawlies with their own fascinating part to play in the drama of daily life.'[18]

When Aboriginal people appear, they do so as part of this ecology, 'part of the environment'; but again this is not mere repetition of earlier ways of figuring Aborigines as part of the landscape, more nature than culture. The ecological framework makes a difference. From the Aborigines as 'gentle custodians' of the land, Butler derives a notion of the unique Australian environment as a *heritage*. The programs are thus overtly 'responsibilising'—of the nation and the individual—'bringing Australia to its senses about what will be lost if we do not manage our environment intelligently, learning from the past and applying what we learn now for the future.'[19]

Thus the nationing effects of the two series. The programs were enormously popular, and Butler was made Australian of the Year for 1979. I would argue they played a decisive part in opening up for non-Aboriginal Australians the possibility for a new and indeed original 'Australian' kind of identification with Australian landscapes. Despite their contemporaneity with David Attenborough's *Life on Earth*, there was something here that could not be contained within the colonialist frames of European landscape or its narratives of settlement, a sense of responsibility that came from nowhere else. In a certain manner, Butler's Australian landscape resists being made national according to any of the predictable tropes because of the way it is shown as having its own kind of 'integrity' which human destiny can probably only destroy. Butler explicitly turns 'exploration' into 'exploitation', again marking off his distance from the earlier genres. As to the red centre: 'Australians have built up a sort of mystical feeling about the Outback, a sort of folk-culture idea which like most such ideas has some basis in truth, and a whole lot of nonsense in it'.[20] The ecosystems he presents are uniquely Australian in a way that makes the span of (European) human history look oddly superficial. At the same time, of course, their mediation through the figure of Harry Butler and through the television screen—with its own intimacy, intense local-ness, and exemplary effect—was in its own way newly and deeply nationing.

THE ABORIGINAL

Much less confidently I want to use the *Bush Tucker Man* series (1988, 1990, 1996) as the exemplary text within my fourth phase, the 'Aboriginal'. It is clear that the landscapes in which the Bush Tucker Man moves are saturated with their Aboriginality, and on an overt level the programs are a tribute to Aboriginal knowledge. But my main point is not about this overt attribution or, as some have said, appropriation. The main landscapes featured in the series are the 'new' landscapes of the eighties and nineties, the Aboriginal landscapes of Cape York, the northern wetlands, the north-west: 'from Arnhem Land to the Kimberleys, from the rainforest to Cape York'.[21] Its centre is Darwin, not western New South Wales (perhaps not even Uluru). Moreover it is this access to an Aboriginal landscape, to an Australian landscape that signified Aboriginality, which made the programs a success. It was a particular instance of the general case I suggested earlier—Aboriginality made available, for the first time, to all Australians. Again these landscapes were operating not merely as landscapes but as national landscapes, our 'national natural' for the nineties. Further, the ecological perspective of Butler's programs, while not often explicit in the *Bush Tucker Man*, operates as a kind of foreknowledge, a pre-text, underwriting Major Les Hiddins's respectful relationship to the land.

At the same time, of course, one of the pleasures or pains of the program was to marvel at the Bush Tucker Man's almost perfect embodiment of the older figures of the Australian bushman and explorer. He's like the long-lost third Leyland Brother. On one level, then, Les Hiddins was perfect for the job. He gathered up all the old meanings, the national meanings, of the bush, the outback, the wide brown land, and merged them seamlessly with the new sense of Aboriginal belonging offered to the nation as its own deep secret, its ancient and modern uniqueness. Again I do not want to react cynically to these effects despite their stunning impurity, because they just might have a progressive potential in changing the contiguity of 'Australian' and 'Aboriginal' meanings.

If they do it is because the program's success in representing Aboriginal landscapes and the meanings that these landscapes draw to themselves exceeds the Bush Tucker Man's own signifying power. Their Aboriginality goes beyond the yuppie bush tucker gloss, and cannot be contained by the programs' overarching narrative threads. Certainly it is not too difficult to be struck by a sense of incongruity, anachronism, even violation in the Bush Tucker Man's presence in this landscape and in his assumption of Aboriginal knowledges. Here I'm not so much talking at the level of pure political critique—which might easily be developed in terms of appropriation, speaking for the other, and so on. At a more basic, mundane semiotic level, the programs create an un-ease through clashes in their own signifying systems. As is so often the case, popular culture was quicker than the culture critics in spotting the contradictions, turning them into a witty Foster's Lager ad featuring the Bush Tucker Man at home in the wilderness—with an esky full of Foster's.

In a way, then, it is not surprising, on re-viewing the programs, to note how seldom contemporary Aborigines appear. The discourse is usually about the old people, the knowledge of 10,000 years ago, as it is with Harry Butler. But again repetition produces change. The nationing effect of the later series comes in the way the Bush Tucker Man makes this knowledge *contemporary* and everyday. Unlike Butler, the program turns the landscape back into a part of human history. It's about *living* here, about domesticity and comfort rather than epic struggle. Perhaps that is why Major Les is described as an 'ethno-botanist', not a term I'd come across before.[22] In the process, as suggested earlier, Aboriginality becomes part of the meaning of Australian modernity, not just part of its ancient past. More than that: we participate with the Bush Tucker Man as he engages in the most literal sort of embodiment—*eating* the landscape. The Aboriginal landscape is thus embodied for the viewer; the landscape becomes part of our bodies, part of our inside, not merely a place somewhere 'out there', out back. Even in the third series, which returned to the 'in the footsteps of the explorers' genre, the main dramatic principle is the contrast between what we know now (that is, Aboriginal knowledge) and what they (the Europeans) knew then.[23]

Perhaps. The point I want to rest with is that this still new sense of the landscape as Aboriginal is now one of the potential meanings that any representation of a 'national' landscape must negotiate. This is one thing the *Bush Tucker Man* and *Priscilla* have in common. Moreover these are the landscapes that now bear the fullest burden of national significance, the deepest and most intimate, in the paradox of a 'new' history that has 'always been there'. So much so, perhaps, that non-Aboriginal Australians can only approach this landscape through *incongruity*, silent in the *Bush Tucker Man*, loud in *Priscilla*.

Although at something of a tangent to this paper's focus on images of the landscape, there have also been important shifts in the style of the natural science wildlife documentaries which have been so brilliant over the last decade or so. Among the most successful is the 1993 documentary *Kangaroos: Faces in the Mob*. The program has been criticised for its anthropomorphism, as it names individual kangaroos, invests them with personalities, and inserts a moral in contrasting good and bad mothers.[24] It is difficult to disagree with this reading. And yet the anthropomorphism here is not that of *Wild Kingdom* from three decades earlier and from another place. Against the seductive identifications which the cinematography and narrative encourage is another discourse that refuses domestication, that keeps us at a distance even when we shed tears for Jaffa—the joey who won't return next year a happier and a wiser kanga. The program's emphasis on the social organisation of the 'mob' is part of it. But, strangely, so too is the very intimacy that the new filming technologies allow—the intimacy creates a kind of distance for the viewer, a close-up view that is in a sense *non-human* in its perspective and so works quite differently from the more panoramic, imperial gaze of the *Wild Kingdom* genre. For all its anthropomorphising, *Kangaroos* creates an unusual, original relationship between human and non-human—perhaps anthropological or ecological rather than merely domesticating. While the program makes us feel that these kangaroos are intimately 'of us', there is nothing left of the cute antipodean relationship.

CONCLUSION

It is not possible to predict the political effects of the kinds of changes I've described. No doubt European desires for the exotic, the authentic and the primitive, for myths of belonging that need constant renovation, underwrite these representations of land, nature and nation. Appropriation and assimilation are in a sense the only tools we have to work with, rough as they are. Changes in visual imagery and rhetoric might have a real significance beyond style or beyond the moment of viewing, but then again they might not. Sudden reverses are always possible. But there are optimistic ways of reading the changes, in particular the shift to a situation in which, despite everything, it is more and more possible for non-Aboriginal Australians to identify aspects of Aboriginal culture as defining an Australian culture to which they also belong. Even changes in 'mere' style should not be underestimated. Perhaps the new myth of belonging will depend on knowing just the ways in which we do *not* belong, at least not by birthright or just by being here. Television has played a decisive role in the circulation and recognisability of new ways of apprehending the landscape. Less spectacular and in some ways less memorable than the cinema, television's very mundaneness defines the mode of its effectivity and, most important, its ability to reproduce itself, prodigiously but inexactly.

GOOD READERS
AND GOOD CITIZENS
Literature, Media and the Nation

In recent decades nationalism has sometimes been classed in the same category of immoral behaviours as racism and sexism. Reading from the historical and literary record, nationalism often appears to have been little other than racism and sexism. Race was the very basis of the national settlement in early twentieth-century Australia; how profoundly, I think, is something we still have to learn. How far are we from thinking in terms of First Nations as a way of acknowledging Indigenous Australia? Our easy familiarity with and moral superiority to pre-1967 Australia and the White Australia Policy means that there are many degrees of Australian racism that remain hidden from commonplace historical knowledge. Australians still tend to think of South Africa as belonging to another time and place altogether, another moral universe and historical trajectory. This was not a mistake that colonial Australians made. The parallels will become less and less resistible.

The critique of nationalism has been a defining enterprise of both Australian studies and Australian literary studies since the 1970s.[1] One side of the work has been the recovery of writers, texts and genres excluded from the nationalist canon; another has been the recovery of an adequate 'national' literary history against the exclusions of post-war ethico-formalist criticism. Both kinds of work, the former no less than the latter, have often been motivated by the idea of the nation, by the possibility of repairing or completing the national history or culture, even when rejecting utterly the forms that nationalism had taken. Feminist criticism has been the single most important force reshaping Australian literary studies since the 1970s, but much of its work, too, has inevitably been work on the nation.[2] Even though the steps in the argument exposing nationality's homogenising and exclusionary effects are by now thoroughly familiar and routine, we still need to renew the critique because we are still discovering the range of the nation's historical and textual forms. Their weight and pressure still bear on the present, and not merely as a residual force.

This critical anti- or post- or neo-nationalism took new forms in the 1980s and 1990s under the influence of postmodern and postcolonial theories. To the critique of specific nationalisms was added a general critique, a general grammar, of the category of 'nation'. While postcolonial criticism has often found itself productively in the very midst of the historical, textual and theoretical ambiguities of 'anti-colonial nationalism', in Leela Gandhi's term, both theories have in certain of their manifestations defined themselves *against* nationalism—nationalism, for example, in its mode as an exemplary modernising grand narrative or as a new imperialism.[3] From one perspective, nationalism and imperialism—not to mention modernism and imperialism—begin to look more like each other than like categorical opposites. The earlier project of 'completing' the national cultural history was problematised by this rendering of nationality as a form of imposed and therefore oppressive identity, singular and organic, the very opposite of the multiple, shifting or hybrid subjectivities that both postmodernism and postcolonialism learnt to celebrate. The assumption that there was an ideal form of Australian culture towards which we were evolving, which each text manifests or ought to manifest, has thankfully disappeared almost without trace.

But this rich and necessary sense that nationalism belongs in the sin bin of history, at least in these essentialist and homogenising forms, has sometimes been taken to mean that *any* dealing with the idea of nation is retrograde; as if, for example, the very idea of a history of Australian literature were hopelessly complicit with all the ghosts of nationalisms past. In an age of micro-politics, micro-subjectivities and borderless media flows, it can seem as if the idea of nation is at best nostalgic, and at worst—much worse.

This is a caricature, but not too far from some views I've heard expressed in moments of postmodern, postcolonial or 'post-national' hyperbole. But surely it involves a kind of category error. In the simplest terms, nationalism does not equal the nation, and problematising the category of nation does not equal its historical transcendence, although this way of putting it does not express the positive dimension of my argument. Nor does the nation necessarily mean the (oppressive) imagined community. There are ways of talking about culture 'in the nation' or about culture and the state which are not exhausted by this kind of pure critique of nationality or nationalism.

To show the oppressive, homogenising and frankly racist operations of nationalism—to suggest why historically and as a mode of 'culturalist' thinking nationalism always tends this way—leaves a great deal still unsaid about the way the category of the nation organises and enables the production, circulation and evaluation of culture, and how it does so in specific ways in this place. Having said that, we should also say, on the other side, that to argue that the idea of the nation and its institutions have a massive effect in organising culture in Australia is by no means equivalent to seeing nationality as an exhaustive or even a necessary category. Most culture happens either below or beyond the horizon of nation. Nonetheless, if we are interested in cultural history, there will be limits to what we can say before bumping up against the nation as an idea or, better, an institutional structure.

The most common way the nation features in contemporary literary criticism is probably still as the 'oppressive dominant' against which difference or diversity must be asserted. This idea organises a great deal of current work on Australian literature, and the grammar of its critique has structured most of the major books and articles in the area over the last decade or so. Contemporary literary studies and cultural history are unthinkable without this critical 'technology'. Nonetheless I want to argue that this negative critique is less than the whole story and, further, that is in danger of becoming an impediment. Its insights can produce their own forms of blindness, in both an over-emphasis and an under-emphasis on nation: an over-emphasis, I think, on the homogeneity and dominance of forms of Australian cultural nationalism, for example in turn of the century literary and journalistic circles or the ambiguous, minority position of mid-century nationalist intellectuals. Australian cultural nationalism has often been turned into a one-dimensional dominant principle, continuously present from the 1890s to the 1990s. Such characterisation renders it an uninteresting subject. Strangely, for all our obsessive concern with putting nationalism in its historical place, the definitive history of Australian cultural nationalism and of relations between literature and national institutions remains to be written. It does so partly because of over-familiarity, because we 'know all about' nationalism. Hence, in part, the *under*-emphasis on nation and nationalism: for example, the under-emphasis on its modernity. Susan Sheridan's work is important here, tracing the complex investments in the idea of nation made by early-twentieth century women writers in Australia.[4]

The historical and theoretical critiques of nationalism have produced a useful anxiety about deriving any value from the category of nation, but this anxiety is sometimes transformed into a kind of triumphalist *transcendence* of the national. This is the effect of romantic-aesthetic categories persisting in literary criticism. The procedures of negative critique slide all too easily into a generalisable aesthetics or a utopian principle based—currently—on notions of transgressive or hybrid subjectivities. The critique of nationalist forms, like the critique of racist and sexist forms to which it is so closely tied, is often exemplary. But in one sense nothing is easier for criticism at this point in time, nothing more routine, than finding that literary or other texts are subversive of the dominant or the normative, whether despite or because of themselves, *or* that despite or because of themselves they end up affirming and reproducing the dominant. Either way, literature's transcendence, or literary criticism's, is assured. These points lead off into another argument.[5] My point for the present is that we still need to think and work through the category of the nation, not just negatively because it is there as a stubborn historical fact that we can't avoid, but *positively* as well, because the nation is a political and cultural formation around which value and meaning are accrued, projects formulated and principles defended. While neither the essence nor the whole, the national is a crucial dimension through which cultural producers, critics, consumers, policy-makers and marketers work, partly through necessity and partly through choice, and with a whole range of effects that can scarcely be summed up as simply 'oppressive' or 'dominant'.

To proceed as if we could transcend or dismiss the nation seems to me not only bad history, but also a kind of institutional bad faith. It involves a forgetting of the conditions of our own work—for one thing, for many of us, within a state institution which we are presently trying to defend and quite possibly in the name of the nation. Such negative positions represent the continuation of a radical anti-institutionalism that has been a persistent thread in modern literary studies from Coleridge on. Except for those embarrassing examples from the mid-nineteenth century or during times of war, literary studies has never been very good at thinking about its relation to the state either. But clearly the state, mobilised in part around the idea of nation, has been one enabling condition for contemporary Australian literature and literary criticism, for example through state patronage.

More broadly, if we want to defend or reform the role of the Australia Council or local content and foreign ownership regulations, or for that matter multiculturalism or notions of a redefined 'republican citizenship', we have to commit ourselves to some version of the nation and the state. What is to be rendered 'multicultural' if not the nation? (Other forms of community, perhaps, but the point remains.) If we want to urge our fellow citizens—as fellow citizens not merely as individuals—to take responsibility for the treatment of Indigenous Australians (if we see a political usefulness and appropriateness in terms such as 'Indigenous Australians' and Indigenous Australians as fellow citizens) then we are already working within the framework of the nation, although not exclusively or exhaustively. The complexities of the situation are nicely untangled in Ken Gelder and Jane Jacobs's recent book *Uncanny Australia*, in which they show how the category of the nation enables and legitimises the 'Aboriginal sacred', even as it disables and delegitimises.[6] It seems to me that one of the effects of the nation, which is not an effect of the state, is that there are certain histories we *cannot opt out of*: here and now, for instance, the history of relations between Indigenous and non-Indigenous Australians, the history of assimilation and multiculturalism, or the history of Australia's relations to Asia, both the Asia within and the Asia without.

It might be possible inside certain forms of aesthetic or linguistic discourse to proceed as if the nation did not exist or existed only for the worse and never for the better. But any kind of talk about literature or culture that claims something more—some purchase on history—has to take on the idea of the nation including its positive meanings. We have become expert at the absolutely necessary task of demythologising the nation, although we still struggle to keep up with the nation remythologising itself. For good reasons, we—and I guess by 'we' I mean the 'middle generation' of critics who began to write and think about Australian culture in the decade from the late-1970s—are distinctly uncomfortable in thinking about literature or talk about literature as playing a positive role in, say, forming a national identity or a national community (I hesitate to use the terms and just manage to resist quotation marks). But this is part of what I want to hypothesise here, at least at the end of my essay. Might we, for example, draw on the language of citizenship to talk about literature as a kind of 'public good'? Can we imagine literature not merely as subversive of national identity, but producing versions of national community to which we might give our assent? Can we take seriously the idea of literature having a role to play in forming good citizens? We needn't be shy of the idea, despite the disciplinary and flag-saluting resonances it carries with it. It seems to me that the idea of forming good citizens might in fact be much closer to what we do as teachers and critics of literature than are many of the fantasies surrounding the notion of textual politics—although textual politics will remain one of our principal 'disciplinary' techniques.

II

I want to approach some of these issues now from another angle, drawing on recent work on popular culture and media in Australia. For much of its modern life, the cultural significance of literature and literary criticism has been defined by their relationship to print journalism (and, pre-cinema, to the theatre). The public life of literature is now governed by its more complex relationship to the media and the media industries. One effect of this repositioning within culture is that notions of cultural decline have been circulating widely—both in the media and the academy— with blame attributed to theory or postmodernism, globalisation or the marketplace (and sometimes odd combinations of these things). The innocent pleasures or profound truths once available through literature, it is felt, are being lost or denied in contemporary culture. The academy has been accused of having abandoned aesthetic values and literary tradition for theory, ideology or pop. In the pages of the 'higher journalism' there have been more than faint echoes of US debates about the destruction of the canon.[7]

Against the notion of cultural decline it could be argued, instead, that literature, and especially Australian literature, is more prominent than it has ever been before: in newspapers and magazines, in the bookshops, at literary festivals and in literary prizes, in cinema and on television. One paradoxical example is the proliferation of essays by public intellectuals about the decline of public intellectuals. This 'rise and rise' goes together with the remarkable boom in essays and books of essays directed at the educated general reader, surely evidence that the public intellectual is flourishing, though also, crucially, that the modes and media of the public intellectual life are shifting.[8] Another example might be the genre of reflective ficto-memoirs or memoir-essays developed by Robert Dessaix and Drusilla Modjeska. Highly aesthetic, possibly postmodernist, acutely niche-marketed, their books have rediscovered a public *ethical* mode for literature at once old and new.

Literature's markets and media have diversified and their effects multiplied, but such proliferation has more often than not been beyond traditional notions of the literary and beyond the normal range of literary criticism. Thus its effect on the cultural prestige of literature has been ambiguous, especially compared to that of the cinema (and perhaps popular music too). In Graeme Turner's words, 'although the literary field has broadened over the 1970s and 1980s—through the extent of its output and the diversification of its genres, sub-genres and modes of writing—this does not seem, in the 1990s, to have much affected its purchase on the national imagination.'[9] Whether or not we judge that to be a problem, I can't think of an account of Australian literature outside Turner's essay and Mark Davis's *Gangland* that makes a sustained attempt to re-think its subject in the light of these kinds of changes.

Although cultural studies has seldom been as different from literary studies as it has claimed, it *is* much more practised in thinking about culture in terms of the culture industries, institutions and the 'everyday'. Necessarily a great deal of cultural studies work, too, is invested in a critique of the ideological effects of national cultures or the cultural effects of national ideologies. If modern print culture has played the role that Benedict Anderson claims for it in the formation of new nations, how much more so, the argument goes, for the new electronic media cultures, with their capacities for nation-wide simultaneous dissemination.[10] Working with the very mundaneness of these cultural forms as well as their technological and institutional dimensions has been an aspect of cultural studies from the start. Further, and this is the point for the present argument, they have enabled or forced cultural studies to come up with some new ways of thinking about culture and the nation.

Literature, by contrast, has traditionally been defined by its transcendence of these mundane or technological realities through a commitment to texts and to high principles, to texts regarded as formal bundles of ethical effects, and even with the cultural turn in literary criticism over the last three decades this historical legacy remains. The great sophistication of textual critique and its extension into the reading of historical discourses has not altogether compensated for the lack of attention to the institutional and 'industrial' side of literature's existence. Despite 'the history of the book' and similar projects, it is still possible to think of these aspects of production, distribution and governance as inessential, almost accidental, in relation to literature—even *opposed* to literature—in ways that do not even begin to make sense in other fields of culture.[11] In short, we have scarcely begun to talk about literature as a form of public-commercial-aesthetic institution comparable to cinema, television or popular music. More precisely, we *have* considered literature this way, and uncontroversially, when it has been removed from the realm of immediate cultural value: the further removed the texts are from cultural capital the more easily we read historically and institutionally—hence the really interesting ongoing work on the nineteenth century in Australia or the interwar years which seems to proceed in quite a different way from work on, say, post-1960s writing.

III

As a publishing phenomenon, Australian literature in the last decade or two has in many ways followed a similar trajectory to the media cultures, to Australian cinema, television and popular music.[12] While its institutional context has been characterised by the increasing globalisation or multi-nationalisation of publishing and distribution, the market as suggested above has also been progressively localised and diversified. As with rock bands and film-makers since the 1970s, works can be produced and careers pursued wholly with reference to a local audience but (increasingly) without that audience having to be conceived as 'the people', the nation or the universe.

The effort to talk to a local audience no longer needs to be based on a low-key populist sense of its presence, as say for Alan Marshall, or a high camp gothic attempt to overcome its absence, as for Patrick White. The kinds of novels once thought to comprise Australian literature—'serious' literary novels addressing a serious national readership—are now only one small part of the Australian literary marketplace. As Susan Lever has commented, 'novels no longer form part of the cultural binding of society: they now are marketed to the same variety of consumer groups as other products, so they are not only for children or adults, but for women, feminists, Aborigines, migrants, gays, lesbians, liberals—or, even, men'.[13] We need not, though, see market differentiation as the opposite of 'cultural binding' so much as a moment in its transformation. The situation of literature, in the weighted sense of the term, is a particular instance of John Frow's general remark that high culture 'is no longer "the dominant culture" but is rather a *pocket* within commodity culture'.[14] This fact does not necessarily devalue or 'reduce' high culture, but it does seriously complicate talk of *the* dominant culture, forcing critics and historians to ask structural questions: 'dominant' for whom, where and under what conditions, and with what effects? It does not negate talk of power or cultural authority but draws attention to their uneven, variable distribution.

The field of possibility in which literature operates has thus been fundamentally altered, restructuring the constraints and stresses in the system, but also, and no less, the opportunities, the spaces for growth. Of course, neither internationalisation nor market diversification are managed for the benefit of artists/producers and not necessarily for consumers either. Both can kill. Distribution remains a serious, often mortal, problem for the publishing industry, as it does in the film industry.[15] The Australian market—and in many ways that means Australian culture—is in a structurally vulnerable position in most areas. Loss of independence and local knowledge is a constant threat. But the vulnerabilities have less to do with terminal cultural decline than with transformations in the system, from within and from without, that also produce new structures, new possibilities and new desires towards both internationalisation and local diversification. In literature as in film, television and music, a mature, sophisticated system has come into being since the mid-eighties, defined by the presence of an established and diverse local production and publishing industry, a diverse (though relatively small) local market, an established (though never secure) regime of regulation and intervention, a professional (though often exploitative) infrastructure of agents, critics, administrators, magazines and commercial outlets, and an amateur infrastructure of fans and wannabes. Of course this does not necessarily translate into wealth or celebrity. Nevertheless, although many cultural projects in Australia share something of the 'one off' quality of Australian cinema—of developments that *could have been* followed up[16]—there is now a substantial ecology of Australian film, television, popular music and literature; that is, cultures which, however fragile, have their own dynamics, their own diversity and density, their own 'self-sustainability'.

This has meant that the relationship between the national and the international, the local and the imported, has also fundamentally altered, both in economic and industrial terms, and in how it is possible to think or criticise the relationship. Australian culture in all these fields is more integrated than ever before within international cultures and markets—and by 'integrated' I do not mean absorbed or taken over. In terms of modes of production, styles of marketing and ways of conceiving creative projects, the national and the international no longer function as opposites. Perhaps, as history is beginning to suggest, the national and the international never did operate just in this simple fashion. Our nationalist intellectuals, for example, while never modernists, were often modernising internationalists of a sort, and newer studies are revealing the complexity of earlier patterns of 'dependence'.[17] But the dynamics of the relationship have changed dramatically in the last decade or so. As a consequence, criticism has been forced to read both the present and past in new ways, and to seek out new models to account for the formation and transformation of national cultures.

In the late 1990s we witnessed the delicious spectacle of Hollywood movie-workers demonstrating about the number of movie projects going off shore, particularly to Australia.[18] Of course the American industries remain massively powerful and pervasive. But the nature of the Australian relationship to that power has shifted, at least in what seem to be its emergent tendencies. Rather than sheer opposition or imitation, the Australian culture industries are increasingly 'shuffled into' the international networks as part of a system of transnational flows that do not work simply in the one direction. Elizabeth Jacka has used the movie *Babe* as a way of exemplifying one dimension of this shift, describing the film as 'international as well as national, imbricated with other audiovisual industries and with new media technologies and with a narrative style and theme that is different from a Hollywood blockbuster but sits comfortably alongside it'.[19]

Alongside cases such as *Babe* or *Dark City* are the 'small' movies that burrow out a place for themselves within the dominant system, movies such as *Love and Other Catastrophes*, *Head On* or *Praise*, addressing their local audiences without anxiety or apology, and, we might say, without nationalism. They also achieve success in the international festival market, and sometimes beyond. We are approaching the situation in which— positively—Australia can afford to have a cinema that is 'bad' as well as 'good', surely a sign of a mature system.[20] In popular music the two-way or multiple flows are perhaps even more striking. The point is not just the export success of a handful of Australian acts, significant though that is, but rather the way that, here, too, local and international no longer function simply as opposites. Most significant is that bands in the two, three or four rungs of celebrity below the A-list stars like Savage Garden tour around Europe or the States and have fan bases there, and their equivalents from Denver or Dallas might do the same in Brisbane. Brisbane isn't the worst place in the world for a band like Regurgitator to establish and maintain local, national and international fan bases.

In the literary domain too, imaginative or professional relations between writers, kinds of writing and kinds of readers are likely to be transnational in this sense. Although the relations of power remain seriously unequal, the integration of the Australian market into international publishing has, ironically perhaps, assisted the integration of Australian publishing into international markets, not least for newer publishers such as Melbourne's Text Publishing. Together with the increasing diversity and specialisation of local writing and local markets—even more I think than the spectacular international success of Australian writing in the 1980s and 1990s—these developments have reduced almost to insignificance that stubbornly persistent colonialist sense of Australian culture as out of place and out of time. The 'international' is no longer something we need to catch up with or import in order to remedy an essential lack in local culture; not something we might proclaim in order to distinguish our taste from the parochial local norm. It is *here* as well as there, inside as well as out. It doesn't necessarily mean London (almost certainly not) or New York or Paris; it might mean Beijing or Bali or Buenos Aires.[21] As Lever puts it, in the course of making a slightly different argument, 'the Australian writer in the 1990s is likely to be acutely aware of an international literary scene, in which Australians must participate as equals, rather than as the favoured patriots or ridiculed provincials of the past'.[22] And again, this isn't just about the stars on the A-list such as David Malouf or Peter Carey who, if symptomatic, are also atypical; nor is it just about successful genre writers. I'm thinking no less of more 'local' writers such as Nick Earls, Venero Armanno or Richard Flanagan. The nearest evidence to hand is a feature piece in the *Weekend Australian*'s Review pages. Novelist and teacher of creative writing Antoni Jach, interviewed by journalist Helen Elliot, lists the writers he admires: 'American Richard Ford, Austrian Thomas Bernhard, Frenchman Michel Butor, Italian Roberto Calasso'.[23] Jach has a dream of Europe, to be sure, but there's no cringe involved, only a sense that these writers speak to him of what the contemporary novel—here and now and in Melbourne—might be. Here, too, the new internationalism works sideways and crossways rather than in a linear relation to a single (European) cultural centre. My point is that these local and international dynamics do not diminish the significance of the nation so much as re-fashion it beyond the old linear relationships that produced the old nationalism and its opposites. They allow for and perhaps even demand a new (positive) sense of culture within the nation.

It is odd, in fact, how little contemporary criticism is interested in 'overseas influences' on contemporary Australian literature (postcolonial comparative work is another question). For a moment in the 1970s it looked as if this was going to be a major new theme that would revitalise the whole critical field with what appeared to be a rise in American and European influences. But on the whole I think there are *good* reasons why, apart from some passing references to magic realism or postmodern fiction, this interest in overseas influence has not been sustained or why it has been shuffled back into more routine ways of thinking about our literature.[24] These have to do with the coming into being of the local cultural ecology or mature system as described above, the new density that both the literary culture and the national history now carry, and the sense that the international is now part of a shifting set of relationships—between local, regional, national and international co-ordinates—rather than an absolute other.[25] Literary culture, like Australian history, is, at best, now both more self-reflexive and more cross-cultural (for want of a better word).[26] By 'self-reflexive' I mean that the central questions for writing and thinking Australian history are no longer those circulating around the relationship between Australian and Britain but are, we might say, about Australia's relationship with itself: about Aboriginal history, histories of gender, sexuality, race and colonialism, and histories of memory, space and place, all of which have become part of literary history too. These are shifts that I would dare to call postcolonial (in the relative rather than absolute sense of the term).

Something similar has happened in the realm of theory too. Again from a structurally 'weak' position, Australia has become an exporter of original theory in the fields of cultural studies, feminism, postcolonialism, multiculturalism and more. Australian theory circulates through and as part of international networks. Like novels and pop music, it almost always has its own local twist, its distinctive Australian inflection, which arises from the everyday and institutional worlds in which it must operate, from the circulation of both national and international dynamics, and from productive work on both local and international 'raw materials'.[27]

IV

Intensification of the local and the national has thus occurred alongside and often in the same trajectory as intensification of the international (in some spheres, the American). There is a sense in which Australia can now be seen as exemplary not merely as supplementary; exemplary, that is, of the condition of a postmodern, multicultural and postcolonial nation. This is at least a possibility that our best film, visual art, pop music, literature, history-writing, theory and criticism can make its own and make known to us. Of course, there are contrary political forces that want to exemplify something very different. Nonetheless, what has emerged on the positive side might be called a relative rather than an absolute sense of national culture, a sense that Australian culture, at whatever point we approach it, *is* distinctive, but relatively so, simultaneously the same and different in the formulation Tom O'Regan uses to describe both Australia's television culture and Australian cinema.

The story, in other words, has little to do with essences, organic growth or autochthonous evolution. It demands a model of cultural *transfer* rather than cultural becoming. For example, Australia's is 'a film and television milieu configured by flows and transfers (of concepts, genres, styles, texts, fashions etc.) which shape film-making, criticism and consumption'; in this model 'cultural imports are connected to local cultural production and its export, while unoriginality and derivation is (sic) connected to the very possibility of originality'.[28] O'Regan develops Yuri Lotman's five-stage model of cultural transfer which he connects to Meaghan Morris's argument about the 'positive unoriginality' of Australian culture.[29] Let me quote O'Regan, but replacing his references to cinema with references to literature:

> Lotman and Morris emphasise the agency of the receiving culture in any cultural transfer relationship. They draw attention to a culture's necessary orientation toward 'imports' and how imports and local texts restructure each other. Both direct our attention to the international participation inherent in all national [literatures] and to the different sorts of participation on offer. National audiences, critics and [writers] appropriate, negotiate and transform the international [literatures] in various ways. The centrality of cultural transfers in the Australian context suggests that the distinctiveness of Australian [literature] may be found in its *negotiation* of cultural transfers. Any claims we may make about the space of—and distinctiveness of—Australian [literature] must turn on the participation, negotiation, adaptation and hybridisation following on from unequal cultural transfers.[30]

McKenzie Wark has given the point an even more positive spin, wresting from it a new way of thinking about the contemporary situation of Australian cultures 'within' international cultural systems. 'The great virtue of Australian culture,' Wark suggests, 'is its unoriginality—that it borrows shamelessly from all manner of foreign sources, that it adapts and collages'.[31]

These shifts in cultural modelling which have gained currency in various domains of media studies in recent years have been driven by work on popular culture, indeed by the attempt to 'keep up' with popular culture itself; also by the visual arts (Wark's formulation is sourced to Paul Taylor). Their necessary pre-condition is the relative dissolution of the boundaries between high culture and the media cultures. The point is not that cultural markets and cultural institutions are no longer structured through the division between high and low culture, or that high culture no longer carries prestige. Rather there has been a shift in social relations, in markets, technologies and institutions, and in the relations of value between the different domains:

> High culture is fully absorbed within commodity production ... Works of high culture are now produced in exactly the same serial forms as those of low culture: the paperback book, the record or disk, film, radio and television (where there now exist specifically high-cultural channels). Within the overall cultural market high culture forms a 'niche' market—but this is also true of many, increasingly differentiated, low cultural products.
>
> [R]ather than designating definite domains of texts, the terms 'high' and 'low' represent a division that is operative within all cultural domains.[32]

The 'modernist fantasy of self-definition through opposition to a degraded mass culture ... has been replaced by rather different practices of fusion or play between high and low genres and traditions'.[33] If this is now a (too) familiar way of defining postmodernism, it is not just a postmodernist utopian fantasy. More significantly, it is a quite 'pragmatic' way of understanding what is going on in contemporary artistic practice. After all, for the vast majority of the post-sixties generations popular culture has been learnt as a first language, high culture as a second. The dissolution of the barriers between high and low cultures for these age groups was a mundane reality before it was, for some, a principled intellectual project.

This development has had its consequences, too, for an Australian culture so often defined and self-defined as irredeemably 'low' in relation to European high culture. The dissolution of the boundaries between high and low has, in the same process, dissolved the Australian colonial sense of cultural inferiority, distance or time-lag. Again, Australia becomes exemplary rather than supplementary. Many of the central issues which drove talk about Australian culture from the mid-nineteenth to the mid-twentieth century—debates about whether Australian culture was local or universal, original or oppressed, youthful or mature, raw or belated—quite suddenly disappeared sometime in the 1980s because quite suddenly they stopped being important or interesting questions. Earlier forms of nationalism (and anti-nationalism) born from the *absence* of a convincing sense of local cultural density have thus been disappearing too, as the presence of a national culture, in the ecological sense suggested above, has become both a creative possibility and an everyday reality. The process does not involve any transcendence of the nation.

V

In studies of popular culture or media in Australia, the problem of the national culture has taken a significantly different form from in literary studies, not just because of the different technology or chronology involved, but because of the imposing presence in these fields of popular, mass-mediated cultures, especially but never exclusively American in provenance. American culture has dominated in cinema, television and popular music in ways that are not paralleled in literature (by American or British literature). I suppose there was a sense for many in the nineteenth century that British literature was literature, but not in the same way that in the twentieth century American cinema structurally and industrially is the cinema. In film and popular music Australian cultural production and reception have been shaped at every turn by the relationship to the United States. O'Regan's definition of Australian cinema as a 'medium-sized English-language cinema' is not merely a statement of the obvious, but rather a way of defining precisely Australia's structural relationship to American cinema and, then, to other national cinemas.[34] Both adjectives define the advantages and the disadvantages, the constraints and the possibilities, structured into Australia's situation.

O'Regan's point is that the USA (like the market) is a structural condition of Australian culture's operation, not its inevitable doom. Australia's is a condition of relative cultural weakness, 'permanently unequal', but O'Regan wants to resist seeing Australian culture, cinema in this instance, either as the abject victim of America or as its wholesome, triumphant opponent.[35] The fact that Hollywood has long been part of Australian cinema is cause for neither rejoicing nor despair, but a condition of its being to which we must attend. It says nothing about cultural value or, for that matter, originality. Australian cinema in response has adopted a range of strategies to 'compete with, imitate, oppose, complement and supplement' the dominant international cinema.[36] From this perspective it is more useful to emphasise Australia's participation in a transnational film industry than its separation. It is routinely rather than exceptionally difficult in Australian cinema to see where the local ends and the international begins.

Borrowing, repetition and appropriation have long been recognised as the normal condition of making culture in the domain of popular culture, in contrast to the realm of high art with its celebration of originality and uniqueness. Hence the search, too, for a unique and original Australian art which is unlike everybody else's mass culture. Perhaps literary criticism is still uncomfortable with the idea, despite the postmodern celebration of genre-bending or postcolonial theories of (textual) hybridity. The hybridity that literary criticism celebrates tends to be of a high and worthy aesthetic variety, the very definition of literariness rather than an historical circumstance. Literature is thus still accorded a privileged position, its capacity for representing or performing hybridity given a special ethical status. For O'Regan, by contrast, diversity and hybridity are in the first instance *mundane* properties of Australian culture; that is, merely structural consequences of its position as a medium-sized, predominantly English-language culture in a larger international system. At this level, there is nothing to be celebrated; hybridity in itself guarantees nothing (a useful correction to some uses of the notion as an absolute aesthetic principle). Nonetheless, it is the description of this diversity, argued against essentialist notions of the national culture, which underwrites the return of a more positive, more inclusive sense of national culture as an object of critical interest. Thus the point is not that literature—or cinema or television—can't elevate this mundane hybridity into an aesthetic or political principle. On the contrary, it's about defining the conditions under which this can occur, the ways in which the necessities of Australian culture can be turned into virtues.

These are the kind of arguments that I find interesting to shift across to the literary domain: first because of the way they bring to the fore the structural or institutional aspects of culture in Australia; second because of the way they model the integration of Australian cultures into international cultures; and third because they bring back into play a positive sense of the nation and the state. I'm not suggesting that this is all or always what criticism should do. Literary criticism has many uses, many different occasions for its aesthetic, ethical, political and historical modes. We need therefore to be modestly pluralistic towards the ends of criticism, while remaining rigorously sceptical towards its ultimate claims about getting outside or above or beyond or between anything. Without being prescriptive, then, I want to argue for the usefulness of attempting to map just how literature is both like and unlike other fields of culture in Australia; or the ways in which the shape of Australian literature, too, is defined by the fact of its being 'medium-sized and predominantly English-language' within an international system; or, again, the way it functions *through* national boundaries. Again, I think we could call these perspectives postcolonial. They can also indicate how literature both is and is not a 'special' domain of culture, revealing both the mundane and the privileged aspects of literature which define its meanings in contemporary Australian society. More strongly, I'd say that without some consideration along these lines we are likely either to under-estimate or over-estimate literature's significance.

The idea of cultural transfer and transformation is critical in renewing ways of thinking about the nation and national cultures. On the one hand it suggests how and why Australian culture *shares* many aspects in common with other multicultural settler cultures, other medium-sized, English-language cultures (and so forth). But it will also suggest the relative distinctiveness that cultural forms have taken within this national space (and within the dynamics that the national boundaries themselves set in motion). It provides a way of talking about Australian originality and distinctiveness which is not tied to idealist notions of a self-originating culture, a pure or essential form. The precondition of Australian culture is seen instead in terms of its dialogue or negotiation with, its implication in, its appropriation, re-combination, indigenisation or hybridisation of, international cultures—even at the most mundane and local level, always in a context structured by local and national dynamics. Think of country music, or Tracey Moffat, or David Foster, or Meryl Tankard, or Circus Oz.

The fit with literature won't be too neat. American literature does not play the same role here as Hollywood or American music; the technologies involved mean that literature has a different relationship to its individual creators (more like popular music than film); and what we do with literature isn't exactly the same as what we do with cinema, television or music. Within the general model, each form can be shown to have its own relationship to its local market, its local traditions and its international contemporaries.

Interestingly, 'high' art—literature and the visual arts, even dance—has been much more open to Indigenous and ethnic minority influences than have the popular cultures of film and television. Popular music lies somewhere in between. It is virtually impossible now to think 'Australian literature' without also thinking 'Aboriginal' and 'multicultural' as inseparable parts of its contemporary meaning; the same can't be said of television, despite SBS. This new high cultural function exists partly because of the different economics involved, but also because of the 'minority' (but no longer simply elite) cultural space they occupy and the ways in which these high prestige forms can be pre-disposed, by cultural producers, policy-makers, critics and audiences, towards kinds of 'national' responsibility. Again, notions of the dominant or of essentialising, homogenising nationalism are inadequate to explain these cultural dynamics.

VI

One tendency in recent cultural and political studies is to see globalisation as boosting the international *and* the local at the expense of the national. This clearly has its point, and fits with much of what I've said above. But its disappearing of the nation is too slick by half, and we should probably be sceptical of any notion that manages so neatly to combine two favourite intellectual fantasies, the rootless cosmopolitan and the rooted community. The boundaries of the nation do make a difference. They act as a kind of 'interference' for both incoming and outgoing messages. They define one crucial and contested level in the circulation of meanings and values. They define one set of institutional structures which also help determine what happens above and below their own horizon.

The national *is* a productive way of conceiving of an audience, a critical community, a 'society', a market, a history, a polity. Nothing can guarantee that such conceptions will not be exploitative but, equally, nothing guarantees in advance that they won't be useful, strategic, progressive, democratic. National cultural institutions like the Australia Council, sometimes despite their rhetoric, tend to be biased *towards* diversity and inclusiveness, although we will still want to scrutinise the balance or reach of their programs. The idea of the nation motivates creative, critical and pedagogic projects. We don't have to like all of these projects—we almost certainly won't—but they will define the nation as a crucial framework for competition between projects. As Simon During has written, 'to reject nationalism absolutely or to refuse to discriminate between nationalisms is to accede to a way of thought by which intellectuals—especially postcolonial intellectuals—cut themselves off from effective political action'.[37] We do not need to romanticise this 'political action'. It need not be anything more than what we do when we use literature or other forms of culture as critics or teachers to 'responsibilise' our audience—as good readers and good citizens.

The national is still one of the most important, one of the least avoidable, concepts through which this process can occur, but it is of course by no means the only one. Questions of gender or sexual identity, or postcolonial or regional histories, are just some of the other options. We can agree with Richard White, that 'to write the richest and fullest Australian history, we need to write against the notion of a national history, the sort of history that takes the nation as its subject and teleological dynamic'.[38] But my point in relation to nationality is, again, that we cannot afford to theorise or to activate negative critique alone, as if nationality were always and everywhere a useless or pernicious notion. White, too, is suggesting a constitutive history not merely a deconstructive one ('Only then will we be able to give the nation its proper place in its history'). We need to be able to theorise and activate a positive account of the nation, not in a simple celebratory sense, but in the sense of substantive histories, institutions or cultural possibilities that we want either to maintain or to bring into being. *Australian literature* is one way of defining such histories, institutions and cultural possibilities.

Notes

INTRODUCTION

1   David Carter, 'Structures, Networks, Institutions: The New Empiricism, Book History and Literary History', in Katherine Bode and Robert Dixon (eds), *Resourceful Reading: The New Empiricism, eResearch and Australian Literary Culture* (Sydney: Sydney University Press, 2009), pp. 31–52.

2   Pascale Casanova, trans. M.B. DeBevoise, *The World Republic of Letters* (1999; Cambridge, Mass., and London: Harvard University Press, 2004). A.A. Phillips, 'The Cultural Cringe', *Meanjin* 9.4 (Summer 1950): 299–302.

3   Robert Dixon, *Photography, Early Cinema and Colonial Modernity: Frank Hurley's Synchronized Lecture Entertainments* (London: Anthem, 2012); Robert Dixon and Veronica Kelly (eds), *Impact of the Modern: Vernacular Modernities in Australia 1870s–1960s* (Sydney: Sydney University Press, 2008).

4   Tom O'Regan, *Australian National Cinema* (London: Routledge, 1996), p. 77.

5   The modernity of both the Jindyworobaks and Ern Malley has been asserted: see Peter Kirkpatrick, 'Jindy Modernist: The Jindyworobaks as Avant Garde', in Peter Kirkpatrick and Robert Dixon (eds), *Republics of Letters: Literary Communities in Australia* (Sydney: Sydney university Press, 2012), pp. 99–112; Philip Mead, *Networked Language: Culture & History in Australian Poetry* (Melbourne: Australian Scholarly Publishing, 2008), ch. 2.

6   Humphrey McQueen, *The Black Swan of Trespass: The Emergence of Modernist Painting in Australia to 1944* (Sydney: Alternative Publishing Cooperative, 1979).

7   Helen Topliss, *Modernism and Feminism: Australian Women Artists 1900–1940* (Sydney: Craftsman House, 1996); Ann Stephen, Philip Goad and Andrew McNamara (eds), *Modern Times: The Untold Story of Modernism in Australia* (Melbourne: Miegunyah Press, 2008).

8   In addition to those referenced: Liz Conor, *The Spectacular Modern Woman: Feminine Visibility in the 1920s* (Bloomington: Indiana University Press, 2004); Laurie Duggan, *Ghost Nation: Imagined Space and Australian Visual Culture 1901–1939* (St Lucia: University of Queensland Press, 2001); Peter Kirkpatrick, *The Sea Coast of Bohemia: Literary Life in Sydney's Roaring Twenties* (St Lucia: University of Queensland Press, 1992); Angela Woollacott, *To Try Her Fortune in London : Australian Women, Colonialism, and Modernity* (Oxford: Oxford University Press, 2001).

9   David Carter, *Dispossession, Dreams and Diversity: Issues in Australian Studies* (Sydney: Pearson, 2006), ch. 10: 'Australian Modernity'.

10 Richard Waterhouse, *Private Pleasures, Public Leisure: A History of Australian Popular Culture since 1788* (Melbourne: Longman, 1995); Veronica Kelly, 'A Complementary Economy? National Markets and International Product in Early Australian Theatre Managements', *New Theatre Quarterly* 21.1 (February 2005): 77–95.

11 Jill Julius Matthews, *Dance Hall & Picture Palace: Sydney's Romance with Modernity* (Sydney: Currency Press, 2005), p. 1.

12 Matthews, *Dance Hall & Picture Palace*, pp. 1–2, 8.

13   Mead, *Networked Language*, p. 30.

14   Dixon, *Photography, Early Cinema and Colonial Modernity*, pp. xxiii-xxiv.

15   Kelly, 'A Complementary Economy?', p. 77.

16   See my 'Modernising Anglocentrism: *Desiderata* and Literary Time' in Kirkpatrick and Dixon (eds), *Republics of Letters*, pp. 85–98 and 'Transpacific or Transatlantic Traffic? Australian Books and American Publishers', in Robert Dixon and Nicholas Birns (eds), *Reading Across the Pacific: Australia-United States Intellectual Histories* (Sydney: Sydney University Press, 2010), pp. 339–59.

17   David Carter, 'Magazine Culture: Notes Towards a History of Australian Periodical Publication 1920–1970' in Alison Bartlett, Robert Dixon and Christopher Lee (eds), *Australian Literature and the Public Sphere* (Toowoomba: University of Southern Queensland/ASAL, 1998), pp.69–79 and 'Magazine History', *Media International Australia* 99 (May 2001): 9–14.

18   Philip Mead has emphasised the local and regional elements beneath or beyond national/transnational frames: 'Nation, Literature, Location', in Peter Pierce (ed.), *The Cambridge History of Australian Literature* (Melbourne: Cambridge University Press, 2009), pp. 549–67.

WEIRD SCRIBBLINGS ON THE BEACH

This essay first appeared as 'Modernity and Belatedness in Australian Cultural Discourse' in Southerly 54.4 (Summer 1994–1995): 6–18.

1   Paper delivered to the British Australian Studies Association conference on Australian Popular Culture, London, September 1992. Published as 'On the Beach: Apocalyptic Hedonism and the Origins of Postmodernism', in Ian Craven (ed.), *Australian Popular Culture* (Cambridge: Cambridge University Press, 1994), pp. 190–204.

2   A.D. Hope, 'Australia', *Meanjin* 2.1 (Autumn 1943): 42.

3   Marcus Clarke, 'Preface to Gordon's *Poems*' (1876), in John Barnes (ed.), *The Writer in Australia* (Melbourne: Oxford University Press, 1969), pp. 35–36. Clarke's phrases first appeared in commentaries he wrote on paintings by Louis Buvelot and Nicholas Chevalier published in 1874.

4   From Clarke's commentary on Chevalier's *Buffalo Ranges*, in Bernard Smith (ed.), *Documents on Art and Taste in Australia 1770–1914* (Melbourne: Oxford University Press, 1975), p. 139.

5   P.R. Stephensen, 'The Foundations of Culture in Australia' (1935–36), in Barnes (ed.), *The Writer in Australia*, p. 205.

6   A.G. Stephens, 'Introduction to *The Bulletin Story Book*' (1901), in Barnes (ed.), *The Writer in Australia*, pp. 107–8.

7   D.R. Jarvis, 'The Development of an Egalitarian Poetics in the *Bulletin*, 1880–1890', *Australian Literary Studies* 10.1 (May 1981): 22–34.

8   See Ch. 6, 'Paris, Moscow, Melbourne', below.

9   'Foreword', *Vision* I (May 1923): 2.

10   Humphrey McQueen, *The Black Swan of Trespass: The Emergence of Modernist Painting in Australia to 1944* (Sydney: Alternative Publishing Cooperative, 1979), p. 19.

11   A.A. Phillips, 'The Craftsmanship of Lawson', in *The Australian Tradition: Studies in a Colonial Culture*, (1958; Melbourne: Longman Cheshire, 1980), p. 1. The essay first appeared in *Meanjin* 7.2 (Winter 1948): 80–90. The original opening was less dramatic, although it still describes the work of Lawson, Furphy and their contemporaries as a 'landmark in the history of Anglo-Saxon culture'.

12   In 'The Democratic Theme', Phillips links the writers' proletarianism and realism to 'the simplicity and directness which belonged to the way of life [they were] revealing': *The Australian Tradition*, p. 53.

13   Herbert Piper 'The Background of Romantic Thought', *Quadrant* 2.1 (Summer 1957–1958): 49–55.
14   H.P. Heseltine, 'The Literary Heritage', *Meanjin* 21.1 (1962): 35–49. My emphasis.
15   Lionel Trilling, 'On the Modern Element in Modern Literature', *Partisan Review* 28.1 (January-February 1961): 9–35.
16   Bernard Smith, 'The Myth of Isolation' (1962), in *The Death of the Artist as Hero: Essays in History and Culture* (Melbourne: Oxford University Press, 1988): 220–21. The quotations are from Robert Hughes in the Exhibition Catalogue and the review of the *London Times* art critic.
17   Milner, 'On the Beach', p. 192.
18   For a critique of Milner see Ann Curthoys and Stephen Muecke, 'Australia, For Example', in Wayne Hudson and David Carter (eds), *The Republican Debate* (Sydney: UNSW Press, 1993), pp. 196–200.
19   I was delighted to discover a magic realist version of the genre: 'What appears to be romantic or surrealist at the centre of civilisation may take on a realistic quality at the periphery. The so-called "magic realism" of Latin American fiction has taught us that. There has always been a similar strain in Australian culture though it is yet to be clearly discerned.' Bruce Clunies Ross, 'Australian Literature and Australian Culture', in Laurie Hergenhan (ed.), *The Penguin New Literary History of Australia* (Ringwood: Penguin, 1988), p. 13.

CRITICS, WRITERS, INTELLECTUALS

A version of this essay was first published in Elizabeth Webby (ed.), The Cambridge Companion to Australian Literature *(Cambridge: Cambridge University Press, 2000), pp. 258–93.*

1   Since this essay first appeared there has been a significant 'reclaiming ' of the discipline, a renewed confidence about literary studies on its own ground, even as that ground is constantly redefined by developments such as 'the new empiricism', 'transnationalism' or world literature. See for example Katherine Bode and Robert Dixon (eds), *Resourceful Reading: The New Empiricism, eResearch, and Australian Literary Culture* (Sydney: Sydney University Press, 2009); Robert Dixon, 'Australian Literature-International Contexts', *Southerly* 67.1–2 (2007): 15–27.
2   Frederick Sinnett, 'The Fiction Fields of Australia ' (1856), in John Barnes (ed.), *The Writer in Australia, 1856–1964* (Melbourne: Oxford University Press, 1969), p. 19; Marcus Clarke, 'Preface to Gordon's *Poems*' (1876), in Barnes (ed.), *The Writer in Australia*, p. 34; H.G. Turner and Alexander Sutherland, *The Development of Australian Literature* (Melbourne: George Robertson, 1898), p. vii; A.G. Stephens, 'Henry Lawson's Poems', *Bulletin*, 15 February 1896, in Leon Cantrell (ed.), *A.G. Stephens: Selected Writings* (Sydney: Angus & Robertson, 1978), p. 220; Vance Palmer, 'An Australian National Art' (1905), in Barnes (ed.), *The Writer in Australia*, p. 170; P.R. Stephensen, *The Foundations of Culture in Australia: An Essay Towards National Self Respect* (1935–36; Sydney: Allen & Unwin, 1986), p. 22; Vincent Buckley, 'The Image of Man in Australian Poetry' (1957), in Barnes (ed.), *The Writer in Australia*, p. 294; Miles Franklin, *Laughter, Not For a Cage* (Sydney: Angus & Robertson, 1956), p. 217, published posthumously based on CLF lectures delivered in 1950.
3   Brian Kiernan, *Criticism* (Melbourne: Oxford University Press, 1974), pp. 11–12.
4   Nettie Palmer, 'The Arts in Australia' (1929), in Vivian Smith (ed.), *Nettie Palmer* (St Lucia: University of Queensland Press, 1988), p. 378. Palmer is paraphrasing a lecture by Will Dyson.
5   Palmer, 'The Arts in Australia', p. 377.
6   Kiernan, *Criticism*, p. 9.

7   Turner and Sutherland, *The Development of Australian Literature*, p. 30. For this common phrase, combining the meanings of 'racially characteristic ' and 'organically rooted', see also Elizabeth Webby, 'Before the *Bulletin*: Nineteenth Century Literary Journalism', in Bruce Bennett (ed.), *Crosscurrents: Magazines and Newspapers in Australian Literature*, (Melbourne: Longman Cheshire, 1981), pp. 3 & 25.

8   Anon., 'The Characteristics of Australian Literature' (1890), in Barnes (ed.), *The Writer in Australia*, p. 45.

9   Ken Stewart, 'Journalism and the World of the Writer: The Production of Australian Literature, 1855-1915', in Laurie Hergenhan (ed.), *The Penguin New Literary History of Australia* (Ringwood: Penguin, 1988), pp. 174-79; George Nadel, *Australia's Colonial Culture: Ideas, Men and Institutions in Mid-Nineteenth Century Eastern Australia* (Melbourne: Cheshire, 1957).

10   Turner and Sutherland, *The Development of Australian Literature*, p. x.

11   Sylvia Lawson, *The Archibald Paradox: A Strange Case of Authorship* (Ringwood: Penguin/Allen Lane, 1983); John Docker, *The Nervous Nineties: Australian Cultural Life in the 1890s* (Melbourne: Oxford University Press, 1991), pp. 26-69.

12   Richard White, *Inventing Australia: Images and Identity 1688-1980* (Sydney: Allen & Unwin, 1981), p. 88.

13   A.G. Stephens, 'Australian Literature I' (1901), in Cantrell (ed.), *A.G. Stephens*, p. 77. In 'Fashions in Poetry' (1899) Stephens writes: 'Beyond all other verse writers [Tennyson] embodied the spirit of his time. But his time is gone, and the spirit of his time is gone, and with them has gone the force of much of Tennyson's poetry.' Cantrell (ed.), *A.G. Stephens*, p. 52.

14   Lawson, *The Archibald Paradox*, p. 171.

15   H.M Green, *A History of Australian Literature: Pure and Applied Volume I 1789-1923* (Sydney: Angus & Robertson, 1962), pp. 762-74, especially p. 773.

16   Stephens, 'Introduction to *The Bulletin Story Book*' (1901), in Cantrell (ed.), *A.G. Stephens*, p. 109.

17   Stewart, 'Journalism', p. 189.

18   Leon Cantrell, 'A.G. Stephens, the *Bulletin*, and the 1890s' in Leon Cantrell (ed.), *Bards, Bohemians and Bookmen: Essays in Australian Literature* (St Lucia: University of Queensland Press, 1976), p. 110.

19   Stephens, 'Australian Literature I', p. 82.

20   Stephens, 'A Book of Sunlight', in Cantrell (ed.), *A.G. Stephens*, p. 213. Also 'Lawson and Literature' in the same volume, p. 228.

21   Stephens, 'Literary Criticism of Art', in Cantrell (ed.), *A.G. Stephens*, pp. 346 & 348.

22   Christopher Brennan, 'Studies in French Poetry, 1860-1900', *Bookfellow* (January 1920): 44-46.

23   From the *Bulletin*: Vance Palmer, 'Fiction for Export', 1 June 1922; 'The Missing Critics', 26 July 1923; 'The Writer and his Audience', 8 January 1925; Louis Esson, 'Nationality in Art', 1 February 1923. Responses include: Wallace Nelson, 'Art and Nationality', 1 March 1923; Frank Morton, 'Art and Nationality', 5 April 1923. Morton was a powerful, witty critic in his own right, mainly in the pages of the *Triad*. He argued that 'The fetich (sic) of Nationality is just as bad and damned a thing in Art as in Affairs... Art, like true greatness, has no nationality'.

24   Phrases quoted from Pictor, 'The Purpose of Art', *Bulletin*, 13 September 1923; and R.H.M., 'A Celt in a Kilt', *Bulletin*, 20 September 1923.

25   White, *Inventing Australia*, ch. 7.

26   Vivian Smith, *Vance and Nettie Palmer* (Boston: Twayne, 1975); David Walker, *Dream and Disillusion: A Search for Australian Cultural Identity* (Canberra: ANU Press, 1976); Drusilla Modjeska, *Exiles at Home: Australian Women Writers 1925-1945* (Sydney: Angus & Robertson, 1981); Ivor Indyk, 'Vance Palmer and the Social Function of Literature', *Southerly* 50.3 (September 1990): 346-58; Craig Munro, *Wild Man of Letters: The Story of P.R. Stephensen* (Melbourne: Melbourne University Press,

1984).

27   Rex Ingamells, *Conditional Culture* (1938), in Barnes (ed.), *The Writer in Australia*, pp. 245–65.

28   Nettie Palmer, *Modern Australian Literature* (1924), in Smith (ed.), *Nettie Palmer*, p. 293.

29   Vance Palmer, 'Novels for Men', *Bulletin*, 19 April 1923.

30   Vance Palmer, 'The Narrative Faculty', *Bulletin*, 5 January 1922; 'Fact and Its Proper Place', *Bulletin*, 17 January 1924.

31   Quotations from Vance Palmer, 'The Missing Critics' and 'The Writer and his Audience'; Rann Daley [Vance Palmer], 'Undemocratic Democracy', *Aussie* (16 August 1920): 13.

32   Quotations from letters by Nettie Palmer (1936) in Vivian Smith (ed.), *Letters of Vance and Nettie Palmer 1915–1963* (Canberra: National Library of Australia, 1977), pp. 135 & 138.

33   Ian Reid, *Fiction and the Great Depression: Australia and New Zealand 1930–1950* (Melbourne: Edward Arnold, 1979): 77–84; and see Ch. 9, 'Realism, Documentary and Socialist Realism', below.

34   John Tregenza, *Australia's Little Magazines 1923–1954* (Adelaide: Libraries Board of SA, 1964); and see Ch. 6, 'Paris, Moscow, Melbourne', below. Examples of pamphlets/booklets include Stephensen, *The Foundations of Culture* (1936); Frank Dalby Davison, *While Freedom Lives* (1938); the unpublished 'Writers in Defence of Freedom ' (1939) (see Modjeska, *Exiles at Home*, pp. 259–60); and Brian Penton, *Think—Or Be Damned* (1941).

35   Stephensen, *Foundations of Culture*, pp. 8, 84, 66 (my emphasis).

36   The Crisis issue of *Meanjin* [1.8 (1942)] published Vance Palmer's 'Battle' and 'Australian Outlook' by Ingamells.

37   C.B. Christesen, 'The Wound as the Bow', *Meanjin* 10.1 (1951): 4.

38   Kiernan, *Criticism*, p. 30. Stuart Lee, '*Southerly*' in Bennett (ed.), *Crosscurrents*, pp. 161–71.

39   M. Barnard Eldershaw, *Essays in Australian Fiction* (Melbourne: Melbourne University Press, 1938). Writers treated are Richardson, Prichard, Davison, Palmer, Mann, Boyd, Stead, and Dark.

40   Manning Clark, 'Letter to Tom Collins: Mateship', *Meanjin* 2.3 (1943): 40; 'Tradition in Australian Literature', *Meanjin* 8.1 (1949): 16. New books included J.K. Ewers's *Creative Writing in Australia* (1945), Colin Roderick's surveys of fiction (1947 & 1950), and the republication of Furphy's *Such is Life* (1944).

41   Vance Palmer, *The Legend of the Nineties* (Melbourne: Melbourne University Press, 1954); A.A. Phillips, *The Australian Tradition: Studies in a Colonial Culture* (Melbourne: Cheshire, 1958); Russel Ward, *The Australian Legend* (Melbourne: Oxford University Press, 1958). See Phillips, 'Cultural Nationalism in the 1940s and 1950s' and Andrew Wells, 'The Old Left Intelligentsia 1930–1960', in Brian Head and James Walter (eds), *Intellectual Movements and Australian Society* (Melbourne: Oxford University Press, Melbourne, 1988).

42   A.A. Phillips, 'Preface to the 1966 Edition', *The Australian Tradition*, p. xxv.

43   David Carter, 'Capturing the Liberal Sphere: *Overland's* First Decade' in Carter (ed.), *Outside the Book: Contemporary Essays on Literary Periodicals* (Sydney: Local Consumption Publications, 1991), pp. 177–92. John McLaren, *Writing in Hope and Fear: Literature as Politics in Postwar Australia* (Melbourne: Cambridge University Press, 1996).

44   Jack Beasley, *Red Letter Days: Notes from Inside an Era* (Sydney: Australasian Book Society, 1979); David Carter, *A Career in Writing: Judah Waten and the Cultural Politics of a Literary Career* (Toowoomba: ASAL, 1997); Susan McKernan [Lever], *A Question of Commitment: Australian Literature in the Twenty Years After the War* (Sydney: Allen & Unwin, 1989), pp. 23–49.

45 Phillips, 'The Democratic Theme', *The Australian Tradition*, p. 70.

46 Leigh Dale, *The English Men: Professing Literature in Australian Universities* (Toowoomba: ASAL, 1997), pp. 148–51.

47 *Meanjin* 13.2–4 (1954): 165–69, 429–36, 591–96.

48 Dale, *The English Men*, pp. 92ff; Docker, *In A Critical Condition: Reading Australian Literature* (Ringwood: Penguin, 1984), pp. 86–92; Patrick Buckridge, 'Intellectual Authority and Critical Traditions in Australian Literature 1945–1975' in Head and Walter, *Intellectual Movements*, pp. 200–2.

49 Vincent Buckley, 'Towards an Australian Literature', *Meanjin* 18.1 (1959): 64, 68, 61. An important precursor was A.D. Hope, 'Standards in Australian Literature' (1956), reprinted in Grahame Johnston (ed.), *Australian Literary Criticism* (Melbourne: Oxford University Press, 1962).

50 For example G.A. Wilkes, *New Perspectives on Brennan's Poetry* (1953); Leonie Gibson [Kramer], *Henry Handel Richardson and Some of Her Sources* (1954); Vincent Buckley, *Henry Handel Richardson* (1961); Dorothy Green, *Ulysses Bound: Henry Handel Richardson and Her Fiction* (Canberra: ANU Press, 1973).

51 Docker, *In a Critical Condition*, pp. 90–107.

52 For example, Vincent Buckley, '*Capricornia*', in Johnston (ed.), *Australian Literary Criticism*, pp. 169–86; G.A. Wilkes, 'The Progress of Eleanor Dark', *Southerly* 12.3 (1951): 139–48 and 'The Novels of Katharine Susannah Prichard', *Southerly* 14.4 (1953): 220–31.

53 G.A. Wilkes, 'The Eighteen Nineties' (1958) in Johnston (ed.), *Australian Literary Criticism*, p. 40.

54 Vincent Buckley, *Essays in Poetry, Mainly Australian* (Melbourne: Melbourne University Press, 1957). 'The Image of Man in Australian Poetry', in Barnes (ed.), *The Writer in Australia*, pp. 273, 275, 283–84.

55 Thomas Shapcott, 'Douglas Stewart and Poetry in the *Bulletin*, 1940–1960' in Bennett (ed.), *Crosscurrents*, pp. 148–57. John Thompson, Kenneth Slessor and R.G. Howarth (eds), *The Penguin Book of Australian Verse* (Ringwood: Penguin, 1958).

56 Buckley, 'The Image of Man', pp. 292, 293, 295.

57 H.P. Heseltine, 'The Literary Heritage', *Meanjin* 21.1 (1962): 35–49. See Phillips's reply, 'The Literary Heritage Re-Assessed', *Meanjin* 21.2 (1962): 172–80.

58 Buckridge, 'Intellectual Authority and Critical Traditions', pp. 206–208.

59 Vincent Buckley, 'Patrick White and his Epic', in Johnston (ed.), *Australian Literary Criticism*, pp. 187–97.

60 But see James McAuley's anti-romantic discussion of White's style as Mannerism: 'Literature and the Arts', in Peter Coleman (ed.), *Australian Civilization* (Melbourne: Cheshire, 1962), p. 131.

61 Carter, 'Capturing the Liberal Sphere', pp. 188–91; McLaren, 'The Image of Reality in Our Writing', *Overland* 27–28 (July–September 1963): 45; Phillips, *The Australian Tradition*, p. 111.

62 Geoffrey Dutton (ed.), *The Literature of Australia* (Ringwood: Penguin, 1964). The revised 1976 edition goes further, dropping some of the broader essays while adding chapters on Stead, Webb and Boyd.

63 G.A. Wilkes, *Australian Literature: A Conspectus* (Sydney: Angus & Robertson, 1969), p. 11.

64 Judith Wright, *Preoccupations in Australian Poetry* (Melbourne: Oxford University Press, 1965); Brian Elliott, *The Landscape of Australian Poetry* (Melbourne: Cheshire, 1967).

65 Docker, *In a Critical Condition*, chs 3 & 4. Vincent Buckley, 'Unequal Twins: A Discontinuous Analysis', *Meanjin* 40.1 (1981): 9.

66 James McAuley, 'Comment: By Way of Prologue', *Quadrant* 1 (Summer 1956–1957): 3.

67 Susan McKernan [Lever], 'The Question of Literary Independence: *Quadrant* and Australian Writing', in Carter (ed.), *Outside the Book*, pp. 165–76.

68   Quoted phrase from Christesen, 'The Wound as the Bow'.

69   Christopher Lee, ""Sinister Signs of Professionalism"? Literary Gang Warfare in the 1950s and 1960s' in Alison Bartlett, Robert Dixon and Chris Lee (eds), *Australian Literature and the Public Sphere* (Toowoomba: ASAL, 1999), pp. 187–93.

70   Buckley, 'Towards an Australian Literature', p. 62. See also his essay 'Intellectuals' in Coleman (ed.), *Australian Civilization*, pp. 89–104.

71   Patrick Buckridge, 'Clearing a Space for Australian Literature 1940–1965', in Bruce Bennett and Jennifer Strauss (eds), *The Oxford Literary History of Australia* (Melbourne: Oxford University Press, 1998), p. 186.

72   Brian Matthews, *The Receding Wave: Henry Lawson's Prose* (Melbourne: Melbourne University Press 1972); Brian Kiernan, *Images of Society and Nature: Seven Essays on Australian Novels* (Melbourne: Oxford University Press, 1971).

73   Humphrey McQueen, *The New Britannia: An Argument Concerning the Social Origins of Australian Radicalism and Nationalism* (Ringwood: Penguin, 1970).

74   See Richard Gordon (ed.), *The Australian New Left: Critical Essays and Strategy* (Melbourne: Heinemann, 1970).

75   John Frow, 'The Chant of Thomas Keneally', *Australian Literary Studies* 10.3 (1982): 291–99.

76   Don Anderson, 'Christina Stead's Unforgettable Dinner Parties', *Southerly* 39.1 (1979): 28–45 and 'A Severed Leg: Anthropophagy and Communion in Patrick White's Fiction', *Southerly* 40.4 (1980): 399–417.

77   Peter Botsman et al. (eds), *The Foreign Bodies Papers* (Sydney: Local Consumption Publications, 1981).

78   See reviews listed in Dale, *The English Men*, p. 224 (note 97) and Docker, *In a Critical Condition*, pp. 163–79.

79   ASAL 1982 Conference Program and Abstracts (University of Adelaide, May 1982). Graeme Turner and Delys Bird, 'Australian Studies: Practice Without Theory', *Westerly* 3 (1982): 51–56.

80   Carole Ferrier (ed.), *Gender, Politics and Fiction: Twentieth Century Australian Women's Novels* (St Lucia: University of Queensland Press, 1986).

81   Graeme Turner, *National Fictions: Literature, Film and the Construction of Australian Narrative* (Sydney: Allen & Unwin, 1986), p. 2 (my emphasis); Kay Schaffer, *Women and the Bush: Forces of Desire in the Australian Cultural Tradition* (Cambridge: Cambridge University Press, 1988); Adam Shoemaker, *Black Words, White Page: Aboriginal Literature 1929–1988* (St Lucia: University of Queensland Press, 1989); Mudrooroo Narogin, *Writing from the Fringe: A Study of Modern Aboriginal Literature* (Melbourne: Hyland House, 1990).

82   Ken Gelder and Paul Salzman, *The New Diversity: Australian Fiction 1970–88* (Melbourne: McPhee Gribble, 1989).

83   Note the sub-titles of Robert Dixon, *Writing the Colonial Adventure: Race, Gender and Nation in Anglo-Australian Popular Fiction 1875–1914* (Cambridge: Cambridge University Press, 1995) and Susan Sheridan, *Along the Faultlines: Sex, Race and Nation in Australian Women's Writing 1880s–1930s* (Sydney: Allen & Unwin, 1995).

84   Dixon, *The Course of Empire: Neo-Classical Culture in New South Wales 1788–1860* (Melbourne: Oxford University Press, 1986); *Writing the Colonial Adventure* (reference above).

85   Simon During, *Patrick White* (Melbourne: Oxford University Press, 1996), p. 15. Peter Craven, 'The Kingdom of Correct Usage is Elsewhere', *Australian Book Review* 179 (April 1996): 36–41.

86   Sneja Gunew and Kateryna O. Longley (eds), *Striking Chords: Multicultural Literary Interpretations* (Sydney: Allen & Unwin, 1992); Bob Hodge and Vijay Mishra, *Dark Side of the Dream: Australian Literature and the Postcolonial Mind* (Sydney: Allen & Unwin, 1990).

87   Bill Ashcroft, Gareth Griffiths and Helen Tiffin, *The Empire Writes Back: Theory and Practice in Post-Colonial Literatures* (London: Routledge, 1989).

88   Wark, 'Media Policy and Law to Suit All', *Australian*, 6 December 1995.

89   Delys Bird, Robert Dixon and Susan Lever (eds), *Canonozities: The Making of Literary Reputation in Australia*, *Southerly* 57.3 (Spring 1997); Martin Lyons and John Arnold (eds), *A History of the Book in Australia, 1891–1945: A National Culture in a Colonised Market* (St Lucia: University of Queensland Press, 2001); *Journal of the Association for the Study of Australian Literature* 4 (2005), special issue devoted to ethics.

DRAWING THE LINE

1   Newspaper proprietors John Fairfax & Sons Ltd bought Art in Australia Ltd in November 1934; Ure Smith resigned from Fairfax in November 1938 at which point his connection with *Art in Australia* ceased. Nancy D.H. Underhill, *Making Australian Art 1916–49: Sydney Ure Smith Patron and Publisher* (Melbourne: Oxford University Press, 1991), pp.164–67. Other magazines such as the *Lone Hand* (1907–21), the *Triad* (1915–27) and *Table Talk* (1885–1939) covered art shows and included occasional reproductions and articles on modern art; *Undergrowth* (1925–29) was an important arena for discussions of modernism but circulated primarily among art students; *Art and Architecture* (1904–12) was the journal of the NSW Institute of Architects and the 'most informative magazine on the arts' but was virtually restricted to Institute members. Continued as *Salon* and then *Architecture*. Ure Smith published it 1924–26: Underhill, *Making Australian Art*, p. 157.

2   Underhill, *Making Australian Art*, pp. 36–45, 134–38.

3   Ibid., p. 37.

4   Ibid., p. 156.

5   Initially the magazine cost 12s 6d or £2.10s annually. In February 1922 its new series in a larger format was 6s or £1.4s annually. In February 1923, the original format was resumed but at a reduced cost, 7s 6d or £1.1s annually. The bi-monthly was 3s 6d or £1.10s, and from March 1934 the new quarterly was 5s and 20s annually. Underhill, *Making Australian Art*, p. 156.

6   Underhill, *Making Australian Art*, p. 5.

7   Introduction, *Art in Australia* 7 (1919): 1.

8   Roger Osborne, 'A National Interest in an International Market: The Circulation of Magazines in Australia during the 1920s', *History Australia* 5.3 (December 2008): 75.1–16.

9   See the discussion of *Aussie* in the following chapter.

10   Humphrey McQueen, *The Black Swan of Trespass: The Emergence of Modernist Painting in Australia to 1944* (Sydney: Alternative Publishing Cooperative, 1979), p. 6.

11   Katharine Susannah Prichard, 'The Grey Horse', *Art in Australia* 3.10 (December 1924) and 'The Curse', *Art in Australia* 3.17 (September 1926): 22–26.

12   'Roland Wakelin', *Art in Australia* 3.11 (March 1925): n.p.

13   Editorial, *Art in Australia* 17 (September 1926): 6.

14   Underhill, *Making Australian Art*, pp. 22–23.

15   McQueen, *The Black Swan*, p. 81n.

16   Underhill, *Making Australian Art*, p. 200.

17   *Art in Australia* 3.27 (March 1929): n.p.

18   Ibid. For the *Home* see Robert Holden, *Cover Up: The Art of Magazine Covers in Australia* (Sydney: Hodder & Stoughton, 1995).

19   Caroline Jordan, 'Designing Women: Modernism and its Representation in *Art in Australia*', in Jeanette Hoorn (ed.), *Strange Women: Essays in Art and Gender* (Melbourne: Melbourne University Press, 1994), pp. 28 & 30.

NOTES

20 Jane E. Hunt, "'Victors" and "Victims"? Men, Women, Modernism and Art in Australia', *Journal of Australian Studies* 27 (2003): 68.

21 For example, in Basil Burdett, 'Some Contemporary Australian Artists', *Art in Australia* 3.29 (September 1929): n.p.

22 Helen Topliss, *Modernism and Feminism: Australian Women Artists 1900–1940* (Sydney: Craftsman House, 1996).

23 Orpen was Irish but was understood primarily in *Art in AUstralia* as a 'British' painter.

24 Norman Lindsay's polemics and criticism (and art works) appeared regularly in the magazine's early numbers. Articles include: 'A Modern Malady' (1), 'The Creator and the Parasite' (2), 'Elliott Gruner's Morning Light' (5), 'The Inevitable Future' (2.1), 'The Quick and the Dead' (3.1–2) and 'Social Purpose as a Manifestation of Art' (3.3).

25 Editorial, *Art in Australia* 3.22 (December 1927): n.p.

26 Laurie Duggan, *Ghost Nation: Imagined Space and Australian Visual Culture 1901–1939* (St Lucia: University of Queensland Press, 2001), p. 71.

27 A. Radcliffe-Brown, 'Margaret Preston and Transition', *Art in Australia* 3.22 (December 1927): n.p.

28 Lindsay continues: 'Not to its immediate protagonists, or the herd of true believers— but to artists of assured standing who, mediating certain abstract notions, loosed by the movement, were enabled to add to their achievements certain qualities in which their art was lacking'. 'Will Ashton', *Art in Australia* 3.12 (June 1925): n.p.

29 'Society of Artists' Exhibition', *Art in Australia* 3.6 (December 1923): n.p.

30 P.G. Konody, 'The Australian Exhibition in London', *Art in Australia* 3.7 (March 1924): n.p. Extracts from reviews are included later in the same number. See also 'Roland Wakelin' (3.11, March 1925) where Wakelin describes the Australian Exhibition at Burlington House as showing 'sameness of treatment and a lack of individuality in outlook'.

31 Christopher Brennan, 'Form, Idea and Expression', *Art in Australia* 3.6 (December 1923): n.p. 'Bolshevism' was one of Howard Ashton's favourite terms for modernism too: 'Percy Lindsay's Landscapes', *Art in Australia* 11 (December 1921): n.p.

32 P.G. Konody, 'The Art of Gerald Moira', *Art in Australia* 11 (December 1921): n.p.

33 Basil Burdett, 'Roi de Mestre', *Art in Australia* 3.16 (June 1926): 13.

34 H.H. Fotheringham, 'The Importance of Design and its Relation to the Student', *Art in Australia* 3.21 (September 1927): 45.

35 George W. Lambert, 'A Painter's Advice to Students: A Talk by G.W. Lambert to the Students of the Sydney Art School on his Return to Sydney Recently', *Art in Australia* 2.1 (February 1922): 9.

36 Ibid., p. 11.

37 Anne Gray, *George W. Lambert Retrospective: Heroes and Icons* (Canberra: National Gallery of Australia, 2007), pp. 41–43.

38 Ibid., p. 31.

39 Ibid., pp. 28–29.

40 George W. Lambert, 'The European Art Exhibition', *Art in Australia* 3.5 (August 1923): n.p.

41 Basil Burdett, 'Some Contemporary Australian Artists', *Art in Australia* 3.29 (September 1929): n.p.

42 Basil Burdett, 'The Later Work of Elioth Gruner', *Art in Australia* 3.27 (March 1929): n.p.

43 Burdett, 'Roi de Mestre', p. 14.

44 Editorial, *Art in Australia* 3.17 (September 1926): 5.

45 Ibid., p. 6.

46 Burdett, 'Some Contemporary Australian Artists'.

47 A. Radcliffe-Brown, 'Margaret Preston and Transition'. There was nothing 'feminine' in the Editorial's definition of Preston's 'chief assets' as 'strength, vitality and an indubious originality in aesthetic values'.

48   A.G. Stephens, 'The Craft of Art', *Bookfellow* V.9 (July 1920): 141.

49   *Art in Australia*, 3.31 (March 1930): plates 33 & 34.

50   Editorial, *Art in Australia* 2 (1917): n.p.

51   Bernard Smith with Terry Smith and Christopher Heathcote, *Australian Painting 1788-2000* (Melbourne: Oxford University Press, 2001), p. 182. Smith describes the artists shaping taste in the 1920s in the following terms: 'Still deeply respectful of Royal Academy tradition, they nevertheless reflected the post-war interest in bright colours, crisp painting and decorative emphasis given currency by such British painters as Augustus John, Sir William Orpen, Eric Kennington, Gerald Kelly, Algernon Talmage, William Strang and Dame Laura Knight' (182).

52   Lambert, 'A Painter's Advice', pp. 9 & 13.

53   Margaret Preston, 'From Eggs to Electrolux', *Art in Australia* 3.22 (December 1927): n.p.

54   J.F. Bruce, 'The Younger Generation', *Art in Australia* 3.2 (May 1922): 45. Bruce's essay is in fact an attempt to wrest this dictum about craft from the hands of a 'resolute orthodoxy', to turn it towards the future following Lambert's example.

55   Lionel Lindsay, 'William Blake, the Artist', *Art in Australia* 3.4 (May 1923): n.p.; Margaret Preston, 'Australian Artists Versus Art', *Art in Australia* 3.26 (December 1928): n.p.

56   Roy de Mestre, 'Modern Art and the Australian Outlook', *Art in Australia* 3.14 (December 1925): n.p.

57   Editorial, *Art in Australia* 3.29 (September 1929): n.p.

58   Fotheringham, 'The Importance of Design', p. 45.

59   Thea Proctor, 'An Artist's Appreciation of Margaret Preston', *Art in Australia* 3.22 (December 1927): n.p.

60   Editorial, *Art in Australia* 3.29 (September 1929): n.p.

61   G.H.P [George Patterson], 'Art and the Ford Cars', *Art in Australia* 3.30 (December 1929): n.p.

'ESPRIT DE NATION' AND POPULAR MODERNITY

This essay first appeared in History Australia *5.3 (2008): 78.1–78.23.*

1   Stuart Macintyre, *The Succeeding Age: The Oxford History of Australia Volume 4 1901–1942* (Melbourne: Oxford University Press, 1986), p. 182. See also Pat Grimshaw et al., *Creating a Nation* (Melbourne: McPhee Gribble, 1994), chs 9 & 10 and Stuart Macintyre, *A Concise History of Australia* (Cambridge: Cambridge University Press, 1999), ch. 7.

2   See Liz Conor, *The Spectacular Modern Woman: Feminine Visibility in the 1920s* (Bloomington: Indiana University Press, 2004); Jill Julius Matthews, *Dance Hall and Picture Palace: Sydney's Romance with Modernity* (Sydney: Currency Press, 2005); Gail Reekie, *Temptations: Sex, Selling and the Department Store* (Sydney: Allen & Unwin, 1993); Richard Waterhouse, *Private Pleasures, Public Leisure: A History of Australian Popular Culture Since 1788* (Melbourne: Longman, 1995).

3   Pat Lawlor, *Confessions of a Journalist* (Auckland: Whitcombe & Tombs, 1935), ch. 12.

4   Phillip L. Harris, 'The Story of Aussie', in Harris (ed.), *Aussie: A Reprint of All the Numbers of the Diggers' Own Paper of the Battlefield* (Sydney: Phillip L. Harris on behalf of the Australian War Museum, 1920); Lawlor, *Confessions*, p. 100; Vane Lindesay, *The Way We Were: Australian Popular Magazines 1856–1969* (Melbourne: Oxford University Press, 1983), pp. 86–93; Graham Seal, '"Written in the Trenches": Trench Newspapers of the First World War', *Journal of the Australian War Memorial* 16 (April 1990): pp. 30–38.

5 The most extensive use of the new *Aussie* is in Conor, *The Spectacular Modern Woman*, but she does not discuss the magazine as such. There is a brief reference in H.M. Green, *A History of Australian Literature Pure and Applied Volume I, 1789–1923* (Sydney: Angus & Robertson, 1962), p. 733 and an entry in Lindesay, *The Way We Were*, pp. 94–101.

6 David Walker, *Dream and Disillusion: A Search for Australian Cultural Identity* (Canberra: ANU Press, 1976), p. 214.

7 All the examples in this paragraph are from the May 1922 issue.

8 Lawlor, *Confessions*, p. 120, records that A.A. Catts, proprietor of the New Century Press, estimated he was losing £200 an issue in the magazine's final months.

9 Like *Smith's Weekly*, *Aussie* was populist in style but appealed to middle-class readers. See Peter Kirkpatrick, *The Sea Coast of Bohemia: Literary Life in Sydney's Roaring Twenties* (St Lucia: University of Queensland Press, 1992), pp. 110–17; Humphrey McQueen, 'Shoot the Bolshevik! Hang the Profiteer! Reconstructing Australian Capitalism, 1918–21', in E.L. Wheelwright & Ken Buckley (eds), *Essays in the Political Economy of Australian Capitalism Volume 2* (Sydney: Australian & New Zealand Book Company, 1978), p. 190; R.B. Walker, *Yesterday's News: A History of the Newspaper Press in New South Wales from 1920* (Sydney: Sydney University Press, 1980), p. 8.

10 Tim Rowse, *Australian Liberalism and National Character* (Malmsbury: Kibble Books, 1978); Gregory Melleuish, *Cultural Liberalism in Australia: A Study in Intellectual and Cultural History* (Melbourne: Cambridge University Press, 1995), pp. 38–49.

11 The crisis of the Depression provided *Aussie* with parallels to the war years. There had been too much talk of hardship among politicians and the press (April 1930). 'Never, perhaps, in the history of Australia has so much dissatisfaction been felt with politics as is felt to-day', but 'most of the uproar comes, of course, from the mob, who think like sheep and vote like asses' (April 1931).

12 Editorial, 'Opening the Federal Parliament', *Aussie*, April 1927. This piece begins with a satirical paraphrase of newspaper effusions over the Duke of York's visit, but it is sympathetic to him as a 'fine fellow' having to suffer the outpourings of 'ultra-loyal politicians'.

13 See also editorials for January and May 1929.

14 'Honestly, you could almost see the gum leaves in Walter Jago's thick, curly brown hair. He enjoyed the hurly-burlies of the Decade, but in a faintly puzzled way, belonging in spirit to an earlier tradition'. Dulcie Deamer in Peter Kirkpatrick (ed.), *The Queen of Bohemia: The Autobiography of Dulcie Deamer* (St Lucia: University of Queensland Press, 1998), p. 96.

15 Probably the best account we have for the nineteenth century is still Sylvia Lawson's *The Archibald Paradox: A Strange Case of Authorship* (Ringwood: Allen Lane, 1983).

16 'Making Australia Safe for the (American) Talkies' (August 1931) talks about the worship of American speech in Australia through the influence of the movies, although it also holds out the possibility that 'we may Australianise this "New Revelation"'.

17 Books by these authors reviewed in February, March and October 1922, and March 1923.

18 Woolacott was associate editor of the *Triad* from late 1924 and proprietor and editor from August 1926.

19 The terms are from Alfred Kazin, *On Native Grounds: An Interpretation of Modern American Prose Literature* (New York: Harcourt, Brace, 1942).

20 Sharyn Pearce, *Shameless Scribblers: Australian Women's Journalism, 1880–1995* (Rockhampton: Central Queensland University Press, 1998), p. 71.

21 Pearce, *Shameless Scribblers*, p. 79.

22 Dulcie Deamer, 'The Clouded Glory', *Aussie*, March 1927.

23 Conor, *The Spectacular Modern Woman*, p. 213.

'SCREAMERS IN BEDLAM'

1   'Foreword', *Vision* I (March 1923): 2–3.
2   'Screamers in Bedlam II. The Literary Lombroso: A Gallery of Modernists', *Vision* III (November 1923): 59.
3   This is a key point in Marshall Berman's *All That is Solid Melts Into Air: The Experience of Modernity* (London & New York: Verso, 1983), p. 91ff. 'Marx's prose [in the *Communist Manifesto*] suddenly becomes luminous, incandescent; brilliant images succeed and blend into one another; we are hurtled along with a reckless momentum, a breathless intensity. Marx is not only describing but evoking and enacting the desperate pace and frantic rhythm that capitalism imparts to every facet of modern life.'
4   Jack Lindsay, *The Roaring Twenties: Literary Life in Sydney, New South Wales in the Years 1921–6* (London: The Bodley Head, 1960), p. 98n. The full sentence reads: 'Emotionally we were close to Dadaism and early Surrealism in our violent rejection of the society which had begotten the 1914–18 war; but aesthetically we took the opposite viewpoint'. He adds, 'In Europe it was possible to identify the bourgeoisie with effete "traditional culture"; in Australia that was impossible. On the contrary we identified it with a total ignorance of tradition.'
5   Norman Lindsay, 'The Sex Synonym in Art: "Ulysses" and the Conquest of Disgust', *Vision* I (March 1923): 27. An extended critique of *Ulysses* as a 'gabble of vulgar sex synonyms', not a truly liberating celebration of sex, the essay again has the 'attack' of a modernist manifesto.
6   Hugh McCrae, 'Hunt's Up!', *Vision* II (August 1923): 6.
7   Peter Bürger, *Theory of the Avant-Garde*, trans. Michael Shaw (Manchester: Manchester University Press; Minneapolis: University of Minnesota Press, 1984), p. 50.
8   K.K. Ruthven, 'Appropriating a Space for Modernism: Ezra Pound and the *New Freewoman*', in David Carter (ed.), *Outside the Book: Contemporary Essays on Literary Periodicals* (Sydney: Local Consumption Publications, 1991), pp. 217–18.
9   Jack Lindsay, 'Vision of the Twenties', *Southerly* 2 (1952): 66–67. In *The Roaring Twenties*, Lindsay describes his enthusiasm for Aldous Huxley (p. 198) and the Sitwells (p. 126), also his less enthusiastic reading of Ezra Pound (p. 65). Peter Kirkpatrick suggested to me the point about Lindsay testing out the possibilities and limitations of *Creative Effort* even as he pursued its ideals in *Vision*.
10   Berman, *All That is Solid Melts Into Air*, p. 91.
11   From his later Marxist position, Jack Lindsay claimed that the magazine 'did hold potentially a strong humanist element', '*Vision* and the *London Aphrodite*', in Bruce Bennett (ed.), *Crosscurrents: Magazines and Newspapers in Australian Literature* (Melbourne: Longman Cheshire, 1981), p. 96; and he interpreted their opposition to 'abstract art and stylistic formalisms' as 'standing out for a humanist realism as well as our own brand of idealist abstraction disguised as "sensuousness"': '*Vision* of the Twenties', p. 67. 'Humanist realism' is not a phrase one can imagine Norman Lindsay ever using positively.
12   Humphrey McQueen, *The Black Swan of Trespass: The Emergence of Modernist Painting in Australia to 1944* (Sydney: Alternative Publishing Cooperative, 1979), p. 19.
13   Peter Kirkpatrick, *The Sea Coast of Bohemia: Literary Life in Sydney's Roaring Twenties* (St Lucia: University of Queensland Press, 1992), ch. 9. Jack Lindsay, 'Vision of the Twenties'; '*Vision* and the *London Aphrodite*'; *The Roaring* Twenties, ch. 8.
14   Jack Lindsay, 'Vision of the Twenties', p. 66.
15   Kirkpatrick, *The Sea Coast of Bohemia*, p. 66.
16   Norman Lindsay, *Creative Effort: An Essay in Affirmation* (1920; London: Cecil Palmer, 1924), p. 1. See Kirkpatrick, *The Sea Coast of Bohemia*, pp. 63–69.

17   John Docker, *Australian Cultural Elites: Intellectual Traditions in Sydney and Melbourne* (Sydney: Angus & Robertson, 1974), p. 30.

18   Norman Lindsay, *Creative Effort*, p. 176.

19   Kirkpatrick, *The Sea Coast of Bohemia*, p. 69.

20   Docker, *Australian Cultural Elites*, pp. 22–24. Kirkpatrick, *The Sea Coast of Bohemia*, pp. 206–7. Jack Lindsay, *The Roaring Twenties*, pp. 74–75. Kosmas Tsokhas, 'Modernity, Sexuality and National Identity: Norman Lindsay's Aesthetics', *Australian Historical Studies* 107 (October 1996): 219–41.

21   Tsokhas, 'Modernity, Sexuality and National Identity', p. 226.

22   Docker, *Australian Cultural Elites*, p. 30.

23   Jack Lindsay remembers that the title came from Norman ('Vision of the Twenties', p. 62), although letters by Norman state that 'Vision' as the name for a new literary magazine originally came from Sydney Ure Smith. See Nancy D.H. Underhill, *Making Australian Art 1916–49: Sydney Ure Smith Patron and Publisher* (Melbourne: Oxford University Press, 1991), pp. 75–76. Underhill traces the struggle of wills between Lindsay and Ure Smith, pp. 74ff.

24   Norman Lindsay, 'The Inevitable Future', *Art in Australia* 2.1 (February 1922): 22–40.

25   Jack Lindsay, 'Two Directions in Modern Poetry', *Art in Australia* 2.2 (May 1922): 42–44.

26   Norman Lindsay, 'A Modern Malady', *Art in Australia* 1 (1916): n.p. See also 'The Creator and the Parasite' in the second issue.

27   Jack Lindsay, 'Vision in the Twenties', p. 62.

28   Jack Lindsay, *The Roaring Twenties*, p. 83.

29   Kirkpatrick, *The Sea Coast of Bohemia*, pp. 210 & 214.

30   Ibid., p. 89.

31   Norman Lindsay, 'The Shelley Myth', *Vision* III (November 1923): 31–37; Jack Lindsay, 'Two Dimensional Poetry', *Vision* III (November 1923): 38–41.

32   Advertisement for the magazine in *Vision* III (November 1923).

33   The quoted phrase is from Hugh Kenner, *The Pound Era* (London: Faber, 1975), p. 131.

34   Kenner, *The Pound Era*, p. 30.

35   Hugh McCrae, 'Song', *Vision* II (August 1923): 7.

36   Quotations in order from Kenneth Slessor, 'Thieves' Kitchen' (II, p. 10) and 'Rubens' Innocents' (I, p. 8), and Jack Lindsay, 'Beethoven' (III, p. 10).

37   Kenneth Slessor, 'The Embarkation for Cythera', *Vision* IV (February 1924): 10. Slessor is clearly having great fun with costume drama in this poem, hardly taking it seriously.

38   Philip Mead has recently pursued this point much further, analysing the modernism of Slessor's greatest poem 'Five Bells' in relation to the cinema, and in particular Slessor's own close professional interest in the cinema as a journalist and film reviewer: *Networked Language: Culture & History in Australian Poetry* (North Melbourne: Australian Scholarly Publishing, 2008), ch. 1.

39   Kirkpatrick, *The Sea Coast of Bohemia*, pp. 78–97.

40   Ibid., p. 270.

41   Quotations from reviews are reprinted in 'These Liberties', *Vision* II (August 1923): 58.

42   Advertisement/Editorial Announcement in *Vision* II.

43   Jack Lindsay, 'Australian Poetry and Nationalism', *Vision* I (May 1923): 30.

44   Richard White, *Inventing Australia: Images and Identity 1688–1980* (Sydney: George Allen & Unwin, 1981), ch. 7. And see John F. Williams, *Quarantined Culture: Australian Reactions to Modernism 1913–1939* (Cambridge: Cambridge University Press, 1995), esp. ch. 8.

45   David Walker, 'Modern Nerves, Nervous Moderns: Notes on Male Neurasthenia', in S.L. Goldberg and F.B. Smith (eds), *Australian Cultural History* (Cambridge: Cambridge University Press, 1988), pp. 123–37.

46   Norman Lindsay, 'The Inevitable Future', p. 25.
47   James Cunninghame (Jack Lindsay), 'France the Abyss', *Vision* II (August 1923): 35.
48   Norman Lindsay, 'Hyperborea I: On Men and Not-Men, the Conspiracy of Tailors, and Some Pictures', *Vision* II (August 1923): 13.
49   Norman Lindsay, 'Hyperborea II: Of the Hyperborean Landscape', *Vision* III (November 1923): 17.
50   Ibid., p. 18.
51   Jack Lindsay, 'Shakespeare and Milton', *Vision* IV (February 1924): 33.
52   F.S. Burnell, 'At the Sign of the "Golden Basket"', *Vision* IV (February 1924): 23.
53   Robert D. Fitzgerald, 'The Dark Rose', *Vision* IV (February 1924): 7.
54   'These Liberties', *Vision* II (August 1923).
55   Advertisement, *Vision* III (November 1923); Kirkpatrick, *The Sea Coast of Bohemia*, p. 211.
56   Advertisement, *Vision* III (November 1923).
57   'These Liberties', *Vision* II (August 1923).
58   Kirkpatrick, *The Sea Coast of Bohemia*, p. 211.
59   Bürger, *Theory of the Avant-Garde*, p. 52.
60   Kirkpatrick, *The Sea Coast of Bohemia*, p. 214–15.
61   John Tregenza, *Australian Little Magazines 1923–1954* (Adelaide: Libraries Board of South Australia, 1964), p. 18.
62   See Stephen Garton, *The Cost of War: Australians Return* (Melbourne: Oxford University Press, 1996) and Marina Larsson, *Shattered Anzacs: Living with the Scars of War* (Sydney: UNSW Press, 2009).
63   'These Liberties', *Vision* II (August 1923).
64   Kirkpatrick, *The Sea Coast of Bohemia*, ch. 5.
65   Ibid., p. 211.
66   For a more recent analysis see Jill Julius Matthews, *Dance Hall & Picture Palace: Sydney's Romance with Modernity* (Sydney: Currency Press, 2005).
67   The closest comparison would be with the Sydney *Triad*, whose key figures Frank Morton and L.L. Woolacott were close to Norman Lindsay and Sydney bohemianism. See Ch. 7, 'The Mystery of the Missing Middlebrow', below and Kirkpatrick, *The Sea Coast of Bohemia*, pp. 103–6.

PARIS, MOSCOW, MELBOURNE

This essay first appeared as 'Paris, Moscow, Melbourne: Some Avant-Garde Australian Little Magazines' in Australian Literary Studies *16.1 (May 1993): 57–66.*

1   *Stream* 1.2 (August 1931): inside front cover.
2   As Humphrey McQueen has argued, the metaphor of arrival can be misleading as it allows no space for the local conditions of reception. Hence the use of 'emergence' in the subtitle of his book, *The Black Swan of Trespass: The Emergence of Modernist Painting in Australia to 1944* (Sydney: Alternative Publishing Cooperative, 1979). The avant-garde projected modernism's arrival as being 'all at once' although it is more accurate to talk of multiple arrivals and threads of development across the first four decades of the century.
3   Contributors to *Strife* include Waten, McClintock (as art editor), Brian Fitzpatrick (then a journalist and poet), Colin Wills and Bernard Burns (both journalists), Huffshi Hurwitz (a young Jewish communist), and artists Nutter Buzacott and James Flett. See David Carter, *A Career in Writing: Judah Waten and the Cultural Politics of a Literary Career* (Toowoomba: ASAL, 1997), pp. 3–20; Charles Merewether, 'Social Realism: The Formative Years', *Arena* 46 (1977): 67; Don Watson, *Brian Fitzpatrick: A Radical Life* (Sydney: Hale & Iremonger, 1979), pp. 32–35.

NOTES

4   Proletarian writing had some presence in the late 1920s in the *Workers' Weekly*, the paper of the Communist Party of Australia. See Carter, *A Career in Writing*, p. 27.

5   Merewether, 'Social Realism', p. 67. David Elliott, *New Worlds: Russian Art and Society 1900–1937* (London: Thames & Hudson, 1986), pp. 20–21 & 84–117.

6   The point applies no less to the *Communist Manifesto*, 'the archetype of a century of modernist manifestos and movements': Marshall Berman, *All That is Solid Melts Into Air: The Experience of Modernity* (London: Verso, 1983), p. 89.

7   Mike Gold quoted in Daniel Aaron, *Writers on the Left* (Oxford: Oxford University Press, 1977), p. 207.

8   Peter Bürger, *Theory of the Avant-Garde*, trans. Michael Shaw (Manchester: Manchester University Press; Minneapolis: University of Minnesota Press, 1984), p. 50.

9   Ibid., pp. 22, 49.

10 Ibid., p. 22.

11 Ibid., pp. 72–82.

12 Ibid., p. 52.

13 Ibid., p. 22.

14 Berman, *All That is Solid*, p. 91.

15 'An Important Booklet!', *Strife*, p. 8.

16 Elliott, *New Worlds*, p. 117.

17 'Notes of the Month: War', *Strife*, p. 7.

18 'Notes of the Month: Literature', *Strife*, pp. 7–8.

19 'Notes of the Month: Soviet Russia', *Strife*, p. 7.

20 Charles Merewether, *Art & Social Commitment: An End to the City of Dreams 1931–1948* (Sydney: Art Gallery of NSW, 1984), p. 56.

21 Local contributors to *Stream* include Cyril Pearl (editor), Alwyn Lee, Edgar Holt, David Lockhart, Gino Nibbi, Bertram Higgins, A.R. Chisholm, Sacha Youssevitch, Jack Maugham, Fritz Hart, and once, reviewing Edmund Wilson's *Axel's Castle*, Nettie Palmer. See Carter, *A Career in Writing*, pp. 30–34; John Tregenza, *Australia's Little Magazines 1923–1954* (Adelaide: Libraries Board of South Australia, 1964), pp. 39–44.

22 *Stream* 1.1 (July 1931): inside front cover.

23 *Stream* 1.1 (July 1931): 4.

24 Sacha Youssevitch, 'Hunger and Love', *Stream* 1.2 (August 1931): 23–26; Lvovsky, 'Soviet Literature', *Stream* 1.3 (September 1931): 13–14; Glaeser & *Union des artistes moderns*, 'Montages', *Stream* 1.2 (August 1931): 4, 47.

25 *Stream* 1.3 (September 1931): 45.

26 *Stream* 1.3 (September 1931): title page.

27 Other magazines include the left/realist *Yesterday and Most of Today* (Sydney, 1932–34); *Pandemonium* (Melbourne, 1934–35), a magazine of social and cultural commentary with modernist interests; and *Manuscripts* (Geelong and Melbourne, 1931–35), a fine production journal which developed an interest in contemporary European literature. See Tregenza, *Australia's Little Magazines*, ch. 3.

28 Winston Rhodes, 'The New Realism', *Proletariat* 1.1 (April 1932): 13. See Merewether, *Art & Social Commitment*, pp. 57–58 for the magazine's striking cover images.

29 'Art is a Weapon', *Masses* 1.1 (November 1932). See Merewether, *Art & Social Commitment*, pp. 11–14, 50.

30 Tregenza, *Australia's Little Magazines*, ch. 4.

31 See Carter, *A Career in Writing*, ch. 7.

THE MYSTERY OF THE MISSING MIDDLEBROW

This essay first appeared as 'The Mystery of the Missing Middlebrow or The C(o)urse of Good Taste' in Judith Ryan and Chris Wallace-Crabbe (eds), Imagining Australia: Literature and Culture in the New New World, (Cambridge, Mass.: Harvard University Press, 2004), pp. 173–202.

1 Foundational work includes, on the American side, Joan Shelley Rubin, *The Making of Middlebrow Culture* (Chapel Hill: University of North Carolina Press, 1992) and Janice Radway, *A Feeling for Books: The Book-of-the-Month Club, Literary Taste, and Middle-Class Desire* (Chapel Hill: University of North Carolina Press, 1997); and on the British side: Rosa Maria Bracco, *'Betwixt and Between': Middlebrow Fiction and English Society in the Twenties and Thirties* (Melbourne: University of Melbourne History Monograph Series, 1990) and *Merchants of Hope: British Middlebrow Writers and the First World War, 1919–1939* (Providence & Oxford: Berg, 1993), and Nicola Humble, *The Feminine Middlebrow Novel* (Oxford: Oxford University Press, 2001). Australian work on art patronage includes Nancy D.H. Underhill, *Making Australian Art 1916–49: Sydney Ure Smith, Patron and Publisher* (Melbourne: Oxford University Press, 1991) and Heather Johnson, *Sydney Art Patronage 1890–1940* (Sydney: Bungoona, 1997).

2 John Frow, *Cultural Studies and Cultural Value* (Oxford: Clarendon Press, 1995), pp. 22–28.

3 Fortunately this claim is rapidly becoming untenable. See Erica Brown and Mary Grover (eds), *Middlebrow Literary Culture: The Battle of the Brows 1920–1960* (Basingstoke & New York: Palgrave Macmillan, 2011); Jaime Harker, *America the Middlebrow: Women's Novels, Progressivism, and Middlebrow Authorship Between the Wars* (Amherst: University of Massachusetts Press, 2007); Gordon Hutner, *What America Read: Taste, Class, and the Novel* (Chapel Hill: University of North Carolina Press, 2009); Kate Macdonald (ed.), *The Masculine Middlebrow, 1880–1950: What Mr Miniver Read* (Basingstoke & New York: Palgrave Macmillan, 2011).

4 Radway, *A Feeling for Books*, pp. 1–14 & 129–37; Bracco, *'Betwixt and Between'*, pp. 1–14.

5 Bracco, *'Betwixt and Between'*, p. 13. John Feather, *A History of British Publishing* (Abingdon: Routledge, 2006), chs 9–11; Joseph McAleer, *Popular Reading in Britain 1914–1950* (Oxford: Clarendon Press, 1992), chs 2–3; Jonathan Rose, 'Modernity and Print I: Britain 1890–1970', in Simon Eliot and Jonathan Rose (eds), *A Companion to the History of the Book* (Malden & Oxford: Blackwell, 2007), pp. 341–47.

6 Bracco, *Merchants of Hope*, p. 10.

7 Stefan Collini, *Absent Minds: Intellectuals in Britain* (Oxford: Oxford University Press, 2006), p. 112.

8 F.R. Leavis, *Mass Civilisation and Minority Culture* (Cambridge: The Minority Press, 1930); Q.D. Leavis, *Fiction and the Reading Public* (1932; London: Pimlico, 2000).

9 Virginia Woolf, 'Middlebrow', *The Death of the Moth and Other Essays* (London: Hogarth Press, 1942), p. 182.

10 Q.D. Leavis, *Fiction and the Reading Public*, p. 39.

11 As recorded in the *Oxford English Dictionary*. Two earlier uses have since been found: in the Irish *Freeman's Journal*, 3 May 1924 (http://www.middlebrow-network.com/DefiningtheMiddlebrow.aspx) and *Queenslander* (Brisbane), 12 May 1923, p. 7, quoting the London *Daily Chronicle* (no date reference).

12 Bracco, *Merchants of Hope*, pp. 12–13 & 52–56.

13 See books listed above by Humble, Harker, Brown and Grover, Macdonald; and Faye Hammill, *Women, Celebrity, and Literary Culture Between the Wars* (Austin: University of Texas Press, 2007).

14 Radway, *A Feeling for Books*, p. 15.

15 Ibid., p. 283.

16   Rubin, *The Making of Middlebrow Culture*, pp. 14–33.
17   Radway, *A Feeling for Books*, pp. 146–47 & 205–20; Rubin, *The Making of Middlebrow Culture*, pp. 27–29 & 164–78.
18   For Morton see Peter Kirkpatrick, *The Sea Coast of Bohemia: Literary Life in Sydney's Roaring Twenties* (St Lucia: University of Queensland Press, 1992), pp. 103–7. The *Triad* was superseded by the *New Triad* which lasted only one year, August 1927-July 1928.
19   H.M. Green, *A History of Australian Literature Pure and Applied Volume I 1789–1923* (Sydney: Angus & Robertson, 1962), p. 731.
20   See Ch. 3, 'Drawing the Line', above.
21   While the *Home* maintained an interest in surrealism and modern design, its governing discourse remained 'good taste'; only in its later years, as a John Fairfax publication and after Ure Smith's resignation, did it become more thoroughly 'avant-garde' in appearance.
22   Underhill, *Making Australian Art*, pp. 35–8 and passim.
23   Jonathan Wild, *The Rise of the Office Clerk in Literary Culture, 1880–1939* (Basingstoke: Palgrave Macmillan, 2006).
24   David Carter, 'Modernising Anglocentrism: *Desiderata* and Literary Time' in Peter Kirkpatrick and Robert Dixon (eds), *The Republic of Letters: Literary Communities in Australia* (Sydney: Sydney University Press, 2012), pp. 85–98.
25   Radway, *A Feeling for Books*, pp. 261ff.
26   Patrick Buckridge, '"Good Reading" in the *Australian Women's Weekly*, 1933–1970', *Journal of the Association for the Study of Australian Literature* 1 (2002): 36.
27   *Man* (June 1937): 7.
28   Richard White, 'The Importance of Being *Man*,' in Peter Spearritt and David Walker (eds), *Australian Popular Culture* (Sydney: Allen & Unwin, 1979), p. 156.
29   J.O. Anchen, *The Australian Novel: A Critical Survey* (Melbourne: Whitcombe & Toombs, 1940). His top ten lists novels by Henry Handel Richardson, G.B. Lancaster, Xavier Herbert, Tarlton Rayment, Christina Stead, Michael Innes, Leonard Mann, Arthur Upfield, Kylie Tennant and Myra Morris.
30   Mary Mansfield, Editorial, *Australian Books* 1.1 (September 1946): 1.
31   R.J.F. Boyer, 'Why We Publish *Talk*,' *Talk* 1.1 (April 1946): 8.
32   Eric Ashby, 'Give the Highbrow a Fair Deal,' *Talk* 1.1 (April 1946): 37.
33   Max Harris, 'The Current Literary Scene,' *Angry Penguins* (July 1946): 60–61.
34   Henry Seidel Canby, *A New Land Speaking: An Essay on the Importance of a National Literature* (Melbourne: Melbourne University Press, 1946), p. 27.
35   George Mackaness, 'Are We Australians Book-Conscious?', *Australian Books* 2.1 (December 1946): 1.
36   Helen Topliss, *Modernism and Feminism: Australian Women Artists 1900–1940* (Sydney: Craftsman House, 1996).
37   Jim Collins (ed.), *High-Pop: Making Culture into Popular Entertainment* (Oxford & Malden: Blackwell, 2002).
38   David Carter, 'Public Intellectuals, Book Culture and Civil Society,' *Australian Humanities Review* 24 (December 2001–February 2002): http://www.lib.latrobe.edu.au/AHR/.
39   Peter Craven, 'Nothing if not Dappled,' *Australian Book Review* (August 2001): 11–12.
40   Andrew Reimer, 'When East Meets West,' *Age*, 7 October 2000, p. 11.
41   *Australian Author* 33.2 (August 2001): 4.
42   For 'cultural omnivores' see R. Peterson and R. Kern, 'Changing Highbrow Taste: From Snob to Omnivore,' *American Sociological Review* 61 (October 1996): 900–7; for 'neo-consumers' see R. Honeywill, 'Neo-Consumers Set the Agenda for Booksellers,' *Australian Bookseller and Publisher* (October 2002): 16–17.
43   Jim Collins, Introduction, *High-Pop*, p. 7.

'SOME MEANS OF LEARNING OF THE BEST NEW BOOKS'

This essay first appeared in Australian Literary Studies *22.3 (2006): 329–41.*

1   'Introduction', *All About Books* (December 1928): 1. The magazine continued monthly through to March 1938.

2   When the magazine invents a competition inviting readers to nominate their ten desert island books—a characteristic strategy of highlighting both reader choice *and* ranking—it limits the field to living authors and twentieth century books (and this was in January 1929). The results are printed in May 1919, p. 187. They include novels by John Galsworthy, Christopher Morley, Rudyard Kipling, J.M. Barrie, Australians Erle Cox and Aeneas Gunn, and Nettie Palmer's *Australian Story Book*.

3   Arthur Thrush, 'Pocket Editions of Today', *All About Books* (December 1928): 42.

4   Nettie Palmer wrote a two-page column monthly for the magazine from June 1929 to December 1934, largely reviewing new Australian books and commenting on developments in publishing and bookselling; her place was taken by Frederick Macartney.

5   Peter D. McDonald, *British Literary Culture and Publishing Practice 1880–1914* (Cambridge: Cambridge University Press, 1997), pp. 1–21. Janice Radway, *A Feeling for Books: The Book-of-the-Month Club, Literary Taste, and Middle-Class Desire* (Chapel Hill: University of North Carolina Press, 1997), pp. 127–53.

6   Between 1914 and 1939, the number of books published in the UK almost doubled, and in the decade from 1928 sales more than tripled. Clive Bloom, *Bestsellers: Popular Fiction Since 1900* (Basingstoke: Palgrave Macmillan, 2002), p. 37.

7   The heading is 'BooksBooksBooksBooks'.

8   Under the heading 'What England and America are Reading'. Bestselling lists were less records of sales than ways of guiding readers and consumers. See Laura J. Miller, 'The Best-Seller List as Marketing Tool and Historical Fiction', *Book History* 3 (2000): 286–91.

9   See 'Commence an AAB Book Club', *All About Books* (July 1932): 104. A John O'London's (see note 14 below) Literary Circle was created in Sydney around 1932 and was reported by *All About Books*.

10   Radway, *A Feeling for Books*, p. 222.

11   D.W. Thorpe with Joyce Thorpe Nicholson, *A Life of Books : The Story of D.W. Thorpe Pty Ltd., 1921–1987.* (Middle Park, Vic.: Courtyard Press, 2000), p. 71.

12   Gail Reekie, *Temptations: Sex, Selling and the Department Store* (Sydney: Allen & Unwin, 1993), pp. 44–62.

13   Thorpe, *A Life of Books*, p. 55.

14   F.R. Leavis, *Mass Civilisation and Minority Culture* (Cambridge: Gordon Fraser, 1930). Q.D. Leavis, in *Fiction and the Reading Public*, sees *John O'London's* as epitomising the lowbrow, in terms that might almost describe *All About Books*: 'merely a resume of publishers' advertisements [and] literary gossip' (1932; London: Chatto & Windus, 1965, p. 10).

15   Radway, *A Feeling for Books*, pp. 187–90; Joan Shelley Rubin, *The Making of Middlebrow Culture* (Chapel Hill: University of North Carolina Press, 1992), pp. 94–147. See Ch. 7, 'The Mystery of the Missing Middlebrow', above.

16   Phil Grim, 'Russia, England, British Guiana (sic), Mexico', *All About Books* (May 1934): 94.

17   In Vivian Smith (ed.), *Letters of Vance and Nettie Palmer 1915–1963* (Canberra: National Library of Australia, 1977), p. 61. She reports the remark as having been made to her by Furnley Maurice (62). The final remark is from 'Australian Literary Journals' (1929), in Vivian Smith (ed.), *Nettie Palmer* (St Lucia: University of Queensland Press, 1988), p. 357.

18   'We Turn Six', *All About Books* (January 1934): 3.

19   'Books for Your Christmas Gifts', *All About Books* (December 1929): 407.

20   T.R. Adam, 'The Renaissance of Self', *All About Books* (March 1929): 116.

21   'Views, News and Reviews: High-Brow or Low?', *All About Books* (September 1929): 313–14.

22   Quotations in order: 'Novels for Holiday Reading and Christmas Gifts: Warwick Deeping in Good Form', *All About Books* (December 1937): 193; Phil Grim, 'What is a High-Brow?' *All About Books* (March 1933): 42.

23   Quotations in order: 'Books for Your Christmas Gifts', p. 407; 'Novel of Distinction for Discriminating Readers', *All About Books* (September 1929): 325; S.M. Macfarlane, 'Novels I Think You Would Like to Read', *All About Books* (December 1928): 4.

24   In May 1929 the magazine wondered, 'What Present-Day Authors will be Read in 1975?'.

25   'We Turn Six', p. 3.

26   Rubin, *The Making of Middlebrow Culture*, pp. 31–33.

27   Vance Palmer, 'The Future of Australian Literature' *Age*, 9 February 1935, p. 6.

28   Rubin, *The Making of Middlebrow Culture*, p. 35.

29   Nettie Palmer, 'Australian Books of 1930', *All About Books* (December 1930): 307; 'A Reader's Notebook', *All About Books* (October 1933): 158.

30   Nettie Palmer, 'Australian Books of 1930', p. 309.

31   The occasion was the bestseller success of Henry Handel Richardson's *Ultima Thule* as a Book-of-the-Month Club selection, 'A Reader's Notebook', *All About Books* (October 1929): 337. 'Believing that the reading public does not know what it wants, such clubs decide to distribute books that they believe in.' She lists unlikely bestsellers distributed by the Book-of-the Month Club including *The Bridge of San Luis Rey*, *All Quiet on the Western Front*, and now *Ultima Thule*. '[I]t is by this real greatness in the books they recommend that the judges are prepared to stand'.

32   G.H. Cowling, 'The Future of Australian Literature', *Age*, 16 February 1935, p. 6. Interestingly in this piece Cowling argues that the first task 'is to build up a tradition that Australians are a *reading* people, and that they read with a discrimination that is bred by much reading'.

33   Leigh Dale, *The English Men: Professing Literature in Australian Universities* (University of Southern Queensland: ASAL Literary Studies series, 1997), pp. 54–55.

34   G.H. Cowling, 'What is Good Literature?' *All About Books* (May 1931): 107.

35   G.H. Cowling, 'Arnold Bennett, Ellen Terry and Others', *All About Books* (September 1933): 140.

36   G.H. Cowling, 'The Novel', *All About Books* (February 1934): 23–24.

37   C.H. Peters, 'Reading With a Purpose', *All About Books* (July 1933): 99. Capt. C.H. Peters had a weekly books talk on ABC Radio, 'The Literary Log Book' (in 1931–2) and later 'Books—Wise and Otherwise' (1935). He was the first general manager of booksellers Robertson & Mullens from 1921.

38   'Some Views, News and Reviews: Recreational Reading—and a Warning', *All About Books* (October 1929): 348.

39   Jonathan Rose, *The Intellectual Life of the British Working Classes* (New Haven & London: Yale University Press, 2002), pp. 187–89.

40   The notion of books as 'personalising' is from Radway, *A Feeling for Books*, p. 283.

41   *All About Books* (May 1929): 178; Stella M. Macfarlane, 'Novels I Think You Would Like to Read', *All About Books* 15 September 1930: 238.

42   For example: 'What are the books that we cannot afford to miss this year? Nearly all that I have noted here are such as we shall want to have at hand in years to come … either in our homes or in our libraries' (Palmer, 'Australian Books of 1930', p. 307).

REALISM, DOCUMENTARY, SOCIALIST REALISM

This essay first appeared as 'Documenting and Criticising Society' in Laurie Hergenhan (ed.),
The Penguin New Literary History of Australia, *(Ringwood: Penguin, 1988), pp. 370–89.*

1   See Ch. 6, 'Paris, Moscow, Melbourne', above. The one issue of *Strife* is dated 13
      October 1930.

2   Drusilla Modjeska, *Exiles at Home: Australian Women Writers 1925–1945* (Sydney:
      Angus & Robertson, 1981); Ian Reid, *Fiction and the Great Depression: Australia and
      New Zealand, 1930–50* (Melbourne: Edward Arnold, 1979).

3   M. Barnard Eldershaw, *Tomorrow and Tomorrow and Tomorrow* (1947; London:
      Virago, 1983): 317. The Virago edition restores cuts made to the 1947 edition (which
      had the reduced title *Tomorrow and Tomorrow*) because of war-time censorship.

4   Barnard Eldershaw, *Tomorrow and Tomorrow and Tomorrow*, p. 81.

5   *Australian New Writing*, edited by George Farwell, Katharine Susannah Prichard
      and Bernard Smith, appeared 1943–46 (I have quoted from the foreword to the first
      issue). See Smith's 'Reds and Other Colors', *Age Monthly Review* (October 1981):
      7–8 and John Tregenza, *Australian Little Magazines 1923–1954* (Adelaide: Libraries
      Board of South Australia, 1964), pp. 58–60.

6   Frank Dalby Davison, 'What is Literature?' in *Australian Writers Speak: Literature
      and Life in Australia* (Sydney: Angus & Robertson, 1942): 12.

7   Alan Marshall, 'Australian Picture-Book II', in *Alan Marshall's Battlers* (Sydney: Pan,
      1983): 39–40. The sketch first appeared in *Left Review* (December 1937).

8   See Charles Merewether 'Social Realism: The Formative Years', *Arena* 46 (1977):
      65–80; Julie Wells, 'The Writers' League: A Study in Literary and Working Class
      Politics', *Meanjin* 46.4 (1987): 527–34; Ken Harper, 'The Useful Theatre: The New
      Theatre Movement in Sydney and Melbourne, 1935–83', *Meanjin* 43.1 (1984): 56–71;
      Angela Hillel, *Against the Stream: Melbourne New Theatre, 1936–86* (Clifton Hill:
      New Theatre Melbourne, 1986).

9   David Carter, 'Re-Viewing Communism: *Communist Review* (Sydney) 1934–1966',
      Australian Literary Studies 12.1 (1985): 93–105.

10   John Morrison, 'Tons of Work', *Sailors Belong Ships* (Melbourne: Dolphin, 1947),
      reprinted in *Stories of the Waterfront* (Ringwood: Penguin, 1984), p. 12.

11   Jean Devanny, *Sugar Heaven* (1936; Melbourne: Redback, 1982), pp. 41–42.

12   Alan Marshall, *How Beautiful Are Thy Feet* (1949; Ringwood: Penguin, 1979), p. 1.
      Marshall's novel, originally titled *Factory*, was completed by 1937 (Harry Marks,
      I Can Jump Oceans: The World of Alan Marshall, Melbourne: Nelson, 1976). The
      passage quoted appeared first in *Communist Review* (February 1938): 17.

13   Humphrey McQueen, *The Black Swan of Trespass: The Emergence of Modernist Painting
      in Australia to 1944* (Sydney: Alternative Publishing Cooperative, 1979), p. 35.

14   Patrick White, 'The Prodigal Son', *Australian Letters* 1.3 (1958): 39.

15   H.M. Green, *A History of Australian Literature, Pure and Applied Volume II 1923–
      1950* (Sydney: Angus & Robertson, 1961), p. 934.

16   J.M. Harcourt, *Upsurge* (1934; Nedlands: UWA Press, 1986), pp. 33–34.

17   From a newspaper review quoted on the front cover of the 1986 re-issue of the novel.

18   L. Harry Gould, review of *Sugar Heaven*, *Workers Weekly*, 19 June 1936, p. 2.

19   Modjeska, *Exiles at Home*, p. 228.

20   Prichard's comment on *Upsurge* cited in Richard Nile's introduction to the 1986 re-issue
      of the novel; Devanny's description of *Sugar Heaven* from 'The Worker's Contribution
      to Australian Literature' in *Australian Writers Speak*, p. 58. See Carole Ferrier, 'Jean
      Devanny, Katharine Susannah Prichard, and the "Really Proletarian Novel"', in Carole
      Ferrier (ed.), *Gender, Politics and Fiction: Twentieth-Century Australian Women's Novels*
      (St Lucia: University of Queensland Press, 1992), pp. 101–17.

21   A.A. Zhdanov, 'Speech at the First All-Union Congress of Soviet Writers' in Thomas

Riha (ed.), *Readings in Russian Civilization Volume 3: Soviet Russia 1917-Present* (Chicago: University of Chicago Press, 1969), p. 695.

22   Carter, 'Re-Viewing Communism', p. 97.

23   Jack Beasley, 'Questions of Australian Literature', *Communist Review* (January 1960): 31–36.

24   Patrick Buckridge, 'Katharine Susannah Prichard and the Literary Dynamics of Political Commitment', in Ferrier, *Gender, Politics and Fiction*, pp. 85–100.

25   Buckridge, 'Katharine Susannah Prichard', p. 97.

26   Prichard, *Working Bullocks* (1926; Sydney: Angus & Robertson, 1972), p. 204.

27   Jack Lindsay, 'The Novels of Katharine Susannah Prichard', in his *Decay and Renewal: Critical Essays on Twentieth Century Writing* (Sydney: Wild & Woolley, 1976), p. 323.

28   Sneja Gunew, 'Katharine Prichard's Political Writings and the Politics of Her Writing', in John Hay and Brenda Walker (eds), *Katharine Susannah Prichard: Centenary Essays* (Nedlands: Centre for Studies in Australian Literature, UWA, 1984), pp. 49–60.

29   Drusilla Modjeska, Introduction, Katharine Susannah Prichard, *Winged Seeds* (1950; London: Virago, 1984), p. ix.

30   T. Inglis Moore *Social Patterns in Australian Literature* (Sydney: Angus & Robertson, 1971), pp. 15–16, 134; Cecil Hadgraft, *Australian Literature: A Critical Account to 1955* (London, Heinemann, 1960), p. 259.

31   Kylie Tennant, *Tiburon* (1935; Sydney: Sirius/Angus & Robertson, 1981), pp. 222–29.

32   For example, Green, *A History of Australian Literature*, p. 1097.

33   Brian Matthews, '"A Kind of Semi-Sociological Literary Criticism": George Orwell, Kylie Tennant and Others', *Westerly* (June 1981): 67.

34   Adrian Mitchell, 'Fiction', *The Oxford History of Australian Literature* (Melbourne: Oxford University Press, 1981), p. 129.

35   Eleanor Dark, *The Little Company* (1945; London: Virago, 1985), p. 128.

36   Vance Palmer, 'Battle', *Meanjin* 1.8 (1942): 5–6.

37   Eleanor Dark, *Waterway* (1938; Sydney: Angus & Robertson, 1979), p. 33.

38   Modjeska, *Exiles at Home*, p. 238.

39   Dark, *The Little Company*, p. 19.

40   See Ch. 9, 'Current History Looks Apocalyptic', below.

41   For more recent assessments see Christopher Lee and Paul Adams (eds), *Frank Hardy and the Literature of Commitment* (Melbourne: Vulgar Press, 2003).

42   A.D. Hope, 'The Sty of Circe: Judah Waten's *The Unbending*', in his *Native Companions: Essays and Comments on Australian Literature 1936–1966* (Sydney: Angus & Robertson, 1974), pp. 277–87.

43   Dorothy Hewett, *Bobbin Up* (1959; London: Virago, 1985).

44   Veronica Brady's comments are in a review of the 1985 Virago reprint of *Bobbin Up*: 'Rites of Passage', *Australian Society* (February 1986).

'CURRENT HISTORY LOOKS APOCALYPTIC'

This essay first appeared in Australian Literary Studies *14.2 (October 1989): 174–87.*

1   H.G. Wells, *A Modern Utopia* (1905; Lincoln & London: University of Nebraska Press, 1967), p. 99.

2   M. Barnard Eldershaw, *Tomorrow and Tomorrow and Tomorrow* (London: Virago, 1983), pp. 163–69. The novel was written c. 1941–44. It was first published as *Tomorrow and Tomorrow* in a form abridged by the war-time censor and/or the publisher in 1947 (Melbourne: Georgian House). See Introduction by Anne Chisholm to the Virago edition. All subsequent references are to this, the first complete edition, although the shorter title will be used for convenience.

3   Cited in Drusilla Modjeska, *Exiles at Home: Australian Women Writers 1925–1945* (Sydney: Angus and Robertson, 1981), p. 115.

4   Jill Roe, 'The Historical Imagination and its Enemies: M. Barnard Eldershaw's *Tomorrow and Tomorrow and Tomorrow*', *Meanjin* 43.2 (1984): 245.

5   Gary Saul Morson, *The Boundaries of Genre: Dostoevsky's 'Diary of a Writer' and the Traditions of Literary Utopia* (Austin: University of Texas Press, 1981), p. 182. See also Peter Ruppert, *Reader in a Strange Land: The Activity of Reading Literary Utopias* (Athens & London: University of Georgia Press, 1986), pp. 34–53.

6   H.M. Green, *A History of Australian Literature Pure and Applied, Volume II 1923–1950* (Sydney: Angus & Robertson, 1961), p. 1104.

7   J.D.B. Miller, 'A Footnote on Tomorrow', *Meanjin* 7.2 (1948): 125; Frank Dalby Davison, '*Tomorrow and Tomorrow*' and P.H. Partridge, 'The Shape of Things to Come', *Meanjin* 6.4 (1947): 249–52.

8   Ruppert, *Reader in a Strange Land*, p. 52.

9   Darko Suvin, *Metamorphoses of Science Fiction: On the Poetics and History of a Literary Genre* (New Haven: Yale University Press, 1979), p. 52.

10   Raymond Williams, 'Utopia and Science Fiction', in *Problems in Materialism and Culture: Selected Essays* (London: Verso & New Left Books, 1980), p. 205.

11   Williams, 'Utopia', pp. 205–8.

12   Anne Freadman, 'Anyone for Tennis?', in Ian Reid (ed.), *The Place of Genre in Learning: Current Debates*, (Geelong: Centre for Studies in Literary Education, Deakin University, 1987), p. 116.

13   Marjorie Barnard, 'How *Tomorrow and Tomorrow* Came to be Written', *Meanjin* 29.3 (1970): 328.

14   Modjeska, *Exiles at Home*, pp. 100–15.

15   See Richard Nile and David Walker, 'Marketing the Literary Imagination: Production of Australian Literature, 1915–1965', in Laurie Hergenhan (ed.), *The Penguin New Literary History of Australia*, (Ringwood: Penguin, 1988), pp. 284–302. Robert Darby in an unpublished paper, 'An Age of Memorials: *Plaque with Laurel* and the Question of a National Literature', shows how Barnard Eldershaw's *Plaque with Laurel* (1937) works to distinguish the 'serious writer' from the journalist, the populariser, and the academic.

16   Quoted by Barnard herself in 'How *Tomorrow and Tomorrow* Came to be Written', p. 328.

17   Including *A History of Australia* (Sydney: Angus & Robertson) in 1962. The exception was a critical study, *Miles Franklin* (New York: Twayne, 1967).

18   As Jill Roe and Humphrey McQueen have pointed out, comparisons with *War and Peace* are not far-fetched. See McQueen, 'What is in a Name?', *Australian Book Review* (December 1988): 24–25.

19   Dymphna Cusack, 'Culture in Wartime', in *Culture in War Time* (Sydney: Central Cultural Council, 1940), pp. 16–17. See also Barnard, 'Our Literature', in *Australian Writers Speak: Literature and Life in Australia* (Sydney: Angus & Robertson, 1942), pp. 102–15.

20   [C.B. Christesen], 'Editorial Note: War on the Intellectual Front', *Meanjin Papers* 1.8 (1942): 3.

21   William Morris, 'Art and Socialism' (1884) in A.L. Morton (ed.), *Political Writings of William Morris* (London: Lawrence and Wishart, 1973), p. 121.

22   Frank Dalby Davison, *While Freedom Lives* (Sydney: The Author, 1938), p. 24.

23   This distinction was formulated by Ian Hunter and Jeff Minson during collaborative course writing at Griffith University. William Morris's *News from Nowhere* can stand as an expression of aesthetic utopianism (and see the quotations above from Cusack and Christesen); programmatic utopianism could be located, in utopian fiction, in Edward Bellamy's *Looking Backward*. Clearly the two forms are not discrete and are not confined to works of fiction.

24 A position similar to the novel's is expressed, interestingly enough, in an *Angry Penguins* editorial: '[post-war reconstruction] should not fall exclusively into the hands of technical specialists, but should, as far as possible, be the concern of the community at large'. Max Harris and John Reed, *Angry Penguins* (December 1944): 2.

COMMUNISM AND CARNIVAL

I would like to acknowledge the assistance of Allan Gardiner in the preparation of this essay which first appeared in Russell McDougall (ed.), To the Islands: Australia and the Caribbean, *Special Issue of* Australian Cultural History *21 (2002): 97–106.*

1 For the ABS see Jack Beasley, *Red Letter Days: Notes from Inside an Era* (Sydney: Australasian Book Society, 1979), pp. 129–88; Allan Gardiner, 'Ralph de Boissiere and Communist Cultural Discourse in Cold War Australia', PhD thesis, University of Queensland, 1993; Ralph de Boissiere, 'On Writing a Novel', *Journal of Commonwealth Literature* 17.1 (1982): 11; Paul Adams, *The Stranger from Melbourne: Frank Hardy: A Literary Biography 1944–1975* (Nedlands: UWA Press, 1999), pp. 62–67.

2 Ralph de Boissiere, *Crown Jewel* (Melbourne: Australasian Book Society, 1952).

3 See David Carter, *A Career in Writing: Judah Waten and the Cultural Politics of a Literary Career* (Toowoomba: ASAL, 1997): 170–73. It should be noted that among the ABS's first books were also Walter Kaufmann's *Voices in the Storm* (1953) and Judah Waten's *The Unbending* (1954).

4 Beasley, *Red Letter Days*, pp. 137 & 139.

5 Gardiner, 'Ralph de Boissiere', p. 28. Chapter 1 of Gardiner's thesis provides rich detail on de Boissiere's Trinidad years. See also de Boissiere, 'On Writing a Novel', pp. 1–4 and Gardiner's interview with de Boissiere, 'Comrades in Words: Ralph de Boissiere Interviewed by Allan Gardiner', *Kunapipi* 15.1 (1993): 32–41.

6 Gardiner, 'Ralph de Boissiere', p. 30.

7 In Stuart Sayers, 'Writers & Readers: Better Late than Never', *Age*, 8 August 1981, p. 26.

8 Gardiner, 'Comrades in Words', p. 38.

9 See Deirdre Moore, 'The Realist Writers', *Overland* 156 (1999): 24–29, which is followed by de Boissiere's essay, 'Leaving the Realist Writers to Themselves', pp. 30–34; David Martin, *My Strange Friend* (Sydney: Picador, 1991), pp. 233–39; Adams, *The Stranger from Melbourne*, pp. 162–66.

10 Sayers, 'Writers & Readers'.

11 De Boissiere, 'On Writing a Novel', p. 10.

12 David Carter, 'The Story of Our Epoch, A Hero of Our Time: The Communist Novelist in Postwar Australia', in Paul Adams and Christopher Lee (eds), *Frank Hardy and the Literature of Commitment*, (Melbourne: Vulgar Press, 2003), pp. 89–111.

13 Gardiner, 'Ralph de Boissiere', pp. 82–83.

14 Beasley, *Red Letter Days*, pp. 171–84; Carter, *A Career in Writing*, pp. 108–16 and 'Reviewing Communism: *Communist Review* (Sydney) 1934–1966', *Australian Literary Studies* 12.1 (1985): 93–97.

15 Susan McKernan [Lever], *A Question of Commitment: Australian Literature in the 20 Years after the War* (Sydney: Allen & Unwin, 1989), p. 42.

16 Frank Hardy 'Author's Note', *Power Without Glory* (Melbourne: Realist Printing and Publishing, 1950).

17 De Boissiere, 'On Socialist Realism', *Communist Review* (March 1960): 122.

18 Hardy, 'Author's Note'.

19   A phrase borrowed from Ien Ang, *On Not Speaking Chinese: Living Between Asia and the West* (London: Routledge, 2001), p. 62.
20   De Boissiere, 'Leaving the Realist Writers to Themselves', p. 30.
21   Salman Rushdie, 'Exemplary Lives', *Times Literary Supplement*, 7 August 1981, p. 910.
22   Louis James, 'Review: *Crown Jewel* by Ralph de Boissiere', *Journal of Commonwealth Literature* 17.1 (1982): 15.

O'GRADY, JOHN *SEE* 'CULOTTA, NINO'

This essay first appeared in Maggie Nolan and Carrie Dawson (eds), Who's Who? Hoaxes, Imposture and Identity Crises in Australian Literature, Special Issue of Australian Literary Studies 21.4 (2004): 56–73.

1   For an overview of Australian literary hoaxes see Maggie Nolan and Carrie Dawson (eds), *Who's Who? Hoaxes, Imposture and Identity Crises in Australian Literature*, *Australian Literary Studies* 21.4 (2004).
2   Janis Wilton and Richard Bosworth, *Old Worlds and New Australia: The Post-War Migrant Experience* (Ringwood: Penguin, 1984), p. 24.
3   Bob Hodge and Vijay Mishra, *Dark Side of the Dream: Australian Literature and the Postcolonial Mind* (Sydney: Allen & Unwin, 1990), pp. 191–92.
4   Ruth Brown, 'From Nino Culotta to Simon During', *Australian Studies* 9 (November 1995): 35–44.
5   Patrick Buckridge, 'Clearing a Space for Australian Literature 1940–1965', in Bruce Bennett and Jennifer Strauss (eds), *The Oxford Literary History of Australia* (Melbourne: Oxford University Press, 1998), p. 185.
6   Lindsay Barrett, 'The Self-Made Man: Narrative and National Character in Post-War Australia', *Southern Review* 25 (March 1992): 93.
7   John Hetherington, *Forty-Two Faces* (Melbourne: Cheshire, 1962), pp. 97–102. See also: Anne Scollan, 'The House that Nino Built', *Australian Home Beautiful* (August 1963): 18–23; John Yeomans, 'Nino Today', *Walkabout* (March 1963): 24–27.
8   These points are based on extensive reading of the O'Grady papers in the National Library of Australia (NLA MS 8046) and the Ure Smith Pty Ltd papers in the Mitchell Library, State Library of NSW (ML MSS 1590); confirmed by correspondence with John O'Grady Jnr (JO'G Jnr) and in interview with Sam Ure Smith (SUS), 1 February 2003.
9   Interview with SUS; see also full-page advertisement in *Ideas*, 10 October 1958.
10   SUS to H. Hewett, 18 December 1957, Ure Smith papers Box 7.
11   John O'Grady (JO'G) to JO'G Jnr, 22 January 1958; refers to Ure Smith's intention to 'break the story of Nino's identity', NLA (Box 1).
12   Nino Culotta, *They're A Weird Mob* (Sydney: Ure Smith, 1957), p. 7.
13   OED Online.
14   Information on sales figures is scattered throughout the O'Grady and Ure Smith papers, and on the books themselves. By March 1958 it is clear from the correspondence that the author's 'cover' was no longer a secret.
15   JO'G to JO'G Jnr, 16 August 1957. NLA (Box 1).
16   Jacqueline Kent, *A Certain Style: Beatrice Davis, A Literary Life* (Ringwood: Viking/ Penguin, 2001), p. 212.
17   O'Grady's notebooks are among his papers at the NLA. They include prose sketches, diaries, notes on foreign languages etc. Stage plays are included in Box 7. He published a story in the March 1957 issue of the *Australian Journal*. The *Oxford Companion to Australian Literature* notes his earlier literary work.

18 JO'G to JO'G Jnr, 17 October 1957. NLA (Box 1).

19 JO'G to JO'G Jnr, 22 January 1958. NLA (Box 1).

20 JO'G Jnr, correspondence with the author.

21 These figures have been assembled from Ure Smith publicity, details in the Ure Smith and O'Grady papers, *Ideas* magazine (the booksellers' and publishers' trade journal), and publishing information included in successive editions of the novel. For the book's publishing history, see David Carter 'They're a Weird Mob and Ure Smith', in Craig Munro and Robyn Sheahan-Bright (eds), *Paper Empires: A History of the Book in Australia 1946–2005* (St Lucia: University of Queensland Press, 2006), pp. 24–30.

22 *Ideas*, 5 December 1958, p. 1304. In the November issue of the same year, *Ideas* recorded that Ure Smith had offered prizes for the purchaser of the 100,000th copy of the book. The winner was, of course, an Italian-Australian fisherman, Mr G. Travia, from Geraldton, WA, who wrote: 'I like reading when not engaged in catching crayfish. My opinion of *They're a Weird Mob* is that it would do a lot of good if some of these new Australians would read it and take notice'.

23 Reliable sales figures are virtually impossible to establish before the introduction of the Bookscan tracking system in January 2001. However the *Australian Bookseller and Publisher* best-seller lists from the 1990s suggest that each new Bryce Courtenay title sold between two hundred and three hundred thousand copies over its first two to three years. Raw figures, then, are similar to *They're a Weird Mob*, but from a much larger population base, and the scanty figures available suggest that no single title has sold as well for as long as O'Grady's book did. A new edition was released in 2012 by Text Publishing in a new Text Classics series.

24 Typescript in O'Grady papers. NLA (Box 1).

25 JO'G to JO'G Jnr, 1 May 1958. NLA (Box 1).

26 Items collected in O'Grady papers, esp. Box 1.

27 John Frow, 'Signature and Brand', in Jim Collins (ed.), *High-Pop: Making Culture into Popular Entertainment* (Malden: Blackwell, 2002), pp. 56–74.

28 Reviewed by J.H. Mullett and J.D. McLaren, *Overland* (June 1958): 38–39; A.G. Mitchell, *Meanjin* 17.2 (June 1958): 216–17. Much later, it would appear in Geoffrey Dutton's *The Australian Collection: Australia's Greatest Books* (Sydney: Angus & Robertson, 1985).

29 JO'G to JO'G Jnr, 16 December 1957 and 22 January 1958. NLA (Box 1).

30 JO'G to JO'G Jnr, 2 February 1958. NLA (Box 1).

31 JO'G to JO'G Jnr, 12 February 1958. NLA (Box 1).

32 JO'G to JO'G Jnr, 6 March 1958; Toongabbie event reported in the *Advertiser*, 16 June 1960, cutting in NLA (Box 1).

33 Jennifer Rutherford, *The Gauche Intruder: Freud, Lacan and the White Australian Fantasy* (Melbourne: Melbourne University Press, 2000).

34 SUS to JO'G, 3 March 1959, Ure Smith papers (Box 47). See also typescript of O'Grady interview with Hazel de Berg (NLA) in which he claims the sequel was written purely because his publisher demanded a sequel and his contract meant he owed them another book. NLA Hazel de Berg Collection, http://nla.gov.au/nla.oh-vn221809

35 Newspaper cutting from *Daily Telegraph* in Ure Smith papers (Box 47).

36 JO'G to JO'G Jnr, from Italy, 8 July 1959. NLA (Box 1).

37 Ross Chambers, *Story and Situation: Narrative Seduction and the Power of Fiction* (Minneapolis: University of Minnesota Press, 1984).

38 As in the Foreword to *Gone Gougin'* (1975): 'Quite a lot of this story is factual and true. Quite a lot is fictional, and untrue. The rest of it is in between, and combines fact and fiction in about equal proportions'.

39 Hetherington, *Forty-Two Faces*, p. 98.

40   The jokes, though, got worse. *Gone Fishin'* was described as 'Netted by Nino Culotta. Scaled by "Wep". Published Ungutted by Ure Smith.' *Gone Gougin'* was described as 'Noodled by Nino Culotta. Ground and Polished by Benier [the illustrator]. Set and Mounted by Ure Smith.' Seriality isn't always a virtue.

41   Frow, 'Signature and Brand', p. 63.

42   Details compiled from scattered newspaper cuttings and correspondence in O'Grady (Box 1) and Ure Smith papers (Box 47).

43   Frank Devine comment, newspaper cutting in Ure Smith Papers (Box 47); no source recorded.

44   SUS to John McCallum, 19 January 1959, and song lyrics, Ure Smith Papers (Box 47); 'No Musical' and Lancaster as Nino, letter to JO'G Jnr, 22 January 1958, NLA (Box 1); details of film rights and multiple drafts of scripts, NLA (Boxes 1, 2, 10).

45   Postcard to SUS from Italy (1959), Ure Smith Papers; notes/diary on Vietnam tour in NLA (Box 1).

46   Quotation from National Museum of Australia curator, correspondence with author, 17 February 2003.

THE WIDE BROWN LAND ON THE SILVER SCREEN

This essay brings together two earlier pieces: 'Crocs in Frocks: Landscape and Nation in the 1990s', Journal of Australian Studies *49 (1996): 89–96 and 'The Wide Brown Land on the Small Grey Screen: The Nature of Landscape on Australian Television',* Journal of Australian Studies *58 (1998): 116–26.*

1   See Tony Bennett et al. (eds), *Celebrating the Nation: A Study of Australia's Bicentenary* (Sydney: Allen & Unwin, 1992).

2   Ross Gibson, 'The Nature of a Nation: Landscape in Australian Feature Films', in *South of the West: Postcolonialism and the Narrative Construction of Australia* (Bloomington: Indiana University Press, 1992), p. 73.

3   David Carter, *Dispossession, Dreams and Diversity: Issues in Australian Studies* (Sydney: Pearson, 2006), ch. 8.

4   Stephen Muecke, *Ancient & Modern: Time, Culture and Indigenous Philosophy* (Sydney: UNSW Press, 2004).

5   See Peter McKay, 'The Fine Art of Selling a Car', *Sydney Morning Herald*, 4 March 1995.

6   Meaghan Morris, 'Tooth and Claw: Tales of Survival, and *Crocodile Dundee*', in *The Pirate's Fiancée: Feminism, Reading, Postmodernism* (London & New York: Verso, 1988), p. 247.

7   Tom Griffiths, *Hunters and Collectors: The Antiquarian Imagination in Australia* (Melbourne: Cambridge University Press, 1996), p. 152.

8   Graeme Turner, *Making it National: Nationalism and Australian Popular Culture* (Sydney: Allen & Unwin, 1994).

9   For an account of changes see David Carter, 'Future Pasts', in David Headon, Donald Horne and Joy Hooton (eds), *The Abundant Culture: Meaning and Significance in Everyday Australia* (Sydney: Allen & Unwin, 1994), pp. 3–15.

10   Griffiths, *Hunters and Collectors*, pp. 127–49; quotation p. 134.

11   Information from the Healesville Sanctuary Souvenir booklet. On 1920s–1930s conservation movements see Griffiths, *Hunters and Collectors*, pp. 141–45.

12   Accounts of programming based on Sydney edition of *TV Week*.

13   Albert Moran, 'Crime, Romance, History: Television Drama', in Albert Moran and Tom O'Regan (eds), *The Australian Screen* (Ringwood: Penguin, 1989), pp. 236–55; Tom O'Regan, *Australia's Television Culture* (Sydney: Allen & Unwin, 1993).

14   Peter Beilby (ed.), *Australian TV: The First 25 Years* (Melbourne: Nelson, 1981);
      Paul James, 'Australia in the Corporate Image: A New Nationalism', *Arena* 63 (1983):
      65–106.
15   Griffiths, *Hunters and Collectors*, pp. 176–79.
16   Julie Marcus, 'The Journey Out to the Centre: The Cultural Appropriation of Ayer's
      Rock', in Anna Rutherford (ed.), *Aboriginal Culture Today* (Sydney: Dangaroo, 1991),
      pp. 254–74; Carter, *Dispossession*, ch. 8.
17   Harry Butler *In the Wild* (Sydney: ABC/Hodder & Stoughton, 1977) and *In the Wild
      (Part Two)* (Sydney: ABC/Hodder & Stoughton, 1979). Quotation from *Part Two*, p.
      119.
18   Both quotations from Butler, *In the Wild*, Foreword.
19   Butler, *In the Wild (Part Two)*, p. 126.
20   Ibid., p. 122.
21   The quotations are the titles of the first two *Bush Tucker Man* series. Major Les
      Hiddins was originally assigned by the Australian Army to survey the north and
      north-west for bush tucker, bush medicine etc. that might be useful in times of
      national need.
22   Hiddins is described in this way in the National Library of Australia catalogue, a
      description drawn it appears from the 'blurb' accompanying his earliest films/videos
      (pre-ABC).
23   A fascinating twist to these themes was given in 2006–2007 by the two series of
      Going Bush on SBS TV, featuring 'urban' Aborigines Cathy Freeman, Deborah
      Mailman (Series 1) and Luke Carroll (Series 2) travelling into the 'unknown'
      outback.
24   Maree Delofski, 'Beastly Stories', *Metro Magazine* 104 (1995), pp.104–05.

GOOD READERS AND GOOD CITIZENS

This essay first appeared in Australian Literary Studies *19.2 (October 1999): 136–51.*

1   This is clear in an early survey text, James Walter (ed.), *Australian Studies: A Survey*
     (Melbourne: Oxford University Press, 1989).
2   Two of the founding works of Australian studies were the key feminist texts, Anne
     Summers's *Damned Whores and God's Police: The Colonization of Women in Australia*
     (Ringwood: Penguin, 1975) and Miriam Dixson's *The Real Matilda: Woman and
     Identity in Australia, 1788–1975* (Ringwood: Penguin, 1976).
3   Leela Gandhi, *Postcolonial Theory: A Critical Introduction* (Sydney: Allen & Unwin,
     1998), p. 115.
4   Susan Sheridan, *Along the Faultlines: Sex, Race and Nation in Australian Women's
     Writing 1880s–1930s* (Sydney: Allen & Unwin, 1995).
5   I have pursued aspects of this argument in various places: 'Tasteless Subjects: Post-
     Colonial Literary Criticism, Realism and the Subject of Taste', *Southern Review* 25.3
     (November 1992): 292–303; 'After Postcolonialism', *Meanjin* 66.2 (2007): 114–19.
6   Ken Gelder and Jane Jacobs. *Uncanny Australia: Sacredness and Identity in a
     Postcolonial Nation* (Melbourne: Melbourne University Press, 1998).
7   See David Carter (ed.), *The Ideas Market: An Alternative Take on Australia's
     Intellectual Life.* (Melbourne: Melbourne University Press, 2004); Mark Davis,
     Gangland: Cultural Elites and the New Generationalism (Sydney: Allen & Unwin,
     1997); McKenzie Wark, *The Virtual Republic: Australia's Culture Wars of the 1990s*
     (Sydney: Allen & Unwin, 1997).
8   See David Carter, 'The Conscience Industry: The Rise and Rise of the Public
     Intellectual', in Carter (ed.), *The Ideas Market*, pp.15–39 and 'Public Intellectuals,

Book Culture and Civil Society', *Australian Humanities Review* 24 (December 2001–February 2002), http://www.lib.latrobe.edu.au/AHR/

9   Graeme Turner, 'Film, Television and Literature: Competing for the Nation', in Bruce Bennett and Jennifer Strauss (eds), *The Oxford History of Australian Literature* (Melbourne: Oxford University Press, 1998), p. 350. This situation has changed again in the 21st century with a relative decline in 'big' Australian films, the rise of a new culture of books and reading as anticipated in the present essay, and significant media coverage given to literary works such as Kate Grenville's *The Secret River* (2005). See Ken Gelder and Paul Salzman, *After the Celebration: Australian Fiction 1989–2007* (Melbourne: Melbourne University Press, 2009), pp. 80–94.

10   Benedict Anderson, *Imagined Communities: Reflections on the Origin and Spread of Nationalism* (London: Verso, 1983).

11   See David Carter and Kay Ferres, 'The Public Life of Literature', in Tony Bennett and David Carter (eds), *Culture in Australia: Policies, Publics and Programs* (Melbourne: Cambridge University Press, 2001), pp. 140–60; David Carter, 'Structures, Networks, Institutions: The New Empiricism, Book History and Literary History', in Katherine Bode and Robert Dixon (eds), *Resourceful Reading: The New Empiricism, eResearch and Australian Literary Culture* (Sydney: Sydney University Press, 2009), pp. 31–52.

12   David Carter, 'Publishing, Patronage and Cultural Politics: Institutional Changes in the Field of Australian Literature from 1950', in Peter Pierce (ed.), *The Cambridge History of Australian Literature* (Melbourne: Cambridge University Press, 2009), pp. 360–90.

13   Susan Lever, 'Fiction: Innovation and Ideology', in Bennett and Strauss (eds), *The Oxford History of Australian Literature*, p. 330.

14   John Frow, *Cultural Studies and Cultural Value* (Oxford: Clarendon, 1995), p. 86.

15   For a gloomy assessment of literary and scholarly publishing in Australia see Michael Wilding, 'Australian Literary and Scholarly Publishing in Its International Context', *Australian Literary Studies* 19.1 (May 1999): 57–69. Wilding does conclude by emphasising the dynamics in the system which generate positive developments. For more recent views see David Carter and Anne Galligan (eds), *Making Books: Contemporary Australian Publishing* (St Lucia: University of Queensland Press, 2007); my essay in that volume examines literary fiction publishing.

16   Tom O'Regan, *Australian National Cinema* (London and New York: Routledge, 1996), p. 232.

17   Richard Nile, 'Literary Democracy and the Politics of Reputation', in Bennett and Strauss (eds), *The Oxford Literary History of Australia*, pp. 130–46.

18   For a more recent study see Ben Goldsmith, Susan Ward and Tom O'Regan, *Local Hollywood* (St Lucia: University of Queensland Press, 2010).

19   Elizabeth Jacka, 'Film', in Stuart Cunningham and Graeme Turner (eds), *The Media in Australia: Industries, Texts, Audiences* (Sydney: Allen & Unwin. 1997), p. 88.

20   O'Regan *Australian National Cinema*, p. 353.

21   David Carter, 'Going, Going, Gone? Britishness and Englishness in Contemporary Australian Culture', *Overland* 169 (Summer 2002): 81–86.

22   Lever, 'Fiction', p. 310.

23   Elliott, Helen. 'Tales of a City', *Weekend Australian* Review 8–9 May (1999): 10.

24   And, more recently, why the question of 'influence', which suggests *importation* first and foremost, has been subsumed within the broader framework of transnationalism, more open to models of cultural flows in multiple directions. See Robert Dixon, 'Australian Literature-International Contexts', *Southerly* 67.1–2 (2007): 15–27.

25   Tom O'Regan *Australia's Television Culture* (Sydney: Allen & Unwin, 1993), p. xxiv.

26   As indicated above, 'transnational' is probably the word I needed.

27   See my essay 'An Australian Accent? From Textual Politics to Cultural History in Australian Literary Studies', in Wolfgang Zach and Michael Keneally (eds),

NOTES

Literatures in English: Priorities of Research (Tübingen: Stauffenburg Verlag, 2008), pp. 383–93.

28   O'Regan *Australian National Cinema*, p. 213.

29   Meaghan Morris, 'Tooth and Claw: Tales of Survival, and Crocodile Dundee', in her *The Pirate's Fiancée: Feminism, Reading, Postmodernism* (London: Verso, 1988), pp. 241–69.

30   O'Regan *Australian National Cinema*, p. 231.

31   McKenzie Wark, 'Media Law and Policy to Suit All', *Australian* 6 December 1995.

32   Frow, *Cultural Studies*, pp. 23–25.

33   Ibid., p. 25.

34   O'Regan, *Australian National Cinema*, ch. 4.

35   Ibid.

36   Ibid., p. 49. See also O'Regan, '"Knowing the Processes But Not the Outcomes": Australian Cinema Faces the Millennium', in Bennett and Carter (eds), *Culture in Australia*, pp. 18–45.

37   Simon During, 'Literature—Nationalism's Other? The Case for Revision', in Homi Babha (ed.), *Nation and Narration* (London and New York: Routledge, 1990), p. 139.

38   Richard White, '*Inventing Australia* Revisited', in Wayne Hudson and Geoffrey Bolton (eds), *Creating Australia: Changing Australian History* (Sydney: Allen & Unwin, 1997), pp. 21–22.

INDEX

INDEX

Babe 263
Bail, Murray 149-50
Bakhtin, Mikhail 188, 214
Balzac, Honoré de 208
Baracchi, Guido 123
Barbusse, Henri 173
Barjai 125
Barnard Eldershaw, M. xiii, 26, 80, 168, 181, 183, 186-201
Barnard, Marjorie 28, 141, 144, 147-48, 187, 193-95
Barrett, Lindsay 216
Barthes, Roland 38
Batt, Leon 141
Baudelaire, Charles 106
Baudrillard, Jean 38
Beardsley, Aubrey 109
Beasley, Jack 203
Beethoven, Ludwig Van 90, 95, 178
belatedness viii-xii, 3-8, 10-12, 14, 49, 54, 57, 67. 104, 115, 263-64, 267
Bell, Graeme 229
Benjamin, Walter 38
Bennett, Arnold 159, 164
Bernhard, Thomas 264
Better Homes and Gardens 150
Bifur 121
Bird, Delys 39
Blake, William 93-94
Blast 115
Bookfellow 20, 135
Book-of-the-Month Club 132-33, 145
Booksellers, Stationers and Fancy Goods Journal 156
Booth, E.C. 164
Bosworth, Richard 216
Botticelli, Sandro 106
Boyd, Arthur 10
Boyd, Martin 33, n277, n278
BP Magazine 51
Bracco, Rosa Maria 132-33
Brady, E.J. 69
Brady, Veronica 185
Brennan, Christopher 19, 28, 30-33, 35, 37, 57
Brereton, John Le Gay 69, 79
Brett-Young, Francis 164
Broomfield, Fred 69, 80

Bruce, J.F. 63
Bucharin, Nikolai 173
Buckley, Vincent 15, 29-35, 44
Buckridge, Patrick 35, 142, 176-77, 216
Bulletin 5, 17-20, 25, 31, 67, 79, 80, 110, 138, 145, 169, 220
Bunting, Basil 120
Burdett, Basil 57, 59-60, 62, 64
Bürger, Peter 91, 112, 115-6, 125
Bush Tucker Man 249-51
bush 22, 24, 27, 40, 69, 73, 81, 103-4, 147, 162-3, 224, 233-35, 241, 244-51
Butler, Harry 245, 247-49, 250
Butor, Michel 264
Byron, George Gordon 95, 99

Calasso, Roberto 264
Canby, Henry Seidel 133, 145-46, 149
Carey, Peter 149-50, 264
Carlyle, Thomas 79
Casanova, Pascale viii
Casey, Gavin 183
Cassell & Co. 220
Catullus 93, 99
centre, the, 'red centre' 42, 233-41, 245-47, 249
Cézanne, Paul 50, 57, 106
Chambers, Ross 226
Chaplin, Charlie 120, 136, 188
Christesen, C.B. 26, 34, 140, 196, 205
Churchill, Winston 187
cinema ix-xi, xiii-xiv, 21, 36, 40, 68, 70, 73, 78, 84, 102, 110, 116, 123, 136, 151, 194, 223, 230, 232-43, 252, 259-70
Circus Oz 270
Clancy, Tom 223
Clark, Manning 27
Clarke, Marcus 2-5, 9-11, 15-16, 32
class 7, 21, 27, 31, 72-77, 110, 124-25, 129, 131, 133, 137-38, 141, 147, 151-52, 155-56, 160, 165, 168, 173-78, 180-85, 190, 200, 202-13
Clendinnen, Inga 149
Clune, Frank 139, 142, 194, 246
Cold War 1, 27, 34-35, 176, 178, 208
Coleridge, Samuel Taylor 257
Collini, Stefan 131
Collins, Dale 69
Collins, Jim 151

INDEX

INDEX